Gnuplot in Action

Gnuplot in Action

Understanding Data with Graphs

PHILIPP K. JANERT

MANNING

Greenwich
(74° w. long.)

For online information and ordering of this and other Manning books, please visit www.manning.com. The publisher offers discounts on this book when ordered in quantity. For more information, please contact

Special Sales Department
Manning Publications Co.
Sound View Court 3B   fax: (609) 877-8256
Greenwick, CT 06830   email: orders@manning.com

⊗ Recognizing the importance of preserving what has been written, it is Manning's policy to have the books we publish printed on acid-free paper, and we exert our best efforts to that end. Recognizing also our responsibility to conserve the resources of our planet, Manning books are printed on paper that is at least 15 percent recycled and processed without the use of elemental chlorine.

Manning Publications Co.
Sound View Court 3B
Greenwick, CT 06830

Development editor: Nermina Miller, Tom Cirtin
Copyeditor: Benjamin Berg
Proofreader: Katie Tennant
Typesetter: Dottie Marsico
Cover designer: Marija Tudor

ISBN 978-1-933988-39-9
Printed in the United States of America
1 2 3 4 5 6 7 8 9 10 – MAL – 14 13 12 11 10 09

The purpose of computing is insight,
not numbers.
—R. W. Hamming

The purpose of computing is insight,
not pictures.
—L. N. Trefethen

brief contents

contents

foreword

Thomas Williams was a CS undergrad and I was an EE/CS undergrad at Villanova University. The EE department had just built a VLSI design lab and we were both immediately drawn to it. The campus had two existing computer labs, both depressing. They were crammed into dingy basements filled with rows of VT100 terminals and the acrid smell of burnt coffee. By contrast, the new VLSI lab was on the top floor of the engineering building in a room with high ceilings and plenty of light. Better still, it had a brand-new Pyramid minicomputer—right there in its own air conditioned room—that ran Unix. The lab had a dozen AED color displays and a huge HP plotter. Dr. Richard Perry ran the lab and was happy to let us hack away as much as we wanted. Together we got a UUCP link that dialed out nightly to Princeton. We got sendmail and a news reader running. After a few months, the administrators discovered that the phone bill had skyrocketed due to nightly long distance calls to New Jersey! But we had Villanova on the Arpanet.

I'd been taking classes in electromagnetism and signal processing and really wanted to visualize the equations. Tom had a similar need to visualize differential equations. There were no reasonable tools on campus to do so. At home I had an early PC clone with a bootlegged copy of Lotus 123 that could graph data, but graphing a simple equation was a clumsy process to first fill a spreadsheet with data points and then plot them. And Lotus 123 was never going to work with the HP plotter or AED terminals we had right there. In the fall of 1986, I suggested to Tom that we write the program we really wanted. He agreed. We settled on calling it *gnuplot* as a pun on a lame program at school that predated ours called "newplot." It wasn't until a month later that we read Richard Stallman's Gnu Manifesto. That resonated with us and matched our thinking perfectly. The common name was simply a lucky coincidence.

Fortran and Pascal were the prevailing languages taught in school then, but neither was portable. C was clearly a better fit and Unix was the right OS to start with. Tom focused on writing the equation parser and P-code evaluator while I focused on the command-line processor and graphics drivers. The command-line approach was patterned after Vax/VMS and chosen out of necessity; there were no portable GUIs then and, besides, we wanted to be able to use dumb terminals to drive the plotters and printers we had nearby. Within a month we had the basics working. After that we started porting to every machine we could find with a C compiler: VMS, MS-DOS, and several flavors of Unix.

By the fall of 1987, we published gnuplot as open source to newsgroups like sci.math. We were surprised by the response we got! Notes of thanks and encouragement came in from all around the world. More importantly, we received bug fixes and patches to make gnuplot more portable to add support for many more terminals and devices. We folded those in while adding features and fixing bugs ourselves.

Tom and I both graduated in 1987 and didn't look at gnuplot much after that. But it took on a life of its own thanks to the dedicated contributions of others, and now it's tremendously more powerful than when we left it. People have continued to add features to it, and now there is this book, *Gnuplot in Action*, to serve as guide to all that gnuplot has to offer. What a great testament to the benefits of open source!

—COLIN D. KELLEY
CTO, RingRevenue, Inc.
Original Gnuplot Author

foreword

I smiled when I learned that there would be a book about gnuplot. It had been a long time since Colin and I were busy compiling new builds, which at the time needed to be cut up into little "packages" to fit on the relatively new USENET. And a long time since we heard from the early customers. To be honest, back then, we were pretty surprised at the actual volume of reactions and the diversity of uses people were finding for it. It made us really happy to realize that universities, researchers, economists, hospitals, and various companies around the world were using it. For me, it was a bellwether for the future power of the Internet and open source software. I still remember when the "University of Free Estonia" sent us an email just days *before* the Baltic States had officially announced their independence. And I remember tracking when we'd been deployed in every inhabited continent (with active websites in Czech, French, German, Indonesian, Japanese, Portuguese, Slovak, Italian, and more). And now this new book, *Gnuplot in Action*, is finally available to help those people starting out with gnuplot or those stepping up to do more complicated things!

There are a few fundamental beliefs I'd like readers to understand about gnuplot. From the beginning, it had to be fun, with no learning curve to create your first few plots. It had to be free and stay free. It had to be easily available and reliable. We wrote it to run on every type of computer, every display, every printer we could get our hands on. But of course we didn't have everything on hand and new devices launched all the time. So there was a requirement for gnuplot to be modifiable, so that one group of users or developers could write new features simply and have the results included in subsequent versions. Ultimately, gnuplot of today owes most of its success to the many volunteers who consistently contribute ideas and time to the development of the project. The result, hopefully, is a product powerful enough to create graphs which convey exactly the information their authors intended.

Enjoy!

—THOMAS "THAW" WILLIAMS
Google
Original Gnuplot Author

preface

I have been using gnuplot for 15 years, and it's an indispensable part of my toolset: one of the handful of programs I can't do without.

Initially, I used gnuplot as part of my academic research work as a theoretical condensed matter physicist. But much later, when I joined Amazon.com, I found myself using gnuplot again, this time to analyze the movement of workers in Amazon's gargantuan warehouses and the distribution of packages to customers. Later yet, I found gnuplot helpful when analyzing web traffic patterns for the Walt Disney Company.

I find gnuplot indispensable because it lets me *see* data, and do so in an easy, uncomplicated manner. Using gnuplot, I can draw and redraw graphs and look at data in different ways. I can generate images of data sets containing millions of points, and I can script gnuplot to create graphs for me automatically.

These things matter. In one of my assignments, I was able to discover highly relevant information because I was able to generate literally *hundreds* of graphs. Putting all of them on a web page next to each other revealed blatant similarities (and differences) between different data sets—a fact that had never before been noticed, not least because everybody else was using tools (mostly Excel) that would only allow graphs to be created one at a time.

While at Amazon, I discovered something else: data is no longer confined to the science lab. In a modern corporation, data is *everywhere*. Any reasonably sophisticated organization is constantly collecting data: sales numbers, web traffic, inventory, turnover, database performance, supply chain details, you name it. Naturally, there's a continuous and ever-increasing demand to make use of this data to improve the business.

What this means is that data analysis is no longer a specialist's job—everybody has a need for it, even if only to monitor one's own metrics or performance indicators. This isn't a bad thing. The way inputs influence outputs is often not obvious, and placing decisions on a firmer, more rational footing is reasonable.

But what I also found at Amazon and elsewhere is that the people doing the data analysis often don't have the right toolset, both in terms of actual software tools and in regard to methods and techniques.

In many ways, my experience in the corporate world has been an influence while writing this book. I believe that graphical methods—which are accessible to anyone, regardless of mathematical or statistical training—are an excellent way to understand data and derive value from it (much better and more powerful than a five-day statistics class, and much more flexible and creative than a standard Six-Sigma program).

And I believe that gnuplot is a very good tool to use for this purpose. Its learning curve is flat—you can pick up the basics in an hour. It requires no programming skills. It handles a variety of input formats. It's fast and it's interactive. It's mature. It's also free and open source.

Gnuplot has always been popular with scientists all over—I hope to convince you that it can be useful to a much larger audience. Business analysts, operations managers, database and data warehouse administrators, programmers: anybody who wants to understand data with graphs.

I'd like to show you how to do it.

acknowledgments

Several data repositories on the web were helpful, either because of the data sets available there or merely as a source of inspiration. Among the most helpful were

- The data set collection and the Data and Story Library (DASL) at StatLib (http://lib.stat.cmu.edu)
- The UCI Machine Learning Repository at UC Irvine (http://www.ics.uci.edu/~mlearn/MLRepository.html)
- R. J. Hyndman's Time Series Data Library (http://www-personal.buseco.monash.edu.au/~hyndman/TSDL)
- The Exploring Data site at Central Queensland University (http://exploring-data.cqu.edu.au)

Wherever specific data sets have been used, detailed attribution is given in the text.

Two resources I relied on more than on any other: the excellent collection of the University of Washington libraries (Seattle), and the amazingly comprehensive store of information available at Wikipedia.

Writing a book is a long process, *much* more involved than writing a collection of independent papers of equal length. One of the lessons I learned during the preparation of this book is this: even if you know that writing a book will take longer than you expect, it *still* takes longer than you expect!

Handling projects of such nature takes true dedication and courage. I would like to express special appreciation to Marjan Bace and his team at Manning publications for taking this project on and guiding it to completion.

I'd like to thank the original gnuplot authors Colin Kelley and Thomas Williams for sharing their reminiscences about the early history of gnuplot. I also would like to thank Professor Nick Trefethen for giving me permission to use his maxim 22 as motto for this book. It can't be said any better.

While writing this book, I enjoyed conversations or correspondence with Nick Chase, Austin King, and Richard Kreckel. Professor Ethan Merritt answered many of my questions about gnuplot internals and has been very helpful in a variety of ways.

Many readers pointed out errors in the manuscript, or provided thoughtful comments and helpful suggestions. Reviewers who took time out of their busy schedules to read the manuscript at different stages in its development and to provide invaluable feedback included Mark Pruett, Nishant Sastry, Dawid Weiss, Hans-Bernhard Bröker, Petr Mikulík, Bas Vodde, Daniel Sebald, Maxim Belushkin, and Scott White. Mitchell Johnson painstakingly verified the correctness of all gnuplot commands in the text. I'm grateful for the care and effort everyone expended on behalf of this project.

Special thanks go to PAUL Schrader (Bremen).

Finally, this book is about an open source project and has been written using tools from other open source projects: I'd like to mention iceWM, tcsh, XEmacs, Perl, and of course gnuplot itself. I'm indebted to their creators, maintainers, and contributors—without their efforts this book wouldn't exist.

My final thoughts go to Angela, who got me started and kept me going. Without her, nothing would be much worth doing.

about this book

This book is intended to be a comprehensive introduction to gnuplot: from the basics to the power features and beyond. Besides providing a tutorial on gnuplot itself, it demonstrates how to apply and use gnuplot to extract insight from data.

The gnuplot program has always had complete and detailed reference documentation, but what was missing was a continuous presentation that tied all the different bits and pieces of gnuplot together and demonstrated how to use them to achieve certain tasks. This book attempts to fill that gap.

The book should also serve as a handy reference for more advanced gnuplot users, and as an introduction to graphical ways of knowledge discovery.

And finally, this book tries to show you how to use gnuplot to achieve surprisingly nifty effects that will make everyone say, "How did you *do* that?"

Contents of this book

This book is divided into four parts.

The first part provides a tutorial introduction to gnuplot and some of the things you can do with it. If you're new to gnuplot, start here. Even if you already know gnuplot, I suggest you at least skim the chapters in this part: you might pick up a few new tricks. (For example, did you know that you can use gnuplot to plot the Unix password file? No? Thought so.)

The second part is about *polishing* and describes the ways that we can influence the appearance of a plot: by using different styles (chapter 5); using labels, arrows, and other decorations (chapter 6); and by changing the axes and the overall appearance of a graph (chapter 7). The material in these chapters has the character of a refer-ence—this is the place to look up some detail when you need it.

In part 3, we move on to more advanced concepts. Here's where we talk about fun topics such as color (chapter 9) and three-dimensional plots (chapter 8). Chapter 10 introduces more specialized topics, such as plots-within-a-plot, polar coordinates, and curve fitting. In chapter 11 we'll talk about gnuplot *terminals* and ways to export our work to common file formats, and chapter 12 is about ways to use gnuplot in conjunc-tion with, or instead of, a programming language.

In the last part, I'll take gnuplot for granted, and focus instead on the things you can do with it. In chapter 13 I'll present fundamental types of graphs and discuss when and how to use them. I'll also show you how to generate such graphs with gnu-plot. In the remaining two chapters, I focus on the discovery and analysis process itself, and describe some techniques that I've found helpful.

There are three appendixes. Appendix A describes how to obtain and install gnu-plot if you don't already have it. It also contains some pointers in case you want to build gnuplot from source.

Appendix B is a command and options reference, grouped by topic, not alphabet-ically. So if you know that you want to change the appearance of the tic labels, but you've forgotten which option to use, this appendix should point you in the right direction quickly.

In appendix C, I list some additional resources (books and web sites) that you might find helpful. I also give a brief overview of a few tools that are comparable to gnuplot.

I've tried to be comprehensive in my coverage of gnuplot's features, with two exceptions. I don't cover obsolete or redundant features. I also don't discuss features that would only be of interest to a very limited group of users: all material in this book should (at least potentially) be useful to *all* readers, no matter what their situation. Where appropriate, I refer to the standard gnuplot reference documentation for details not discussed here.

As far as the examples are concerned, I've tried to present fresh or at least unfa-miliar data sets. This means you won't find a plot of the Challenger O-Ring data here, nor Napoleon's march, nor Playfair's charts regarding trade with the West Indies. (The one classic I would've liked to include is Anscombe's Quartet, but I couldn't find a suitable context in which to present it. If you've never seen it before, go and look it up yourself.)

How to read this book

This book presents a continuing narrative, and the material is arranged as if the reader were going to read the book sequentially, cover to cover.

But I know that most people reach for a piece of documentation when they need to "get something done, now!" Therefore, I tried to make this book as *diveable* as possi-ble: once you've mastered the essential gnuplot basics, you should be able to open this book on any chapter that's relevant to your current task and start reading, without loss of continuity.

While the chapters are conceived as largely independent of each other, each chapter presents a continuous, progressive exposition, which is best read in order, and from start to finish. The nature of the topic demands that concepts need to be introduced early in a chapter and not brought to completion until the end, after necessary circumstantial material has been introduced.

My advice to you is that you should feel free to pick any chapter you're interested in, but that you should attempt to read each chapter in its entirety, end-to-end, to get the maximum out of this book. I know that the temptation is great to just read a relevant figure caption and then to take it from there, but I'd advise you against that. Gnuplot has many odd quirks, and many useful little tricks as well, which you will not learn about by just skimming the headlines and the captions. I tried to keep the chapters short—try to take them in as a whole.

One caveat: gnuplot is very connected, and explaining one feature often requires knowledge of some other feature. The most proper way to introduce gnuplot would have been to follow a strict bottom-up approach: first, introduce string handling and number formats, followed by the syntax for option management and styles, and finally, in the last chapter, bring it all together by talking about the plot command. This would've been easy to write, perfectly organized—and excruciatingly boring to read!

I take a different approach: explain the most common use early, and leave more exotic variants and applications of commands for later. The price we have to pay is an increased number of forward references. This is an *In Action* book: I want to get you going quickly, without burdening you with unnecessary details early on.

Intended audience

This book was written with two groups of people in mind: those who already know gnuplot, and those who don't.

If you already know gnuplot, I hope that you'll still find it a useful reference, in particular in regard to some of the more advanced topics in the second half of this book. I've tried to provide the big-picture explanations and the examples that have always been missing from the standard gnuplot reference documentation.

If you're new to gnuplot, I think you'll find it easy enough to pick up—in fact, I can promise you that by the end of chapter 2 you'll be productive with gnuplot, and by the end of chapter 3 you'll be well equipped for most day-to-day data graphing tasks that may come your way. A flat learning curve was one of the design objectives of the original gnuplot authors, and the ease with which you can get started is one of the great strengths of gnuplot today.

This book doesn't require a strong background in mathematical methods, and none at all in statistics: anybody with some college level (or just high-school) math should be able to read this book without difficulty. (Some familiarity with basic calculus is advantageous, but by no means required.)

This book should be accessible and helpful to anybody who tries to understand data. This includes scientists and engineers—in other words the kinds of people who've always been using gnuplot. If this describes you, I think you'll find this book a helpful reference and handbook for gnuplot.

But I think this book will also be helpful to readers who don't have a primary background in analytical methods, yet need to deal with data as part of their jobs: business analysts, technical managers, software engineers. If this is your situation, you may find the discussions on graphical methods in part 4 particularly helpful.

Conventions

I spell the name of the program in all lowercase, except at the beginning of a sentence, when I capitalize normally. This is in accordance with the usage recommended in the gnuplot FAQ.

The gnuplot documentation is extensive and I refer to it occasionally, for additional detail on topics covered briefly or not at all here. Traditionally, the gnuplot documentation has been called the *online help* or *online documentation*, owing to the fact that it's available "online" during a gnuplot session. But since the advent of the Internet, the word *online* seems to suggest network connectivity—falsely in this context. To avoid confusion, I'll always refer to the *standard gnuplot reference documentation* instead.

Gnuplot commands are shown using a typewriter font, like this: `plot sin(x)`. Single command lines can get long; to make them fit on a page, I occasionally had to break them across multiple lines. If so, a gray arrow (➡) has been placed at the beginning of the *next* line, to indicate that it is the continuation of the previous one:

```
plot "data" using 1:2 smooth csplines title "data" with lines,
➡ sin(x) title "model"
```

The break in the original line is not indicated separately. When using gnuplot in an interactive session, your terminal program should wrap a line that is too long automatically. Alternatively, you can break lines by escaping the newline with a backslash as usual. This is useful in command files for batch processing, but you don't want to do this during an interactive session, since it messes with the command history feature.

Gnuplot has a large number of options, and keeping all of them, and their suboptions and optional parameters, straight is a major theme running through this book. Throughout the text, and in the reference appendix B, you'll find summaries of gnuplot commands and their options and suboptions.

Within these summaries, I use a few syntactic conventions. My intent is to stay close to the usage familiar from the standard gnuplot reference documentation, but also to follow more general conventions (such as those used for Unix man pages):

```
[ ... ]        # Square brackets for optional parts
[ | ]          # Vertical bars to separate alternatives
{ ... }        # Curly braces for user-supplied input
```

For parameters supplied by the user, it's not always clear from the context what *kind* of information the command expects: is it a string or a number? If it's a number, is it an index into some array or a numerical factor? And so on. I've tried to clarify this situation by prefixing each user-supplied input parameter with a type indicator, terminated by a colon. I summarize the prefixes and their meanings in table 1.

Table 1   Type indicators for user-supplied parameters

Prefix	Description
str:	A string
int:	An integer number
flt:	A floating-point number
idx:	An integer number, which is interpreted as index into an existing array
clr:	A color specification—for example, rgbcolor "red" or rgb "#FFFF00"
pos:	A pair of coordinates, comma separated, optionally containing coordinate system specifiers—for example, 0,0 or first 1.1, screen 0.9
enum:	A gnuplot keyword as unquoted string

Many gnuplot options and directives have abbreviated forms, some of which I use frequently in the latter parts of the book. Table 2 lists both the abbreviated and the full forms. Also keep in mind that an empty filename inside the plot command uses the most recently named file in the same command line again.

Hardware and software requirements

This book describes version 4.2.x of gnuplot, which was initially released in March 2007. The most current bug-fix release at the time of this writing is version 4.2.5, released in March 2009.

After being stagnant for a long time, gnuplot development has picked up again in the last few years, so that things have changed significantly since gnuplot version 3.7. I won't explain obsolete or deprecated features, and only make cursory remarks (if that) regarding backward compatibility.

Table 2   Abbreviations for the frequently used directives to the plot command and for the most important options

Abbreviation	Full
i	index
ev	every
u	using
s	smooth
s acs	smooth acsplines
t	title
w l	with lines
w linesp or w lp	with linespoints
w p	with points
set t	set terminal
set o	set output
set logsc	set logscale

Some installations and distributions still use gnuplot 4.0 (or older). *Not all examples in this book will work with version 4.0 of gnuplot or earlier.* If this is your situation, you should upgrade, either by installing a precompiled binary of version 4.2, or by compiling gnuplot from source. Appendix A tells you how to do it.

The current development version is gnuplot 4.3, which will be released eventually as minor gnuplot release 4.4 (or potentially as major 5.0 release). Except for some features that I've worked on myself (such as the `smooth cumul` and `smooth kdens` features I'll introduce in chapter 14), I won't have much to say about upcoming features in the next gnuplot release.

I assume you have access to a reasonably modern computer (not older than five years or so), running any flavor of Unix/Linux, a recent release of MS Windows, or Mac OS X. Although gnuplot has been ported to many other platforms in the past, most of them are by now obsolete, and I won't talk about them in this book.

About the author

My education is in physics, and I've worked as technology consultant, software engineer, technical lead, and project manager, for small startups and in large corporate environments, both in the U.S. and overseas.

I first started using gnuplot when I was a graduate student, and it has become an indispensable part of my toolbox: one of the handful of programs I can't do without. Recently, I've also started to contribute a few features to the gnuplot development version.

I provide consulting services specializing in corporate metrics, business intelligence, data analysis, and mathematical modeling through my company, Principal Value, LLC (www.principal-value.com). I also teach classes on software design and data analysis at the University of Washington.

I hold a Ph.D. in theoretical physics from the University of Washington.

Author online

Purchase of *Gnuplot in Action* includes free access to a private web forum run by Manning Publications where you can make comments about the book, ask technical questions, and receive help from the author and from other users. To access the forum and subscribe to it, point your web browser to www.manning.com/GnuplotinAction. This page provides information on how to get on the forum once you are registered, what kind of help is available, and the rules of conduct on the forum. It also provides links to the source code for the examples in the book, errata, and other downloads.

Manning's commitment to our readers is to provide a venue where a meaningful dialog between individual readers and between readers and the author can take place. It is not a commitment to any specific amount of participation on the part of the author, whose contribution to the Author Online remains voluntary (and unpaid). We suggest you try asking the author some challenging questions lest his interest stray!

The Author Online forum and the archives of previous discussions will be accessible from the publisher's website as long as the book is in print.

About the title

By combining introductions, overviews, and how-to examples, the *In Action* books are designed to help learning and remembering. According to research in cognitive science, the things people remember are things they discover during self-motivated exploration.

Although no one at Manning is a cognitive scientist, we are convinced that for learning to become permanent it must pass through stages of exploration, play, and, interestingly, retelling of what is being learned. People understand and remember new things, which is to say they master them, only after actively exploring them. Humans learn in action. An essential part of an *In Action* guide is that it's example-driven. It encourages the reader to try things out, to play with new code, and explore new ideas.

There is another, more mundane, reason for the title of this book: our readers are busy. They use books to do a job or solve a problem. They need books that allow them to jump in and jump out easily and learn just what they want just when they want it. They need books that aid them in action. The books in this series are designed for such readers.

About the cover illustration

The figure on the cover of *Gnuplot in Action* is captioned "A peer of France." The title of Peer of France was held by the highest-ranking members of the French nobility. It was an extraordinary honor granted only to few dukes, counts, and princes of the church. The illustration is taken from a 19th-century edition of Sylvain Maréchal's four-volume compendium of regional dress customs published in France. Each illustration is finely drawn and colored by hand.

The rich variety of Maréchal's collection reminds us vividly of how culturally apart the world's towns and regions were just 200 years ago. Isolated from each other, people spoke different dialects and languages. In the streets or in the countryside, it was easy to identify where they lived and what their trade or station in life was just by their dress.

Dress codes have changed since then and the diversity by region, so rich at the time, has faded away. It is now hard to tell apart the inhabitants of different continents, let alone different towns or regions. Perhaps we have traded cultural diversity for a more varied personal life-certainly for a more varied and fast-paced technological life.

At a time when it is hard to tell one computer book from another, Manning celebrates the inventiveness and initiative of the computer business with book covers based on the rich diversity of regional life of two centuries ago, brought back to life by Maréchal's pictures.

Part 1

Basics

Gnuplot is a tool for visualizing data and analyzing it using graphical methods. This first part provides an introduction to all those features of gnuplot that you are going to need on a daily basis.

Chapter 1 introduces gnuplot and describes the kinds of problems it is designed to solve. I also define some important terms and provide a brief overview of gnuplot's history.

Chapter 2 is a quick start tutorial on gnuplot—you will learn everything to become productive with gnuplot right here.

Chapter 3 goes into more depth on the way gnuplot handles data. We will talk about file handling, data transformations, and math.

Chapter 4 discusses a variety of practical matters, from string handling to gnuplot's help feature.

Prelude: Understanding data with gnuplot

This chapter covers

- Warm-up examples
- What is graphical analysis?
- What is gnuplot?

Gnuplot is probably the most widely used open source program for plotting and visualizing data. In this book, I want to show you how to use gnuplot to make plots and graphs of your data: both quick and easy graphs for your own use and highly polished graphs for presentations and publications.

But I also want to show you something else: how to solve data analysis problems using graphical methods. The art of discovering relationships in data and extracting information from it by visual means is called *graphical analysis* and I believe gnuplot to be an excellent tool for it.

As a teaser, let's take a look at some problems and how we might be able to approach them using graphical methods. The graphs here and in the rest of the book (with very few exceptions) have been, of course, generated with gnuplot.

1.1   *A busy weekend*

To get a feeling for the kinds of problems that we may be dealing with, and for the kinds of solutions that gnuplot can help us find, let's look at two examples. Both take place during a long and busy weekend.

1.1.1   *Planning a marathon*

Imagine you're in charge of organizing the local city marathon. There will be more than 2,000 starters, traffic closed around the city, plenty of spectators—and a major Finish Line Festival to celebrate the victors and help the wounded. The big question is: when should the Finish Line crew be ready to deal with the majority of runners? At what point do we expect the big influx of the masses?

You still have the results from last year's event. Assuming that the starters haven't improved dramatically over the last year (probably a safe assumption), you do a quick average on the completion times and find that last year's average was 172 minutes. To be on the safe side, you calculate the standard deviation as well, which comes out to about 15 minutes. So you tell your crew to be ready for the big rush starting two and a half hours (150 minutes) after the start, and feel reasonably well prepared for the event.

So it comes as a surprise when on the big day, plenty of runners start showing up on the finish line after only 130 minutes—a good 20 minutes earlier than the expected onset of the rush. In terms of event management, being off by 20 or 30 minutes isn't catastrophic, yet it is a bit strange. The next day you wonder: what went wrong?

Let's look at the data to see what we can learn about it. So far, all we know of it is the mean and the standard deviation.

The mean is convenient: it is easy to calculate and it summarizes the entire data set in a single number. But in forming the mean, we lost a lot of information. To understand the whole data set, we have to *look* at it. And since we can't understand data by looking at more than 2,000 individual finish times, this means we'll have to *plot* it.

It will be convenient to group the runners by completion time and to count the number of participants that completed during each full minute. The resulting file might start like this:

```
# Minutes Runners
133 1
134 7
135 1
136 4
137 3
138 3
141 7
142 24
...
```

Now we plot the number of runners against the completion (see figure 1.1).

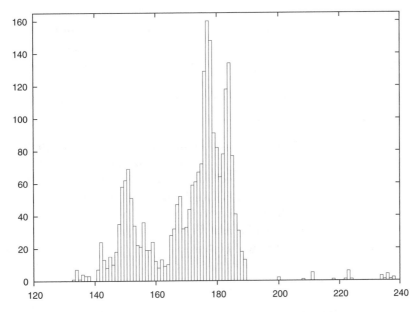

Figure 1.1 Number of finishers versus time to complete (in minutes)

It is immediately obvious where we went wrong: the data is *bimodal*, meaning it has two peaks. There is an early peak at around 150 minutes, and a later main peak at 180 minutes.

Actually, this makes sense: a major sporting event such as a city marathon attracts two very different groups of people: athletes, who train and compete throughout the year and are in it to win, and a much larger group of amateurs, who come out once a year for a big event and are mostly there to participate.

The problem is that for such data, the mean and standard deviation are obviously bad representations—so much so that at the time when we expected the big rush (170 minutes), there's actually a bit of a lull at the finish line!

The take-home message here is that it is usually not a good idea to rely on summary statistics (such as the mean) for unknown data sets. We *always* should investigate what the data looks like. Once we've confirmed the basic shape, we can choose how to summarize our findings best.

And of course, there is always more to learn. In this example, for instance, we see that after about 200 minutes, almost everybody has made it, and we can start winding down the operation. The actual "tail" of the distribution is quite small—actually, a bit surprisingly so (I would've expected to see a greater number of stragglers, but possibly many runners who are *really* slow drop out of the race when they realize they'll place badly).

USING GNUPLOT

Let's look at the gnuplot command that was used to generate figure 1.1. Gnuplot is command-line–oriented: after you start gnuplot, it drops you into an interactive command session, and all commands are typed at the interactive gnuplot prompt.

Gnuplot reads data from simple text files, with the data arranged in columns as shown previously. To plot a data file takes only a single command, plot, like this:[1]

```
plot "marathon" using 1:2 with boxes
```

The plot command requires the name of the data file as argument in quotes. The rest of the command line specifies which columns to use for the plot, and in which way to represent the data. The using 1:2 declaration tells gnuplot to use the first and second column in the file called marathon. The final part of the command, with boxes, selects a box style, which is often suitable to display counts of events.

Gnuplot handles most everything else by itself: it sizes the graph and selects the most interesting plot range, it draws the border, and it draws the tic marks and their labels. All these details can be customized, but gnuplot typically does a good job at anticipating what the user wants.

1.1.2   *Determining the future*

The same weekend when 2,000 runners are running through the city, a diligent graduate student is working on his research topic. He studies diffusion limited aggregation (DLA), a process wherein a particle performs a random walk until it comes in contact with a growing cluster of particles. At the moment of contact, the particle sticks to the cluster at the location where the contact occurred and becomes part of the cluster. Now, a new random walker is released to perform a random walk, until *it* sticks to the cluster. And so on.

Clusters grown through this process have a remarkably open, tenuous structure (as in figure 1.2). DLA clusters are fractals, but rather little is known about them with certainty.[2]

The DLA process is very simple, so it seems straightforward to write a computer program to grow such clusters in a computer, and this is what our busy graduate student has done. Initially, all seems well, but as the simulation progresses, the cluster seems to grow more and more slowly. Excruciatingly slowly, in fact. The goal was to grow a DLA cluster of N=100,000 particles. Will the program ever finish?

Luckily, the simulation program periodically writes information about its progress to a log file: for each new particle added to the cluster, the time (in seconds) since the start of the simulation is recorded. We should be able to predict the completion time

---

[1] Depending on your gnuplot setup and initialization, your graphs may look slightly different than the figures shown in this chapter. We'll discuss user-defined appearance options starting in chapter 5.

[2] The original paper on DLA was "Diffusion Limited Aggregation, A Kinetic Critical Phenomenon" by T. A. Witten and L. M. Sander, and appeared in *Physical Review Letters* Vol. 41, p. 1400 in 1981. It is one of the most quoted papers from that journal of all time. If you want to learn more about DLA and similar processes, check out *Fractals, Scaling, and Growth Far From Equilibrium* by Paul Meakin (1998).

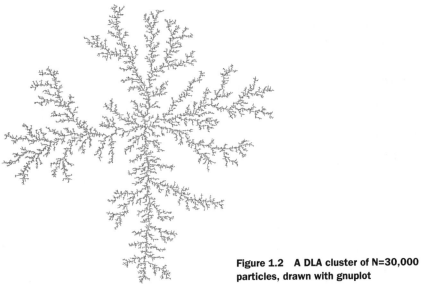

Figure 1.2   A DLA cluster of N=30,000 particles, drawn with gnuplot

from this data, but an initial plot (figure 1.3) is just not very helpful; there are too many ways that this curve can be extrapolated to larger cluster sizes.

The time consumed by many computer algorithms grows as a simple power of the size of the problem. In our case, this would be the number N of particles in the cluster $T \sim N^k$, for some value of k. Our research student therefore plots the running time of

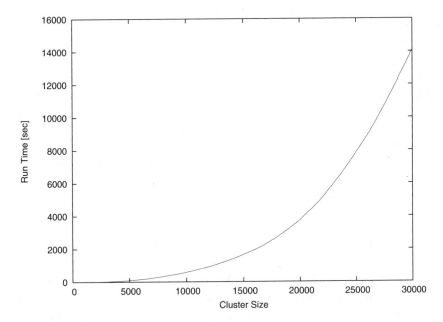

Figure 1.3   Time required to grow a DLA cluster

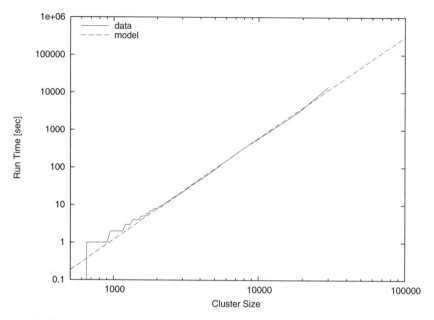

Figure 1.4   Time required to grow a DLA cluster in a double-logarithmic plot, together with an approximate mathematical model

his simulation program on a double logarithmic plot versus the cluster size (see figure 1.4). The data points fall on a straight line, indicating a power law. (I'll explain later how and why this works.) Through a little trial and error, he also finds an equation that approximates the data quite well. The equation can be extended to any cluster size desired and will give the time required. For N=100,000 (which was the original goal), we can read off T=300,000 seconds (or more), corresponding to 83 hours or four days, so we can tell our friend that there is no point in spending the weekend in the lab—he should go out (maybe run a marathon), and come back on Monday. Or perhaps work on a better algorithm. (For simulations of DLA cluster growth, dramatic speedups over the naive implementation are possible. Try it if you like.)

USING GNUPLOT

Again, let's see how the graphs in this section were created. The easiest to understand is figure 1.3. Given a file containing two columns, one listing the cluster size and the other listing the completion time, the command is simply

```
plot "runtime" using 1:2 with lines
```

The only difference compared to figure 1.1 is the style: rather than boxes, I use line segments to connect consecutive data points: `with lines`.

Did you notice that figure 1.3 and figure 1.4 contain more than just data? Both axes are now labelled! Details such as labels and other helpful decorations often make the difference between a mediocre and a high-quality graph, because they provide the observer with the necessary context to fully understand the graph.

In gnuplot, all details of a graph's appearance are handled by setting the appropriate options. To place the labels on the x and y axes in figure 1.3, I used

```
set xlabel "Cluster Size"
set ylabel "Run Time [sec]"
```

Figure 1.4 is drawn using double-logarithmic axes. This is another option, which is set as follows:

```
set logscale
```

Figure 1.4 shows two curves: the data together with a best "fit." Plotting several data sets or mathematical functions together in one plot is easy: we just list them one after another on the command line for the `plot` command:

```
plot "runtime" using 1:2 title "data" with lines,
➨    1.2*(x/1000)**2.7 title "model"
```

This command introduces a further gnuplot feature: the `title` directive. It takes a string as argument, which will be displayed together with a line sample in the plot's key or legend (visible in the upper left of figure 1.4).

Finally, we come to figure 1.2. That's a somewhat different beast. You'll notice that the border and the tic marks are missing. The aspect ratio (the ratio of the graph's width to its height) has been constrained to 1, and a single dot has been placed at the position of each particle in the cluster. Here are the most important commands that I used:

```
unset border
unset xtics
unset ytics

set size square

plot "cluster" using 1:2 with dots
```

You see that gnuplot is really simple to use. In the next section, I'd like to talk more about using graphical methods to understand a data set, before coming back to gnuplot and discussing why it is my favorite tool for this kind of activity.

1.2 What is graphical analysis?

These two examples should have given you an idea of what graphical analysis is and how it works. The basic steps are always the same:

1 Plot the data.
2 Inspect it, trying to find some recognizable behavior.
3 Compare the actual data to data that represents the hypothesis from the previous step (as we did in the second example earlier, when we plotted running time of the simulation program together with a power-law function).
4 Repeat.

We may try more sophisticated things, but this is the basic idea. If the hypothesis in the second step seems reasonably justified, we'll often try and *remove* its effect, for instance by subtracting a formula from the data, to see whether there is any recognizable pattern in the residual. And so on.

Iteration is a crucial aspect of graphical analysis: plotting the data this way and that way; comparing it to mathematical functions or to other data sets; zooming in on interesting regions or zooming out to detect the overall trend; applying logarithms or other data transformations to change its shape; using a smoothing algorithm to tame a noisy data set; and so on. During an intense analysis session using a new but promising data set, it's not uncommon to produce literally *dozens* of graphs.

None of these graphs will be around for long. They're transient, persisting just long enough for us to form a new hypothesis, which we'll try to justify in the next graph we draw. This also means that these graphs won't be "polished" in any way, since they're the graphical equivalent to scratch paper: notes of work in progress, not intended for anyone but ourselves.

This isn't to say that polishing doesn't have its place. But it comes later in the process: once we know what the results of our analysis are, we need to communicate them to others. At this point, we'll create "permanent" graphs, which will be around for a long time—maybe until the next departmental presentation, or (if the graph will be part of a scientific publication, for instance) possibly forever!

Such permanent graphs have different requirements: other people must be able to understand them, possibly years later, and most likely without us there to explain them. Therefore, graph elements such as labels, captions, and other contextual information become very important. Presentation graphs must be able to stand by themselves.

Presentation graphs also should make their point clearly. Now that we know the results of our analysis, we should find the clearest and most easily understood way of presenting our findings. A presentation graph should make one point and make it well.

Finally, some would argue that a presentation graph should "look good." Maybe. If it makes its point well, there is no reason why it shouldn't be visually pleasing as well. But that is an afterthought. Even a presentation graph is about the content, not the packaging.

1.2.1 *Data analysis and visualization concepts*

Data analysis and visualization is a broad field. Besides different graphical approaches, there are of course also other methods, which may do entirely without visual help. I think it will help to introduce and distinguish a number of terms and concepts for different activities in data analysis. At times, the boundaries between these different concepts may be fuzzy, but I think the overall distinctions are clear.

Graphical analysis   Graphical analysis is an investigation of data using graphical methods. The purpose is the discovery of new information about the underlying data set. In graphical analysis, the proper question to ask is often not known from the outset, but is discovered as part of the analysis process.

Presentation graphics   In contrast to graphical analysis, presentation graphics is concerned with communicating information and results that are already understood. The discovery has been made; now it merely needs to be communicated clearly.

Control charts   I use the term control chart somewhat loosely for situations where we already know the questions to ask of the data (as in the case of presentation graphics), but where the primary audience for the graph isn't the public, but the people who created the data themselves. Besides classical control charts (for example in quality engineering), many plots of experimental data fall into this category, because the question is determined at the outset and the graph is drawn to extract specific information to answer it.

Reality representation   What graphical analysis, presentation graphics, and control charts have in common is that they are "digital": some aspect of reality has been measured and translated into numbers, and it is these numbers that are plotted (temperature, stock price, electric field strength, response time... whatever).

Reality representation, by contrast, tries to construct an image that is in some form analogous to the system under consideration. A regular topographic map is a simple form of reality representation. More complex computer-assisted methods include three-dimensional solid body imaging, many ray-tracing systems, most immersive virtual reality methods, and many network flow or relationship-connectivity visualization systems.

Data analysis using reality representation is a large, amorphous, and highly experimental field.

Image analysis   Image analysis takes a two- or (rarely) three-dimensional image of the system under investigation and tries to detect significant structure in this image, often using color variations to indicate changes in value—think medical imaging. Image analysis may either be highly automated (using signal-processing methods) or be done visually. In the latter case, it shares aspects with graphical analysis.

Statistical analysis   This is the classical definition of data analysis. Statistical analysis typically tries to characterize a data set by calculating some mathematical quantity (such as the mean, the median, or the standard deviation) from the data. Statistical analysis gives a quantitative answer to a known, well-posed question.

Statistical analysis works great if we know what questions to ask of the data, and if we want to perform essentially similar analyses repeatedly (for instance, after varying some control parameter in a prescribed fashion). But it's not applicable if the questions to ask are yet unknown. And it can be misleading even otherwise, as our marathon example has shown: statistical analysis always makes some (silent) assumptions about the data that may not be fulfilled in practice. These challenges are well-known in the statistical community.

Exploratory data analysis   Exploratory (or initial) data analysis (EDA or IDA) is a term sometimes used in the statistical literature to describe the initial examination of data to determine its basic characteristics. Graphs typically play a large role. What makes it different from graphical analysis is that it is only seen as precursor to a "real" formal statistical analysis.

1.2.2   *Why graphical analysis?*

Graphical analysis is a discovery tool. We can use it to reveal as-yet unknown information in data. In comparison to statistical methods, it helps us discover *new* and possibly quite unexpected behavior.

Moreover, it helps us develop an intuitive understanding of the data and the information it contains. Since it doesn't require particular math skills, it is accessible to anyone with an interest and a certain amount of intuition.

Even if rigorous model building is our ultimate goal, graphical methods still need to be the first step, so that we can develop a sense for the data, its behavior, and quality. Knowing this, we can then select the most appropriate formal methods.

1.2.3   *Limitations of graphical analysis*

Of course, graphical analysis has limitations and its own share of problems.

- *Graphical analysis doesn't scale.*   Graphical analysis is a manual process that can't easily be automated. Each data set is treated as a separate special case, which isn't feasible if there are thousands of data sets.

  But this problem is sometimes more apparent than real. It can be remarkably effective to generate a large number of graphs and browse them without studying each one in great depth. It's totally possible to scan a few hundred graphs visually, and doing so may already lead to a high-level hypothesis regarding the classification of the graphs into a few subgroups, which can then be investigated in detail. (Thank goodness gnuplot is scriptable, so that preparing a few hundred graphs poses no problem.)

- *Graphical analysis yields qualitative, not quantitative results.*   Whether you regard this as a strength or a weakness depends on your situation. If you're looking for new behavior, graphical analysis is your friend. If you're trying to determine the percentage by which a new fertilizer treatment increases crop production, statistical analysis is the way to go.

- *It takes skill and experience.*   Graphical analysis is a creative process, using inductive logic to move from observations to hypothesis. There is no prescribed set of steps to move from a data set to conclusions about the underlying phenomena, and not much that can be taught in a conventional, classroom format.

  But by the same token, it does not require formal training, either. Ingenuity, intuition, and curiosity are the most important character traits. Everyone can play this game, if they're interested in finding out what the data tries to tell them.

1.3   *What is gnuplot?*

Gnuplot is a program for exploring data graphically. Its purpose is to generate plots and graphs from data or functions. It can produce highly polished graphs, suitable for publication, and simple throw-away graphs, when we're merely playing with an idea.

Gnuplot is command-line–driven: you issue commands at a prompt, and gnuplot will redraw the current plot in response. Gnuplot is also interactive: the output is generated and displayed immediately in an output window. Although gnuplot can be used as a background process in batch-mode, typical use is highly interactive. On the other hand, its primary user interaction is through a command language, not through a point-and-click GUI interface.

Don't let the notion of a command language throw you: gnuplot is easy to use— *really* easy to use! It takes only one line to read and plot a data file, and most of the command syntax is straightforward and quite intuitive. Gnuplot does not require programming or any deeper understanding of its command syntax to get started.

So this is the fundamental workflow of all work with gnuplot: plot, examine, repeat—until you have found out whatever you wanted to learn from the data. Gnuplot supports the iterative process model required for exploratory work perfectly.

1.3.1   *Gnuplot isn't GNU*

To dispel one common confusion right away: gnuplot isn't GNU software, has nothing to do with the GNU project, and isn't released under the GNU Public License (GPL). Gnuplot is released under a permissive open source license.

Gnuplot has been around a long time—a very long time! It was started by Thomas Williams and Colin Kelley in 1986. On the gnuplot FAQ, Thomas has this to say about how gnuplot was started and why it is named the way it is:

> *I was taking a differential equation class and Colin was taking Electromagnetics, we both thought it'd be helpful to visualize the mathematics behind them. We were both working as sys admin for an EE VLSI lab, so we had the graphics terminals and the time to do some coding. The posting was better received than we expected, and prompted us to add some, albeit lame, support for file data.*
>
> *Any reference to GNUplot is incorrect. The real name of the program is "gnuplot." You see people use "Gnuplot" quite a bit because many of us have an aversion to starting a sentence with a lower case letter, even in the case of proper nouns and titles. gnuplot is not related to the GNU project or the FSF in any but the most peripheral sense. Our software was designed completely independently and the name "gnuplot" was actually a compromise. I wanted to call it "llamaplot" and Colin wanted to call it "nplot." We agreed that "newplot" was acceptable but, we then discovered that there was an absolutely ghastly pascal program of that name that the Computer Science Dept. occasionally used. I decided that "gnuplot" would make a nice pun and after a fashion Colin agreed.*

For a long time (about 10 years), the stable major version of gnuplot was version 3.7.x, until version 4.0.0 was released in 2004. As part of the 4.x release, gnuplot has acquired a number of useful new features, including

- Palette-mapped color mode (pm3d), which makes it possible to choose colors for plots from continuous, user-defined color gradients (palettes).
- Much better text-handling capabilities, including the ability to read text from a file and use text as a plot style, support for common string functions, and "enhanced" text mode, allowing the use of formatting commands and special characters in gnuplot graphs.
- New plot styles: filled curves and boxes, histograms, and vectors.
- Improved output handling, including an entirely new interactive terminal based on the wxt widget set using the Cairo and Pango graphics and font libraries, resulting in a dramatically improved visual appearance over previous interactive gnuplot terminals. There are also many marginal improvements to other terminals, including a unified treatment of common pixmap file formats (GIF, PNG, JPG) using libgd.

The current release of gnuplot is version 4.2.5 (released in March, 2009). Gnuplot continues to be actively developed—if you'd like to contribute, subscribe to the developers' mailing list: gnuplot-beta@lists.sourceforge.net.

1.3.2   Why gnuplot?

I have already mentioned the most important reasons why I like gnuplot: easy to learn, easy to use, excellent support for iterative, exploratory use, yet nevertheless scriptable for bulk or offline processing, able to produce publication-quality graphs.

Here are some other reasons why I believe gnuplot is a good tool for many situations. Gnuplot is

- Stable, mature, and actively maintained.
- Free and open source.
- Available on all three platforms currently in use: Linux/Unix, Windows, Mac OS X.
- Able to generate polished, publication-quality graphs, and offering detailed control over the final appearance of plots.
- Supporting all common graphics formats (and quite a few less common ones).
- Able to read regular text files as input, and is tolerant regarding the specifics of the input file format. (No need for the data to be in some special archive file format!)
- Capable of handling large data sets (easily many millions of data points) and fast.
- Modest in its resource consumption.

1.3.3 Limitations

It is important to remember that gnuplot is a data-plotting tool, nothing more, nothing less. In particular, it is neither a numeric or symbolic workbench, nor a statistics package. It can therefore only perform rather simple calculations on the data. On the other hand, it has a flat learning curve, requiring no programming knowledge and only the most basic math skills.

Gnuplot is also no drawing tool. All its graphs are depictions of some data set. It has only very limited support for arbitrary box-and-line diagrams, and none at all for free-hand graphics.

Finally, gnuplot makes no attempt at what I earlier called "reality representation." It is a tool for quantitative analysis, and therefore its bread and butter are dot and line plots. It has no support for three-dimensional solid body imaging, ray-tracing, fisheye functionality, and similar techniques.

Overall, though, I regard these limitations more as strengths in disguise: in the Unix tradition, gnuplot is a rather simple tool, doing (mostly) one thing, and doing it very, very well.

1.4 Summary

In this chapter, I showed you a couple of examples that demonstrate the power of graphical methods for understanding data. I have also tried to suggest a suitable method for dealing with data analysis problems. Start with a plot of the data and use it to identify the essential features of the data set. Then iterate the process to bring out the behavior you're most interested in. And finally (not always, but often) develop a mathematical description for the data, which can then be used to make predictions (which, by their nature, go beyond the information contained in the actual data set).

Our tool in doing this kind of analysis will be gnuplot. And it is gnuplot, and how to use it, that we'll turn to next. Once we have developed the skills to use gnuplot well, we'll return to graphical analysis and discuss useful techniques for extracting the most information possible from a data set, using graphs.

Essential gnuplot 2

In this chapter, we introduce gnuplot's most important features: generating plots, saving them to a file, and exporting graphs to common graphics file formats. In the next chapter, we'll talk about data transformations and the organization of data sets. By the end of the next chapter, you'll know most of the commands you'll use on a day-to-day basis.

Are you surprised that a couple of chapters are sufficient to get us this far? Congratulations, you just discovered why gnuplot is cool: it makes easy things easy, and hard things possible. This chapter and the next cover the easy parts; as to the hard parts... well, that's what the rest of this book is all about.

2.1 Simple plots

Since gnuplot is a plotting program, it should come as no surprise that the most important gnuplot command is `plot`. It can be used to plot both functions (such as

$\sin(x)$) and data (typically from a file). The `plot` command has a variety of options and subcommands, through which we can control the appearance of the graph as well as the interpretation of the data in the file. The `plot` command can even perform arbitrary transformations on the data as we plot it.

2.1.1 Invoking gnuplot and first plots

Gnuplot is a *text-based* plotting program: we interact with it through command-line-like syntax, as opposed to manipulating graphs using the mouse in a WYSIWYG fashion. Gnuplot is also *interactive*: it provides a prompt at which we type our commands. When we enter a complete command, the resulting graph immediately pops up in a separate window. This is in contrast to a graphics *programming language* (such as PIC), where writing the command, generating the graph, and viewing the result are separate activities, requiring separate tools. Gnuplot has a history feature, making it easy to recall, modify, and reissue previous commands. The entire setup encourages you to play with the data: making a simple plot, changing some parameters to hone in on the interesting sections, eventually adding decorations and labels for final presentation, and in the end exporting the finished graph in a standard graphics format.

If gnuplot is installed on your system, it can usually be invoked by issuing the command:

```
gnuplot
```

at the shell prompt. (Check appendix A for instructions on obtaining and installing gnuplot, if your system doesn't have it already.) Once launched, gnuplot displays a welcome message and then replaces the shell prompt with a `gnuplot>` prompt. Anything entered at this prompt will be interpreted as gnuplot commands until you issue an `exit` or `quit` command, or type an end-of-file (EOF) character, usually by hitting Control-D.

Probably the simplest plotting command we can issue is

```
plot sin(x)
```

(Here and in the following, the `gnuplot>` prompt is suppressed to save space. Any code shown should be understood as having been entered at the gnuplot prompt, unless otherwise stated.)

On Unix running a graphical user interface (X11), this command opens a new window with the resulting graph, looking something like figure 2.1.

Please note how gnuplot has selected a "reasonable" range for the x values automatically (by default from -10 to +10) and adjusted the y range according to the values of the function.

Let's say we want to add some more functions to plot together with the sine. We recall the last command (using the up-arrow key or Control-P for "previous") and edit it to give

```
plot sin(x), x, x-(x**3)/6
```

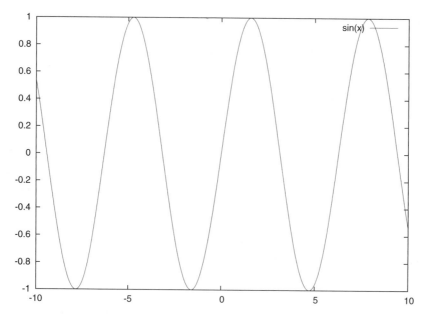

Figure 2.1   Our first plot: `plot sin(x)`

This will plot the sine together with the linear function x and the third-order polynomial $x - \frac{1}{6} x^3$, which are the first few terms in the Taylor expansion of the sine.[1] (Gnuplot's syntax for mathematical expressions is straightforward and similar to the one found in almost any other programming language. Note the ** exponentiation operator, familiar from Fortran or Perl. Appendix B has a table of all available operators and their precedences.) The resulting plot (see figure 2.2) is probably *not* what we expected.

The range of y values is far too large, compared to the previous graph. We can't even see the wiggles of the original function (the sine wave) at all anymore. Gnuplot adjusts the y range to fit in all function values, but for our plot, we're only interested in points with small y values. So, we recall the last command again (using the up-arrow key) and define the plot range that we are interested in:

```
plot [][-2:2] sin(x), x, x-(x**3)/6
```

The range is given in square brackets *immediately after* the `plot` command. The first pair of brackets defines the range of x values (we leave it empty, since we're happy with the defaults in this case); the second restricts the range of y values shown. This results in the graph shown in figure 2.3.

---

[1]   A Taylor expansion is a local approximation of an arbitrary, possibly quite complicated, function in terms of powers of *x*. We won't need this concept in the rest of this book. Check your favorite calculus book if you want to know more.

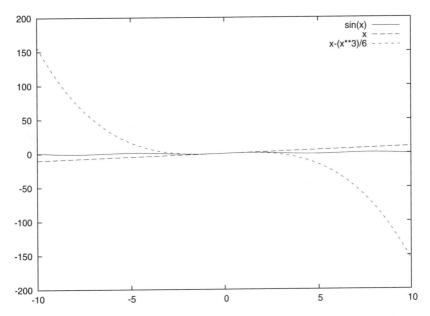

Figure 2.2   An unsuitable default plot range: `plot sin(x), x, x-(x**3)/6`

We can play much longer with function plots, zoning in on different regions of interest and trying out different functions (check the reference section in appendix B for a full list of available functions and operators), but instead let's move on and discuss what gnuplot is most useful for: plotting data from a file.

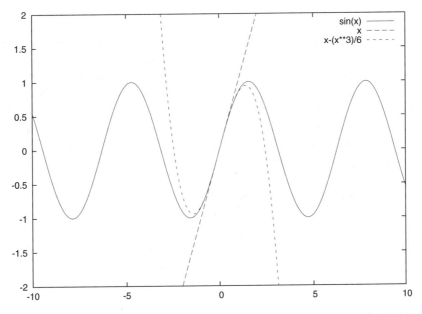

Figure 2.3   Using explicit plot ranges: `plot [][-2:2] sin(x), x, x-(x**3)/6`

2.1.2   *Plotting data from a file*

Gnuplot reads data from text files. The data is expected to be *numerical* and to be stored in the file in *whitespace-separated columns*. Lines beginning with a hashmark (#) are considered to be comment lines and are ignored. Listing 2.1 shows a typical data file containing the share prices of two fictitious companies, with the equally fictitious ticker symbols PQR and XYZ, over a number of years.

> **Listing 2.1   A typical data file: stock prices over time**

```
# Average PQR and XYZ stock price (in dollars per share) per calendar year
1975        49      162
1976        52      144
1977        67      140
1978        53      122
1979        67      125
1980        46      117
1981        60      116
1982        50      113
1983        66       96
1984        70      101
1985        91       93
1986       133       92
1987       127       95
1988       136       79
1989       154       78
1990       127       85
1991       147       71
1992       146       54
1993       133       51
1994       144       49
1995       158       43
```

The canonical way to think about this is that the x value is in column 1 and the y value is in column 2. If there are additional y values corresponding to each x value, they are listed in subsequent columns. (We'll see later that there's nothing special about the first column. In fact, any column can be plotted along either the x or the y axis.)

   This format, simple as it is, has proven to be extremely useful—so much so that long-time gnuplot users usually generate data in this way to begin with. In particular, the ability to keep related data sets in the same file is a big help (so that we don't need to keep PQR's stock price in a separate file from XYZ's, although we could if we wanted to).

   While whitespace-separated numerical data is what gnuplot expects natively, recent versions of gnuplot can parse and interpret significant deviations from this norm, including text columns (with embedded whitespace if enclosed in double quotes), missing data, and a variety of textual representations for calendar dates, as well as binary data (see chapter 4 for a more detailed discussion of input file formats, and chapter 7 for the special case when one of the columns represents date/time information).

Plotting data from a file is simple. Assuming that the file shown in listing 2.1 is called prices, we can simply type

```
plot "prices"
```

Since data files typically contain many different data sets, we'll usually want to select the columns to be used as x and y values. This is done through the using directive to the plot command:

```
plot "prices" using 1:2
```

This will plot the price of PQR shares as a function of time: the first argument to the using directive specifies the column in the input file to be plotted along the horizontal (x) axis, while the second argument specifies the column for the vertical (y) axis. If we want to plot the price of XYZ shares in the same plot, we can do so easily (as in figure 2.4):

```
plot "prices" using 1:2, "prices" using 1:3
```

By default, data points from a file are plotted using unconnected symbols. Often this isn't what we want, so we need to tell gnuplot what *style* to use for the data. This is done using the with directive. Many different styles are available. Among the most useful ones are with linespoints, which plots each data point as a symbol and also connects subsequent points, and with lines, which just plots the connecting lines, omitting the individual symbols.

```
plot "prices" using 1:2 with lines,
➡ "prices" using 1:3 with linespoints
```

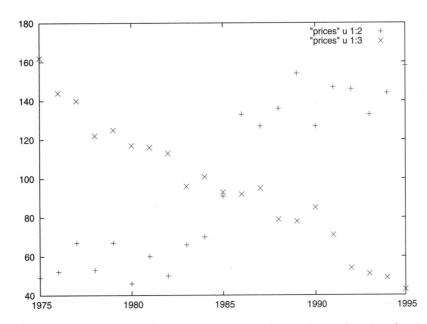

Figure 2.4   Plotting from a file: plot "prices" using 1:2, "prices" using 1:3

This looks good, but it's not clear from the graph which line is which. Gnuplot automatically provides a *key*, which shows a sample of the line or symbol type used for each data set together with a text description, but the default description isn't very meaningful in our case. We can do much better by including a `title` for each data set as part of the `plot` command:

```
plot "prices" using 1:2 title "PQR" with lines,
➥ "prices" using 1:3 title "XYZ" with linespoints
```

This changes the text in the key to the string given as the title (figure 2.5). The `title` has to come after the `using` directive in the `plot` command. A good way to memorize this order is to remember that we must specify the data set to plot *first* and provide the description *second*: define it first, then describe what you defined.

Want to see how PQR's price correlates with XYZ's? No problem; just plot one against the other, using PQR's share price for x values and XYZ's for y values, like so:

```
plot "prices" using 2:3 with points
```

We see here that there's nothing special about the first column. Any column can be plotted against either the x or the y axis; we just pick whichever combination we need through the `using` directive. Since it makes no sense to connect the data points in the last plot, we've chosen the style `with points`, which just plots a symbol for each data point, but no connecting lines (figure 2.6).

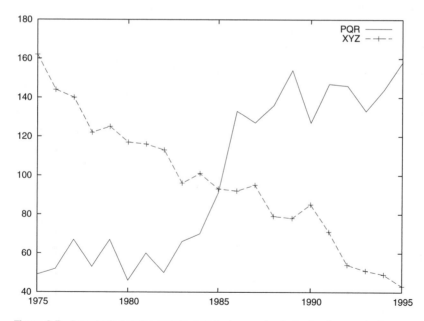

Figure 2.5 Introducing styles and the `title` keyword: `plot "prices" using 1:2 title "PQR" with lines, "prices" using 1:3 title "XYZ" with linespoints`

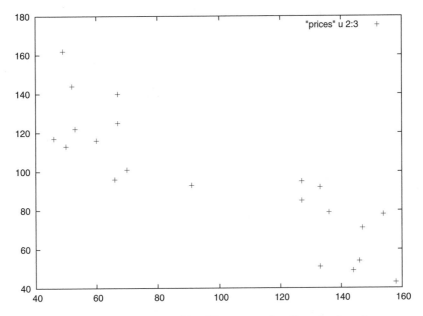

**Figure 2.6 Any column can be used for either x or y axis: `plot "prices"`
`using 2:3 with points`**

A graph like figure 2.6 is known as a *scatter plot* and can show correlations between two data sets. In this graph, we can see a clear negative correlation: the better PQR is doing, the worse XYZ's stock price develops. We'll revisit scatter plots and their uses later in chapter 13.

Now that we've seen the most important, basic commands, let's step back for a moment and quickly introduce some creature comforts that gnuplot provides to the more experienced user.

2.1.3 *Abbreviations and defaults*

Gnuplot is very good at encouraging iterative, exploratory data analysis. Whenever we complete a command, the resulting graph is shown immediately and all changes take effect at once. Writing commands isn't a different activity from generating graphs, and there's no need for a separate viewer program. (Graphs are also created almost instantaneously; only for data sets including millions of points is there any noticeable delay.) Previous commands can be recalled, modified, and reissued, making it easy to keep playing with the data.

There are two more features which gnuplot offers to the more proficient user: *abbreviations* and *sensible defaults*.

Any command and subcommand or option can be abbreviated to the shortest, nonambiguous form. So the command

```
plot "prices" using 1:2 with lines,
➥ "prices" using 1:3 with linespoints
```

would much more likely have been issued as

```
plot "prices" u 1:2 w l, "prices" u 1:3 w lp
```

This compact style is very useful when doing interactive work and should be mastered. From here on, I'll increasingly start using it. (A list of the most frequently used abbreviations can be found in table 2 in the section on conventions in the front of the book.)

But this is still not the most compact form possible. Whenever a part of the command isn't given explicitly, gnuplot first tries to interpolate the missing values with values the user has provided, and, failing that, falls back to sensible defaults. We've already seen how gnuplot defaults the range of x values to [-10:10], but adjusts the y range to include all data points.

Whenever a filename is missing, the most recent filename is interpolated. We can use this to abbreviate the last command even further:

```
plot "prices" u 1:2 w l, "" u 1:3 w lp
```

Note that the second set of quotation marks *must* be there.

In general, any user input (or part of user input) will remain unaffected until explicitly overridden by subsequent input. The way the filename is interpolated in the preceding example is a good example for this behavior. In later chapters, we'll see how options can be built up step by step, by subsequently providing values for different suboptions. Gnuplot helps to keep commands short by remembering previous commands as much as possible.

One last example concerns the using directive. If it's missing entirely and the data file contains multiple columns, gnuplot plots the second column versus the first (this is equivalent to using 1:2). If a using directive is given, but lists only a single column, gnuplot will use this column for y values and provide x values as integers starting at zero. This is also what happens when no using is given and the data file contains only a single column.

Let's close this section with a general comment regarding the syntax of gnuplot commands. Gnuplot syntax is mostly positional, not keyword oriented. This makes for compact commands, since the meaning of an abbreviation can be inferred from the position within the command. The price to pay is that occasionally subcommands that are expected earlier in the command need to be specified, even if we do not want to change their default settings. In this case, they are left blank. We've encountered this in the way empty brackets for the x range have to be supplied, even if we only want to change the y range, or in the way empty quotes indicate that the previous filename should be used again.

2.2   Saving and exporting

There are two ways to save our work in gnuplot: we can save the gnuplot commands used to generate a plot, so that we can regenerate the plot at a later time. Or we can export the actual graph to a file in one of a variety of supported graphics file formats, so that we can print it or include it in web pages, text documents, or presentations.

2.2.1 Saving and loading commands

If we save the commands that we used to generate a plot to file, we can later load them again and in this way regenerate the plot where we left off. Gnuplot commands can be saved to a file simply using the `save` command:

```
save "graph.gp"
```

This will save the current values of all options, as well as the most recent `plot` command, to the specified file. This file can later be loaded again using the `load` command:

```
load "graph.gp"
```

The effect of loading a file is the same as issuing all the contained commands (including the actual `plot` command) at the gnuplot prompt.

An alternative to `load` is the `call` command, which is similar to `load`, but also takes up to 10 additional parameters after the filename to load. The parameters are available inside the loaded file in the variables `$0` through `$9`. Strings are passed without their enclosing quotes, and the special variable `$#` holds the number of parameters to `call`. We can use `call` to write some simple scripts for gnuplot.

Command files are plain text files, usually containing exactly one command per line. Several commands can be combined on a single line by separating them with a semicolon (`;`). The hashmark (`#`) is interpreted as a comment character: the rest of the line following a hashmark is ignored. The hashmark isn't interpreted as a comment character when it appears inside quoted strings.

The recommended file extension for gnuplot command files is .gp, but you may also find people using .plt instead.

Since command files are plain text files, they can be edited using a regular text editor. It's sometimes useful to author them manually and load them into gnuplot, for instance to set up preferences or to imitate a limited macro capability (we'll give an example later in the chapter).

We'll discuss command files in more detail in chapter 12 on batch operations and user configurations.

2.2.2 Exporting graphs

As we've just seen, saving a set of plotting commands to a file is very simple. Unfortunately, exporting a graph in a file format suitable for printing is more complicated. It's not actually difficult, but unnecessarily cumbersome and prone to errors of omission. In this section, we'll first look at the steps required to export a printable graph from gnuplot; then we'll discuss the ways this process can go wrong. Finally, I'll show you a simple script that takes most of the pain out of the experience.

For any graph we want to generate (using gnuplot or anything else), we need to specify two things: the format of the graph (GIF, JPG, PNG, and so on) and the output device (either a file or the screen). In gnuplot, we do this using the `set` command:

```
set terminal png            # choose the file format
set output "mygraph.png"    # choose the output device
```

We'll discuss the set command in much more detail in chapter 4. For now, it's enough to understand that it sets a parameter (such as terminal) to a value. However, and this is often forgotten, it does *not* generate a plot! The only commands to do so are plot, splot (which is used for three-dimensional graphs, which we'll discuss in chapter 8), and replot (which simply repeats the most recent plot or splot command).

So, with this in mind, the complete sequence to export a graph from gnuplot and to resume working is shown in listing 2.2.

Listing 2.2   The complete workflow to generate a PNG file from gnuplot

```
plot exp(-x**2)            # some plot command
set terminal png           # select the file format
set output "graph.png"     # specify the output filename
replot                     # repeat the most recent plot command,
                           #    with the output now going to the
                           #    specified file.
set terminal x11           # restore the terminal settings
set output                 # send output to the screen again,
                           #    by using an empty filename.
```

This example demonstrates an important point: after exporting to a file, gnuplot does *not* automatically revert back to interactive mode—instead, all further output will be directed to the specified file. Therefore, we need to explicitly restore the interactive terminal (x11 in this example) *and* the output device. (The command set output without an argument sends all output to the interactive device, usually the screen.) This should come as no surprise. As we've seen before, gnuplot remembers any previous settings, and so neither the terminal nor the output setting change until we explicitly assign them a different value.

Nevertheless, this behavior is rather different than what we've come to expect from user interfaces in most programs: we usually do not have to restore the interactive session explicitly after exporting to a file. It's also unexpected that three separate commands are required to generate a file (set terminal, set output, and replot), making it easy to forget one.

It's helpful to understand the technical and historical background for this particular design. Gnuplot was designed to be portable across many platforms, at a time (late 1980s!) when graphic capabilities were much less dependable than today. In fact, it wasn't even safe to assume that the computer had an interactive graphics terminal at all (only an attached hardware plotter, for example). So all graphics generation was encapsulated into the terminal abstraction. And since it wasn't safe to assume that every installation would have a graphics-capable interactive terminal as well as a plotter or a file-based output device, the same terminal abstraction was used for both the interactive session as well as the printable export, requiring you to switch between different modes in a way that seems so cumbersome today.

Nevertheless, what we really want most of the time is a simple export routine, which takes the name of a file to export to, as well as the desired file format, and does all the required steps in one fell swoop. In the next section, I show you how to build one yourself.

2.2.3 One-step export script

The multistep process we just described to generate printable graphics from gnuplot is clearly a nuisance. Luckily, we can use the `call` command introduced earlier to bundle all required steps into one handy *macro*.

The `call` command executes all commands in a single file. Therefore, we can put all commands required to generate (for example) a PNG file *and* to restore the gnuplot session back to its original state into a command file, which we can then invoke through a single `call` command. And because `call` can take arguments, we can even pass the name of the desired output file as part of the same command.

If the commands shown in listing 2.3 are placed into a file, this file can be executed using `call` and will write the most recent plot to a PNG file and restore the initial session to its original state.

> **Listing 2.3 A useful script to export the current plot to file**

```
set terminal push    # save the current terminal settings
set terminal png     # change terminal to PNG
set output "$0"      # set the output filename to the first option
replot               # repeat the most recent plot command
set output           # restore output to interactive mode
set terminal pop     # restore the terminal
```

Here we've used the two pseudoterminals push and pop to help with the back-and-forth between the interactive and file terminals. The former (push) saves the current terminal settings onto a stack; the latter (pop) restores the terminal to the state saved on the stack. Neither makes any assumptions about the choice of interactive terminal, and therefore both can safely be used in scripts that must be portable across architectures.

Assuming the file shown in listing 2.3 was named export.gp in the current directory, we would call it like this, to write the current plot to a file called graph.png:

```
call "export.gp" "graph.png"
```

Here, both arguments are quoted. Quoting the second argument isn't strictly necessary, but highly recommended to avoid unexpected parsing of the output filename. The quotes are stripped before the argument is made available to the command file in the $0 variable.

Before leaving this section, one last word of advice: always save the commands used to generate a plot to a command file *before* exporting to a printable format. Always. It's almost guaranteed that you'll want to regenerate the plot to make a minor modification (such as fixing the typo in a label, or adding one more data set, or adjusting the plot range slightly) at a later time. This can only be done from the commands saved to file using save, not from plots exported to a graphics file. In chapter 11, section 11.1, I'll give an improved version of the export script which does both at the same time—that's how I generate all of my graphs.

2.3 *Summary*

In this chapter, we learned how to do the most important things with gnuplot: plotting, saving, and exporting. In detail, we discussed

- How to plot functions or data with the `plot` command: `plot sin(x)`
- How to restrict the plot range using bracket notation: `plot [0:5] sin(x)`
- How to select which columns from a data file to plot through `using`: `plot "data" using 1:2`
- How to save our work to file with the `save` command and how to load it again using `load`
- How to export a graph to a printable file format using `set output`, `set terminal`, and `replot`
- How to write simple scripts and use them through the `call` command

This means that we can do the three most important things for day-to-day work already: generate a plot, save it to file, and export it. In the next chapter, we'll learn about further things we can do with data in gnuplot: smoothing and filtering.

Working with data

3

Working with data is what gnuplot is all about. In this chapter, we look at three blocks of functionality, all of which help us to perform increasingly complicated operations on data. First we look at some special gnuplot syntax to pick out only parts from a larger file—often useful when dealing with data sets that are larger or more complicated than the straightforward ones we've considered so far. Then we discuss commands to smooth or otherwise clean up messy data sets. And finally, after taking a quick look at its math capabilities, we introduce gnuplot's data transformation features, which allow us to perform arbitrary data manipulations when generating a plot. These are particularly useful, and we'll make use of them many times going forward.

Everything I describe in this chapter is part of the plot command, similar to the using or title directives we've encountered before. Actually, there's even *more* to the `plot` command than this: we'll encounter some additional features in the following chapters on style and coordinate systems (axes). You can check appendix B for a full list of available directives. All directives to the `plot` command can be used together (potentially leading to long command lines), but they have to occur in proper order. Check the appendix for details.

3.1   *Managing large data sets*

Sometimes data sets have more internal structure than the simple one-record-per-line model we used in the previous chapter. Two cases in particular are reasonably common and must be dealt with: files containing data blocks—that is, different data sets one after another in a single file—and files containing records that span several lines each. We'll show how to handle each case in turn.

3.1.1   *Multiple data sets per file: index*

Here is a common scenario: some long-running program is performing a complex calculation. Periodically, it summarizes its results up to that point and appends them to an output file; it then continues its calculations. We want to use gnuplot to look at the contents of the resulting file.

The important issue here is that each intermediate result isn't a single data *point*, but an entire data *set*, spanning many rows (and, potentially, many columns as well) in the data file. Say the program simulates the structure of a liquid undergoing a freezing transition and writes the correlation function to file every 1,000 timesteps. The file might then look something like the file shown in listing 3.1.

Listing 3.1   A data file containing several sets

```
# Liquid/Solid transition simulation - density=0.0017
# x: first col; corr(x): second col
# t=0
0    0.99
1    0.03
2    0.01
3    0.02
4    0.01

# t=1000
0    0.98
1    0.10
2    0.05
3    0.01
4    0.02

# t=2000
0    0.99
1    0.32
2    0.14
3    0.08
4    0.03
```

This data file looks as if several distinct data files (for different times *t*) had been appended to one another. Since this situation is sufficiently common, gnuplot provides a way to handle it. But first, we need to look at the meaning of *blank lines* in a data file.

For gnuplot, blank lines in a data file are significant. A *single blank line* indicates a *discontinuity* in the data. The data above and below the blank line will be treated as belonging to the same data set (and be shown using the same line color and line style), but no connecting line will be drawn between the record before and after the blank.

In contrast, *double blank lines* are used to distinguish *data sets* in the file. Each set can be addressed in the `plot` command as if it were in a separate file using the `index` directive to `plot`.

The `index` directive follows immediately after the filename in the plot syntax and takes at least one numeric argument specifying which data set from the file to select. In line with the C language convention for indexing into arrays, `index` counts from 0 (zero). Therefore, to plot only the correlation function for *t*=1000, we could use

```
plot "data" index 1 using 1:2 w linespoints
```

This picks out only the data set with `index` 1 and shows it with `linespoints`.

The `index` directive can take up to three arguments, separated by colons (similar to the syntax familiar from `using`):

```
index {int:start}[:{int:end}][:{int:step}]
```

If only a single argument is given, only the corresponding data set is plotted. If two arguments are present, they're treated as the index of the first and last data set (inclusive) to be shown: `plot "data" index 2:5` will plot four data sets total. A third argument is interpreted as a step size. Accordingly, `plot "data" index 2:5:2` will plot only the data in sets 2 and 4. Only the first argument is mandatory.

So, in summary, the `index` directive lets us select consecutive sets of data from a file. The `every` option, which we discuss next, solves a different problem.

3.1.2 *Records spanning multiple lines: every*

Imagine that the data file mixes (in a regular fashion) different records in the same data set, for instance temperature and pressure readings, as in listing 3.2.

Listing 3.2 A data file containing interleaved data sets

```
# time - value
0     100.03      # temperature
0       2.10      # pressure
1     100.26      # t
1       2.02      # p
2     101.34      # t
2       1.95      # p
3     102.41      # t
3       1.87      # p
```

Here, each record for a single time really spans two lines: the first line gives the temperature and the second the pressure. If we want to plot only the temperature against time, we can use the every directive to pick up only the relevant subset of all lines:

```
plot "data" every 2 using 1:2 with lines
```

Using the every directive, we can control how we step through individual lines. The syntax looks similar to the syntax used for index, except that individual arguments are separated by two colons. Unfortunately, this similarity is somewhat deceiving, because the order of the arguments isn't the same for every as it is for index:

```
every {int:step}[::{int:start}[::{int:end}]]
```

The first argument is the increment, followed (optionally) by the first and last line number. Line numbers are counted from zero. Don't forget to use double colons with the every directive: single colons won't generate an error message, but will lead to strange and hard-to-predict behavior.[1]

The index and every directives can be used to pick out certain parts from a data file. But what do we do if the data itself is noisy or otherwise not fit to plot directly? That's the job of the smooth directive, which is the topic of the next section.

3.2   Smoothing and summarizing data

Gnuplot provides the smooth directive to the plot command as a simple tool to plot noisy or otherwise messy data files. For more sophisticated operations, check out section 3.4 on data transformations.

The smooth directive takes an additional parameter, which must be one of the following:

```
unique, frequency, bezier, sbezier, csplines, acsplines
```

(The current development version of gnuplot, version 4.3, contains two additional algorithms: cumul and kdens. Since they aren't part of the current release, I'm not going to talk about them here, but we'll discuss them in section 13.2 of chapter 13.)

The first two are different from the rest—they provide means to summarize (or otherwise sanitize/clean) data from messy files. The last four provide smooth approximations to noisy data. We'll look at them second, but first we'll discuss unique and frequency.

3.2.1   Plotting unsorted data files

The unique directive sorts the values chosen by the using statement for the x axis. If any x value occurs more than once, it will be replaced with a *single* data point having

---

[1] I am simplifying here. Gnuplot recognizes an additional concept known as a *data block* in a file, as a set of consecutive lines delimited from each other using single blank lines. Data blocks are functionally redundant with data sets (delimited by double blank lines). Data blocks can be selected through additional arguments to the every directive, which are placed between the double colons. This is why it's not illegal to use single colons in this context. If you want to know more about data blocks, check the standard gnuplot reference documentation.

the average of all corresponding y values. The `frequency` directive works the same way except that it forms the sum of all y values for each x value (instead of the average).

There are two different uses for `unique`. The first is a convenient shorthand to deal with unsorted data files such as the file in listing 3.3.

Listing 3.3 An unsorted data file: the years are not in ascending order

```
1970 1
1974 4
1979 4
1971 3     # out of order!
1973 6
1978 5
1980 2
```

When plotting such a file with a style that connects subsequent data points with lines (such as `lines` or `linespoints`), the graph won't look right because gnuplot by default joins points according to their order in the file, not according to the order of the x values (see figure 3.1)

```
plot "jumbled" u 1:2 smooth unique with linespoints
```

We could sort the file externally, but `unique` does this for us on the fly (compare figure 3.2).

The second use for `unique` is to deal with messy data files, such as the one in listing 3.4, which contains the temperature in three different cities, measured over a number of years. Note how the file isn't in a particularly good format (see the comments in the file).

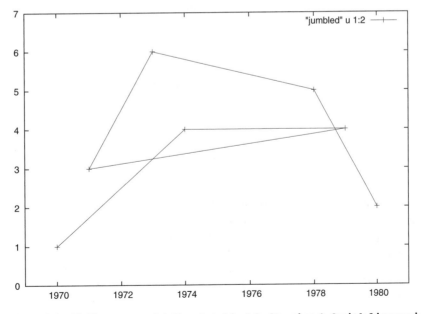

Figure 3.1 Plotting a messy datafile: `plot "jumbled" using 1:2 with linespoints`

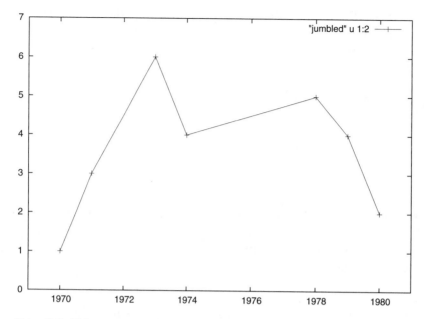

Figure 3.2   Using `smooth unique` lets us sort x values on the fly:
`plot "jumbled" u 1:2 smooth unique with linespoints`

Listing 3.4   A messy data file

```
# Temperature for three cities.
# City codes (column 3): Portway (=1), Abermore (=2), Flagwell (=3)
# Format: Year Temperature City
# ... Portway and Abermore only, annually
1990 32 1
1990 29 2
1991 33 1
1991 27 2
1992 31 1
1992 29 2
1993 32 1
1993 26 2
# ... now Flagwell tacked on, bi-annually
1991 27 3
1993 29 3
```

If we just want to get a general sense of the temperature development overall, `unique` will do this for us in a snap. The following command shows us both the original data points (unconnected), and the trend of the average temperature (compare figure 3.3):

```
plot [1989:1994][25:34] "messy" using 1:2 smooth uniq with linesp,
                        "" using 1:2 with points
```

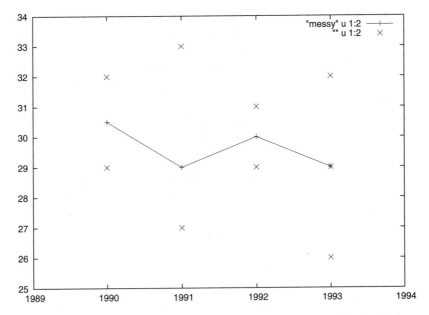

Figure 3.3　Using smooth unique can also find the averages for multi-valued data sets: `plot [1989:1994][25:34] "messy" using 1:2 smooth unique with linespoints, "" using 1:2 with points`

The `frequency` option has a different purpose: together with data transformations, it can be used to generate histograms of statistical data. We'll see an example later in section 13.2 of chapter 13.

3.2.2　*Smoothing noisy data*

While both `unique` and `frequency` summarize existing data, the remaining modes of the `smooth` directive generate smooth representations of the data by replacing the raw data with a mathematical description and plotting its values instead. The different modes generate different mathematical approximations to the data.[2]

- `bezier` calculates and plots a Bézier approximation of order n (where n is the number of data points). The curve is guaranteed to pass through the first and last data point exactly, but in general won't pass through any of the internal points. The resulting curve usually appears particularly smooth.
- `sbezier` first applies the `unique` transformation to the data, then calculates and plots a Bézier approximation to the results.

---

[2] Bézier curves are usually explained in books on computer graphics. A standard is *Computer Graphics: Principles and Practice in C* by James D. Foley, Andries van Dam, Steven K. Feiner, and John F. Hughes (2nd ed, 1995). Splines are a topic in numerical analysis. A popular title is *Numerical Recipes in C: The Art of Scientific Computing* by William H. Press, Brian P. Flannery, Saul A. Teukolsky, and William T. Vetterling (2nd ed, 1992). Material for both Bézier curves and splines can easily be found on the web as well.

- csplines applies a unique transformation, then calculates natural cubic splines to the result and plots these. The resulting curve passes exactly through all data points. As opposed to the Bézier curve (which is defined for the entire data set), splines are defined locally (between any two consecutive data points) and joined smoothly at the points. They're therefore most suited for data that's already quite smooth.

- acsplines applies the unique transformation to the raw data, then forms a *weighted* cubic splines approximation. The weight is taken from a mandatory third argument to the using directive.

Before going any further, an example will help. Let's consider again PQR's stock from section 2.1.2. As usual for share prices, the data is quite noisy, making it hard to see the overall trend. So we smooth it:

```
plot "prices" using 1:2 with linespoints,
➥    "" using 1:2 title "bezier" smooth bezier,
➥    "" using 1:2 title "csplines" smooth csplines
```

The results are shown in figure 3.4. We see both the raw (noisy) data, as well as the Bézier curve and the spline approximation. Note how the Bézier curve is a global approximation, providing a smooth representation of the *entire* data set. In contrast, splines are *local* approximations, smoothly connecting adjacent segments individually.

The weighted spline approximation (that is, smooth acsplines) modifies the local character of the spline approximation. Using weighted splines, each point contributes

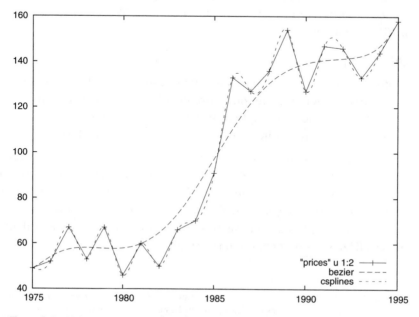

Figure 3.4 Using the smooth directive: plot "prices" using 1:2 with linesp, "" using 1:2 title "bezier" smooth bezier, "" using 1:2 title "csplines" smooth csplines

only according to its *weight* to the approximation, but the interpolation curve is no longer forced to pass through every point in the data set exactly. The weight is taken from a mandatory third column in the using specification, and can either be a constant (the same for all points in the data set) or vary from point to point.

In general, the greater the weight, the more each individual data point contributes to the interpolation curve. In the limit of infinite weight, the spline passes through all points exactly, recovering the behavior of the smooth csplines algorithm. In the opposite extreme, as the weight goes to zero, each point's individual contribution is reduced and the curve becomes smoother. In the limit of zero weight, the curve degenerates into a straight-line fit of the data. Figure 3.5 demonstrates this effect.

In figure 3.5, all weights were constants, but it's also possible to give each data point its own weight factor. This gives us the ability to take into account the uncertainty in each particular data point. Let's assume a data file contains not only x and y values, but also the standard error in each y value. We may then plot a weighted spline curve using this information like so: plot "data" u 1:2:(1/$3**2) s acs. Points with larger errors are quadratically suppressed when forming the spline approximation. (This was a first example of inline data transformations, which we'll formally introduce in section 3.4 later in this chapter.)

The ability to adjust the "stiffness" of an interpolation curve continuously through a control parameter, as we've done in figure 3.5, can help us understand the structure of a data set. We'll see some applications of this technique in chapters 13 and 14.

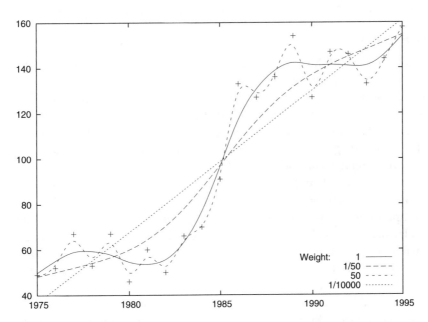

Figure 3.5 The effect of different weights on the acsplines algorithm: plot [1975:1995] [40:160] "prices" using 1:2 with points, "" u 1:2:(1) smooth acsplines 1, "" using 1:2:(1/50.) smooth acsplines 2, "" using 1:2:(50) smooth acsplines 3, "" using 1:2:(1/10000.) smooth acsplines 4

3.3   Math with gnuplot

Not surprisingly, gnuplot can evaluate mathematical expressions and includes support for many mathematical functions. Gnuplot's syntax for mathematical expressions is straightforward and similar to the conventions found in other programming languages.

Gnuplot ships with its own math library, which these days is only used when the system math library is found insufficient. The most notable extension that gnuplot's math library provides is support for complex numbers.

3.3.1   Mathematical expressions

Gnuplot uses standard infix syntax for mathematical expressions, including the normal operators for the four basic arithmetical operations, as in most C-like languages. Parentheses can be used to change the order of evaluation. Gnuplot has the exponentiation operator (`**`), found in Fortran and Perl. All these operate either on floating-point values or on integers. Integer division truncates, so that $3/2$ yields 1. Integers are promoted to floating-point values in mixed expressions, but in some situations truncation occurs in expressions involving variables. If nontruncating division is desired, it's always safer to force the use of floating-point arithmetic by writing `x/2.` or `x/2.0`. Two mathematical operators exist that accept only integer arguments: the familiar modulo operator `%`, and a unary factorial operator: `n! = 1 * 2 * ... * (n-1) * n`.

All the usual relational and logical operators are available as well, including the ternary conditional operator (`?:`). A full list can be found in appendix B.

3.3.2   Built-in functions

Gnuplot provides all the mathematical functions you've come to expect on any scientific calculator: square root, exponential function and logarithms, and trigonometric and hyperbolic functions. It also supports some less-standard functions related to the Bessel functions, the error integral, and the gamma function. You can execute `help functions` from within gnuplot or check appendix B for the full list.

The standard gnuplot distribution contains a file called stat.inc in the demo/ folder, which defines many additional functions, most of them related to various probability distributions. You can load this file into your current gnuplot session using `load`, and then use these functions the same way you would use built-ins.

Gnuplot also includes a random number generator, which can be quite useful at times. It can be accessed through the function `rand(x)`. If called with an argument that is equal to zero, the function returns a pseudo random number between zero and one.

The algorithm used to generate the pseudo random numbers requires two seeds to be set; given the same values for the seeds, exactly the same sequence of numbers will be returned. Gnuplot doesn't have a separate function to set the seeds; instead this is accomplished by providing special values as arguments to `rand(x)`. Check table 3.1 for details. Keep in mind that `rand(x)` is a function, and therefore must be called as an expression, even if only setting the seeds. The command `print rand(-1)`, for example, can be used to reset the seeds to their default values.

Table 3.1 The `rand(x)` function is used both to access the random number generator and to set its seeds, depending on the value of the argument.

Invocation	Description
`rand(0)`	Returns the next pseudo random number, using the current values of both seeds
`rand(-1)`	Resets both seeds to a standard value
`rand(x)`	For x>0,sets both seeds to a value based on the value of x
`rand({x,y})`	For x,y>0, sets the first seed to x and the other seed to y

3.3.3   User-defined variables and functions

It's easy to define new variables simply by assigning an expression to a name. For instance, we might want to define some useful mathematical constants. (We don't need to define pi, since it's already defined by gnuplot—the only such predefined constant.) Listing 3.5 shows some more useful constants we may want to define.

Listing 3.5   Examples of user-defined variables (constants)

```
e = 2.71828182845905       # The base of the natural logarithm
sqrt2 = sqrt(2)            # The square-root of 2
euler = 0.57721566490153   # The Euler-Mascheroni constant
```

Here, `euler` is the Euler-Mascheroni constant (usually represented using the Greek letter gamma), which is "the most important number that you've never heard of before" (J. Stopple).[3]

Functions can be defined in a similar fashion, as shown in listing 3.6.

Listing 3.6   Examples of user-defined functions

```
f(x) = -x * log(x)

gauss( x, m, s ) = exp( -0.5*( (x-m)/s )**2 )/sqrt(2*pi*s**2)

# Using the factorial operator to generate binomial coefficients
binom( n, k ) = n!/(k!*(n-k)!)

min( a, b ) = ( a < b ) ? a : b # Using the ternary "?" operator
step( x ) = ( x < 0 ) ? 0 : 1   # A piece-wise defined function
```

Functions can have up to 10 variables and can contain other functions and operators. We use them as we would use any other function. Assuming we had issued the definitions in listing 3.6, we could then simply write `plot sin(x), f(x)`.

By default, gnuplot assumes that the independent dummy variable, which is automatically replaced by a range of x values when plotting a function, is labeled x, but this can be changed using the `set dummy` command. For example, `set dummy t` will make t the independent variable.

---

[3] Read his wonderful *A Primer of Analytic Number Theory* (2003) to find out why you should care. The quote can be found on page 49.

All other variables occurring in a function definition (parameters) must have been assigned values before we can plot (that is, evaluate) the function. For convenience, it's possible to assign values to parameters as part of the plot command. The following code snippet draws two lines, one for a=1 and one for a=2 (also compare figure 3.6):

```
g(x) = cos(a*x)/a
plot a=1, g(x), a=2, g(x)
```

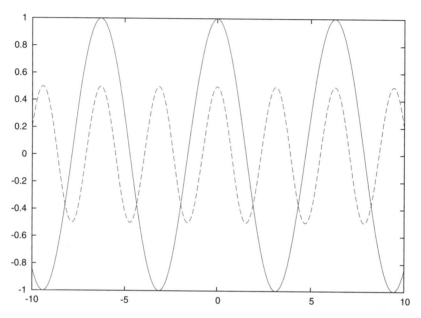

Figure 3.6   Assigning to variables as part of the plot command:
`plot a=1, g(x), a=2, g(x)`

All functions and variables have global scope. There's no such thing as a private variable or local scope!

Lists of all user-defined variables and functions can be generated using the following two commands:

```
show variables
show functions
```

3.3.4   *Complex numbers*

I mentioned earlier that gnuplot has limited support for complex numbers, so let's take a quick look. (If you don't know what complex numbers are, you probably want to skip this section.)

Complex numbers are pairs of numbers, the so-called *real* and *imaginary* parts. In gnuplot, a complex number is indicated using curly braces ({}). The following expression would be interpreted as the complex number $z = 1 + i$, where i is the imaginary unit.

```
z = { 1, 1 }
```

Gnuplot can perform simple arithmetic on complex numbers, such as { 1, 1 } + { -1, 0 }. Furthermore, many of the built-in mathematical functions (such as sin(x), exp(x), and so forth) can accept complex arguments and return complex numbers as results. We can use the special functions real(x) and imag(x) to pick out the real and imaginary parts, respectively.

One important limitation of gnuplot's complex numbers is that both parts must be numeric *constants*—not variables, not expressions! We can always work around this limitation, though, by using a complex constant as part of a more general expression. For example, the following command will plot real and imaginary parts of the exponential function, evaluated for imaginary argument:

```
plot real( exp(x*{0,1}) ), imag( exp(x*{0,1}) )
```

Complex numbers are of fundamental importance in mathematics and theoretical physics, and have important applications in signal processing and control theory. Gnuplot's ability to handle them makes it particularly suitable for such applications.

Now that we've seen what mathematical operations we can perform, let's see how we can apply them to data.

3.4 Data transformations

As stated before, gnuplot is first and foremost a *plotting* tool: a program that allows us to generate straightforward plots of raw data in a simple and efficient manner. Specifically, it's *not* a statistics package or a workbench for numerical analysis. Large-scale data transformations are not what gnuplot is designed for. Properly understood, this is one of gnuplot's main strengths: it does a simple task and does it well, and does not require learning an entire toolset or programming language to use.

Nevertheless, gnuplot has the ability to perform arbitrary transformations on the data as part of the plot command. This allows us to apply filters to the data from within gnuplot, without having to take recourse to external tools or programming languages.

3.4.1 Simple data transformations

An arbitrary function can be applied to each data point as part of the using directive in the plot command. If an argument to using is enclosed in parentheses, it's not treated as a column number, but as an expression to be evaluated. Inside the parentheses, you can access the values of the column values for the current record by preceding the column number with a dollar sign ($) (as in shell or awk programming). Some examples will help to clarify.

To plot the square root of the values found in the second column versus the values in the first column, use

```
plot "data" using 1:( sqrt($2) ) with lines
```

To plot the average of the second and third columns, use

```
plot "data" using 1:( ($2+$3)/2 ) with lines
```

To generate a log/log plot, we can use the following command (although the `logscale` option, discussed in section 3.6, is the preferred way to achieve the same effect):

```
plot "data" using ( log($1) ):( log($2) ) with lines
```

Here are some more creative uses. To plot two data sets of different magnitude on a similar scale, use this (assuming that the data in column three is typically greater by a factor of 100 than the data in column two):

```
plot "data" using 1:2 with lines, "" using 1:( $3/100 ) with lines
```

If the data file contains the x value in the first column, the mean in the second, and the variance in the third, we can plot the band in which we expect 68 percent of all data to fall as

```
plot "data" using 1:( $2+sqrt($3) ) with lines,
➡    "" using 1:( $2-sqrt($3) ) with lines
```

All expressions involving operators or functions can be part of `using` expressions, including the conditional operator:

```
plot "data" using 1:( $2 > 0 ? log($2) : 0 ) with lines
```

Finally, it should be kept in mind that the expression supplied in parentheses can be a *constant*. The following command uses the `frequency` directive to count the number of times each of the values in the first column (assumed to be integers) has occurred. The resulting plot is a *histogram* of the values in the first column (remember that `smooth frequency` sums up the values supplied as y values and plots the sum):

```
plot "data" using 1:(1) smooth frequency with lines
```

A fundamental limitation to all these transforms is that they can only be applied to a *single record at a time*. If you need aggregate functions over several records (sums or averages, for example), or across different data sets, you'll have to perform them externally to gnuplot. Nevertheless, the ability to apply an arbitrary filter to each data point, and to combine different data points for the same x value, is often tremendously useful.

3.4.2 *Pseudocolumns and the column function*

Gnuplot defines two pseudocolumns that can be used together with data transformations. The column 0 contains the line number in the current data set; the column -2 contains the index of the current data set within the data file. When a double blank line is encountered in the file, the line number resets to zero and the index is incremented. We could use these pseudocolumns, for instance, like this:

```
plot "data" using 0:1  # Plot first column against line number
plot "data" using 1:-2 # Plot data set index against first column
```

Another way to pick out a column is to use the `column(x)` function. This function evaluates its argument and uses the value (which should be an integer) to select a column. For instance, we may have a variable x (possibly obtained through some complicated expression) and want to use x as column specifier. No problem: `plot "data" u 1:(column(x))`. The `column(x)` function is only available inside parenthetical expressions when used as part of the `using` directive.

The `column(x)` function and pseudocolumns work together quite well. For instance, in this example, we plot all values from a file, but add a constant vertical offset of 1.5 to values from different data sets (to separate curves from different data sets from each other, so that we can distinguish them more easily):

```
plot "data" using 1:($2 + 1.5*column(-2)) with lines
```

There's one other function we should mention in this context: `valid(x)`. It returns true only if the value of the column with column number x is a valid number. We can use this function to test values from messy files, and only plot those that are valid.

3.5   *Plotting functions and data*

There are two options that we might want to know about when plotting functions and data: `set samples` and `set clip`.

The `set samples` controls the number of points at which a function is evaluated to generate a plot. It defaults to 100 points, but this may not be sufficient for curves including cusps or singularities. A value of 300–500 works well—it rarely makes sense to set a sampling rate higher than the horizontal number of pixels of the output device (which is usually around 600). This option has no effect when plotting data, unless one of the smoothing algorithms is used; the smooth curve will be sampled according to the value of the `set samples` option.

Changing the number of sampling points is easy: simply give an integer argument to set samples:

```
set samples 300    # Now 300 points are used
```

The `set clip` option controls how gnuplot plots points that are too close to or outside the plot range:

```
set clip points set clip [ one | two ]
```

The first version, `set clip points`, is only relevant when using a style that shows discrete plotting symbols (such as `with points`, `with linespoints`, and so on). If it's active, symbols that would touch or overlap the borders of the plot are suppressed. Exactly how many points are clipped depends on the symbol size: for larger symbols, more points need to be clipped. (See chapter 5 for more detail on styles and ways to influence the symbol size.)

The second version controls how gnuplot plots line segments connecting points if at least one of the points falls outside the currently visible plot range. If `set clip one` is active, line segments are drawn if at least one of the end points falls into the visible plot range. If `set clip two` is active, line segments are drawn even if both end points are outside the current plot range, but a straight line connecting them crosses the visible range. In no case are parts of the line segment drawn outside the visible range. By default, `set clip one` is on, but `set clip two` is off.

3.5.1   *Tricks and warnings*

Gnuplot math allows for a few tricks, which can be used to good effect in some situations—or which may trip up the unwary.

- First, remember that *integer division truncates!* This means that 1/4 evaluates to 0 (zero). If you want floating-point division, you must promote at least one of the numbers to floating point: 1/4.0 or 1.0/4 will evaluate to 0.25, as expected.

- Gnuplot tends to be pretty tolerant when encountering undefined values: rather than failing, it just doesn't produce any graphical output for data points with undefined values. This can be used to suppress data points or generate piecewise functions. For example, consider the following function:

  ```
  f(x) = abs(x) < 1 ? 1 : 1/0
  ```

  It's only defined on the interval [-1:1], and a plot of it will only show data points for this interval.

- A similar method can be used to exclude certain data points when plotting data from a file. For example, the following command will only plot data points for which the y value is less than 10:

  ```
  plot "data" using 1:( $2 < 10 ? $2 : 1/0 ) with linespoints
  ```

This 1/0 technique is a good trick that's frequently useful, in particular in conjunction with the ternary operator, as in these examples.

3.6   *Logarithmic plots*

Lastly, let's see how we can generate logarithmic plots. Logarithmic plots are a crucial technique in graphical analysis. In gnuplot, it's easy to switch to and from logarithmic plots:

```
set logscale       # turn on double logarithmic plotting
set logscale x     # turn on logarithmic plotting for x-axis only
set logscale y     #                              for y-axis only

unset logscale     # turn off logarithmic plotting for all axes
unset logscale x   #                              for x-axis only
unset logscale y   #                              for y-axis only
```

We can provide a base as a second argument: set logscale y 2 turns on binary logarithms for the y axis. (The default is to use base 10.)

We'll talk some more about uses for set logscale in chapter 13.

3.6.1   *How do logarithmic plots work?*

Logarithmic plots are a truly indispensable tool in graphical analysis. Fortunately, it's possible to understand what they do even without detailed understanding of the mathematics behind them. However, the math isn't actually all that hard, so in this section, I'll try to explain how logarithmic plots work and how they're used.

Let's just quickly recapitulate the most relevant properties of logarithms. The defining relation for the log function is

$$n = \log_b b^n$$

There isn't a single log function, but infinitely many; we always need to specify the *base* b, with respect to which the logarithm needs to be taken.

Logarithms with respect to different bases are related to one another in a simple way:

$$\log_a x = \log_a b \log_b x$$

Logarithms to two specific bases are used most often: the logarithm to base 10 (typically abbreviated log) and the so-called natural logarithm to base e=2.7818... (abbreviated ln). Be aware that the notation just introduced ($\log(x)$ and $\ln(x)$) is common in mathematical contexts, but when using gnuplot's built-in functions, `log(x)` refers to the natural logarithm; you must use `log10(x)` for the logarithm to base 10.

Logarithms have many interesting properties, two of which are of fundamental importance:

$$\log(xy) = \log(x) + \log(y)$$

and

$$\log(x^k) = k \log(x)$$

We can see that the logarithm of a product equals the sum of the logarithms, so these two relations can be summarized by saying that logarithms turn products into sums and powers into products. We'll see how these relationships are at the core of logarithmic plots.

In a logarithmic plot, we don't plot the actual values; instead we plot their logarithms. But tic marks on the axes are usually labeled with the actual values (not their logarithms). Here's an example: we want to plot the values of 1, 10, 100, and 1000. Their logarithms (to basis 10) are 0, 1, 2, and 3, respectively (since $10^3 = 1000$ and so on). In a logarithmic plot, we'll place tic marks at equal distance from each other (at the locations 0, 1, 2, and 3), but *label* them 1, 10, 100, and 1000.

In figure 3.7 we demonstrate these aspects. The y axis on the left is scaled logarithmically. Comparing the values on the left-hand y axis to the units of the right-hand y axis shows how a logarithmic axis is linear in the exponent to which the base must be raised to obtain the actual value (that is, it's linear in the logarithm). Also note how the same *relative* change results in the same visual length when using logarithmic scales: both scale arrows have the same length and represent a 100 percent change, although the absolute change is different for both arrows (1 to 2 on the left, 100 to 200 on the right).

We can switch on logarithmic plotting either on only a single axis (usually the y axis) or on both, yielding a single or double logarithmic plot, respectively. Single logarithmic plots are sometimes referred to as *semi-log plots*, and double logarithmic plots are also known as *log-log plots*. Both plots are used for different purposes.

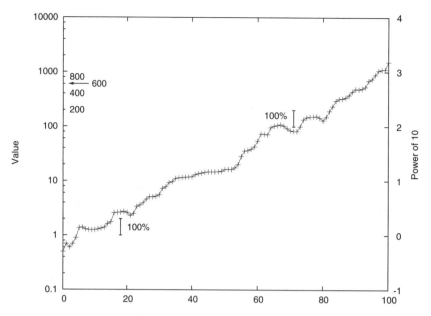

Figure 3.7   A semi-log plot. See the text for details. (Labels for some of the minor tic marks on the left axis have been provided.)

There are two uses for single logarithmic plots. First of all, if we have data with exponential behavior, showing it on a single logarithmic plot will let the data fall onto a straight line:

$$y(x) = e^{a\,x} \Rightarrow \log(\,y(x)\,) = a\,x$$

In other words, if $y(x)$ is an exponential function of x, then $\log(\,y(x)\,)$ is a linear function (straight line) of x. We can use single logarithmic plots in this way to determine, for instance, the half-life of a radioactive substance from measured decays.

The other use for single logarithmic plots is common in finance: on a single logarithmic plot, all *relative* changes have the same size, no matter how large the underlying absolute changes.

Here's an example: If a stock we own falls by $10 in a single day, our reaction will be different depending on whether we paid $20 or $100 initially. In the first case, we lost 50 percent of our money, but in the second, we lost only 10 percent. What we really care about are relative changes, not the absolute ones. What we therefore want is a plot in which all changes of the same relative magnitude result in the same distance on the graph. That's exactly what *semi-log plots* do for us. If the value before the change is y_1 and the value after the change is $y_2 = g\,y_1$, where g equals 1.1 (corresponding to a 10 percent gain), then the change in absolute terms is

$$y_1 - y_2 = y_1 - g\,y_1 = (\,1 - g\,)\,y_1$$

which depends on the overall size of the value y_1. But if we consider logarithms, we find

$$\log(\,y_1\,) - \log(\,y_2\,) = \log(\,y_1\,) - \log(\,g\,y_1\,) = \log(\,y_1\,) - \log(\,g\,) - \log(\,y_1\,) = -\log(\,g\,)$$

which is *independent* of the overall value and depends only on the relative size of the change, *g*. This is why long-term charts of, for example, the Dow-Jones index are usually shown as semi-log plots: a 10 percent drop today or in 1929 results in the same distance covered on the graph, despite the fact that the Dow-Jones is over 13,000 today,[4] but stood around 300 then.

Double logarithmic plots serve a different purpose: they help us identify power law behavior—that is, data that follows an equation such as the following (*C* is a constant):

$$y(x) = C x^k$$

The analysis goes through as previously, but we end up with logarithms now on *both* sides of the equation:

$$\log(y(x)) = k \log(x) + \log(C)$$

The resulting graph is a straight line, with a slope that depends on the exponent *k*. We've seen an example of this in chapter 1, when estimating the completion time of a long-running computer program.

Double logarithmic plots are very important. Power laws occur in many different contexts in the real world, but aren't always easy to spot. Go back to figure 1.3 in chapter 1: many different curves will seem to fit the data about equally well. But once plotted on a double-log plot (see figure 1.4), the linear shape of the data stands out and provides a strong and easily recognizable indicator of the underlying power law behavior.

Log and log-log plots are part of the standard toolset. When faced with a new data set, I typically plot it both ways, just to see whether there's some obvious (exponential or power law) behavior in it that wasn't apparent immediately. They're also useful when dealing with data that changes over many orders of magnitude. Learn how to use them!

3.7 *Summary*

In this chapter, we covered what's really the "meat" of gnuplot: working with data. We learned special commands to deal with large and with messy data sets. In detail, we've seen

- The `index` specifier to the `plot` command, which lets us pick out only part of a data file
- The `every` specifier to the `plot` command, which allows us to select only a subset of records from a data file
- The `smooth` directive, which helps us summarize or approximate a noisy data set

Even more importantly, we also introduced inline data transformations. They give us the ability to apply a random function to individual data points as they're being

---

[4] This statement was true when this section was first written. As the book went to press, the Dow-Jones index had fallen below 9,000 points. (These two data points indicate the length of time it took to complete the manuscript!)

plotted. This will turn out to be extremely handy in our work. The most important features we've introduced are

- User-defined functions and variables.
- The syntax for inline transformations. If the arguments to the `using` directive are enclosed in parentheses, their contents is evaluated as a mathematical expression. Columns from the data file are available as column numbers, prefixed with a dollar sign: `plot "data" using 1:(sqrt($2))`.
- The pseudocolumn 0 stands for the line number in the data file.

Finally, we introduced logarithmic plots and discussed why and how they work, and what they're good for.

This concludes what we need to know to get started doing data analysis using gnuplot. In the next chapter, we'll turn away from gnuplot's core functionality of dealing with data and generating plots, and instead talk about a host of useful features which make our work with gnuplot easier.

Practical matters

In the previous two chapters, we looked at ways to manipulate and visualize data using gnuplot, which is the core task that gnuplot was designed for. Before moving on to more sophisticated application areas, let's close this introductory part of the book by looking at some features of gnuplot that don't directly have much to do with data and visualization, but that are useful to have around.

First, we'll learn how to view and manipulate *options*, which are gnuplot's way of controlling details of its operation. Then we'll summarize what we've learned about input file formats and show how we can use options to customize some aspects of file handling. From files, it's only a small step to strings: gnuplot can read strings from files and make them part of a graph. We'll see how to do this, and learn about gnuplot's facilities to handle and manipulate strings.

The last part of this chapter talks about useful tricks relating to gnuplot's interactive terminals. In the process, we'll also learn how to use gnuplot's online help system and history feature.

This chapter is a bit of a grab-bag of useful features. What they all have in common is that they help us be more productive with gnuplot, without *directly* being related to the manipulation and plotting of data. This chapter deals with the "other stuff."

4.1   *Managing options*

Gnuplot has relatively few commands (such as the `plot`, `save`, and `load` commands we've already encountered in two preceding chapters), but a large number of *options*. These options are used to control everything, from the format of the decimal point to the name of the output file. There are more than 100 such options available, and countless suboptions for each. Check appendix B for a complete categorized reference of available options.

The three commands used to manipulate individual options are

- `show` to display the current value of an option
- `set` to change the value of an option
- `unset` to disable a specific option, or to return it to its default value

There's also a fourth command, `reset`, which returns *all* options to their default values. The only options not affected by `reset` are the ones directly influencing output generation: `terminal` and `output`.

We've already encountered the `set` command, when we discussed output file formats in chapter 2:

```
set terminal postscript
set output "graph.ps"
```

The syntax of all three commands is straightforward. Here, we first set the global style for functions to unconnected points, then display the current settings for the `style function` option, and finally return it to its default value:

```
set style function points
show style function
unset style function
```

The `show` command is also used more generally to display all kinds of information about gnuplot's internal state, not just options which can be changed using `set`. In the previous chapter, we already encountered `show variables` and `show functions`, which display all user-defined variables and functions.

Another useful command is

```
show version long
```

This prints the current version of gnuplot, together with a copyright notice and some pointers to the online documentation. More importantly, it also shows the compile-time flags that gnuplot was compiled with. This is particularly relevant, since some features have only recently been added to gnuplot, and may not be enabled on all platforms. You can use `show version long` to see which flags your version of gnuplot was built with.

Finally, we can use `show all` to see a listing of all possible options and their values. Be prepared for a long listing!

4.2 Data files

By default, gnuplot data files are ASCII text files that contain data in whitespace-separated columns. We can pick out any column and print its values against any other column by means of the `using` directive. All of this should be old hat by now (or go back and check section 2.1.2 to refresh your memory).

Using text files as primary data store has a number of advantages: we don't need special tools to generate or read them, and it's easy to write scripts to pre- or postprocess them. If necessary, we can even load them into any text editor and manipulate them by hand. In addition, text files are largely portable across most current computer architectures (so that files generated on Unix, say, can be opened and read on Windows)—except for the choice of the linebreak indicator (newline character). Gnuplot expects lines in input files to be terminated by whatever the local operating system (or rather, the local C library) considers the "native" newline character. If you encounter problems reading files generated on a different platform, try converting newlines to the local format. (The same argument applies to the files gnuplot writes: lines are terminated with the native newline character on the given system.)

Besides the regular, column-oriented file format, gnuplot can also read files in a packed *matrix* layout, with n rows of m columns each, representing data on a regular n-by-m grid. We'll discuss them in chapter 8 on multidimensional plots.

4.2.1 Permissible formats and options

Several aspects of the file format can be controlled through options. For instance, we can choose additional characters to indicate comment lines in data files. In this section, we look at the fine points of input file formats: numbers and missing values, comments, and strings.

NUMBER FORMATS

Gnuplot can read both integers and floating point numbers, as well as numbers in *scientific notation*: a floating-point number, followed by an upper- or lowercase character `'e'`, followed by an integer, which is interpreted as a power of 10. The numeric value of such a field is obtained after multiplying the floating-point part by 10 raised to the appropriate power. An example will make this clear: in scientific notation, the value 35,100 would be encoded `3.51e4`; the value -0.0001 would be written `-1e-4`.

We can also allow the letters `'d'` or `'q'` (both upper- and lowercase) instead of `'e'` or `'E'` for Fortran D or Q constants, by setting

```
set datafile fortran
```

This option is off by default, since it requires additional parsing, and should only be enabled if actually needed.

COMMENTS

Comments can be included in a data file on lines starting with the comment character (#). The line must *start* with the comment character and is ignored entirely. If gnuplot encounters a # in any location other than the first one in the line, it isn't interpreted as a comment character, and any text following it is interpreted as additional data. This isn't a problem as long as only columns preceding it are specified in the `using` declaration of the `plot` command.

We can make gnuplot interpret additional characters as comment characters by using the `set datafile commentschars` command:

```
set datafile commentschar ["{str:chars}"]
```

For example, to tell gnuplot that the exclamation point indicates a comment line in a data file, we'd say

```
set datafile commentschar "!"
```

The string can contain any number of characters, all of which will be interpreted as a comment character if found at the beginning of a line, which will result in the line being ignored. Resetting this option to a new value overrides all previous settings.

FIELD SEPARATOR

By default, fields (columns) are separated from one another by whitespace, which means any number of space or tab characters. We can change the field separator using the `set datafile separator` command:

```
set datafile separator [ "{str:char}" | whitespace ]
```

For example, to make the comma a field separator, we'd use

```
set datafile separator ","
```

Separator characters aren't interpreted as separators when inside quoted strings: quoted strings are always interpreted as the entry of a single column.

Only a *single* character can be defined as field separator at any given time. (This isn't true when using `whitespace`.)

To reset, we can issue `set datafile separator whitespace` or simply `set datafile separator`, so that columns will be split on whitespace again.

MISSING VALUES

We can use the `set datafile missing` command to specify the string that will be used in a data file to denote missing data:

```
set datafile missing ["{str:str}"]
```

An example would be `set datafile missing "NaN"`, which interprets the IEEE floating-point indicator NaN ("Not-a-Number") as missing value. There is no default value for this parameter.

Having an indicator for missing values is important when using a whitespace-separated file format: if the missing value were just left blank, gnuplot wouldn't recognize it as a column value at all, and use the value from the *next* column instead.

The interpretation of missing values in a data set depends on the precise syntax of the using directive. Let's look at two examples. Listing 4.1 shows a file containing a missing value.

```
1     10
2     10
3     11
4     12
5     NaN
6     11
7     11
8     10
9     10
```

If we plot this file using

```
plot "data" using 1:2 with linespoints
```

the fifth record (containing the missing value) will be ignored and the data will be plotted with one continuous, unbroken line. On the other hand, the command

```
plot "data" using 1:($2) with linespoints
```

will also ignore the fifth record, but will treat it as a blank line, and therefore not draw a connecting line across the gap (see figure 4.1).

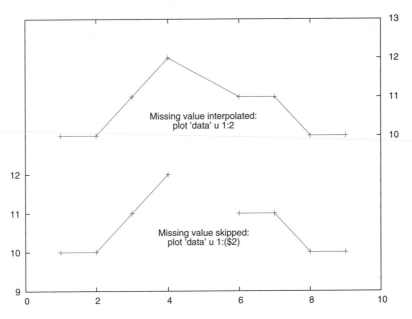

Figure 4.1   Gnuplot treats missing values differently, depending on the plot syntax. The file is the same as in listing 4.1.

STRINGS AND TITLE STRINGS

If gnuplot has been built with support for data strings (see section 4.3 in this chapter), gnuplot can read and process text fields found in input files. A valid text field can be any string of printable characters not including blank spaces. If the string contains blanks, it must be enclosed in *double* quotes to prevent gnuplot from interpreting the blanks as column separator. (Single quotes don't work!) The enclosing double quotes are stripped off and aren't part of the field's value. If a field contains whitespace and is protected by enclosing double quotes, it must not contain double quotes as part of the string value. If you need to use quotation marks and blanks in the same string, you must use single quotes inside the string and double quotes to enclose the entire field. If you have designated a non-whitespace character as column separator using `set datafile separator`, the same considerations apply: strings containing the separator must be protected with double quotes. Listing 4.2 shows some ways that strings can be used in a data file.

Listing 4.2　Strings in data files need only be quoted if they contain whitespace.

```
# Year  Title
1965    Yesterday                   # Bare string without blanks
1966    "Yellow Submarine"          # Blanks require double quotes
1969    "Maxwell's Silver Hammer"   # Sgl quote inside dbl quotes
```

Strings can be placed directly onto the plot, either using the `with labels` style (see section 4.3.4 later in this chapter) or the `ticslabels()` family of functions (see section 7.3.4 in chapter 7, and the examples in section 13.3 in chapter 13). Finally, it's possible to use the values of the first line in an input file as entries into the legend or *key* of a plot (see section 6.4.4 in chapter 6).

For more information on string handling, check section 4.3 on string handling later in this chapter.

MORE TRICKS WITH DATA FILES

For the most part, input file parsing with gnuplot is very robust and works without much tinkering. One good piece of advice is to always specify all required columns explicitly via the `using` directive. If this is done, gnuplot silently skips any garbage (fields it can't parse) in the file, treating them as missing values. If one relies on the default columns (without the `using` directive), gnuplot will instead silently bail when it encounters an unparseable field. This is most likely to happen when doing casual work with small files containing only two columns, sometimes leading to mysterious failures. My advice: make it a habit *always* to specify all columns with `using`.

For the sake of completeness, I want to mention two additional features related to the handling of data files.

It's possible to parse more complicated record formats than the ones we've discussed so far by passing a format string, which describes the format of each record, to `using`. The format string must be compatible with the `scanf()` family of functions, familiar from the standard C library. Check the standard gnuplot reference documentation if you believe this is of relevance to you, but given the well-known fussiness of scanf(), this is rarely the best path forward. If a file has a format that can't be parsed normally by gnuplot, it's usually a better idea to convert it to a gnuplot-compatible format using a small conversion program in Perl, awk, or a similar tool. Also, time and date strings are handled in a special way: don't attempt to parse them using a scanf()-like format string. Use the special commands described in section 7.5 in chapter 7 instead to parse and process such data.

Finally, gnuplot can read certain binary packed file formats. Again, if this is of relevance to you, I suggest the standard gnuplot reference documentation. Unless you have very special needs, I recommend you stick with text files.

4.3   Strings

String handling is a new feature in the 4.2 release of gnuplot and may not be enabled in all installations. Before proceeding, you should check whether your version of gnuplot is built with support for strings by running show version long. Among the compile-time options, you want to find +DATASTRINGS and +STRINGVARS (both with a plus sign). If gnuplot on your system is built without support for strings, you might have to compile your own—appendix A tells you how to.

In this section, we'll first look at the way strings are quoted, and then introduce operations that gnuplot can perform on strings. We conclude with some example applications that demonstrate what we just learned.

4.3.1   Quotes

You can assign a string constant to a gnuplot variable. String constants must be enclosed in quotes, either single or double quotes. The difference is that escaped control characters (such as \n) are interpreted as control characters within *double* quoted strings, but are treated literally (that is, not interpreted) inside of *single* quoted strings. (Reminiscent of the behavior of Perl strings, for instance.)

A double-quoted string can contain single quotes; to obtain a double quote inside of a double quoted string, it must be escaped with a preceding backslash. Within single-quoted strings (which don't recognize the backslash as escape operator), we can get a single quote by doubling it:

```
a = 'This is a string.'
b = "First Line\nSecond Line."

c = "Double quote\" escaped."
d = 'Single quote'' escaped.'
```

4.3.2   String operations

Strings can be assigned to variables just as numbers can. Strings are converted to numbers silently, if possible; only integers (not floating-point numbers) are promoted to strings:

```
x = '3.14'     # String
y = 2 + x      # Promotes to number: now y = 5.14
```

```
a = 4            # Number (integer!)
b = 'foo' . a    # Promotes to string: now b = foo4
```

There are three operators acting on strings and a handful of functions. The first of the operators is the concatenation or "dot" operator:

```
a = 'baz'
b = "foo" . 'bar'
c = b . a           # c is now "foobarbaz"
```

The other two operators are comparison operators, for use in conditionals: eq (equals) returns true if both of its arguments are equal, and ne (not equals) returns true if they differ.

```
a = 'foo'
b = 'bar'

c = a eq 'foo' ? 'equal' : 'different'
```

Strings can be indexed like arrays, using a syntax similar to the syntax used to indicate plot ranges:

```
a = "Gnuplot"
b = a[2:4]          # b is now "nup"
c = a[4:]           # c is now "plot"
```

The first character in the string has index 1 (not zero!). If we leave either the beginning or the end of the substring empty, it will default to the beginning or the end of the entire string, as shown.

There are a small number of functions to analyze and parse strings (see table 4.1) and we can define our own string functions, in the same way that we define functions operating on numbers:

```
head( s ) = s[1:3]
a = head( "January" )     # a is now "Jan"
```

Table 4.1 String functions

Function	Description
strlen("str")	Takes a string and returns the number of characters in the string.
substr("str", i, j)	Takes a string and two integers. Equivalent to str[i:j].
strstrt("str", "key")	Takes two strings. Returns the index of the first character of the string key in the string str, or zero if not found.
words("str")	Takes a string. Strips leading and trailing whitespace, then breaks the string into tokens on whitespace. Returns the number of tokens found. Newlines and tabs are interpreted as whitespace only if the string was double-quoted.

Table 4.1   String functions *(continued)*

Function	Description
word("str", n)	Takes a string and an integer. Strips leading and trailing whitespace, then breaks the string into tokens on whitespace. Returns the *n*th token found. (Tokens are counted starting at 1, not at zero.) Newlines and tabs are interpreted as whitespace only if the string was double-quoted.
sprintf("format", ...)	Returns a formatted string. Equivalent to the sprintf() function in the C standard library.
gprintf("format", ...)	Returns a formatted string. Similar to sprintf(), but uses gnuplot's format specifiers. See section on 7.3.3 on set format for details.
system("string")	Takes a shell command as string and executes it in a subshell. Returns the output of the shell command. (More detail in chapter 12.)

4.3.3   String applications

Let's conclude this section on strings and string handling with a brief look at practical uses for strings within gnuplot.

There are two different ways to place strings onto a graph: either as individually (or manually) placed options using the set command, or read from a data file and placed automatically by gnuplot. We'll discuss manual placement of labels and tic marks in chapters 6 and 7 on decorations and axes.

In regards to automatic placement of strings, three different uses stand out. First of all, we can use labels as data and place strings, rather than symbols, onto a plot using the with labels style (see listing 4.3). When using this style, we must supply a third column to the using directive (see section 5.2.5 for details). Values in this column will be interpreted as strings and placed onto the plot at the position specified by the values from the first and second colum.

Listing 4.3   Printing strings from the data file using with labels

```
plot 'data' using 1:2:3 with labels
```

We can apply inline data transformations to the with labels style. Of course, the only possible operations are string operations. The stringcolumn(n) function is often useful in this context: it returns the value of column n as a *string* (whereas the column(n) function returns the value of column n as a *number*). We'll show an example for all of this in the next section.

We can also read the labels to be used for tic marks from a file, through the ticlabels() family of functions, which we'll describe in section 7.3.4, when we discuss axes labeling in general. You can find an example of its use in listing 4.4.

```
plot "data" using 1:2:xticlabels(3) with lines
```

Finally, we can use the first noncomment entry in the data file as label for the data set in the plot's legend (the key), by giving the column number as argument to the `title` option of the `plot` command (see listing 4.5—more details in section 6.4.4).

Listing 4.5   Reading text for the graph's key from the data file

```
plot "data" using 1:2 title 2 with lines
```

4.3.4   *Crazy example: plotting the Unix password file*

As a crazy example of what is possible, let's plot a typical Unix password file with gnuplot!

Here is the file (see listing 4.6). (For non-Unix users: each line in the file describes a user. Each line consists of several fields, separated by colons. The first field is the username, the third field is a numeric user ID, and the fifth field is a textual description of the user. The other fields are of no relevance to us here.)

Listing 4.6   A text file that can be plotted by gnuplot

```
at:x:25:25:Batch jobs daemon:/var/spool/atjobs:/bin/bash
daemon:x:2:2:Daemon:/sbin:/bin/bash
ftp:x:40:49:FTP account:/srv/ftp:/bin/bash
games:x:12:100:Games account:/var/games:/bin/bash
ldap:x:76:70:User for OpenLDAP:/var/lib/ldap:/bin/bash
lp:x:4:7:Printing daemon:/var/spool/lpd:/bin/bash
mail:x:8:12:Mailer daemon:/var/spool/clientmqueue:/bin/false
man:x:13:62:Manual pages viewer:/var/cache/man:/bin/bash
mysql:x:60:108:MySQL database admin:/var/lib/mysql:/bin/false
news:x:9:13:News system:/etc/news:/bin/bash
ntp:x:74:103:NTP daemon:/var/lib/ntp:/bin/false
postfix:x:51:51:Postfix Daemon:/var/spool/postfix:/bin/false
sshd:x:71:65:SSH daemon:/var/lib/sshd:/bin/false
uucp:x:10:14:Unix-to-Unix CoPy system:/etc/uucp:/bin/bash
wwwrun:x:30:8:WWW daemon apache:/var/lib/wwwrun:/bin/false
```

To plot this file, we need to set the field separator to be the colon (`:`) and are then able to plot it using the `with labels` style (see section 5.2.5 in chapter 5).

Just for fun, we also make the letter `'m'` the comment character. Verify how the records starting with an `'m'` don't show up in the graph!

In the plot (see listing 4.7; the resulting graph is shown in figure 4.2), we use the numeric user ID as the x coordinate and the line number in the file as the y coordinate. The label, printed at the resulting position, consists of each user's login name, stacked (by virtue of a newline character) on top of the textual description of the user.

> **Listing 4.7   Plotting a text file (the Unix password file) with gnuplot**

```
set datafile separator ':'
set datafile commentschar "m"
plot [-20:150][:27] "/etc/passwd"
➡ u 3:($0+2):( stringcolumn(1) . "\n" . stringcolumn(5) ) w labels
```

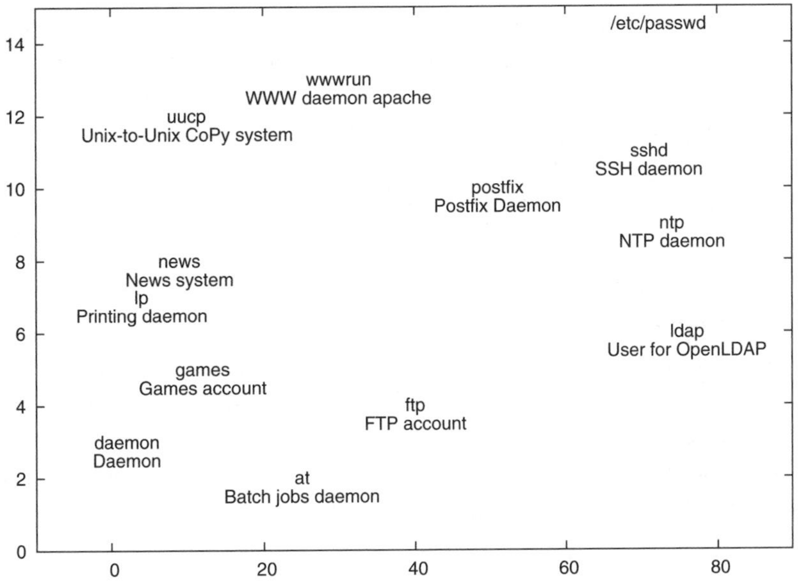

Figure 4.2   Demonstrating string functions and the `with labels` plot style

4.4   Generating textual output

Gnuplot creates graphs—after all, that's the whole point! Nevertheless, sometimes it can be useful to have gnuplot create textual output. For example, we may want to export the results from gnuplot's spline interpolation algorithm to a file, so that we can use them in another application. Or we may have applied some inline data transformation and want to get our hands on the resulting data for some reason.

Gnuplot has two different facilities for generating text: the `print` command and the `set table` option.

4.4.1   The print command

The `print` command evaluates one or more expressions (separated by commas) and prints them to the currently active printing channel—usually the screen:

```
print sin(1.5*pi)
print "The value of pi is: ", pi
```

The device to which `print` will send its output can be changed through the `set print` option:

```
set print                              # print to STDERR
set print "-"                          # print to STDOUT
set print "{str:filename}" [ append ]  # print to file
```

By default, print sends its output to standard error (usually the current terminal if gnuplot is run interactively). But output can be redirected either to standard output (using the special filename -), or to a regular file (simply by giving the filename as argument to set print). Each invocation of set print creates a new file (clobbering any existing file of the same name), unless the additional keyword append has been specified. On systems that support input/output redirection, it's possible to specify a shell command as recipient of the output from the print command, by starting the filename with the pipe symbol (|) (see section 12.2.3).

Some gnuplot commands that generate textual output use the set print option internally to determine where to send their output (an example is the show palette palette command; check section 9.1.2).

4.4.2   *The set table option*

The set table facility gives us access to the data that makes up a graph *as text*. In other words, using set table, we can obtain the values of all points shown in a plot as numeric expressions.

The command to generate output as numbers, as opposed to graphics, is the set table command:

```
set table ["{str:filename}"]
```

As long as set table is active, all output will be directed to the specified file (or to the current value of set output if no file was named). To return gnuplot to creating graphics, use unset table. (Don't forget!)

Similar to what we found for the set terminal command, it's important to remember that set table doesn't generate any output: it merely selects a channel to which the output will be sent. Only plot or replot commands generate actual output. One of them must be issued after set table; otherwise the resulting file will be empty. (In fact, in previous versions of gnuplot, what is now the set table facility was exposed as one of the terminals: set terminal table.)

Both x and y values will be printed to the file as two separate columns. If the plot contains several curves, they'll be written to the file one after another, as separate data sets. The data format is taken from the value of the set format option, which is also used for formatting axis tic labels (see section 7.3.3). The third column contains a marker indicating whether this data point was within the plot range or outside of it: an i for "inside," an o for "outside", or u if the point is undefined.

For data from a file, only the data points read from the input file will be written to the output file. For functions, including Bézier and Spline approximations, the number of data points depends on the value of the set samples option (see section 3.5).

4.5   Interacting with gnuplot

By now, you should be familiar with the basic gnuplot edit-view workflow. In this section, I introduce some convenience features that can help make the work go more smoothly. First, we learn how to access the built-in help system and the command history feature. Then I explain how to use keyboard shortcuts (hot keys) and the mouse to interact with gnuplot. Finally, we look at ways to read data from the interactive terminal, rather than from a file.

4.5.1   Getting help

Gnuplot has an extensive, built-in online help system ("online" in the sense that it's accessible from within the gnuplot session; it has nothing to do with network connectivity to the Internet). To get started, enter `help` at the gnuplot prompt. Alternatively, you can go directly to the reference page for a specific command by entering the name of the command as argument to the `help` command. For example, to learn about the `plot` command, you'd use

```
help plot
```

The online help is very detailed and comprehensive, so you should become familiar with it. But keep in mind that it's a *reference*, not a tutorial. If you know the name of the command or option you are looking for, it's great. But if you want to find all relevant options for a specific task, navigating the online help can be very frustrating.

This is what appendix B of this book is for: there, you'll find all commands and options, grouped by topic. The appendix can therefore be used as a roadmap to the online help system.

4.5.2   Command history

Gnuplot has a history feature, making it possible to recall the most recent commands. (The size of the history buffer is controlled by the `set historysize` option.) The history feature is bound to the up- and down-arrow keys, as well as to the `Ctrl-p` and `Ctrl-n` key combinations.

If you want more control over the command history, you can use the `history` command. The `history` command can be used in three ways: to print all or parts of the command history, to search it, or to reexecute a command:

```
history [quiet] [{int:max}] ["{str:filename}" [append]]   # show
history ?"{str:cmd}"                                       # search
history !"{str:cmd}"                                       # execute
```

The first line shows how to print the command history to the screen, or (if a filename is given) to a file. Optionally, `history` clobbers any existing file of the same name, unless the `append` keyword is used. By default, the command history is shown together with line numbers, but they can be suppressed through the `quiet` option. Finally, we can restrict the output to the last `max` entries by providing a numerical argument. For example, the command `history quiet 5` will plot the last five commands to screen, suppressing line numbers. The current output on my system is shown in listing 4.8.

Listing 4.8   Typical output from the command: `history quiet 5`

```
plot sin(x)
plot [-2:2] sin(x)
plot [-2:2] sin(x), x
plot [-2:2][-1:1] sin(x), x
history quiet 5
```

Alternatively, we can give a command, or just its beginning, as argument to `history`, prefixed by either a question mark (?) or an exclamation point (!). If the question mark is used, gnuplot will search the command history and show only those entries that start with the string provided. If the exclamation point is used, the most recent matching entry in the command history will be executed again. For example, `history ?"set term"` will show all commands that changed the `terminal` setting.

4.5.3   *Hot keys and mousing*

When we issue a `plot` command, gnuplot pops up a new window containing the plot (assuming of course that we're working with one of the interactive terminals, and not currently exporting graphs to file). The new window containing the graph is automatically *raised* or active.

When a graphics window is active like this, we can invoke gnuplot commands through keyboard shortcuts or mouse clicks. In this section, we look at some of the default bindings provided by gnuplot. In chapter 12, we'll see how to define our own keyboard or mouse shortcuts.

HOT KEYS

Hitting the spacebar when the plot window is active raises the gnuplot command window. This is convenient when doing actual work: you can iteratively continue working on a single graph without ever having to take your hands off the keyboard!

Grid lines can be toggled on or off through the hot key `g`. Logarithmic plotting is bound to `l` (y axis only) and `L` (in this case, gnuplot scales only the axis closest to the mouse pointer logarithmically). Hitting `q` closes the current plot window.

Some other interesting default bindings are listed in table 4.2, and we can get a display of *all* currently defined key bindings by pressing `h` while the plot window is active.

I don't find most of the default bindings all that useful, but in chapter 12 I'll show you how to install a set of convenient hot key bindings yourself.

Table 4.2   Selected default hot key bindings

Key	Function
Spacebar	Raise command window and switch keyboard focus to it
q	Close the current plot window
g	Toggle grid lines on the plot
r	Toggle crosshair (ruler) at current mouse position

Table 4.2 Selected default hot key bindings *(continued)*

Key	Function
l (lowercase letter L)	Toggle y axis logarithmic scale
L	Toggle logarithmic scaling for the axis closest to the mouse pointer
u	Unzoom (after zooming using the mouse)
h	Help: show all key bindings

MOUSING

In interactive terminals, we can use the mouse to navigate the graph. By default, mouse actions should be enabled, but in case they aren't, we can enable them using the command

```
set mouse
```

When the mouse is active, the current coordinates are always displayed at the bottom of the plot window. We can place a temporary crosshair at the current mouse position by hitting the r key. Hitting r again switches the crosshair off. While the crosshair is active, its location and the relative distance of the mouse pointer from the crosshair coordinate are shown in the plot window, together with the absolute coordinates of the mouse pointer.

We can use the mouse to zoom in on a graph by dragging the mouse while holding mouse button 3 (often the right mouse button). Click into the graph with mouse button 3 and drag while holding the button down, then click with mouse button 1 to replot only the section of the graph in the indicated region. Hit u (unzoom) to return to the previous setting. When using the mouse to set the plot range in this way, both the x and the y range are fixed according to the mouse coordinates.

The mouse can be used for additional effects. The current mouse coordinates are written to gnuplot variables whenever we click in the plot windows, and are therefore available in user-defined functions. In chapter 12, we'll look at some cool macros that make use of this to place arrows onto the plot using only the mouse.

4.5.4 *Reading data interactively*

All data that's rendered by the plot command must be read from a file: gnuplot doesn't maintain any data sets in memory. Nevertheless, sometimes you want to plot just a few points without creating a file for them. In situations like this, it's possible to enter the data in the command window.

When given the special filename -, gnuplot attempts to read data from standard input, which in an interactive session is the command window. Gnuplot will show a prompt at which data can be typed. Finish each line by hitting the return key. Gnuplot will keep prompting for data until either an end-of-file (EOF) character (typically Ctrl-D) is encountered or the character e is entered on a line by itself.

It's even possible to read data from standard input multiple times within the same plot command: `plot '-', '-'` will read data until an end-of-file character is encountered and then expect to read *more* data (for the second "file") until finding a second EOF character. Of course, the data entered at a prompt this way can have multiple columns, from which we can select some with `using`, and all the other features of the `plot` command can be used as well.

Although this feature can be used interactively, it's mostly intended for situations where gnuplot is used in batch-mode as part of larger scripts (we'll talk more about that in chapter 12). When used interactively, this feature quickly becomes inconvenient, because (as explained earlier), gnuplot doesn't maintain data sets in memory and therefore all data has to be manually reentered every single time one wants to plot or replot the graph.

4.6   *Summary*

This chapter was somewhat of a grab-bag of useful features that make life easier. In particular, we talked about

- Gnuplot's commands for option management: `set`, `unset`, and `show`.
- The file format for gnuplot data files. We also introduced all the options that can be used to customize aspects of input file handling.
- String handling in gnuplot.
- Obtaining textual instead of graphical output.
- The online help system and how to use it.
- Special key bindings, which we can use when the plot window is active.
- How to use the mouse with gnuplot.

This concludes the first part of the book. We now have all features and commands at our disposal to work efficiently with gnuplot. In the next part, we'll take the basics for granted, and instead talk in detail about the different ways that we can affect the appearance of a graph: the "looks." Stay tuned.

Part 2

Polishing

This part is about all the different features gnuplot provides to make a graph both pretty and informative.

Chapter 5 talks about different styles with which to represent data, such as lines, symbols, or bars. I'll also explain how to define your own custom styles.

Chapter 6 introduces all kinds of decorations that we can use to make a graph more informative. You will learn about arrows, labels, and ways to customize the graph's legend.

Chapter 7 describes how to control the way axes and tic marks are drawn. This chapter also explains how to handle timeseries data and how to use calendar dates as tic labels.

Doing it with style

This chapter covers

- Choosing plot styles
- Plot style gallery
- Customizing styles

The following three chapters describe the different ways to control the appearance of a plot: how to make it look just right. In this chapter, we'll discuss the various ways to display *data*, and in the next chapter we'll talk about all the *other* stuff that goes onto a plot, such as labels, borders, arrows, and similar decorations. Since axes and their labels can provide so much relevant information about a plot, they've been given their own chapter (chapter 7) which is the third and last in this part.

This chapter consists of three parts. First I describe the syntax for choosing a specific style for a plot. Then I'll give a comprehensive, illustrated catalog of available styles. And finally, I'll talk about ways you can define your own custom styles.

Only the first section in this chapter is required reading, because here is where I explain how to choose plot styles and where I introduce the important concept of terminal capabilities. For the rest of this chapter, feel free to just look at the figures so that you get a sense for the kinds of plots that gnuplot can create. You can always come back to this chapter when you need a specific plot type.

5.1   *Choosing plot styles*

Different types of data call for different display styles. For instance, it makes sense to plot a smooth function with one continuous line, but to use separate symbols for a sparse data set where each individual point counts. Experimental data often requires error bars together with the data, whereas counting statistics call for histograms. Choosing an appropriate style for the data leads to graphs that are both informative and aesthetically pleasing.

There are two ways to choose a style for the data: inline, as part of the `plot` command, or globally, using the `set style` directive. Let's talk about inline styles first, and then come back to global preferences later, once we've had a chance to introduce the notion of *terminal capabilities*, because it is up to the terminal which styles are actually available.

5.1.1   *Inline style directives*

We have already seen inline styles in chapter 2: by giving the `with` keyword as part of the `plot` command, we can specify which style to use:

```
plot "data" u 1:2 with lines, "" u 1:3 with linespoints,
    "" u 1:4 with points
```

As usual, keywords can be abbreviated to the shortest unambiguous form, so we'd probably write `w l`, `w linesp` or `w lp`, and so on.

In graphical analysis, we often want to plot several similar data sets together on the same plot, usually so that we can compare them directly to one another:

```
plot "data" u 1:2 w l, "" u 1:3 w l, "" u 1:4 w l
```

All of these are plotted using the same style (`with lines`). Now the question is: which curve is which (see figure 5.1)?

Gnuplot helps us here by plotting each curve with a different line pattern (or different symbol, or different color, depending on the specific style chosen). Styles are chosen from a list of available patterns. If we need to plot more data sets than there are different styles, the selection begins again at the beginning.

We can overrule this automatic progression of plot styles by fixing the specific style to use:

```
plot "data" u 1:2 w l 2, "" u 1:3 w l 2, "" u 1:4 w l
```

This will plot the second and third column in the data file using the second style from the list of available styles for the current terminal. Fixing a specific style like this doesn't affect the way the internal style counter is incremented, so the fourth column of the data will be displayed using the third style from the selection.

All this brings up the question: how many styles are there, and what are they? There's no absolute answer to this question; it all depends on the output format, or rather, the `terminal`.

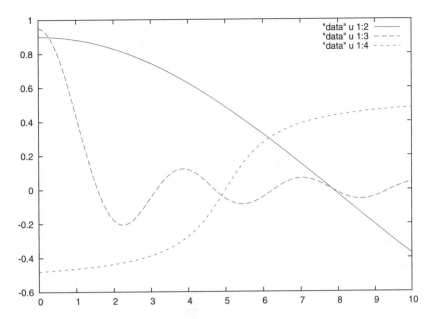

Figure 5.1   Gnuplot chooses a different line style for each curve automatically.

5.1.2   *Terminal capabilities*

Gnuplot itself knows little about rendering a graph—this is left to the individual `terminal` devices. This way, gnuplot itself makes no assumptions about the platform it is running on and can be very portable. Output devices obviously differ widely in their capabilities—we can't get color plots from a black-and-white printer. On the other hand, an interactive color terminal (such as X11) gives us color, but possibly only a smaller selection of patterns and available fonts.

Gnuplot has a built-in command called `test` that generates a standard test image. The test image shows all available line styles and fill patterns, and also attempts to demonstrate more advanced terminal capabilities, such as the ability to rotate text through an arbitrary angle. To use the `test` command, we first need to select the terminal we are interested in and set the name of the output file (if it's not an interactive terminal) like so:

```
set terminal postscript
set output "test.ps"
test
```

Note that the command is `test`—not `plot test`!

Along the right side of figure 5.2 we see the available line and symbol styles, fill patterns along the bottom, and line widths on the left side. We can also see what kinds of arrows the terminal supports, and whether it has the ability to rotate text. For a Post-Script terminal as shown in the figure, all these features are supported.

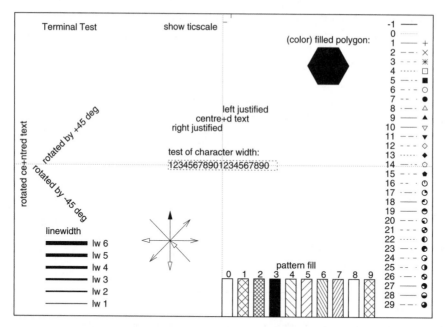

Figure 5.2   The standard test image to demonstrate terminal capabilities, shown here for the PostScript terminal

5.1.3   *Global style directives*

Although inline styles give us a lot of control over the detailed representation of the data, they can be clumsy, in particular in large `plot` commands containing many data sets. This is where *global styles* come in.

By default, data (from a file) is plotted using the `points` style, while functions are plotted with `lines`. We can change these defaults using the `set` command, which we introduced in chapter 4. To specify the global defaults, we can use

```
set style data {enum:style}
set style function {enum:style}
```

Here, the {style} parameter can either be a style family (such as `lines` or `points`), or a specific style (such as `lines 3`). If only the family is indicated, gnuplot will iterate through all available styles in that family as usual, but if we choose one specific style, only that one will be used for all curves. Inline styles override global styles, as you would expect.

Now that we know how to choose styles, it's time to look at the possible choices. So, let's take a tour of the big catalog of available plot styles.

5.2   *Plot styles*

There are well over two dozen styles available in gnuplot. Here we look at those most useful for ordinary, two-dimensional data. We'll encounter some additional styles in chapter 8 on multidimensional plots.

5.2.1 Core styles

There are four styles I would call "core" styles, because they are so generally useful: with points, with lines, with linespoints, and with dots. These styles represent data with simple symbols or lines on the plot (see figure 5.3).

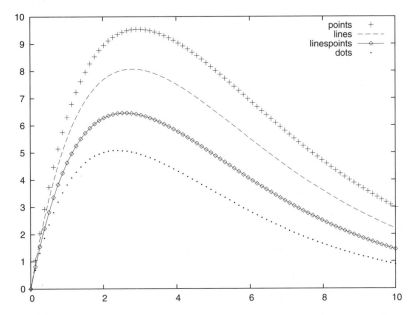

Figure 5.3 The four core styles: with points, with lines, with linespoints, and with dots

POINTS

The points style plots a small symbol for each data point. The symbols aren't connected to each other. This is the default style for data (see figure 5.3).

The size of the symbol can be changed globally using the set pointsize command. The parameter is a multiplier, defaulting to 1.0:

```
set pointsize {flt:mult}
```

It is also possible to change the pointsize inline:

```
plot "data" u 1:2 w points pointsize 3
```

LINES AND LINESPOINTS

The lines style does not plot individual data points, only straight lines connecting adjacent points. This is the default style for functions, and the preferred style for dense data sets without too much noise.

Many aspects of lines, including their width and color, can be customized using set style line. Since lines are such fundamental objects, I have collected all this material in a separate section at the end of this chapter for easier reference (section 5.3).

The `linespoints` style is a combination of the previous two: each data point is marked with a symbol, and adjacent points are connected with straight lines. This style is mostly useful for sparse data sets.

DOTS

The `dots` style prints a "minimal" dot (a single pixel for bitmap terminals) for each data point. This style is occasionally useful for very large, unsorted data sets (such as large scatter plots). Figure 1.2 in chapter 1 was drawn using dots.

5.2.2   Box styles

Box styles, which draw a box of finite width, are sometimes useful for counting statistics, or for other data sets where the x values cannot take on a continuous spectrum of values.

STEPS

Gnuplot offers three styles to generate steplike graphs, consisting only of vertical and horizontal lines (see figure 5.4). The only difference between the three styles is the location of the vertical step:

- `histeps` style places the vertical step midway between adjacent x values.
- `steps` style places the vertical step at the *end* of the bin.
- `fsteps` style places the vertical step at the *front* of the bin.

If in doubt, the `histeps` style is probably the most useful one.

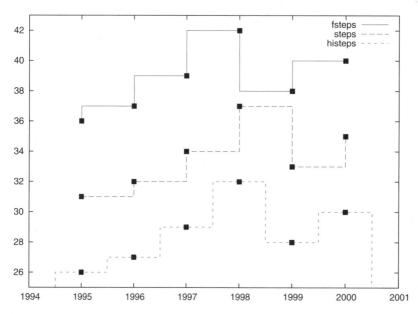

Figure 5.4   The three steps styles. The same data set is shown three times (vertically shifted). Individual data points are represented by symbols; the three steps styles are shown in different line styles. Note how different the same data set can appear, depending on the exact location of the vertical steps.

BOXES AND IMPULSES

In contrast to the step styles from the previous section, the boxes style plots a box centered at the given x coordinate from the x axis (not from the graph border) to the y coordinate (see figure 5.5). The width of the box can be set in one of three ways:

- Supplied as third parameter to using.
- Set globally through the set boxwidth option.
- Otherwise, boxes are sized automatically to touch adjacent boxes.

If a third column is supplied in the using directive, it is interpreted as the total width of the box in the same coordinates that are used for the x axis. The set boxwidth option has the following syntax:

```
set boxwidth [ {flt:size} ] [ absolute | relative ]
```

The size parameter can either be a measure of the absolute size of the box in x axis coordinates, or it can denote a fraction of the default box size, which is the width of the box if it touches adjacent boxes. If absolute mode isn't stated explicitly, relative sizing is assumed. A boxwidth of -2 can be used to force automatic sizing of boxes (with adjacent boxes touching each other). The impulses style is similar to the boxes style with a boxwidth set to zero. The examples in figure 5.5 make this more clear.

Boxes can be filled or shaded, according to the value of the set style fill option. It has the following syntax:

```
set style fill [ empty | solid [{flt:density}] | pattern [{idx:n}] ]
              [ border [ {idx:linetype} ] | noborder ]
```

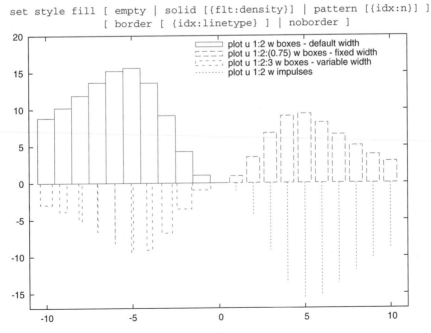

Figure 5.5 Box and impulse styles. The widths of boxes can be set globally or for each box individually. The second data set uses a fixed width (enclosed in parentheses in the using directive); the third one reads values for variable box widths from file.

Density is a numeric value between 0.0 (empty) and 1.0 (solid); the color used is the same as the current line type. Available fill patterns vary from terminal to terminal. Use the `test` command to see what's available. By default, each box is bounded by a border in the current linetype. This can be changed using the `border` attribute. The border can be turned off entirely using `noborder`.

HISTOGRAMS

The `histogram` styles are a recent addition to gnuplot and are somewhat of a departure from gnuplot's usual processing model, in that they have the concept of a *data set*. The overall appearance of the plot depends on both row and column information simultaneously.

Histograms are the result of counting statistics. For the sake of discussion, let's assume that there are three parties (Red, Blue, and Green) and we want to show the number of votes for each party. The outcome of a *single* election can be shown easily using, for instance, the `histeps` style.

But what to do if elections are held annually, and we want to show the results for a number of years in one plot? To make matters concrete, let's consider a specific data file, shown in listing 5.1.

Listing 5.1   Data for figure 5.6 and figure 5.7

```
# Year  Red    Green Blue
1990    33     45    18
1991    35     42    19
1992    34     44    14
1993    37     43    25
1994    47     15    30
1995    41     14    32
1996    42     20    35
1997    39     21    31
```

One possible solution would be to plot the data as a regular time series (see figure 5.6):

```
set style data linesp
plot "histo" u 1:2 t "Red", "" u 1:3 t "Green", "" u 1:4 t "Blue"
```

Often this is exactly what we want, but this format can be clumsy, in particular if there are many competing parties or if there is a lot of variation year over year. The histogram style offers an alternative.

Using `set style histogram clustered` generates a sequence of histograms (see figure 5.7). Each histogram corresponds to *one row* in the input file (in our example, this corresponds to one year):

```
set style fill pattern
set style histogram clustered
plot "histo" u 2 t "Red" w histograms,
  ➥ "" u 3 t "Green" w histograms, "" u 4 t "Blue" w histograms
```

Instead of inline styles, we can use global styles and achieve the same result:

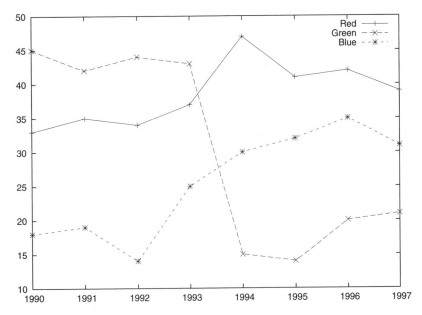

Figure 5.6 **Election results as a time series. The data file is shown in listing 5.1.**

```
set style fill pattern
set style histogram clustered
set style data histograms
plot "histo" u 2 t "Red", "" u 3 t "Green", "" u 4 t "Blue"
```

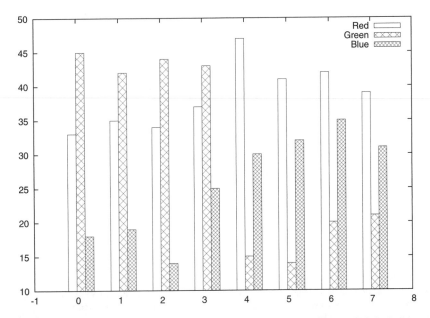

Figure 5.7 **Election results using set style histogram clustered. This is the same data set as in figure 5.6.**

For all of the histogram styles, it is usually a good idea to have the boxes filled to make them more easily distinguishable, and so we have enabled this option here. We can control the spacing between consecutive histograms using the optional gap parameter to the set style command: set style histogram clustered gap 2. The size of the gap is measured in multiples of individual boxes in the histograms. (To create gaps within each histogram, so that neighboring boxes don't touch each other, use set boxwidth.)

Keep in mind that the way gnuplot reads the data file for histograms is a bit unusual: each new row generates a new histogram *cluster*, but the histogram style accepts only a *single* column in the using directive. We therefore have to list the file repeatedly in the same plot command to generate meaningful histograms, as shown previously.

Finally, the labels gnuplot places along the x axis aren't very meaningful. We can either set explicit labels for each histogram using the set xtics add command or we can read a textual label from the data file using the function xticlabels() (or xtic() for short). The effect of the latter is demonstrated in figure 5.8. Both of these commands will be treated in more detail in chapter 7 on axes.

Besides the clustered histogram style we looked at so far, there is also a *stacked* style. Using this style, the individual boxes aren't placed next to one another, but stacked on top of each other, so that each vertical box comprises an entire histogram. By default, adjacent boxes touch each other, but as usual, set boxwidth can be used to control the width of individual boxes (see figure 5.8).

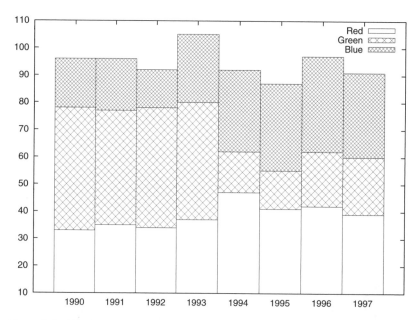

Figure 5.8 Election results using set style histogram rowstacked. This is the same data set yet again. Note the effect of the xtic() function, which is used to read x axis labels directly from the data file.

```
set style fill pattern
set style histogram rowstacked
set style data histograms
plot "histo" u 2:xtic(1) t "Red", "" u 3 t "Green", "" u 4 t "Blue"
```

There are two additional histogram styles, which I won't describe here in detail, since they're similar to the ones we discussed already. The set style histogram errorbars style is similar to the clustered style, except that it reads *two* values for each box, the second being the uncertainty in the data, represented with a standard errorbar. The set style histogram columnstacked style is equivalent to the rowstacked style, except that each vertical box is built from a single *column* (not row) in the input file.

One last directive related to histograms is newhistogram (see figure 5.9). It can be used to have several *sets* of clustered histograms on the same plot. An example will suffice:

```
set style fill pattern
set style histogram clustered
set style data histograms
plot newhistogram "Election Results",
➡        "histo1" u 2 t "Red", "" u 3 t "Green", "" u 4 t "Blue",
➡    newhistogram "Campaign Spending",
➡        "histo2" u 2 t "Red", "" u 3 t "Green", "" u 4 t "Blue"
```

The syntax for the newhistogram command is a bit unintuitive (I *still* tend to get it wrong), so let me point out the salient features: the newhistogram keyword is followed by a *mandatory* string label (an empty string is permitted), a *mandatory* comma, and then the rest of the plot command follows, starting with the filename.

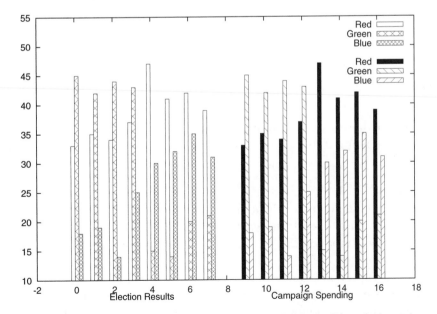

Figure 5.9 Using newhistogram, we can put several histograms into a single graph.

Histograms such as those discussed in this section look good and are frequently used in business presentations or in the media. But they make it difficult to see trends in the data, and in particular quantitative comparison of data can be quite difficult. In section 14.3.5, we'll discuss this matter in more detail.

5.2.3 *Styles with errorbars or ranges*

Sometimes we don't just want to show a single data point, but also want to indicate some range with it. This may be the experimental uncertainty (the *errorbar*), or it may be the range over which some quantity has changed during the observation interval (this is typical of financial charts). Gnuplot offers several styles that place an indicator for such a range onto the plot. First we'll look at styles that draw regular errorbars (both in vertical and in horizontal directions). Then we'll go on to discuss styles that allow us to indicate several ranges at once (but only in the vertical direction).

STYLES WITH ERRORBARS

There are two basic styles to show data with errorbars in gnuplot: `errorbars` and `errorlines`. The `errorlines` style is similar to the `linespoints` style (a symbol for each data point, adjacent points connected by straight lines), while the `errorbars` style is similar to the `points` style (disconnected symbols).

These styles draw errorbars in addition to the actual data. Errorbars can be drawn in either x or y direction, or in both. To select a direction, prefix the style with x, y, or xy respectively, as in `set style data xerrorbars` or `plot "file" with xyerrorlines`. Table 5.1 summarizes all available combinations.

Table 5.1 All possible combinations of `errorbars` and `errorlines` styles

	Errorbars in x direction	Errorbars in y direction	Errorbars in both directions
Unconnected symbols	xerrorbars	yerrorbars	xyerrorbars
Connected symbols	xerrorlines	yerrorlines	xyerrorlines

Errorbars are drawn in the current line style. A tic mark is placed at the ends of each errorbar (see figure 5.10). The size of the tic mark can be controlled using the `set bars` option:

```
set bars [ small | large | fullwidth | {flt:mult} ]
```

The parameter is a multiplier, defaulting to 1.0. The symbolic names `small` and `large` stand for the values 0.0 and 1.0, respectively. The value `fullwidth` is only relevant to histogram styles (more on that in a minute). Finally, the tic marks can be turned off entirely using `unset bars`.

We must supply additional information to styles with errorbars. Just the x and y coordinates aren't enough; we must also provide data about the size of the uncertainties. Usually, this data comes from the data file, in the form of one or two additional columns. If one additional column is given, it's interpreted as a range dy to be added

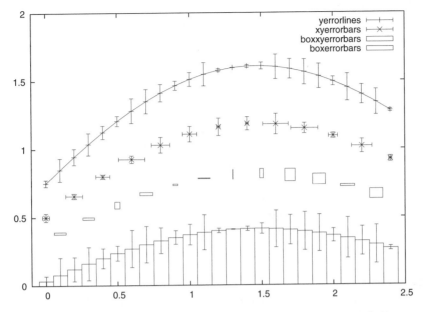

Figure 5.10 Different plot styles showing uncertainty in the data. From top to bottom: connected symbols using `errorlines`, unconnected symbols using `errorbars`, ranges indicated as boxes using `boxxyerrorbars`, and finally errors on top of a histogram using `boxerrorbars`.

and subtracted from the corresponding data value, so that the errorbar would be drawn from $(x, y\text{-}dy)$ to $(x, y\text{+}dy)$. If *two* additional columns are supplied, they are interpreted as the absolute coordinates of the lower and upper end of the errorbar (*not* the ranges), so that errorbars are drawn from $(x, ylow)$ to $(x, yhigh)$. Corresponding logic applies to errorbars drawn in x direction.

As usual, the columns to use are indicated through the using directive to plot:

```
plot "data" using 1:2:3 w yerrorbars        # ( x, y, dy )
plot "data" using 1:2:3:4:5:6 w xyerrorbars # ( x, y, xlow, xhigh,
                                            # ylow, yhigh )
```

Data transformations (see section 3.4 in chapter 3) are often useful in this context. Here are some examples:

- If the input file contains only the variance (instead of the standard deviation, which is usually plotted as error) together with the data, we can apply the necessary square root inline: `plot "data" u 1:2:(sqrt($3)) w yerrorb`.
- If we know that the uncertainty in the data is a fixed number (such as 0.1), we can supply it directly: `plot "data" u 1:2:(0.1) w yerrorl`.
- If the data supplied in the file is of the unsupported form $(x, y, ylow, yhigh, dx)$, we can build up the required plot command manually:
  `plot "data" u 1:2:($1-$5):($1+$5):3:4 w xyerrorl`.

As a final style to visualize data with uncertainty in both directions, there's the boxxy-errorbars style. It's similar to the xyerrorbars style, except that the range of uncertainty is shown as a rectangular box centered at the data point, rather than as a cross of errorbars.

The last style that uses errorbars is boxerrorbars (not to be confused with boxxy-errorbars), which is a combination of the boxes and yerrorbars styles. It is displayed as a box, with a vertical errorbar centered at its top. It might be used, for instance, for histograms that have some uncertainty in their counting statistics. The additional values required for the errorbar are supplied as the third (or third and fourth) arguments to the using directive. In any case, the box width is provided as the last argument to using.

The styles that we've discussed in this section are mostly used to plot data stemming from scientific experiments or calculations, where we want to show the uncertainty in the data clearly. But there are other situations, where we want to indicate a range (or even several ranges) together with the data. Those will be the topic of the next section.

TIME SERIES STYLES

Gnuplot offers two styles that are mostly useful for time series data, although they can be used for other purposes as well: the candlesticks style (also known as *bar-and-whiskers plot*) and the financebars style. Both have the ability to show *two* ranges in a single (the vertical) direction, for instance the typical band of variation and the highest and lowest values ever. Both are frequently used for financial data (such as stock prices) and I'll discuss them in those terms.

Both require five columns of data: the x value, followed (in order) by the opening, low, high, and closing prices. As usual, the appropriate columns are selected through the using directive to the plot command.

Both styles represent the maximum range (low to high) by a vertical line. They differ in the way the secondary (opening to closing) range is displayed: in the candlesticks style, a box of finite width is overlaid the vertical line; in the financebars style, tic marks indicate the opening and closing values. The size of the tic marks is controlled by the set bars option familiar from errorbars styles (see figure 5.11).

Details of the candlesticks can be controlled through some additional options. First of all, if the closing value is greater than the opening one, three vertical lines are drawn inside the box; otherwise, the box is left empty. The width of the box can be changed through the set boxwidth option. (If boxwidth is unset, the value of set bars will be used instead, but this usage is deprecated and should be avoided.) Finally, tic marks can be placed at the ends of the vertical line by appending the keyword whiskerbars (or whisker) to the plot command. The size of these tic marks can be controlled independently from the box width by appending a numerical value to the whiskerbars keyword. This value is interpreted as a multiplier giving the length of the tic mark relative to the box width. Finally, the box will be filled with color or patterns according to the set style fill option.

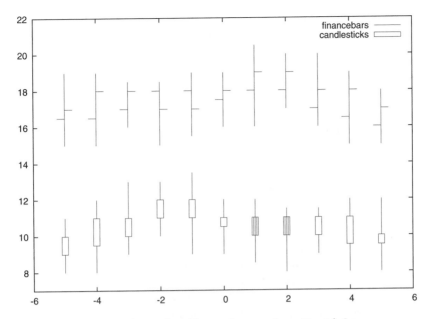

Figure 5.11 Styles for time series: `financebars` and `candlesticks`

A few examples will make this more clear:

```
plot "data" u 1:2:3:4:5 w candlesticks       # Plain
plot "data" u 1:2:3:4:5 w cand whiskerbars   # Tic marks same length
                                             #     as boxwidth
plot "data" u 1:2:3:4:5 w cand whisker 0.1   # Tic marks one tenth
                                             #     of boxwidth
```

Neither the `financebar` nor the `candlesticks` style connect consecutive entries. If that's what we want, we'll have to do so explicitly. Keep in mind that it's not even clear what should be connected in these styles—they don't have a concept of a "middle" value. This is why we have to supply a sixth column containing some form of average value, which can then be connected like so: `plot "data" u 1:2:3:4:5 w cand, "" u 1:6 w lines`.

The `candlesticks` style in particular is quite versatile and can be used to good effect in a variety of situations.

5.2.4   *Filled styles*

As of version 4.2, gnuplot has the ability to fill the area between two curves in two-dimensional plots with color or patterns. This is accomplished through the `filledcurves` style. The appearance of the filled regions is determined by the settings of the fill style, which is controlled by the `set style fill` option, which we discussed earlier in section 5.2.2.

We need to distinguish between different cases, depending on the nature of the boundaries of the fill region:

- Fill the area between two curves.
- Fill the area between one curve and one straight line (which may be one of the coordinate axes or a plot boundary).
- Treat a single curve as a closed polygon and fill its interior.
- Specify an additional point that will be included when constructing the polygon.

The first case is simple. It requires a data set with at least three columns, corresponding to the x value and the y values for both curves (see figure 5.12):

```
plot "data" u 1:2:3 w filledcurves
```

This style is only available when plotting data from a file—it can't be used when plotting functions with gnuplot.

The two lines in this example cross each other, and we can distinguish the enclosed areas depending on whether the first or the second line is greater than (that is, above) the other. In figure 5.12, all enclosed areas are shaded, but we could restrict shading to only one of the two kinds of areas by appending either the keyword `above` or `below`. For example, the command `plot "data" u 1:2:3 w filledcurves above` would shade only the areas indicated in the graph.

Filling the area between a curve and a straight line is more complicated, because we have to specify the location of the straight line, and also have to indicate whether we want to fill on both sides of it or only on one. Figure 5.13 shows both cases. (In all

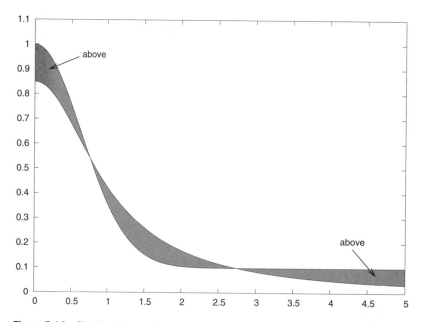

Figure 5.12   Shading the area between two curves: `plot "data" u 1:2:3 w filledcurves`. The areas that would be shaded if the above keyword was given are indicated.

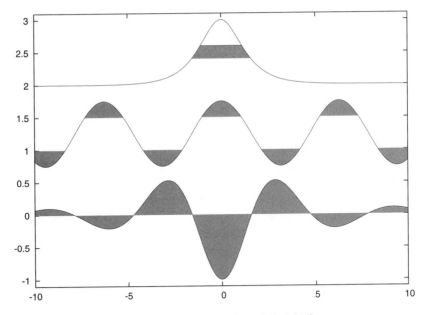

Figure 5.13 **Shading between a curve and horizontal straight lines**

examples in this section, the limiting line is horizontal. The vertical case works in the same way.)

The bottom curve was created using the following:

```
plot -cos(x)/(1+0.1*x**2) w filledc y1=0
```

Here, the bordering straight line is located at y=0 and filling occurs both above and below this line. This is the default. If we want to fill on only one side of the boundary line, we need to indicate this using the keywords above and below. For example, if we had wanted to shade only the areas with positive y values, we could have said

```
plot -cos(x)/(1+0.1*x**2) w filledc above y1=0.
```

What do we do if we want to fill both above *and* below certain thresholds for the same curve, as in the middle curve in figure 5.13? The filledcurves style allows for only one limit at a time, but we can help ourselves by overlaying several plots with different locations for the boundary line. The middle curve in figure 5.13 was drawn using the following command:

```
plot 0.5*cos(x)+1.25 w filledc above y1=1.5,
    0.5*cos(x)+1.25 w filledc below y1=1.0
```

You can see how we draw the same curve twice, once filling above the upper threshold, and once filling below the lower one. For more complicated shading tasks, we can use user-defined functions that are trimmed (using the ternary operator) where we want the shading to end. The top curve in figure 5.13 was generated this way, using the following:

```
plot 1/cosh(x)+2,
➥     1/cosh(x)+2 < 2.6 ? 1/cosh(x)+2 : 2.6 w filledc above y1=2.4
```

After these examples, let's look at all options of the `filledcurves` style:

```
filledcurves [ above | below ] [ x1 | y1 | x2 | y2 ][={flt:limit}]

filledcurves closed
filledcurves xy = {flt:x},{flt:y}
```

The first usage is the one we've been discussing so far. Note how the limiting value can be given with respect to either the first or the second coordinate system (see chapter 6, section 6.2). Specifying a limiting value for x1 or x2 will lead to a vertical boundary line. The limiting value defaults to zero if not specified otherwise.

The second and third uses treat the curve as a closed polygon (if necessary by connecting the leftmost with the rightmost point of the graph) and attempt to fill its interior. The third use specifies an additional point, which will be included in the polygon. Both of these modes make most sense when used together with parametric plots (see chapter 10, section 10.2.1).

5.2.5   *Other styles*

Two styles allow us to encode information by other means than the position on the graph: `with labels` lets us read a test string from the input file and place it on the plot, and `pointsize variable` lets us change the symbol size according to the values in the data set.

Let's look at an example that demonstrates both styles. Listing 5.2 shows a short data file containing the additional information we'll use for labels and symbol sizes as additional columns. Given this file, we can generate the plot in figure 5.14 using the following commands:

```
plot [0:6][0:3.5] "labels" u 1:2:3 w p pt 6 ps var,
➥     "" u ($1+0.25):($2-.25):4 w labels
```

Both styles require a third column as part of the `using` declaration, the contents of which are interpreted as labels or desired symbol sizes, respectively. Variable symbol sizes are most easily recognized if the symbols are circles, which for this terminal setting are chosen by `pointtype 6` (or `pt 6` for short). Then follows the `pointsize variable` (abbreviated `ps var`) specification. Labels are chosen using `with labels`, and I make sure that all labels are offset a little down and to the right, so that they don't overlap with any of the circles.

Listing 5.2   Data for figure 5.14

```
# x      y       size    label
1        2.6     3       ABC
2        2.1     6       EFG
3        1.0     2       PQR
4        1.2     1       UVW
5        1.6     4       XYZ
```

The with labels style in particular is quite versatile and we'll see some examples that use it in chapter 13. On the other hand, you should exercise some caution when using pointsize variable. For instance, it's not necessarily clear to the observer whether the radius or the area of the symbol is proportional to the encoded quantity. More generally, it's not easy to estimate and compare symbol sizes accurately, so that information can easily be lost when encoding it this way. I'll have more to say about visual perception in chapter 14.

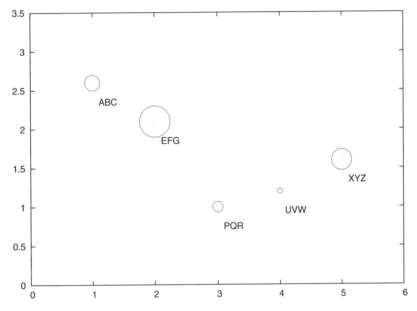

Figure 5.14 Encoding additional information through symbol size or the use of textual labels: pointsize variable and with labels. The corresponding data file is shown in listing 5.2.

This concludes our overview of styles for regular, two-dimensional xy-plots. We'll discuss additional styles for surface and contour plots in chapter 8.

5.3   *Customizing styles*

The drawing elements for data are lines and points. Lines and points come in different types (such as solid, dashed, and dotted for lines, or square, triangular, and circular for points), and different widths or sizes (respectively). Finally, they may have color. Of course, the specific range of possible selections depends on the terminal, and we can use the test command to see all available choices. For portability reasons, though, two line types are guaranteed to be present in any terminal: the linetype -1 is always a solid line in the primary foreground color (usually black). The linetype 0 is a dotted line in the same color.

5.3.1 *Custom line styles*

Besides the predefined line types that exist for a given terminal, we can form our own customized styles as well. In this section, we look at this possibility, and also take the opportunity to talk about the syntax for style specification in more detail.

To define a new line style, use the `set style line` command:

```
set style line {int:index} [ [ linetype  | lt ] {idx:linetype} ]
                           [ [ linewidth | lw ] {flt:linewidth} ]
                           [ [ pointtype | pt ] {idx:pointtype} ]
                           [ [ pointsize | ps ] {flt:pointsize} ]
                           [ [ linecolor | lc ] {clr:colorspec} ]

set style line {int:index} default
```

The command `set style line ...` creates a new entry in a sequence of user-defined line styles. The base for each new style is the corresponding system style; only those properties explicitly named in the `set style line` command are changed.

The `linetype` and `pointtype` options refer to the dash pattern for lines and the shape of the symbol used for data points, respectively. Check the `test` command for your terminal to see the available patterns and symbols.

The `linewidth` and `pointsize` options are measured as multipliers relative to the default size. (In other words, the default for both `linewidth` and `pointsize` is 1.) Values less than 1 are possible.

The `colorspec` must be a valid color specification, using any one of the syntax variants described in the following section.

A user-defined combination of `linetype`, `linewidth`, `pointtype`, `pointsize`, and `linecolor` (even if many of these properties have default values), created using the `set style line` command, is referred to as a `linestyle`, and can be used wherever an individual `linetype`, `linewidth` or similar option is expected. For instance, we can use custom line styles in a plot by specifying their index, like so:

```
set style line 1 lt 3 lw 2
set style line 2 lt 3 lw 4

plot "data" u 1:2 w l ls 1, "data" u 1:3 w l ls 2
```

Finally, we can make gnuplot switch entirely to using our custom styles. As we've seen before, if there is more than one data set, gnuplot cycles through all available plot styles automatically (unless we request a specific style, of course). Usually, gnuplot only uses the predefined styles. However, using the command

```
set style increment [ default | userstyle ]
```

we can choose which set of line types to use. The argument `default` makes gnuplot choose system styles only, while `userstyle` makes gnuplot choose preferentially from custom styles. I say "preferentially" because gnuplot will fall back to a system style if a custom style isn't found for some index.

5.3.2　Specifying color

In the previous section, I referred to a *colorspec*. A colorspec identifies a color in gnuplot. In this section, we look at the syntax for colorspecs.

A colorspec begins with the keyword `rgbcolor` (or abbreviated `rgb`), followed by the actual identifier. Three different formats for the identifier are available:

```
rgbcolor "{str:colorname}"
rgbcolor "{#RRGGBB}"
rgbcolor variable
```

In the first format, we would use an explicit color name, for example `rgbcolor "blue"`. Gnuplot knows 78 distinct colors; you can find a listing of all known color names and their RGB components by issuing this command: `show palette colornames`.

The second format uses an explicit RGB-triple in hexadecimal representation, preceded by a hashmark. This format is familiar, for instance, from cascading style sheet (CSS) indicators. So, to select blue, we could write `rgbcolor "#0000FF"` or `rgb "#0000ff"` (capitalization doesn't matter).

Finally, `rgbcolor variable` means that the color is read together with the actual data from the file. This mode is only available for three-dimensional plots generated using the `splot` command, which we will study in chapter 8. For more details on `rgbcolor variable`, check the standard gnuplot reference documentation.

Although we won't make use of this now, I want to mention that there is yet another way to write a colorspec: we can select a color from a continuous spectrum or *palette* of colors by specifying the position of the color within that spectrum. This allows us to select a color based on the values of the data being plotted, so that we can generate density or other *false-color* plots. We'll come back to them in chapter 9.

5.3.3　Worked example: half-tone shading

Let's look at a quick example that will put many of the topics we've just introduced together.

In section 5.2.2 we drew some figures, such as figure 5.7, which contained boxes filled with different fill patterns to help distinguish them from one another. Instead of fill patterns, we can choose to have boxes filled with different fill colors, simply by saying `set style fill solid` instead of `set style fill pattern`. But what if we want a solid fill style (that is, no patterns), but need to generate output in black and white (as for this book, for example)?

In such a case, we want to replace the different colors with different shades of gray. We also want gnuplot to choose automatically from all available shades, the way it usually cycles through all available colors or line types.

To achieve this effect, we have to set up a sequence of custom styles, consisting entirely of grayscales. We can then use the `set style increment user` command to force gnuplot to choose from this collection of custom styles only. Listing 5.3 demonstrates the required commands and figure 5.15 shows the resulting graph.

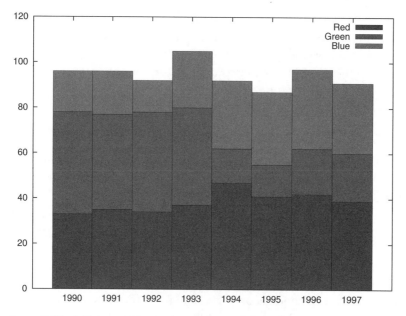

Figure 5.15   A histogram drawn with custom fill styles—see listing 5.3

Listing 5.3   Defining and using custom styles—see figure 5.15

```
set style line 1 lc rgb 'grey30'
set style line 2 lc rgb 'grey50'
set style line 3 lc rgb 'grey70'

set style increment user

set style fill solid 1 border -1

set style histogram rowstacked
set style data histogram

plot "histo" u 2:xtic(1) t "Red", "" u 3 t "Green", "" u 4 t "Blue"
```

Let's step through the commands:

1   Set up three custom styles (labeled 1, 2, and 3), specifying different shades of gray as line color (`lc` for short).

2   Force gnuplot to choose from the custom line styles whenever possible through `set style increment user`.

3   Switch to a solid fill style at full saturation (`solid 1`). This will take the color of each line style and apply it as the fill color.

4   Also request a border to be drawn around the boxes, using the maximally visible default line type `-1` (a solid, black line for almost all terminals).

5   Draw the histogram as usual.

This example employed several of the techniques we learned in this chapter: custom styles, color specs, fill styles, and histograms. The most important aspect is that you understand how to define your own styles and how to make gnuplot use them whenever possible. This will allow you to tailor the appearance of your graphs to your specific needs (as we did in this example).

5.4 *Summary*

This chapter was a bit of an illustrated catalogue: a place where all of gnuplot's major plot styles are demonstrated by way of an example. As such, I'm not disappointed if you didn't read the chapter from start to finish: it's perfectly fine to just look at the figures until you find one that does what you need, and then read the accompanying section.

In the first section, we learned how to choose plot styles (either inline, as part of the `plot` command, or globally, by fixing the appropriate options with `set`).

We also introduced the important topic of terminal capabilities early in this chapter: what we can show on a gnuplot-generated graph depends on the capabilities of the output device or *terminal*. For each possible choice of terminal, we can use the `test` command to generate a test image that demonstrates the chosen terminal's capabilities in a standardized fashion.

Everything we did in this chapter is there to visualize data. By contrast, in the next chapter (chapter 6), we look at things we may want to put on a plot in *addition* to the data: labels, arrows, and other decorations.

Decorations 6

This chapter covers

- Locations on a graph
- Adding arrows, labels, and other decorations
- Providing explanations using a key
- Changing the overall appearance

Data alone doesn't tell a story. To be useful, the data needs to be placed into context: at least, we must tell the observer what the data is (such as position versus time, particle count versus scattering angle, stock price versus date, or whatever) and what units the data is plotted in (centimeters or inches, seconds or minutes, dollars or euros). No plot is complete without this information.

But we can do much more to make a graph useful and informative: we can add arrows and annotations on the graph to point out and explain interesting features. We may also want to provide special tic marks and labels to make quantitative information stand out more. Or we may need to change the overall size and shape of the entire graph to accommodate a specific data set.

In this chapter, we discuss all the means that gnuplot offers to put additional information on a plot (in addition to the actual data). Because much of this material is quite dry, I've gathered the most important commands and options together in the next section. Unless you have special needs, this may be all you need to know right now—gnuplot is quite good at automatically "doing the right thing" in most situations.

6.1   *Quick start: minimal context for data*

For the sake of concreteness, let's go back to the DLA (diffusion limited aggregation) example of section 1.1.2 and in particular figure 1.4. We'll use this plot as our example throughout this section.

The absolute quickest way to add the most important contextual information to the plot is to give it a title, such as

```
set title "Run Time (in seconds)
➡ vs. Cluster Size (in thousands of particles)"
```

This tells the observer both what is plotted (computation time versus system size) as well as the relevant units (time is given in seconds, while particles are counted by the thousands), conveniently packaged into a single command. This is the bare minimum.

The title is centered at the top of the graph (as in figure 6.1—you may want to go back to section 1.1.2 to learn about the context in which this example arose).

With a little additional effort we can put labels on the axes, using the set xlabel and set ylabel commands. This frees up the title for contextual information about the data in the plot, like so:

```
set xlabel "Cluster Size [thousands]"
set ylabel "Running Time [sec]"
set title "DLA Growth Program: Run Time
➡ vs Cluster Size (Double Logarithmic)"
```

Finally, we have the key (or legend), which relates line types to data sets. By default, it's placed in the top-right corner of the graph, but this may not be suitable if it would interfere with data. We can change the position of the key using the keywords

```
left, right, top, bottom, center
```

in the set key command, for example, set key right center, to place the key vertically centered on the right side of the graph. The order of the keywords doesn't matter, and if only one is given, all other options retain their values. Finally, the key can be suppressed entirely using unset key.

We have already seen (in section 2.1.2) how we can change the string describing the data set in the key using the title option to the plot command. To suppress an entry in the key, we can either use the notitle option or provide an empty title string. In the following command, only the actual data curve will have an entry in the key, but the fitted curve won't:

```
plot [0.5:40][.5:30000] "dla-log-short" u 2:6 title "data" w p,
➡ 1.2*x**2.7 notitle
```

Now we can put all of this together. Listing 6.1 summarizes all commands that were used to build figure 6.1.

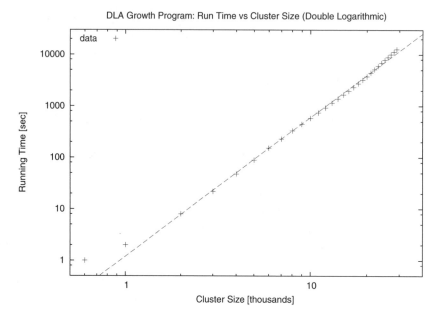

Figure 6.1   Providing minimal context to a plot using a title and axes labels. See listing 6.1.

Listing 6.1   The set of commands used to create figure 6.1

```
set xlabel "Cluster Size [thousands]"
set ylabel "Running Time [sec]"
set title "DLA Growth Program: Run Time
➡ vs Cluster Size (Double Logarithmic)"

set key top left
set logscale

plot [0.5:40][.5:30000] "dla-log-short" u 2:6 title "data" w p,
➡ 1.2*x**2.7 notitle
```

This concludes our quick start, and may be all you need for now. In the rest of this chapter, we'll discuss all the miscellaneous options that are available in case we aren't happy with the defaults. But first I need to describe the different ways you can refer to a location on the plot.

6.2   *Digression: locations on a graph*

First, let's establish some terminology. The entire area of the plot is referred to as the *screen* or the *canvas*. On the canvas there is the actual *graph*, which is surrounded by a *border* (unless we explicitly turn the border off). The region outside the border is called the *margin*. All these are indicated in the figure 6.2.

We can provide up to two different sets of axes to a plot. This is occasionally useful when comparing different data sets side by side: each data set can be presented with its own coordinate system in a single graph. The primary coordinate system (named

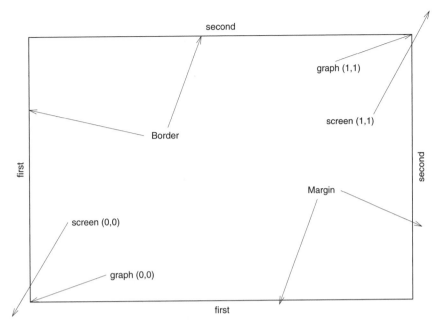

Figure 6.2　The parts of a gnuplot graph: canvas, border, margin

`first`) is plotted along the bottom and left borders. The secondary coordinate system (`second`) is plotted along the top and right borders. By default, the secondary system not shown, instead the primary system is displayed on all four borders. (You'll find more information on axes and coordinate systems in chapter 7.)

Now that we know what all parts of a graph are called, we can talk about the different ways to specify locations. Gnuplot uses *five* different coordinate systems:

`first, second, graph, screen, character`

The first two refer to the coordinates of the plot itself. The third and fourth (`graph` and `screen`) refer to the actual graph area or the entire canvas, respectively, placing the origin (0,0) at the bottom-left corner and the point (1,1) in the top-right corner (see figure 6.2). Finally, the `character` system gives positions in character widths and heights from the origin (0,0) of the screen area. Obviously, positions in this last coordinate system depend on the font size of the default font for the current terminal.

Coordinates are given as pairs of numbers separated by a comma. As necessary, each number in this pair can be preceded by one of the five coordinate specifiers. The default is `first`, and if no coordinate system is given explicitly for y, the one for x is used for both values.[1]

We'll see many examples of coordinate specifications in the rest of this chapter.

---

[1]　Although it may seem weird to use different coordinate systems in the same coordinate pair, this feature is occasionally very useful. For example, we can use the following command to place a vertical line at a fixed x location and let it extend over the full range of the graph, independent of the y range: `set arrow from 1.25, graph 0 to 1.25, graph 1`.

6.3   *Additional graph elements: decorations*

I use the term *decorations* for all additional graphical elements that can be placed onto the graph, but do not (primarily) represent data. The most useful decorations are arrows and text labels, but gnuplot can also draw arbitrary rectangles. (The current development version of gnuplot allows additional shapes.)

6.3.1   *Common conventions*

All decorations are created using the set ... command (see chapter 4). It's very important to remember that this command does *not* generate a replot event: the decorations won't appear on the plot until the next plot, splot, or replot command has been issued!

Keep in mind that decorations aren't taken into account by the autoscale feature, which automatically attempts to adjust the plot ranges in such a way as to display the relevant parts of the data. In other words, if a decoration (or a part of it) falls outside the plot range (either the explicitly given or the automatically selected one), it will *not* appear on the plot. (More on autoscaling in section 7.2.)

So that we can later refer to a specific object (such as an arrow or a text label), we can give each object a numeric tag, for instance set arrow 3 .... Now we can make changes to this arrow only by providing this tag in the next call to set arrow or even eliminate it using unset arrow 3. If we omit the label, gnuplot will assign the next unused number automatically. Arrows, labels, and objects have separate counters.

Finally, all decorations have a number of options that control their appearance on the plot. In general, we specify these options inline as part of the set ... call. For arrows and rectangles, we can also fix these options globally through appropriate set style commands. Inline styles can still be used to override global settings.

6.3.2   *Arrows*

Arrows are generated using the set arrow command, which has the following set of options:

```
set arrow [{idx:tag}] [ from {pos:from} ][ [to|rto] {pos:to} ]
                      [ [ arrowstyle | as {idx:style} ]
                        | [ [ nohead | head | backhead | heads ]
                            | [ size {flt:length} [,{flt:angle}]
                                [,{flt:backangle}] ]
                            [ filled | empty | nofilled ]
                            [ front | back ]
                            [ [ linetype | lt {idx:type} ]
                              [ linewidth | lw {int:width} ]
                              | [ linestyle | ls {idx:style} ] ]
                          ]
                      ]
```

We need to specify the two endpoints of the arrow, using the from and to keywords. When using rto (relative to), the second set of coordinates is interpreted as relative to the first: set arrow from 1,1 rto 2,0 draws a horizontal arrow of length 2.

If we've defined custom arrow styles (see the next section), we can simply choose one of them with `arrowstyle` (as is a synonym for `arrowstyle`). Alternatively, we can provide the required information inline. Let's go through the options in some detail.

CUSTOMIZING ARROW APPEARANCE

By default, arrows have a single head at the destination endpoint. This behavior can be changed using the four keywords explained in the table 6.1.

	From	To	
nohead	none	none	
head	none	head	
backhead	head	none	**Table 6.1 Options to**
heads	head	head	`set arrow ...` **controlling the generation of arrowheads**

We can also change the form of the head using the `size` keyword. This option takes two or three parameters. The `length` gives the length of each side of the head. The units are taken from the x axis of one of the coordinate systems; by default `first` is used.

You can set the angle that the side of the head makes with the arrow's "backbone" using the `angle` argument. The angle is measured in degrees. It's not restricted to values smaller than 90 degrees, so that it's possible to terminate an arrow with a perpendicular crossbar (for example, to create scale indicators as in figure 6.6), or to create even more creative arrowheads.

The `backangle` option only takes effect when either `filled` or `empty` is used. It measures the angle the back of the head makes with the arrow. The `backangle` is measured in the same direction as the `angle` option. Choosing a `backangle` greater than `angle` but less than `90` creates a "feathered" arrowhead. Making `backangle` greater than `90` but less than `180` creates a diamond-shaped head. All these terms are explained in figure 6.3.

The arrowhead can be filled with the current line color using `filled`. Using `empty` just draws the outline of the arrowhead (see figure 6.4).

The arrow is drawn in front of the plotted data if we use `front`; if `back` is given, the arrow is drawn underneath the data.

If we've defined custom line styles, we can choose one of them. Alternatively, we can specify `linetype` and `linewidth` explicitly.

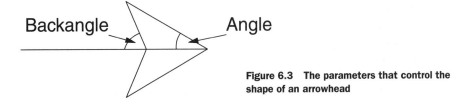

Figure 6.3 The parameters that control the shape of an arrowhead

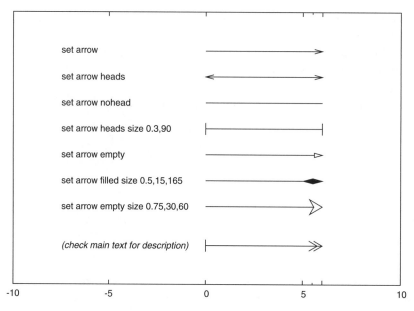

Figure 6.4   Different arrow forms and the commands used to generate them. See listing 6.2 for the last one.

CUSTOM ARROW STYLES

Instead of fixing all options on each arrow individually, we can create custom arrow styles using `set style arrow`. Each arrow style is given an index, and we can choose one of the custom styles when creating an arrow: `set arrow arrowstyle 3 ...` will draw an arrow using style 3. Attempting to create an arrow in a style that has not been explicitly defined will generate an error.

```
set style arrow {idx:index} default

set style arrow {idx:index} [ nohead | head | backhead | heads ]
                            [ size {flt:length} [,{flt:angle}]
                                  [,{flt:backangle}] ]
                            [ filled | empty | nofilled ]
                            [ front | back ]
                            [ [ linetype | lt {idx:type} ]
                              [ linewidth | lw {int:width} ]
                              | [ linestyle | ls {idx:style} ] ] ]
```

The options available for arrow styles are the same as for individual arrows. The `default` keyword resets all arrow properties to their default values.

MORE TRICKS WITH ARROWS

The arrow facility is quite flexible and can be used for purposes other than placing explicit arrows on a plot. Here are some ideas.

Since an arrow without a head is just a straight line, we can use `set arrow ...` to draw arbitrary straight lines on a plot. In particular, arrows can be used to draw *vertical* lines. (We don't need arrows to draw *horizontal* lines of course; just say `plot 1, -1` to draw horizontal lines at y=-1 and y=+1.)

The ability to mix different coordinate systems in the same coordinate specification can come in handy in this context. For example, if we want to draw a vertical line at x=0.5 from the lower to the upper boundary, we can simply say `set arrow from 0.5, graph 0 to 0.5, graph 1`, without having to worry about the exact values of the vertical plot range.

A set of short arrows without heads can be used to draw custom tic marks, if gnuplot's built-in tic marks are insufficient (see chapter 7 for more information on tic marks).

Arrows with customized heads can be used to indicate a scale or range on a graph—figure 6.6 contains such an arrow used for this purpose.

Finally, we can generate an arrow with two *different* heads by generating two single-headed arrows back to back. We can also overlay arrows to generate more sophisticated effects. In listing 6.2, we show the commands used to generate the bottom arrow in figure 6.4.

> **Listing 6.2 Commands used to generate the double-feathered arrow in figure 6.4**

```
set arrow 1 from 0,-9 to 6,    -9 size 0.5,30
set arrow 2 from 0,-9 to 5.75, -9 size 0.5,30
set arrow 3 from 0,-9 to 1,    -9 backhead size 0.3,90
```

As we've seen, arrows are a versatile graph element. But more often than not, we'll want to combine them with some textual explanation. That's what labels are for.

6.3.3 *Text labels*

Text labels are a natural companion to arrows: the arrow shows the observer where to look, and the label explains what is happening. There are fewer options for labels compared to arrows, so let's discuss them quickly.

```
set label [{idx:tag}] [ "{str:text}" ] [ at {pos:location} ]
                      [ left | center | right ]
                      [ rotate [ by {int:degrees} ] | norotate ]
                      [ font "{str:name}[,{int:size}]" ]
                      [ [no]enhanced ] [ front | back ]
                      [ textcolor | tc [ {clr:colorspec}
                                       | lt {idx:type}
                                       | ls {idx:style} ] ]
                      [ point lt|pt {idx:pointtype}
                              | ps {idx:pointsize} | nopoint ]
                      [ offset {pos:off} ]
```

The label text is typically a constant, but it can also be a string variable or any string-valued expression (see chapter 4 for more information about string handling in gnuplot).

By default, the text is placed flush left at the position specified by the `at` ... location, but this can be controlled using the `left`, `center`, and `right` keywords.

Gnuplot allows text to be rotated, but not all terminals support arbitrary angles. Use the `test` command to see what's possible (see section 5.1.2).

We can control the stacking order with `front` and `back` as for arrows.

The color of the text can be selected using textcolor (abbreviated tc), which takes two different kinds of arguments: either a colorspec (see section 5.3) or the index of an existing line type or line style, preceded by one of the keywords lt or ls, respectively. If the latter form is chosen, the color of the indicated line type or line style will be used for the text of the label.

Using point, a symbol can be placed at the position specified with at and the text label is shifted relative to it. The point style and size can be fixed using lt (line type), pt (point type), or ps (point size), and the offset can be customized using offset. The nopoint option suppresses the point.

Finally, a specific font can be chosen using the font option. The keyword noenhanced suppresses the interpretation of enhanced-mode control characters in the text string, even if enhanced mode is active for the current terminal (read chapter 11 for an in-depth discussion of font selection and enhanced text mode).

Besides the fully general set label facility that I just described, gnuplot offers two specialized labelling commands: to add a label to any axis of the plot, or to add a title to the entire graph. Both provide convenient shortcuts for common situations.

TITLE

The title option is a label with some special defaults. For instance, it's automatically placed centered at the top of the graph.

The title option takes the following arguments, which should be familiar from the label discussed previously.

```
set title [ "{str:text}" ]
          [ font "{str:name}[,{int:size}]" ][ [no]enhanced ]
          [ textcolor | tc [ {clr:colorspec}
                             | lt {idx:type}
                             | ls {idx:style} ] ]
          [ offset {pos:off} ]
```

Only the behavior of the offset directive requires an explanation. It can be used to shift the title from its default position by a specified amount. What's unusual is that by default it interprets its argument as given in the character coordinate system. With this in mind, the following commands are entirely equivalent—both shift the title down by the height of a single character:

```
set title "..." offset 0,-1
set title "..." offset character 0,-1
```

AXIS LABELS

The commands that place labels on the axes of a plot are also variants of the standard set label command. Since labels can be placed onto any axis, there's an entire family of related commands, all differentiated by prefixes (such as x and y), that indicate which axis the label belongs to. (We haven't discussed these prefixes yet, but will do so in chapter 7). In the following synopsis, the underscore (_) stands for any of the permissible prefixes.

```
set _label ["{str:text}"] [ offset {pos:offset} ]
                          [ font "{str:name}[,{int:size}]" ]
```

```
[ textcolor | tc [ {clr:color}
                 | lt {idx:type}
                 | lt {idx:style} ] ]
[ [no]enhanced ]
[ rotate by {int:degrees} ]
```

All the options are a strict subset of the ones available for the plain `set label` command.

Finally, always keep in mind that both `set title` and the axis label commands are merely standard text labels with some convenient defaults. If they don't give you sufficient control to achieve the effect you're looking for, you can always use explicit `set label` commands instead.

Besides arrows and labels, which primarily are intended to add explanations to a graph, gnuplot also offers the user the ability to place arbitrary graph *objects* on a plot. This is done using the `set object` command.

6.3.4 *Objects*

The `set object ...` facility can place arbitrary geometrical objects on a graph. At the time of this writing, only rectangles with their sides parallel to the axes of the plot are supported, but future versions of gnuplot will also include circles and ellipses as objects that can be added in this fashion.

```
set object [{idx:tag}] rectangle [ from {pos:from} [to|rto] {pos:to}
                                  | center|at {pos:ctr}
                                    size {pos:extent} ]
                                  [ default ]
                                  [ front | back | behind ]
                                  [ fillcolor | fc {clr:color} ]
                                  [ fillstyle | fs {idx:style} ]
                                  [ linewidth | lw {flt:width} ]

set style rectangle [ front | back | behind ]
                    [ fillcolor | fc {clr:color} ]
                    [ fillstyle | fs {idx:style} ]
                    [ linewidth | lw {flt:width} ]
```

Most of the options are familiar by now, so we only need to discuss placement and sizing in detail.

Rectangles can be specified in two ways. We can either fix two corners that are diagonally across from each other using `from` and `to` or `rto`, or we can fix the center of the rectangle using either `center` or `at`, followed by the width and height. As usual, all positions, as well as the size can be given in any one of the coordinate systems.

The familiar `front` and `back` options exist to control the stacking order. There is also the `behind` option, which will place the current rectangle behind *everything* else on the plot. This is intended primarily to provide colored backgrounds for graphs.

Instead of providing all the detail inline, we can also define a global rectangle style using `set style rectangle`. Currently, only a single rectangle style can be defined in this way and will be used for all rectangles if no specific options are used inline as part of the `set object rectangle` command.

Arrows, labels, and objects are graphical elements that we can use to make graphs more interesting and more informative. But they aren't the only elements that can go on a plot besides data, and aren't even the most useful ones. The single most useful element is probably the graph's *legend* or *key*, which explains what all the lines and symbols on the plot stand for. Gnuplot's set key facility is very powerful, and therefore deserves a section by itself.

6.4   *The graph's legend or key*

We all know the little boxes on hiking maps explaining what all the symbols mean: thick red lines indicate highways, white is for country roads, and thin dashed lines mean unpaved gravel. And the odd-looking symbol with a roof: right, that's an outhouse. In gnuplot, this box is called the *key*.

The key (or legend) explains the meaning of each type of line or symbol placed on the plot. Because gnuplot generates a key automatically, it's the most convenient way to provide this sort of explanation. On the other hand, relying on the key separates the information from the actual data. I therefore often find it preferable to place arrows and labels directly on the graph instead, to explain the meaning of each curve or data set. A separate key excels again when there are so many curves that individual arrows and labels would clutter the graph.

As usual, almost anything about the key can be configured. The full command synopsis is as follows:

```
set key [ on|off ] [ default ]

        [ [ at {pos:position} ]
          | [ inside | lmargin | rmargin | tmargin | bmargin ] ]
        [ left | right | center ] [ top | bottom | center ]

        [ vertical | horizontal ] [ Left | Right ]
        [ [no]reverse ] [ [no]invert ]

        [ [no]autotitle [columnheader] ] [ [no]enhanced ]
        [ samplen {flt:len} ] [ spacing {flt:factor} ]

        [ title "{str:text}" ]
        [ width {int:chars} ] [ height {int:chars} ]
        [ [no]box [ [ linetype | lt {idx:type} ]
                    [ linewidth | lw {int:width} ]
                    | [ linestyle | ls {idx:style} ] ] ] ]
```

As you can see, there are a lot of suboptions! To make information easier to find, I've broken the following explanation into separate sections under their own headings. First we talk about the key as a whole and its position on the plot; then I'll explain the internal layout of information within the key itself. And finally, I'll show you how to affect the overall appearance of the key, and how to restore sanity, if you're in danger of getting lost in all the options.

6.4.1 Turning the key on and off

The entire key can be suppressed using either of the following two commands:

```
set key off
unset key
```

The command set key on enables it again.

6.4.2 Placement

The key can be placed at any position on the entire canvas. The most straightforward (but not necessarily the most convenient) method is to fix a specific location using the at option. The location can be prefixed by any of the standard coordinate system prefixes. The keywords left, right, top, bottom, and center can be used to align the key relative to the specified position. For instance,

```
set key at 0,0 left top
```

places the top-left corner of the key at the origin of the coordinate system.

As usual, with great power comes great responsibility. When using the explicit at option, gnuplot does not rearrange the plot in any way to make room for the key: this must be done explicitly by the user. Instead, we can use several predefined keywords to place the key relative to the graph. When using these keywords, the borders of the graph are automatically adjusted to make room for the key.

We can use the keywords left, right, top, bottom, and center to push the key into the desired position. We can place the key inside the plot using inside (this is the default), or on any one of the margins, using lmargin, rmargin, tmargin, bmargin (meaning the left, right, top, and bottom margin, respectively). We can use combinations of position specifiers, such as set key left top. The effect of these options is cumulative, so that the following two examples will have the same effect:

```
set key bottom left
```

or

```
set key bottom
set key left
```

One surprising exception is that the keyword center by itself is interpreted as the *center of the graph* (both horizontally and vertically).

6.4.3 Layout

The samples in the key can either be stacked vertically or aligned horizontally using the vertical and horizontal keywords. The alignment of the labels within the key is controlled using the Left and Right options (note the capitals). The default is vertical Left.

Usually, the textual description of the line sample is to the left, with the line sample on the right. This arrangement can be interchanged using reverse.

Entries in the key are made in the order in which the corresponding data sets occur in the plot command. If we want to sort entries in some specific way, we need to list the data sets in the appropriate order in the plot command. But we can invert the stacking order of the samples within the key through invert. This is mainly useful to force the ordering of labels in the key to match the order of box types in a stacked histogram (see section 5.2.2).

6.4.4   *Explanations*

The explanation is a bit of text that assigns a meaning to each line sample or symbol type included in the key. The string for the explanation can come from one of two places. The usual (and until recently, the only) source for the explanatory text is the plot command itself. But the most recent versions of gnuplot added the possibility to embed the explanation together with the data in the input file. Let's take a look at both methods.

TAKING EXPLANATIONS FROM THE PLOT COMMAND

Usually, the explanatory text is taken from the plot command, using the title keyword:

```
plot "data" u 1:2 title "Experiment" w l, sin(x) title "Theory" w l
```

If no explicit title has been set in the plot command, gnuplot will generate a standard description, based on the filename and the selection of columns plotted.

There are several ways to suppress key entries. First of all, keep in mind that if an empty string is given as argument to the title keyword, gnuplot will *not* generate a key entry for the corresponding data set. (To generate a key entry without a visible explanation, use a string consisting only of whitespace as argument.) Alternatively, we can use the notitle keyword in the plot command instead. Finally, using the noauto-title option to set key suppresses all key entries that don't have an explicit title string in the plot command.

Interpretation of control characters in the key can be suppressed using the noenhanced flag (see chapter 11 for details on enhanced text mode).

TAKING EXPLANATIONS FROM THE DATA FILE

The option set key autotitles columnhead, which is only available when gnuplot is built with support for data strings, makes gnuplot take the explanations for the key from the first *noncomment* line in the data file.

Let's look at an example. Listing 6.3 shows a data file suitable for use with this option: note how the first line, containing the column headings (which will be used in the key of the plot) isn't a comment line! We can plot this file using the following (see figure 6.5):

```
set style data linesp
set key autotitle columnhead
plot "data" u 1:2, "" u 1:3, "" u 1:4
```

Without the key autotitle columnhead option, we'd have to include the explanations explicitly in the plot command, like so:

```
plot "data" u 1:2 t "Wheat", "" u 1:3 t "Barley", "" u 1:4 t "Rye"
```

| Listing 6.3 | Data for the `set key autotitle columnhead` example (figure 6.5) |

```
Year    Wheat   Barley  Rye     # Not a comment line!
1990    8       6       14
1991    10      5       12
1992    10      7       15
1993    11      5       13
1994    9       6       12
```

There is yet another way to achieve the same effect: if the argument to the `title` keyword in the `plot` command is a number instead of a string, then this number is interpreted as a column number, and the entry in the key is taken from the first noncomment line in this column:

```
plot "data" u 1:2 t 2, "" u 1:3 t 3, "" u 1:4 t 4
```

Note that the title can be taken from a different column than the data, which can be useful in combination with data transformations: commands such as `plot "data" using 1:($2/$3) title 2` are legal.

The ability to take explanations directly from the data file is an interesting new feature, adding significant convenience in particular when plotting many data sets in the same plot. Nevertheless, I am a bit uncomfortable with the way it mixes data and comments in the same file without an easy way to distinguish the two, making files using this format harder to use with data processing filters or as input to other programs. (I'd probably have preferred to make the line containing the column heads a

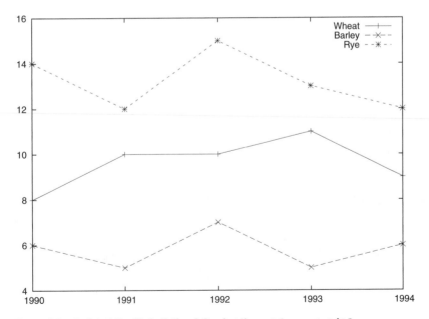

Figure 6.5 A plot of the file in listing 6.3 using the `set key autotitle columnhead` option

comment line, but indicate it through a special marker, such as a doubled hashmark or other comment character at the beginning of the line.) Judge for yourself.

6.4.5   *Appearance*

The length of the line sample in the key can be controlled using `samplen`. The sample length is the sum of the tic length (see chapter 7), and the argument given to `samplen` times the character width. A negative argument to `samplen` suppresses the line sample.

The vertical spacing between lines in the key is controlled using `spacing`. The spacing is the product of the point size, the vertical tic size, and the argument to `spacing`. This parameter does *not* influence the horizontal spacing between entries in `horizontal` mode.

The entire key can be given a title, using the `title` option, and be surrounded by a frame using `box`. In this case, it may be necessary to adjust the size of the box: this can be done using the `width` and `height` parameters. Both take the number of characters to be added or subtracted from the calculated size of the key, before the box is drawn. In particular, if any text label in the key contains control characters for enhanced text mode, the size of the autogenerated box may be incorrect. Finally, the parameters of the lines used to draw the box can be adjusted using the usual options.

6.4.6   *Default settings*

Just to provide a reference, the default settings for the key are

```
set key on right top vertical Right noreverse noinvert autotitle
➥ samplen 4 spacing 1.25 title '' nobox
```

The previous command is equivalent to the much shorter

```
set key default
```

which can occasionlly be helpful to restore sanity when experimenting with key placement and layout.

Now that we've seen all of the different graph elements that can be used in a gnuplot figure, it's time to put everything together and look at a worked example. That's what we'll do next.

6.5   *Worked example: features of a spectrum*

To put all the things we've learned together, let's study a more extensive example (see figure 6.6). The plot shows some (supposedly) experimental data, together with two theoretical curves that might explain the data from the experiment. The data in this example is fake, but the plot is real enough!

Listing 6.4 gives the commands used to generate this graph, as they would have been entered at the gnuplot prompt. Let's step through them in detail—there is much to learn.

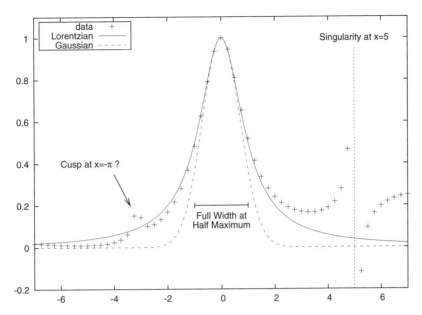

Figure 6.6　A complicated plot. See listing 6.4 for the commands used to generate it.

Listing 6.4　The commands used to generate the plot in figure 6.6

```
set terminal wxt enhanced

set key top left box

set arrow 1 from -4,.35 to -3.4,0.2
set label 1 "Cusp at x=-{/Symbol p} ?" at -6,0.4

set arrow 2 from 5,-.2 to 5,.95 nohead linetype 4
set label 2 "Singularity at x=5" at 5,1 center

set arrow 3 from -1,0.2 to 1,0.2 heads size 0.1,90
set label 3 "Full Width at\nHalf Maximum" at 0,0.15 center

plot [-7:7][-.2:1.1] "spectrum.dat" u 1:2 t "data" w p,
➡ 1/(1+x**2) t "Lorentzian", exp(-x**2) t "Gaussian"
```

1 First, we select our favorite terminal (wxt in this case), making sure to use the *enhanced* mode. We haven't learned about enhanced text mode for terminals yet (we'll do so in chapter 11)—suffice it to say that enhanced mode allows us to use special characters (such as Greek letters) and things such as subscripts and superscripts in our labels.

2 We move the key to the top-left corner, so that it doesn't interfere with the data and surround the key with a box.

3 We place an arrow and a label onto the graph, pointing out an oddity in the data. Note the odd form of the label text: {/Symbol p}. These characters have a special meaning in enhanced text mode. Here, we select the Symbol font for the character p, which is a lowercase Greek letter π.

4 We use an arrow without heads to place a vertical line on the plot. The line shows the vertical asymptote as the data approaches the singularity at x=5.

5 Yet another creative use for an arrow, this time with two customized heads. This arrow isn't used to point out a feature in the graph, but to give an indication of a scale. (The "Full Width at Half Maximum" is commonly used in spectroscopy to measure the width of a spectral line.)

6 The label for the last arrow contains an explicit line break, so that it spreads over two lines. Remember from chapter 4 that escaped characters (such as the \n here) in double-quoted strings are interpreted as control characters.

7 Finally, finally: plot the data!

I hope this example gives you an idea of what can be achieved using decorations. Arrows and labels can be used to explain the data and point out specific features, but nothing prevents us from getting more creative.

Everything we've discussed in this chapter so far related to graphical elements we put on the graph itself: simple decorations, such as arrows, labels, and objects, and complex aggregates, such as the key. But there are other, more global aspects of a graph we may want to control: its overall size and aspect ratio and the way the actual plot is contained within the entire graph. That's what we turn to now.

6.6   *Overall appearance*

Besides the individual decorations we just discussed, there are some features of a plot that determine its general appearance: the overall size and aspect ratio, and the presence or absence of axes and gridlines, borders and margins.

6.6.1   *Size and aspect ratio*

We have to distinguish between the size of the *plot* and the size of the *canvas*. The latter determines the size of the output file (or screen), while the former affects the size of the graph on the canvas. The canvas size is specified using the

```
set terminal {enum:terminaltype} size {flt:x},{flt:y}
```

command, which we'll discuss in chapter 11 on files and output devices. Here, we're interested in the size of the plot on the screen or canvas, which is controlled by the set size command:

```
set size [ [no]square | ratio {flt:r} | noratio ]
         [ {flt:x} [,{flt:y}] ]
```

The numeric values x, y scale the plot with respect to the screen. For values less than 1.0, the graph won't fill the entire screen; for values greater than 1.0, only part of the graph will be shown. If y is omitted, the plot will be scaled in both directions by x. For example, set size 0.5 will reduce the extent of the plot by half along both axes, while keeping the overall canvas size fixed.

If the size of the graph is smaller than the size of the canvas, it's not clear where on the canvas the graph should be located. The graph's position on the screen is fixed using the `set origin` option:

```
set origin {flt:x},{flt:y}
```

The arguments give the origin of the graph in `screen` coordinates.

The `ratio` option and its relatives (`square` and `noratio`) provide a shorthand to control the aspect ratio of the plot; that is, the ratio of the y axis length to the x axis length. Setting `set size ratio 2` will therefore result in a plot that's twice as tall as wide, and `set size square` is a synonym for `set size ratio 1`.

Negative values for the ratio have a special meaning: `set size ratio -1` will scale the graph so that the length of the x axis *unit* is equal to the length of the y axis *unit*. For `ratio -2`, the y axis unit has twice the length of the x axis unit; for `ratio -0.5`, the x axis unit is twice the y axis unit's length. Figure 6.7 demonstrates all these settings.

With `nosquare` and `noratio`, we reset the aspect ratio of the graph to the default value of the terminal (typically a value around 1.25 to 1.5—the postscript terminal defaults to 10/7; the GIF/JPG/PNG terminal defaults to 600/480). Note that neither command resets the scale given by x, y.

It's possible to give contradictory hints to gnuplot when prescribing both scale values in addition to the aspect ratio. In such cases, gnuplot attempts to maintain the

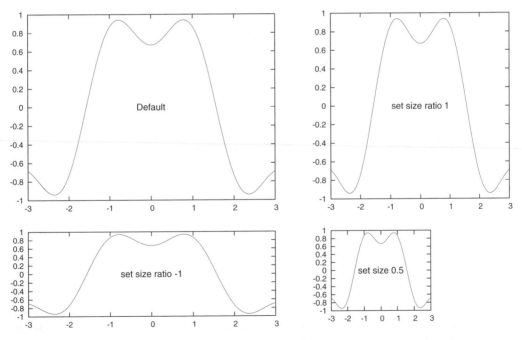

Figure 6.7 Controlling overall image size and aspect ratio with `set size`. Clockwise from top left: default settings, aspect ratio 10/7; full plot size, aspect ratio 1/1; reduced plot on full-size canvas, default aspect ratio; full plot size, x unit with same apparent length as y unit.

desired aspect ratio without exceeding the minimum area given by the scale values. It's always possible to avoid these situations by fixing only two of the values. My recommendation is to control *the size of the plot on the canvas* through the x *or* y scale values, and to control *the aspect ratio* using the `ratio` option. The effect of both of these options is intuitively clear, and no ambiguity is possible.

6.6.2   *Borders and margins*

By default, gnuplot puts borders on all four sides of the plot. This is actually quite suitable if the graph is going to be used in a larger text document (because it gives the plot a "frame" separating it from surrounding text), but can feel cluttered for a stand-alone diagram. And it's simply unsuitable for some special diagrams that don't fit neatly into a rectangular box. For these reasons, gnuplot gives us the ability to control all parts of the border, using the `set border` option:

```
set border [ {int:mask} ] [ front | back ]
           [ [ linetype | lt {idx:type} ]
             [ linewidth | lw {int:width} ]
             | [ linestyle | ls {idx:style} ] ]
```

The only argument that isn't familiar by now is `mask`. This argument is a bit-mask in form of an integer, each bit referring to one side of the border. A mask value of 1 refers to the bottom, 2 to the left, 4 to the top, and 8 to the right, so that 15 (1+2+4+8) paints borders on all four sides. (There are additional bits used for three-dimensional plots using `splot`—we'll discuss them in chapter 8.) To draw borders on some, but not all sides, we first need to unset all borders, and then switch on those we want to see:

```
unset border     # Unset all borders
set border 3     # Switch on bottom and left border: 3=1+2
```

If tic marks are drawn on the border (as is the default), unsetting the border does *not* unset the tic marks: they must be controlled separately using options we discuss in chapter 7.

By default, gnuplot calculates the size of the margins automatically, based on the presence or absence of tics, axis labels, the plot title, and other decorations placed outside the borders. If necessary, we can fix margins manually, using the following commands:

```
set bmargin [ {int:margin} ]    # bottom margin
set lmargin [ {int:margin} ]    # left margin
set tmargin [ {int:margin} ]    # top margin
set rmargin [ {int:margin} ]    # right margin

show margin                     # show current settings
```

If an argument is given, it's interpreted as the desired size of the margins in character widths and heights, using the current terminal's default font. Gnuplot makes a best-effort attempt to determine the average character size for variable-width fonts, either by using the nominal font size in printer points (PostScript) or by sampling the size of a test string (libgd-based bitmap terminals).[2] Omitting the argument restores the default automatic sizing.

6.7 *Summary*

In this chapter, we learned how to decorate our graphs with additional image elements: overall descriptions, such as graph title or key, and additional graphic elements, such as labels and arrows. We also learned how to change the overall size and aspect ratio of the entire graph.

Specifically, we saw

- The set `title` command, to give an overall description to the plot.
- The set `xlabel` and set `ylabel` commands, which can be used to provide labels for the axes.
- The set `arrow` command, which can be used to place arrows and other straight lines directly on the graph.
- The set `label` command, to add text labels to a plot.
- The set `object` facility for adding arbitrary rectangles.
- The complex set `key` command, which allows us to customize the explanation of lines and symbols used to plot data. The most important directives of the set key command are
    - unset key to suppress the key altogether.
    - set key top left, and so on, to move the key to a different spot on the canvas.
- The set `size` command, to change the size of the actual *plot* on the canvas (changing the size of the canvas is done using set terminal size ...; see chapter 11) and to affect the aspect ratio of the plot.
- The set `origin` option determines the position of the actual graph on the canvas.
- The set `border` option, to turn the borders around the plot on or off.

We also studied some ways that these decorations can be used in creative ways to achieve somewhat special visual effects, such as unusual arrowheads, and so forth.

In the following chapter, we'll take a look at the last important thing that gives a plot context: the axes, and their subdivisions and labels. Stay tuned.

---

[2] In the current development version of gnuplot, the position of margins can also be specified explicitly using the screen coordinate system, using a new command syntax: set bmargin at screen .... Check the standard gnuplot reference documentation for details.

All about axes 7

This chapter covers
- Using multiple axes
- Selecting plot ranges
- Customizing tic marks and tic labels
- Plotting time series with gnuplot

In this chapter, we finally come to coordinate axes and their labeling. Treating them last, after discussing plot styles and decorations, may seem surprising, given how critical well-labeled coordinate axes are to achieving an informative graph. On the other hand, gnuplot's default behavior for axes-related options is perfectly adequate in almost all situations, so that explicit customization is rarely required.

One topic deserves special consideration, namely, the use of multiple axes on the same plot, and this is what we'll discuss first. Then we move on and describe all the ways that axes and their labels can be customized. Lastly, we treat the special case when one axis (usually the x axis) represents *time*, in other words, when the plot shows a time series. Time series plots pose special challenges, since now the labels aren't simply numeric. Instead, we need to worry about things such as the names of months and weekdays, potentially in different languages, too! This has long been a problem to gnuplot users, and so I'll devote significant space to this application.

But first, let's talk about multiple axes on the same plot.

7.1 *Multiple axes*

Gnuplot gives us the ability to plot graphs using two different coordinate systems within the same plot. Typically, these coordinate systems will share one axis (otherwise there's no good reason to have them on the same plot), but they may also be entirely independent.

Plots involving two different y axes usually make the most sense when we want to compare two data sets side by side which have very different units. As a typical example, let's study figure 7.1, which compares the average ice cream consumption (in some community) over consecutive four-week periods with the mean temperature during the same period.[1]

Figure 7.1 is a good example of why we might want to use multiple axes on a plot: the two quantities (ice cream consumption and temperatures) have a different nature, and are also numerically quite different. Yet, once we put them next to each other, the correlation becomes clear (not too surprisingly, in this example).

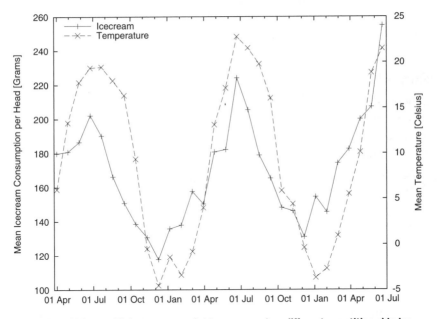

Figure 7.1 Using multiple axes on a plot to compare two different quantities side by side. (See listing 7.2 find out how this plot was made.)

7.1.1 *Terminology*

As we've just seen, gnuplot can handle two sets of axes on a single plot. The consequence is that all commands and options to manipulate axes-related properties come in two versions—one for each set of axes. In this section, we summarize the naming conventions associated with these commands.

---

[1] This example was inspired by the "Ice Cream Consumption" story, found on the StatLib's Data and Story Library (DASL) at http://lib.stat.cmu.edu/DASL/Datafiles/IceCream.html.

The primary coordinate system is usually plotted along the bottom and left borders of the graph. (This corresponds to the `first` coordinate system we introduced in section 6.2.) If the secondary system (`second`) is used, it's plotted along the top and right borders.

Be default, the secondary system isn't used. Instead, the tic marks (but not the labels) of the primary system are mirrored on the opposite sides of the plot.

All options that modify aspects of the coordinate systems can be applied to any of the axes: either the x or the y axis, in either the primary or the secondary coordinate system. The actual commands and options are prefixed to indicate which specific axis a command should be applied to (see table 7.1). Omitting the prefix applies the option to *all* axes.

Table 7.1 Prefixes used to indicate the selected coordinate system

	Primary	Secondary
x axis	x	x2
y axis	y	y2

In the rest of this chapter, I'll frequently discuss only one variant of any option—typically the one for the x axis of the primary coordinate system. It should be understood that everything applies to all other axes as well, just by selecting the appropriate prefix per table 7.1.

7.1.2 *Plotting with two coordinate systems*

The best way to understand how multiple coordinate systems are used in the same plot is through an example. Listing 7.1 shows the beginning of the data file from figure 7.1, and the complete set of commands used to generate the plot from the data file is in listing 7.2.

Listing 7.1 The beginning of the data file from figure 7.1

```
# Date        Consumption[g]   Temperature[Celsius]
1951-04-01    179.8              6.01
1951-04-29    180.8             13.34
1951-05-27    186.5             17.78
1951-06-24    202.1             19.38
1951-07-22    190.1             19.48
...
```

The first three lines (from `set timefmt` to `set xdata`) tell gnuplot how to parse and format the calendar date used along the x axis. We'll discuss them in section 7.5 later in this chapter.

Next, we switch off the mirroring of the primary axis's tic marks on the opposite (right) side of the plot (`set ytics nomirror`) and instead explicitly switch on tic marks for the secondary y axis (`set y2tics`).

We make sure that labels are placed on the graph—this step is crucial when using multiple axes, since otherwise the viewer has no chance of figuring out which data set goes with which axis. We also modify the key from its default location and appearance (see section 6.4 if you need a refresher on any of the options).

Finally, the actual `plot` command. The only thing new here are the axes keywords and their arguments. These directives tell the `plot` command which combination of axes to use for each data set. For example, axes `x1y2` means that the data should be plotted according to the primary x axis, but the secondary y axis.

There are four possible combinations of axes that can be used, and they can be selected using `x1y1`, `x1y2`, `x2y1`, and `x2y2`.

Listing 7.2   The commands used to generate figure 7.1

```
set timefmt "%Y-%m-%d"
set format x "%d%b%y"
set xdata time

set ytics nomirror  # Switch mirroring of primary system OFF
set y2tics          # Switch secondary system ON

set ylabel  "Mean Icecream Consumption per Head [Grams]"
set y2label "Mean Temperature [Celsius]"

set key top left reverse Left

plot ["1951-03-25":]
➥ "icecream" u 1:2 t "Icecream" axes x1y1 w linesp,
➥ "" u 1:3 axes x1y2 t "Temperature" w linesp
```

I hope this example convinced you that using multiple axes in gnuplot is really quite simple (we'll also study a further example in section 7.4). A different question is whether you should do it.

7.1.3   *Should you do it?*

Multiple axes on a single plot are occasionally frowned upon, because they can easily be abused to manipulate the message of a graph. Look at figure 7.2. The middle panel shows both data sets drawn in a single coordinate system. We can see that both curves grow, but also that one grows more strongly than the other.

In the other two panels, we show exactly the *same* data, but how different is the appearance! In the panel on the top, it seems as if both curves are almost identical, while in the panel at the bottom, one seems to be growing much more strongly than the other one. (Look closely—the seemingly strongly growing curve is the one that changed least in the middle panel.)

These dramatically different appearances have been achieved solely by manipulating the plot ranges for each curve individually. Being able to select different plot ranges for the same data on a single plot is what makes dual axes plots open to the kind of abuse you see in figure 7.2.

Also note how in the figure no indication is given which curve is plotted on which axis, making it *impossible* to determine the actual meaning of the graph!

I think dual axes plots have their use, in particular when we want to compare two quantities side by side that are entirely different in nature and are measured in different units. (In this case, we couldn't even plot them "to scale" in a single coordinate

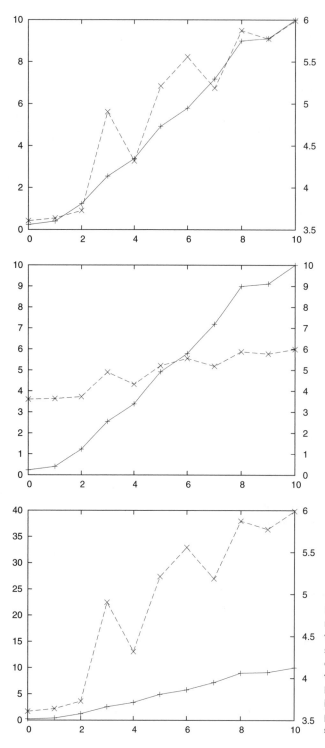

Figure 7.2 **The malicious effect of not-to-scale graphs. The data in all three panels is the same, but the scales have been changed for both curves independently. The scale for the solid curve is always on the left, the scale for the dashed curve is on the right. Only in the middle panel are both curves drawn to the same scale.**

system.) Yet, in all such graphs, care must be taken that the selected plot range is chosen suitably for the data at hand. I'll have more to say about the effect of scales and plot ranges in chapter 14.

7.2 *Selecting plot ranges*

We've already encountered plot ranges in chapter 2, but only in a limited form as an inline specification to the `plot` command, looking something like this:

```
plot [-10:10][-2:2] sin(x)
```

The first pair of numbers in brackets sets the desired x range, while the second (optional) pair of numbers in brackets fixes the y range.

This is enough—most of the time. However, using this syntax, only the plot ranges of the primary coordinate system can be fixed, which is insufficient if we want to use multiple axes on the same plot. Also, the inline syntax doesn't work well when attempting to change the plot range with the mouse.

The inline syntax is a shorthand for the family of _range commands. (Here and in the following, the underscore is intended as a placeholder for any one of the prefixes from table 7.1.) To adjust plot ranges for the primary and the secondary systems independently, we need to issue separate `set _range` commands using different prefixes. Listing 7.3 shows how this is being done.

The explicit `set _range` commands expect a pair of numbers enclosed in square brackets, similar to the syntax for inline range specifications. Besides providing explicit lower and upper boundaries, we can leave one or both of the numbers *blank*, in which case the corresponding value won't be changed. Alternatively, we can supply a star (`*`), which indicates to gnuplot to turn on the `autoscale` feature for that particular value.

If autoscaling is active, gnuplot chooses the plot range so that all of the data (or function) is visible and then extends the plot range to the next full tic mark position. Turning on autoscaling for the independent variable (that is, for the x axis) isn't meaningful unless a data file is being plotted, in which case the plot range is extended to the next full tic mark that includes all data points from the input file. [2]

Listing 7.3 shows some examples of the _range commands in action.

Listing 7.3 Examples for the syntax permissible when setting plot ranges

```
set xrange [-1:5]        # Explicit min and max
set xrange [:10]         # Leave min unaffected, set max explicitly
set yrange [3:*]         # Set min explicitly, use autoscaling for max
set yrange [:sqrt(2)]    # Numeric expressions are legal
set yrange [1:0]         # Inverted axes are possible
```

---

[2] There is also a way to read out the values chosen by the autoscale feature and use them for further computation. Check the standard gnuplot reference documentation on `set _range writeback` and `set autoscale` for more details.

7.3   Tic marks

Tic marks are the subdivision markers placed onto the axes of a plot to indicate the scale of the graph. Only if tic marks are present can a viewer infer *quantitative* informa- tion from a graph. Suitably chosen tic marks are therefore of *critical* importance to any well-constructed graph. Fortunately, gnuplot handles tic marks really well on its own and we rarely need to customize tic mark generation and labeling. But for the few cases when we *do* have special requests, here's how to do it.

Gnuplot distinguishes between major and minor tic marks. The difference is that major tic marks also carry a textual label (normally a number), while minor tic marks don't. By default, only major tic marks are used, except for logarithmic axes, where both major and minor tic marks are drawn by default.

7.3.1   Major tic marks

We can control the appearance of major tic marks using the set xtics family of options. (The usual prefixes for different axes apply.) The command has the follow- ing synopsis:

```
set _tics [ axis | border ]
          [ [no]mirror ]
          [ in | out ]
          [ scale [ default | {flt:major} [,{flt:minor}] ] ]

          [ [no]rotate [by {flt:ang}] ]
          [ offset {pos:offset} | nooffset ]
          [ font "{str:name} [,{int:size}]" ]
          [ textcolor | tc {clr:color} ]

          [ add ]
          [ autofreq
            | {flt:incr}
            | {flt:start}, {flt:incr} [,{flt:end}]
            | ( ["{str:label}"] {flt:pos} [ 0 | 1 ]
               [, ["{str:label}"] ... ] ) ]
```

By default, gnuplot draws tic marks on the border of the plot, and mirrors the primary system on the opposite side. Alternatively, tic marks can be drawn along the zero axis (for instance, set xtics axis will draw tic marks along the line of the plot where y equals 0). If the zero axis isn't within the plot range, the tic marks will always be drawn along the border.

Mirroring of tic marks can be turned off. You probably want to do this when using different coordinate systems for the primary and secondary axes.

Usually, tic marks are drawn on the inside of the border (extending into the plot region), but they can be drawn toward the outside using the out option. This is useful in particular when the tic marks would interfere with the data.

The scale parameter controls the size of both major and minor tic marks. If no size for the minor tic marks is given explicitly, it's set to half the size of the major marks. The size is given relative to the default size of 1.0 for major tic marks.

The text labels associated with major tic marks can be rotated and shifted using rotate and offset. If rotate is used without an explicit angle (in degrees), the labels will be turned by 90 degrees to the left. The position of the labels can be adjusted using offset. The relative shift can be specified in one of the five usual coordinate systems (see section 6.2). Text font and color can be selected in the usual fashion.

Finally, we can control where tic marks will be drawn. If we choose autofreq, gnuplot will automatically generate tic marks based on the plot range. Alternatively, we can provide an increment. Tic marks will be drawn at integer multiples of the increment. Or we can specify a start point, an increment, and (optionally) an endpoint.

Some examples will clarify:

```
pi = 3.1415
set xtics pi         # Draws tic marks at pi, 1*pi, 2*pi, ...
set xtics 1, pi      # Draws tic marks at 1, 1+pi, 1+2pi, ...
set xtics 0,0.1,1    # Draws tic marks at 0, 0.1, 0.2, ... 0.9, 1 only
```

We can also provide a list of explicit labels and locations at which to draw tic marks. The list must be enclosed in regular parentheses, with list entries separated by commas. Each entry in the list consists of the text label for the tic mark (possibly empty), its location, and a third, optional parameter that indicates whether the tic mark should be drawn as a major or minor tic mark: 0 for major and 1 for minor.

Using the add keyword, we can apply additional tic marks, without clobbering previous settings. This can be very useful for adding tic marks for special values to otherwise autogenerated tics, like so:

```
set xtics autofreq
set xtics add ( "pi" 3.1415 )
```

These commands draw an additional tic mark at 3.1415, in addition to the automatically generated ones. Had we omitted the add keyword in the previous example, the second line would have clobbered the first, and the *only* tic mark would have been the one explicitly set at 3.1415.

7.3.2   *Minor tic marks*

Minor tic marks aren't labeled, and are typically drawn smaller than the major tic marks. By default, minor tic marks are disabled for linear axes and enabled for logarithmic axes.

Minor tic marks can be switched on using the m_tics family of options, where the underscore is again used as a placeholder for any of the usual prefixes:

```
set m_tics [ {int:intervals} ]
```

The optional parameter counts the *number of subintervals* between major tics marks; the number of minor tic marks generated is one less than this number.

Minor tic marks are only drawn when there are regularly spaced major tic marks. If all major tics are individually placed, m_tics will have no effect. Minor tic marks can still be created manually, using set _tics.

7.3.3 *Formatting the tic labels*

We can change the formating used for the labels placed at the major tic marks, using
set format:

```
set format [ x|y|xy|x2|y2 ] [ "{str:format}" ]
```

The format can be chosen for each axis individually. Omitting the axis specifier will
apply the format command to all axes at the same time. (Beware: this is a common
mistake leading to often mysterious error messages!)

The format string is similar to the format string familiar from the `printf()` family
of functions from the standard C library. In addition, gnuplot uses extra format (or
conversion) specifiers, which are listed in table 7.2. These conversion specifiers only
apply to *numeric* arguments; for date/time values, check section 7.5.

If the `%` character is encountered in the format string, it's interpreted as the
beginning of a conversion specifier. It must be followed by one of the characters
from table 7.1. A numeric value may be inserted between the `%` and the following
character, which will be interpreted as a desired width. For instance, `set format`
`"%.3f"` will restrict floating-point values to at most three decimal places. (Check the
documentation for the standard C library's family of `printf()` functions for all possible format modifiers.)

**Table 7.2 Conversion specifiers understood by the `gprintf( ... )` function and used to format
numeric values for the `set format` command. See table 7.3 and table 7.4 for conversion specifiers for
date and time values.**

Conversion specifier	Description
%f	Floating point notation
%e or %E	Exponential notation, using 'e' or 'E' (respectively) to indicate exponent
%g or %G	Uses the shorter of %f and %e (or %E)
%x or %X	Hexadecimal representation
%o (lowercase only)	Octal representation
%t	Mantissa to base 10
%l	Mantissa to base of current logscale
%s	Mantissa to base of current logscale; scientific power (restricts power to multiple of 3)
%T	Power to base 10
%L	Power to base of current logscale
%S	Scientific power (restrict power to multiple of 3)
%c	Character replacement for scientific power, such as 'k' (kilo) for 1000, and so on
%P	Multiple of π

Table 7.3 Alphabetically sorted conversion specifiers for date/time information for the `set format` and `set timefmt` commands. See table 7.2 to format numeric values. See table 7.4 for a list sorted by topic.

Conversion specifier	Available for ... input: set timefmt	Available for ... output: set format	Values	Description
%a		✓	Sun, Mon, ...	Abbreviated day of week
%A		✓	Sunday, Monday, ...	Full day of week
%b	✓	✓ (also %h)	Jan, Feb, ...	Abbreviated name of month (3 characters)
%B	✓	✓	January, February, ...	Full name of month
%d	✓	✓	01–31	Day of month (always two digits on output)
%D		✓	e.g. "03/25/08"	Shorthand for "%m/%d/%y" (US date format)
%H	✓	✓	00–24	Hour—24-hour clock (always two digits on output)
%I		✓	00–12	Hour—12-hour clock (always two digits)
%j	✓	✓	001–366	Day of year (always three digits on output)
%k	✓	✓	0–24	Hour—24-hour clock (one or two digits on output)
%l		✓	0–12	Hour—12-hour clock (one or two digits)
%m	✓	✓	01–12	Month (always two digits on output)
%M	✓	✓	00–60	Minute (always two digits on output)
%p		✓	"am", "pm"	a.m./p.m. indicator
%r		✓	e.g. "10:55:48 pm"	Shorthand for "%I:%M:%S %p" (US time format)
%R		✓	e.g. "22:12"	Shorthand for "%H:%M" (24-hour clock time format without seconds)
%s	✓		0–...	Unix epoch seconds (input only!)
%S	✓	✓	00–60	Seconds (always two digits on output)
%T		✓	e.g. "22:12:48"	Shorthand for "%H:%M:%S" (24-hour clock with seconds)
%U		✓	00–53	Week of the year (weeks starting on Sunday; always two digits)
%w		✓	00–06	Day of the week (0=Sunday; always two digits)
%W		✓	00–53	Week of the year (weeks starting on Monday; always two digits)
%y	✓	✓	00–99	Year (two-digit; always two digits on output)
%Y	✓	✓	0000–9999	Year (four-digit; always two digits on output)

Table 7.4 Conversion specifiers for date/time information for the `set format` and `set timefmt` commands, sorted by topic. See table 7.2 to format numeric values. See table 7.3 for a list sorted alphabetically by conversion specifier.

| Conversion specifier | Available for ... | | Values | Description |
	input: set timefmt	output: set format		
%s	✓		0–...	Unix epoch seconds (input only)
%S	✓	✓	00–60	Seconds (always two digits on output)
%M	✓	✓	00–60	Minute (always two digits on output)
%k	✓	✓	0–24	Hour—24-hour clock (one or two digits on output)
%H	✓	✓	00–24	Hour—24-hour clock (always two digits on output)
%l		✓	0–12	Hour—12-hour clock (one or two digits)
%I		✓	00–12	Hour—12-hour clock (always two digits)
%p		✓	"am", "pm"	a.m./p.m. indicator
%j	✓	✓	001–366	Day of year (always three digits on output)
%d	✓	✓	01–31	Day of month (always two digits on output)
%m	✓	✓	01–12	Month (always two digits on output)
%b	✓	✓ (also %h)	Jan, Feb, ...	Abbreviated name of month (3 characters)
%B	✓	✓	January, February, ...	Full name of month
%y	✓	✓	00–99	Year (two-digit; always two digits on output)
%Y	✓	✓	0000–9999	Year (four-digit; always four digits on output)
%w		✓	00–06	Day of the week (0=Sunday; always two digits)
%a		✓	Sun, Mon, ...	Abbreviated day of week
%A		✓	Sunday, Monday, ...	Full day of week
%W		✓	00–53	Week of the year (weeks starting on Monday; always two digits)
%U		✓	00–53	Week of the year (weeks starting on Sunday; always two digits)
%R		✓	e.g. "22:12"	Shorthand for "%H:%M" (24-hour clock time format without seconds)
%T		✓	e.g. "22:12:48"	Shorthand for "%H:%M:%S" (24-hour clock with seconds)
%r		✓	e.g. "10:55:48 pm"	Shorthand for "%I:%M:%S %p" (US time format)
%D		✓	e.g. "03/25/08"	Shorthand for "%m/%d/%y" (US date format)

The format string can also contain arbitrary characters, which are placed verbatim onto the plot. This makes it possible, for instance, to print the units (such as kg or cm) together with the numerical values.

Finally, providing an empty string as format specifier to set format is a way to suppress the generation of tic *labels*, although the tic *marks* will be drawn.

Let's look at an interesting example (listing 7.4 and figure 7.3).

Listing 7.4   The commands used to generate figure 7.3

```
set terminal wxt enhanced

set xtics pi
set format x "%.0P{/Symbol p}"

plot [-3*pi:3*pi][-1:1] cos(x)
```

Let's step through this example:

1   Make sure enhanced text mode is enabled. (You may choose a different terminal, such as x11 if the wxt terminal doesn't work for you, as long as it supports enhanced mode.)

2   Turn on major tic marks at all multiples of π.

3   Choose formatting as a full multiple of π, suppressing any digits to the right of the decimal sign. Also, append the Greek letter for π (namely {/Symbol p}) to the numeric value.

4   Plot. Note the choice of plot range in multiples of π.

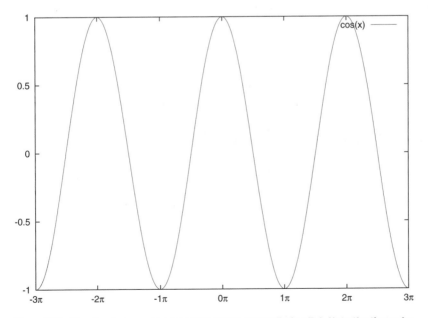

Figure 7.3   The graph generated using the commands in listing 7.4. Note the tic marks at multiples of π and the Greek letters used for the tic labels.

It's important to understand that the format specifier %P will interpret a value as multiple of π, but by itself does *not* ensure that tic marks will only be drawn at integer multiples of π. Instead, we must explicitly choose the locations where tic marks will be drawn using set xtics, then use set format x "%P" to format the labels at those positions accordingly. (Try it both ways to fully understand the difference.)

There are some conversion specifiers in table 7.2 that give us access to the power and mantissa individually. They're intended for situations where you want to build up the combination of power and mantissa yourself; for instance (not using enhanced mode)

```
set format y "%.1t^%T"
```

leads to tic labels of the form 1.5^2. If we use enhanced text mode for the terminal, we might want to use a format specification like

```
set format y "%.1t 10^%T"
```

In enhanced text mode, the caret character will be interpreted as superscript indicator, so that the tic labels will be plotted properly, with the powers as superscripts to 10.

7.3.4   *Reading tic labels from file*

Finally, we can read the tic labels from the input file, using the xticlabels() and yticlabels() functions (or xtic() and ytic() for short) as part of the using directive to the plot command.

Let's look at the data file in listing 7.5. We see that the x values are both present in numeric form (column 1) and as strings. Of course, it would be nice to use the strings for the tic labels. Here's how we do that:

```
plot "months" u 1:2:xtic(3) w linesp
```

The xtic() function takes as argument the number of a column that will be used for the tic labels. Equivalent functions exist for the other coordinate axes (ytic(), x2tic(), and so forth). Labels for the y axis are specified after labels for the x axis.

Listing 7.5   A data file containing a time series—see listing 7.7 and figure 7.4

```
# Month  Data    Month Name
1        3       Jan
2        4       Feb
3        2       Mar
4        5       Apr
5        8       May
6        7       Jun
7        4       Jul
8        5       Aug
9        3       Sep
10       2       Oct
11       4       Nov
12       2       Dec
```

When employing any of the _tic() functions, tic marks and labels will only be drawn at the locations *explicitly* read from the data file—in other words, autogeneration of tic marks is turned off.

In section 7.5.1, we'll see yet another way to plot a file like the one in listing 7.5.

7.3.5 *Grid and zero axes*

In addition (or as alternative) to tic marks along the border of the graph, we can overlay a scale grid on the data. Grid lines are drawn at the position of major and, optionally, minor tic marks.

```
set grid [ [no]_tics ] [ [no]m_tics ]
         [ layerdefault | front | back ]
         [ polar [ {flt:angle} ] ]
         [ [ linetype | lt {idx:majortype} ]
           [ linewidth | lw {flt:majorwidth} ]
           | [ linestyle | ls {idx:majorstyle} ] ]
         [, [ linetype | lt {idx:minortype} ]
           [ linewidth | lw {flt:minorwidth} ]
           | [ linestyle | ls {idx:minorstyle} ] ]
```

We can switch the grid on to be drawn at major or minor tic marks, for the primary or secondary coordinate system. (The underscore again must be replaced by any one of the prefixes from table 7.1.) Tic marks must be enabled—instructions to draw a grid at nonexistent tic locations will be ignored. The grid is either drawn in front (set grid front) or behind the data (set grid back). The lines to use for the grid can be set separately for grid lines drawn at major and minor tic marks. If no style or type is given, the style ls 0, which draws the least visible lines possible (often using a dotted line), is assumed. The polar option is only relevant for plots using polar coordinates, which we'll discuss in chapter 10.

Similar to grid lines, but less obtrusive, are zero axes. These are lines drawn across the graph for all the points where one of the coordinates is equal to zero:

```
set _zeroaxis [ [ linetype | lt {idx:type} ]
               [ linewidth | lw {flt:width} ]
               | [ linestyle | ls {idx:style} ] ]
```

For example, set xzeroaxis switches on a horizontal line at y=0 (representing the x axis). The default line type is ls 0, same as for the grid.

7.4 *A worked example*

You may have wondered how I generated the plot in figure 4.1 using two different y axis scales, each covering only part of the plot. Now we have all the information at hand to lift the secret (shown in listing 7.6).

The plot shows the same data twice, but vertically shifted. I achieve this by adjusting the plot ranges for the primary and secondary coordinate system. Note how the visible range (from min to max) is the same for both systems, but how the two ranges are offset from each other.

Now, the only thing missing are the tic marks. Here, I make sure to specify both a start *and* an end value for tic mark generation—this way, I achieve the partial labeling of each axis, only for the part of the plot that's relevant to each curve. It's all very simple, really...

Listing 7.6   The commands used to generate figure 4.1 in chapter 4

```
set yrange [9:16]
set y2range [6:13]

set ytics 9,1,12 nomirror
set y2tics 10,1,13
```

7.5   *Special case: time series*

Whenever we want to study how some quantity changes over time, we are dealing with a time series. Time series are incredibly common—from stock charts and opinion polls to fever curves. Unfortunately, they pose special challenges, since the tic labels we would like to use for the x axis (such as the names of months or weekdays) aren't strictly numeric.

Worse, they aren't even universal, but locale-dependent. If we want to plot time series data, we therefore need to be able to parse arbitrary date/time formats from a file, and we must have the ability to format timestamps in a suitable, locale-dependent format.

Gnuplot offers three different ways to deal with date/time information as part of axes labels:

- The "classic" way, using `set _data` and `set timefmt`, which allows us to parse and reformat arbitrary date/time information in the input file, and which I'll describe in detail in section 7.5.2.
- The "new" style, which reads fully formatted tic labels directly from the input file using the `_ticlabels()` functions introduced in section 7.3.4.
- For the special cases when we don't require arbitrary date/time labels, but merely want to use the names of *months* or *weekdays* in a plot, gnuplot provides the simplified `set _mtics` and `set _dtics` facilities (see section 7.5.1).

In the next section, we first discuss the simpler case of using month or weekday names as tic labels. Afterwards, we'll tackle the harder problem of dealing with arbitrary date/time information, both for input and for output.

7.5.1   *Turning numbers into names: months and weekdays*

Gnuplot provides two simple commands to turn numbers into the names of months or days of the week. They offer much less flexibility than the general time series commands discussed in the next section, but are easy to use.

Let's look back at the data file in listing 7.5. We want to label the x axis with the names of the month, but without using the explicit names in the third column. We can do this using the `set xmtics` command, which maps numbers to names of months (with 1="January", ..., 12="December"). Don't confuse this command with the `set mxtics` command introduced in section 7.3.2, which switches on minor tic marks!

The sequence of commands in listing 7.7 was used to produce the plot in figure 7.4. Note the dual x axis, with the primary axis showing the names of the month and the secondary showing the index of the corresponding month.

Listing 7.7   Commands used to plot the file in listing 7.5

```
set xtics nomirror # switch off mirrored tic marks on secondary axis
set xmtics         # set primary tic mark formatting to Months
set x2tics 1,1     # switch on secondary tics, starting at 1, not 0
plot [][0:10] "months" u 1:2 w linesp
```

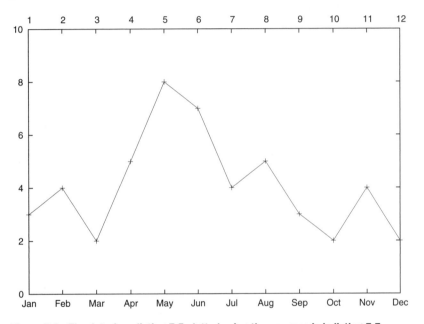

Figure 7.4   The data from listing 7.5 plotted using the commands in listing 7.7

This example demonstrates a general problem when using multiple coordinate systems: the tic marks on the secondary set of axes aren't properly synchronized with the data read from file—they are merely tic marks distributed uniformly over the range inherited from the primary axis of the plot. If we didn't specify the starting value for `x2tics`, gnuplot would distribute 12 units over the range from 0 to 12 (as opposed to 1 to 12), with the result that the primary and secondary tic marks wouldn't even match up with each other! This is true in general for tics on the secondary axes: the plot isn't scaled to them; they're merely aliases for the data in the primary axes, and it's the user's responsibility to make sure the range plotted on the secondary axes matches the data properly.

Besides the names of months, we also can use days of the week (such as "Mon", "Tue", and so on) as tic labels. We enable them using `set xdtics` (with 0="Sunday", ...,

6="Saturday"), similar to what we've seen for set xmtics. Both set xmtics and set xdtics map overflows back into the legal range through a modulo operation (modulo 12 and modulo 7, respectively), as you would expect.

Listing 7.9 shows an interesting application, where we adjust the x values on the fly to align the days of the month with the days of the week. The original data file is shown in listing 7.8.

Listing 7.8   Another time series example—see listing 7.9 and figure 7.5

```
# Day in month     Value
1                   5.080        # First of the month - a WEDNESDAY!
2                   5.310
3                   5.561
4                   5.574
5                   6.008
6                   5.540
7                   5.419
8                   5.519
9                   5.715
...
31                  5.945
```

Listing 7.9   The commands to plot the file in listing 7.8 to generate figure 7.5

```
set xtics nomirror
set xdtics
plot "days" u ($1+2):2 w linesp
```

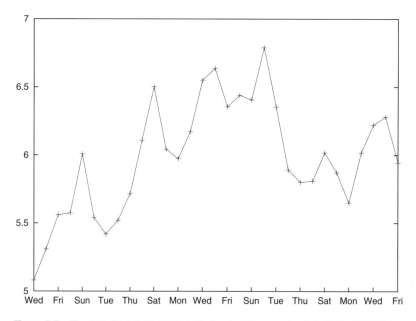

Figure 7.5   The data from listing 7.8 plotted using the commands in listing 7.9. Note the days of the week as tic labels on the x axis.

We can restore normal (numerical) axes labeling through `unset xmtics` or `unset xdtics`.

The actual strings used for the tic labels are determined by the current locale. The default is taken from the `LANG` environment variable, but can be changed using the following command:

```
set locale ["{str:locale}"]
```

The choice of available locales is system-dependent. On Unix systems, you can use the shell command `locale -a` for a list of available locales, or check the directory `/usr/share/locale/`. Note that some locales have country-specific variations (such as `en_AU`, `en_CA`, `en_GB`, and `en_US`). In this case it may not be sufficient to set the general locale (such as `en`), and a more specific locale must be chosen.

Finally, similar commands exist for all other axes, using the usual prefixes per table 7.1.

OLD VERSUS NEW STYLE

If the data file contains a column with suitable strings that can be used for tic labels, the new style (see section 7.3.4) is very convenient. Nevertheless, the old style that we introduced in this section still has its uses. Three points stand out:

- The old style can be used even when the data file doesn't contain explicit tic labels.
- The old style supports internationalization through the `set locale` option.
- The old style gives better results if data points are missing or irregularly spaced. Remember that the new style plots tic marks *only* at the locations found in the data file. So, if for example the entry for the month of May were missing from the file in listing 7.5, no tic mark for May would be generated using the new style. By contrast tic marks (and labels) for all 12 months are drawn when using the old style.

7.5.2 *General time series: the gory details*

For more general time series, we face *two* problems: first we must be able to *read* arbitrary timestamps from the input file, and then *format* them again for output.

First, we must enable time series mode (for the primary x axis) using

```
set xdata time
```

Issuing `set xdata` (without an argument) restores normal operation again. Equivalent commands exist for all other axes, distinguished through the usual prefixes.

In time series mode, input (parsing of timestamps from files) and output (formatting timestamps for inclusion in the plot) are controlled by the two commands `set timefmt` for input and `set format` for output. Both accept a format string using a syntax similar to the one found in the POSIX `strftime()` routine. (We already encountered `set format` in section 7.3.3, but there we only talked about the formatting of plain *numbers*. To this, we now add the possibilities to format complex date/time values.)

Gnuplot assumes all data to be in universal time coordinates (UTC)—it has no facilities to perform time zone changes, adjust for daylight savings, or apply similar transformations. If they are required, they must be applied externally, before attempting to plot the data.[3]

INPUT

Time/date information is parsed in a way reminiscent of the scanf() family of functions, and shares its familiar challenges.

The expected input format is indicated through a format string to set timefmt. The format string may contain several conversion specifiers, all of which begin with the % character, followed by a letter that indicates how an input value should be interpreted. Check tables 7.3 and 7.4 for a list of all possible conversion specifiers and their meanings.

The input format string may contain other characters besides format specifiers, but input strings must match the format *exactly* (with some exceptions regarding whitespace we'll discuss shortly):

```
set timefmt "%Y-%m-%d" # will match 2000-01-01, but also 2000-1-1
set timefmt "%d%b%y"   # will match 1JAN05, 01Jan05, 1jan05
```

If there are no characters separating different fields from one another, gnuplot consumes a fixed number of characters per field (left-to-right), and the fields must be left-zero-padded as necessary:

```
set timefmt "%Y%m%d" # will parse 20020101 as Jan 01st,
                     # but will parse 2002101 as Oct 01st,
                     # and will fail to parse 200211
```

Special rules apply when the date format to be parsed contains whitespace. First of all, gnuplot will interpret whitespace-separated data as occupying several columns. A timefmt format containing whitespace in turn will consume several columns. A blank space (*not* an escaped tab: \t) embedded in a formatting string matches zero or more blanks (not tabs) in the input file. So, "%H %M" matches 1220, 12␣20, and 12␣␣␣20. (The ␣ symbol indicates a whitespace character.)

An example will help. The following input file

```
2005-01-01     8:41    3
2005-01-01     9:17    4
2005-01-01    22:46    2
2005-01-02    03:05    5
```

will be correctly parsed and plotted by the following commands:

```
set timefmt "%Y-%m-%d %H:%M"
plot "data" u 1:3 w linesp
```

---

[3] According to the gnuplot documentation, timestamps are internally represented as seconds since midnight, January 01, 2000 (UTC). Of course, users should not rely on this particular internal representation, but insight into this piece of the implementation helps to understand the way some values default when generating tic marks from dates. For instance, when reading only month and day (using set timefmt "%d %m" for example) but plotting month, day, and year (using set format x "%D" or similar), you'll find that the year defaults to 2000.

Note that the column used for the y values is the *third*, since the time format consumes two columns. Also, the format string contains a single whitespace, but in the data file several blanks separate the date from the time. The file won't parse correctly if the spaces between date and time are replaced by tabs.

Finally, gnuplot won't parse strings enclosed in quotes (see section 4.2.1). Therefore, it's not possible to parse a file that contains date/time information as strings with embedded whitespace:

```
"2005-01-01 8:41"    3  # will NOT parse
"2005-01-01 9:17"    4
```

Gnuplot seems to be tolerant with regard to the locale when it comes to parsing %b and %B fields (abbreviated and full name of months), and appears to parse them on a best-effort basis.

OUTPUT

Compared to parsing time/date information, it's much easier to format it into human-readable tic labels. Simply specify the desired output format using set format _ "..." (where the underscore again is a placeholder for any of the possible prefixes from table 7.1).

Only one word of caution: do not omit the specification of the axis to which this format should be applied. Leaving the axis open will apply the same format to *all* axes. This can lead to mysterious error messages. For instance, if the data for the y axis exceeds the legal range of values for the defined format, this will lead to a Bad format character message. (Gnuplot won't generate a plot in these cases, making it difficult to find the location of the error.)[4]

The format string can contain arbitrary text besides the formatting characters. Here's a useful snippet to stack the time on top of the date (note the embedded newline):

```
set format x "%T\n%D"     # Time stacked on top of date
```

But other text is also possible, such as formatting characters:

```
set format x "%Y-%m-%D %H:%M"     # Date, followed by time
```

and even plain text:

```
set format x "It happened on %A"     # Full day of week
```

In particular when used together with string functions, there is almost no limit to the appearance of tic labels for plots displaying time series.

WORKING IN TIME SERIES MODE

Keep in mind that when working in time series mode (after issuing the set xdata time command), all x coordinates will be interpreted according to the current setting of the set timefmt format option (equivalently for all other axes).

---

[4] If the output formatting routine gets wedged, it may even be necessary to exit gnuplot and restart to reach consistent behavior.

In particular, this means that plotting ranges must be specified as quoted strings, in the format given by `timefmt` (the *input* time format): `plot ["01Jan00":"15Jan00"]` `"data" u 1:2`. Similar concerns hold for the coordinates supplied to `set arrow` or `set label`.

Finally, don't forget that the currently selected locale (as inherited from the environment when gnuplot was started, or set using `set locale`) will affect the tic labels (names of months and of days in week).

7.6   Summary

In this chapter, we talked about all the ways we can control the appearance of the axes on a plot. It's been a long chapter, but axes—or rather, the tic marks and labels placed on them—are important: they enable the viewer to gain *quantitative* insight from the data displayed in the plot.

Before moving on, let's summarize the most important points:

- Most of the time, gnuplot's default behavior is just fine. It will place reasonably spaced tic marks along the axes and label them appropriately.
- We can put an explanatory label on each axis using the `set xlabel` and `set ylabel` commands.
- Tic marks are usually autogenerated, but we can exert great control using the `set _tics` family of commands. We can influence the range and frequency at which tic marks are placed; we can even put individual tic marks onto the plot explicitly.
- Using the same family of commands, we can also customize the appearance of tic marks and tic labels.
- The visible range of a plot is controlled through the `set _range` family of functions. Alternatively, plot ranges can be specified inline as part of the `plot` command.
- Gnuplot supports multiple coordinate systems in a single graph. We can switch them on through the `set x2tics` and `set y2tics` commands, but need to take care not to generate a confusing graph or a graph that distorts the data inappropriately.
- There are several ways to format time and date information for use in tic labels. Numbers can be formatted as names of months or weekdays through the simple `set _mtics` and `set _dtics` commands. For more sophisticated labeling tasks, we can use the `set xdata time` facility, together with the range of formatting options available through the `set format` command.

This chapter concludes our overview of what I would call "basic" gnuplot. In the following chapters, we'll look at some exciting but distinctly more advanced topics, such as color in graphs, multidimensional plots, and other special-purpose features.

We'll also take an in-depth look at ways to script and program gnuplot, and learn everything there is about exporting graphs to standard file formats.

Part 3

Advanced Gnuplot

In this part, we look at several more complicated topics in detail. First we discuss several more sophisticated plotting techniques that we have not encountered before; then we talk about ways to configure gnuplot's terminals and use its scripting capabilities.

Chapter 8 introduces three-dimensional plots.

Chapter 9 is about color plots and also discusses different ways color can be used to convey information in a graph.

Chapter 10 discusses some special techniques, such as graphs containing several subplots, or polar and parametric plots. I also introduce gnuplot's curve-fitting capabilities.

Chapter 11 describes in detail how to export graphs from gnuplot to file, using gnuplot's terminal capabilities.

Chapter 12 explains how to script gnuplot and how to call it from other programs. We also discuss how to use gnuplot to create dynamic graphics for use on a website.

Three-dimensional plots

This chapter covers

- Basics of three-dimensional plots
- Generating surface and contour plots
- Plotting data from a file

In all the plots that we've seen so far, we plotted one variable (y) as a function of another one (x). But what if we want to show how some quantity depends on *two* independent variables? In other words, how can we best visualize a single "output" variable as a function of two "input" variables?

One approach we can take distinguishes the two input variables into the actual independent variable (x) and one *parameter*. We can then generate a plot showing y as a function of x, for different values of the parameter, as shown in figure 8.1. There, we plot the function

```
f(x,a) = 0.5*(x**4)/4! + a*(x**2)/2 + x/2 + 2*a
```

as a function of x—but for three different values of the parameter a.

Quite often, this method turns out to be sufficient, in particular when there's a natural distinction between the independent variable and the parameter. For example, in a biology experiment, we may want to study how the size of a cell

133

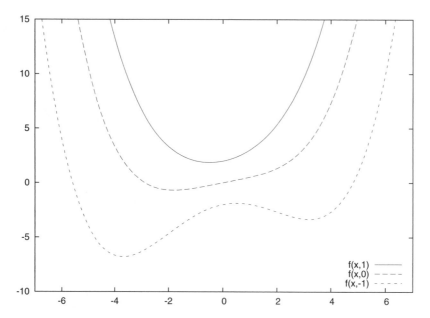

Figure 8.1 Plotting `f(x,a) = 0.5*(x**4)/4! + a*(x**2)/2 + x/2 + 2*a` for three different values of the parameter `a`

culture changes over time, but for three different nutrient solutions. This leads naturally to three different curves, one for each choice of nutrient.

Whenever the second variable assumes only a few distinct values, we're probably better off treating it as a parameter, rather than as a second independent variable. (Such quantities are referred to as *categorical variables* in the statistical literature. Further examples include on/off, male/female/unknown, new account/established account. The choice of nutrient solution is another example.)

But sometimes we have a genuine need to plot a data set as a function of two equivalent variables, neither of which can be declared a parameter. A typical case often occurs whenever we try to show how a quantity is distributed across a spatial area: in such a situation, neither direction is distinguished from the other. The only suitable way to present such data is in a plot that treats both independent variables equivalently.

It's not possible to represent more than two dimensions in a (flat) graph directly, so we have to resort to some form of visual trickery. There are three ways to do this: we can use perspective to create the illusion of depth in our graph. Or we can draw a flat graph, but indicate elevation through the use of contour lines—this is the method familiar from topographic maps. Finally, we can use color to indicate the third dimension. We can even combine some of these techniques in the same graph.

The gnuplot command to generate any one of these graphs is the `splot` command—a close relative of the `plot` command we've been working with so far. In this chapter, we'll learn everything there is to know about it and will also discuss some special gnuplot options that are only relevant for plots generated using `splot`.

A word of caution. Graphs generated with the splot command can be visually very appealing, and we'll see some nice examples in the rest of this chapter and in chapter 9. Nevertheless, my recommendation is to use them sparingly and to also explore other ways of representing multivariate data (such as the one in figure 8.1). Surface plots are often stunning, but (because of the additional need to find a suitable view point) getting them "right" is disproportionately more difficult. Reading *quantitative* (as opposed to qualitative) information off of them is often tricky, if not impossible. Finally, they are simply not suitable for noisy data sets. But they can be effective for conveying the broad aspects of a multidimensional data set, in particular to an audience that has a harder time making sense out of other ways of representing such data (such as false-color plots: for those, see chapter 9).

8.1 Basics

As mentioned previously, the syntax of the splot (short for *surface plot*) command is very similar to the syntax for the plot command. The differences are largely due to the need to handle one additional dimension, which we'll refer to as the z *direction*.

Here's an example of the splot command in action (also see figure 8.2—if your plot doesn't look anything like figure 8.2, keep on reading; I'll tell you about the options you need to adjust manually to get a satisfactory result shortly):

```
splot [-2:2][-2:2]
➥ exp(-(x**2 + y**2))*cos(x/4)*sin(y)*cos(2*(x**2+y**2))
```

We can see how the function must depend on *two* variables, called x and y. Corresponding to the two variables, there are two brackets to limit the plot range. A third bracket can be added to restrict the plot range in the new, "vertical" z direction.

Most of the additional options we know from the plot command are available for the splot command as well. We can plot data from a file as well (see section 8.4 later in this chapter) and use many of the directives familiar from plot. The title option is available to place a descriptive string into the key. The using directive now requires

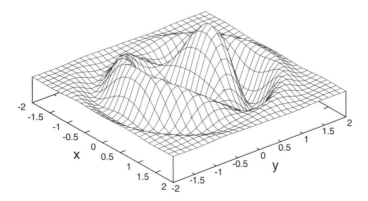

Figure 8.2 Creating three-dimensional plots using the splot command:
`splot [-2:2][-2:2] exp(-(x**2 + y**2))*cos(x/4)*sin(y)*cos(2*(x**2+y**2))`

three arguments to pick out the columns used for the x, y, and z directions, respectively. Similarly, we have to add a third bracket if we want to restrict the z range: `splot [xmin:xmax][ymin:ymax][zmin:zmax]` ... . Although we don't show an example here, nothing prevents us from plotting several functions simultaneously using `splot`: e.g. `splot f(x,y), g(x,y)`.

Finally, we can select the plotting style in the usual form through the `with` option. Not all the styles we described in chapter 5 are available with `splot`. Only `points`, `lines`, `linespoints`, and `impulses` can be used with `splot`. In particular, this means that none of the styles drawing errorbars are available.

Besides `using`, we can use `index` and `every` to plot only parts of a file. The `smooth` directive (see chapter 3) isn't available for `splot`, but we can apply data transformations as part of the `using` directive, as discussed in section 3.4. Furthermore, the `dgrid3d` option provides a way to calculate and plot a smooth approximation to a noisy data set when using `splot` (see section 8.4.3 later in this chapter).

Global options can be used with `splot` in the same way as with `plot`. Both `set style function` and `set style data` have the desired effect. In addition to the familiar `xrange` and `yrange` options (see section 7.2), there's now a `zrange` option to control the plot range globally.

Arrows and labels (but no rectangles) can be placed onto a three-dimensional graph without problems. Just remember to provide a third value to each coordinate for the z value (for example, `set label "text" at -2,-3,1`).

In contrast to `plot`, graphs generated with `splot` can have only a single coordinate system. Therefore, all the options used to control the secondary coordinate system (see section 7.1) have no meaning for graphs generated with `splot`. Also the `axes` directive can't be used with `splot`. We'll study tic marks and axes in more detail later, when we discuss ways to choose the viewpoint for a graph created with `splot`.

8.2   Options for surface and contour plots

In this section, we'll study the options used to generate surface and contour plots. (Density and false-color plots will be discussed in chapter 9, after we've had a chance to talk about color and palettes.)

To keep the discussion simple, we'll focus on plotting functions for now. We'll come back to plotting data from a file toward the end of this chapter, in section 8.4.

8.2.1   Surface plots

There are three options specific to the appearance of a surface plot: `isosamples`, `hidden3d`, and `surface`.

The `isosamples` option controls the number of grid points at which a function will be evaluated when using `splot`. (Keep in mind that this option is only relevant when plotting *functions*—it has no effect when plotting data from a file. But see section 8.4.3 on `dgrid3d` for comparable functionality when plotting data.)

The set isosamples command takes one or two integer values, which specify the number of grid points in x and y direction, respectively. If only a single value is provided, it's used for both directions:

```
set isosamples {int:xlines} [, {int:ylines} ]
```

By default, functions are evaluated on a 10 x 10 grid, which is too coarse to give a good, smooth appearance of the plotted curve. I find values of around 30 to be ideal—using an even finer grid brings little additional smoothness, but leads to grid lines overlapping each other unfavorably. Figure 8.3 shows the same function plotted in figure 8.2, but now plotted with the default setting of set isosamples 10.

In both the figures drawn with splot we've seen so far, the surface was *opaque*: parts closer to the observer obscured parts of the surface further back. By default, this effect is off, and only a transparent wire-mesh of the surface is drawn. To switch to an opaque surface rendering, we use the set hidden3d option. Figure 8.4 demonstrates what a plot looks like if no opaque surface is drawn.

You'll usually want to adjust both of these options explicitly, since their default settings rarely lead to satisfying surface plots. In fact, I include the following lines in my gnuplot startup file (see chapter 12):

```
set hidden3d
set isosamples 30
```

The hidden3d option can take a number of options arguments. The most important of these are offset and trianglepattern.[1]

```
set hidden3d [ offset {int:offset} ] [ trianglepattern {int:mask} ]
```

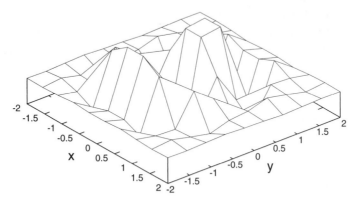

Figure 8.3 The isosamples **option controls the number of nodes used to draw the surface. Here, we use the default value of set** isosamples 10**, whereas in figure 8.2 we used a much finer grid of set** isosamples 30**.**

---

[1] There are a few further options to hidden3d, most of which deal with certain edge cases that may arise when making a surface plot containing undefined points or points outside of the z range. Check the standard gnuplot reference documentation if this is relevant to you.

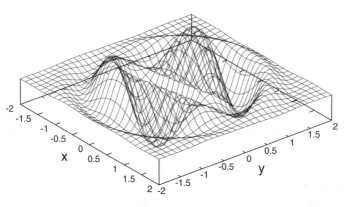

Figure 8.4   The same plot as in figure 8.2, but without the opaque surface effect. Use `set hidden3d` to enable the drawing of an opaque, nontransparent surface.

The `offset` keyword can be used to control the color and line type that will be used for the bottom side of the surface. As we know, gnuplot will cycle through all available plot styles for each new data set. Through the integer argument to `offset`, we can control how far the internal style counter should be advanced from the style used for the top side of the surface. By default, gnuplot chooses the next available style. An argument of zero (`set hidden3d offset 0`) will draw both sides of the surface in the same style.

Through the `trianglepattern` keyword, we can control which lines will be drawn to connect neighboring grid points. The argument to `trianglepattern` is an integer, which will be interpreted as a bitmask (see table 8.1).

Any combination of bits can be selected. The default is 3, so that the surface is made up out of rectangular surface elements. When using a value of 7, diagonal lines are also drawn, so that the surface appears to be made out of triangles. Figure 8.5 compares different settings of this option.

The third option affecting the appearance of the surface is `set surface`. By default, the surface is shown, but it can be switched off entirely using the following command:

```
unset surface
```

Table 8.1   The values used in the mask to the `set hidden3d` option

Bit position	Value	Description
0	1	Lines parallel to x axis
1	2	Lines parallel to y axis
2	4	Diagonal lines, from the southwest to the northeast

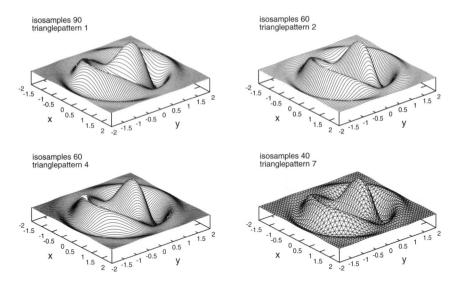

Figure 8.5 **Comparing different values of `isosamples` and `hidden3d trianglepattern`. Except for the values of those two options, these graphs are identical to figure 8.2.**

We switch the surface back on using `set surface`.

For surface plots, this is of course not useful, but we'll see later in this chapter and in chapter 9 other graphs that are generated using `splot`, but in which a surface doesn't play a role.

8.2.2 *Contour lines*

We can add contour lines to a plot generated using `splot`. Contour lines can be a great help when it comes to associating specific z values with surface plots. And, as we'll see toward the end of this section, they can be extremely useful by themselves. (Mapmakers and hikers have known this for a long time!)

One word of caution: when plotting data from a file (instead of functions), the features discussed in this section require that the data be prepared in a "gridded" format: either coming from a file using the *grid* (as opposed to the *matrix*) layout, or by using `dgrid3d` to obtain an on-grid approximation to the actual data. (We'll be talking more about plotting data from files using `splot` in section 8.4.)

We use the `set contour` option to enable contour lines:

```
set contour [ base | surface | both ]
```

By default, contour lines are only plotted on the bottom of the box surrounding the surface plot. But contours can also be drawn on either the plot surface, or on both (base and surface), through the use of the appropriate options to `set contour` (as in figure 8.6).

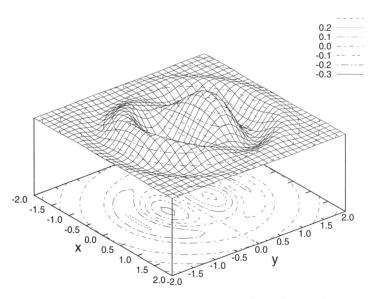

Figure 8.6 Adding contour lines at the base and on the surface using `set contour both` and `set cntrparam levels incremental -0.3,0.1,0.8`. The function is the same as in figure 8.2.

If contours are active (through `set contour`), we can control two aspects of the contours through the `set cntrparam` option: the smoothness of the contour lines, and their spacing.

```
set cntrparam [ linear | cubicspline | bspline ]

set cntrparam [ points {int:q} ]
set cntrparam [ order {int:q} ]

set cntrparam levels [ auto [{int:n}]
                     | discrete {flt:z0} [, {flt:z1} [, ...]]
                     | incremental
                         {flt:start}, {flt:inc} [, {flt:end}] ]
```

To draw contours, gnuplot determines a set of points (called nodes) at which the function (or data) has the same z value. Through the first set of keywords, we can choose how these points will be connected: `linear` (the default) uses straight lines; `cubicspline` uses a smooth curve, which is guaranteed to pass exactly through the nodes; and `bspline` uses a curve that's guaranteed smooth, but isn't guaranteed to pass through the nodes exactly. For "crumply" surfaces, or low resolutions (that is, few grid points), one of the spline options may give significantly better results than the default.

We can specify two additional parameters that are relevant to the way splines are drawn (they have no meaning for `linear` mode). The `points` option controls the number of points for which the interpolation between any two neighboring nodes is evaluated when drawing the contour. More points again mean smoother curves. With `order`, we can set the order of the spline to be used (this option is only relevant for `bspline`). The order must be an integer between 2 and 10. The greater the order, the smoother the contour. Note that both `points` and `order` require *separate* calls to `set cntrparam`—they can't be combined with the type of curve (`linear`, `cubicspline`, or `bspline`) in the same call.

Using `set cntrparam levels`, we can control how many contour lines will be drawn and for which values of z. The different ways we can do this are reminiscent of the options used to place tic marks along the axes (see section 7.3.1). Gnuplot automatically generates an entry in the key (see section 6.4) for each contour line. Calls to `set cntrparam levels` must be made separately from selecting the type of curve and can't be combined into a single command.

When using `auto`, approximately five uniformly spaced contour lines will be drawn. We can pass an integer argument to `auto` to change the number of contour lines that will be generated. All these settings are approximate, because gnuplot will attempt to place contour lines at "round" numbers.

Using `discrete`, we can control exactly where contour lines will be placed. The `discrete` suboption takes a comma-separated list of z values as argument, at which contours should be drawn. All z values for which contours should be shown must be specified in a single call to `set cntrparam levels discrete`.

Lastly, we can fix a starting z value and an increment (and optionally an end value) through the `incremental` keyword.

By default, contour lines change their line type (color or dash pattern) from one consecutive z value to the next, and the line styles, together with the associated z values, are entered into the key of the graph. The `clabel` option gives us a certain amount of control over the appearance of the key:

```
set clabel [ "{str:format}" ]
```

The optional format string, which can be passed to `clabel`, fixes the number format that will be used to print the z values in the key. (See section 7.3.3 for the syntax of the format string.) We can also remove all entries for the contour lines from the key through `unset clabel`. In this case, all contour lines will be drawn with the same line style, but none are entered into the key.

Because contour lines allow us to associate a specific z value with a point on the graph, they allow us to include *quantitative* information into a three-dimensional plot. In fact, we don't even need to make the plot three-dimensional anymore: a flat bird's-eye view showing only contour lines can be a practical representation (as in a topographic map). This brings us to our next topic: the view point.

8.3 Coordinate axes and view point

With three-dimensional plots, we face a new problem that doesn't exist with regular, two-dimensional plots: we can view them from different positions and under different angles. We must therefore choose a *view point*. Closely related is the issue of coordinate axes: we need to provide a clear frame of reference so that the viewer can understand from which position the graph is seen. And finally, we have to provide a scale and tic marks if we want to convey quantitative information. Let's look at all of that.

8.3.1 Borders

A regular (two-dimensional) plot has four borders that we can modify using the set border option, as we've seen in chapter 6. For a surface plot, we can imagine the entire surface embedded in a cube. Now, the set border option can be used to switch each individual *edge* of this cube on or off.

The set border command takes an integer argument, which is interpreted as a 12-bit bitmask, each bit turning one of the edges on or off. Table 8.2 shows the bit positions for each edge of the surrounding cube.

The default value is 31 when using splot, turning on the four sides of the base and the leftmost vertical axis. (No matter what's specified in the set border option, borders other than the base are only drawn if set surface is true.)

Labels can be placed along the borders of the plot in the usual fashion using set xlabel, set ylabel, and (only for splot) set zlabel. In all graphs in this chapter, I've made sure to use explicit labels on both the x and the y axes.

Tic marks are drawn independently of the borders—see chapter 7 for all the options available to control the drawing and placement of tics. Just keep in mind that the secondary coordinate system (x2tics and so on) isn't available, but that instead there's an additional set of options to control the appearance of tic marks in z direction (ztics and so forth).

By default, the surface is elevated a certain distance above the base plan of the surrounding box. We can control this elevation through the xyplane option:

```
set xyplane [ at {flt:zvalue} | {flt:frac} ]
```

There are two ways we can use set xyplane to fix the position of the base relative to the plot surface.

We can simply specify an explicit z value at which the base plan should be drawn, using the keyword at together with xyplane:

```
set xyplane at 0.1
```

Table 8.2   The values of the mask used in the set border option. The fat lines are the ones switched on by the corresponding bit in the mask.

Bit postion	Value	Edge	Bit postion	Value	Edge	Bit postion	Value	Edge
0	1		4	16		8	256	
1	2		5	32		9	512	
2	4		6	64		10	1024	
3	8		7	128		11	2048	

This is the easiest way to fix the location of the base plane if we use an explicit plot range in the vertical direction.

If the z range is dynamically chosen, it doesn't make sense to specify a fixed location for the base plane; instead its position should be chosen as a fraction of the total apparent height of the figure. This is precisely what `set xyplane` *without* the at keyword does: it allows us to control the elevation of the plot surface above the base plane as a *fraction of the total z range.*

A few examples may help to clarify. The command

```
set xyplane 0
```

puts the base plane right at the low end of the z range. Choosing

```
set xyplane 0.5
```

elevates the plotted surface by half the total z range (or half the apparent height of the plot) above the base plane. Using negative arguments to `set xyplane` lifts the base plane so that it intersects with the plot surface. For example, the command

```
set xyplane -0.5
```

places the base plane at the middle of the z range.

The following formula can be used to convert between the two models. It tells us the z value at which the base plane will be drawn, given the fractional parameter f and the z-range [`zmin:zmax`]:

```
z = zmin - f * ( zmax - zmin )
```

8.3.2 *View point*

When creating surface plots using `splot`, we can control one aspect of the graph that has no equivalent in two-dimensional plots as we've seen so far: the view point, that is, the location (relative to the graph) from which the observer appears to be regarding the plotted surface. We can set the view point in two ways: either programmatically with the `set view` option, or interactively using the mouse.

The more convenient way to adjust the viewing angle is of course using the mouse! Grab the plotted surface (by left-clicking into the plot window) and drag it to its desired position. This requires a reasonably fast computer (and works much better if the surfaces are opaque—when `hidden3d` is true). When holding down the Control key while dragging with the mouse, only the box surrounding the graph is shown: this may facilitate this process on slow computers or for surfaces containing many points.

Holding down the middle mouse button and moving the mouse zooms the graph: moving the mouse left to right increases the size of the entire graph (and vice versa). Moving the mouse upward stretches the graph in the z direction only; moving the mouse downward shrinks the graph in z direction. Again, we can suppress rendering of the actual plot surface when dragging by holding down the Control key while moving the mouse.

Finally, holding down the Shift button together with the middle mouse button allows us to move the base plane of the plot (this is equivalent to `set xyplane`).

The `set view` command gives us exactly the same capabilities, but in a noninteractive fashion. The `set view` option takes up to four optional arguments:

```
set view [ {flt:polar} [, {flt:azimuthal}
           [, {flt:scale} [, {flt:z_scale} ]]]]
set view map
```

The first two arguments are the angles (in degrees) of the view point around the horizontal and the vertical axes, respectively. (In spherical coordinates, these are the polar and azimuthal angles.) The first angle is restricted to the range [0:180], while the second angle is restricted to [0:360]. In figure 8.7, we demonstrate how a graph can appear from different view points.

The third and fourth parameter correspond to the zooming effect I've already mentioned in the context of mouse interactions. Both default to 1.0: choosing smaller scale factors results in a smaller graph on the canvas.

Finally, `set view map` is a shorthand for `set view 0, 0, 1, 1`, which places the observer right *above* the plotted surface, so that the observer perceives just the base

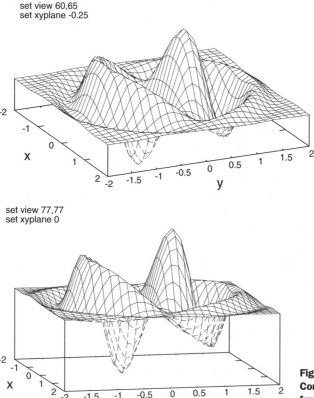

Figure 8.7 Different view points. Compare to figure 8.2 where the same function is shown with `set view` `45,50`.

plane of the plot as a regular, two-dimensional plot. This allows us to show graphs as a contour plot, meaning without the three-dimensional plot surface (which is suppressed through the `unset surface` command). Listing 8.1 summarizes the commands necessary to go from a three-dimensional surface plot to a flat contour plot, and figure 8.8 shows the result.

To get good results when creating contour plots, you might want to increase the number of grid points, using `set isosamples 100` or higher. Alternatively, you can experiment with the spline options on `set cntrparam`.

Listing 8.1 Commands to switch to a contour view—see figure 8.8

```
set view map              # Choose birds-eye view
set size square           # Choose equal units in both directions
unset surface             # Switch off the surface...
set contour               # ... but switch on contours lines
set cntrparam levels 10   # Increase the number of contour lines
set clabel "%.1f"         # Choose format of contour labels in key
set isosamples 150        # Increase sampling frequency
```

The `set view map` command comes in particularly handy when we start discussing false-color plots in chapter 9.

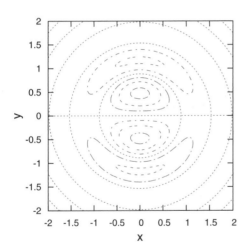

Figure 8.8 The function from figure 8.2 plotted in contour view. See listing 8.1.

8.4   *Plotting data from a file using splot*

Everything we've done so far involved the plotting of functions only. Surely, gnuplot can use data from a file to generate surface and contour plots? Of course it can!

There are two supported data file formats that work with `splot`. For data files in other formats, or for data that's not on a grid, check the `dgrid3d` option described in section 8.4.3.

8.4.1   *Grid format*

If the data file is in *grid format*, each line must contain both x and y coordinates, as well as the z value that is to be plotted. Data must be organized into data blocks, which are separated from each other by a single blank line. Each block must contain all data points for a single row of data points, parallel to the x axis (in other words, within each data block, the x coordinate stays constant, but the y coordinate runs). Listing 8.2 shows a short example file demonstrating this format. The corresponding plot is in figure 8.9.

Listing 8.2   A simple data file suitable for `splot`—see figure 8.9

```
# x       y        z
  0      -1       10
  0       0       10
  0       1       10

  1      -1       10
  1       0        5
  1       1       10

  2      -1       10
  2       0        1
  2       1       10

  3      -1       10
  3       0        0
  3       1       10
```

One very important restriction: *all data blocks must contain the same number of data points.* If the number of data points isn't the same in all data blocks, or if even a single data point is missing or invalid, `splot` can't draw a surface.

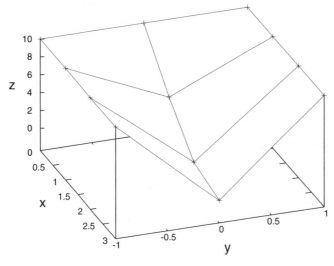

Figure 8.9   The data from listing 8.2 plotted using `splot "data" u 1:2:3 w linesp`

This is a *formal* requirement, only: there's no constraint that the data *values* (that is, the x and y coordinates) form a regular grid. But the resulting plot may look strange or may not be very useful if the underlying grid is too distorted.

It's actually instructive to see what gnuplot does with a "defective" file that doesn't follow this format. Figure 8.10 shows the results of the splot command for a file that's the same as in listing 8.2, except that the last line (the point at (3,1,10)) has been omitted.

The splot command connects all points in one data block consecutively, but doesn't connect data points separated (in the file) by a single blank line—this is exactly what the plot command does when encountering single blank lines in a file. But in addition, splot staggers the plots for successive data blocks (front to back) and thus gives the illusion of optical depth. Finally, cross lines (parallel to the x axis) are only drawn when the data in the input file fulfills the requirements of regular, gridded data blocks, as discussed earlier.

As mentioned in the introduction to this chapter, many of the directives familiar from the plot command are available when plotting gridded data using splot. In particular, we can have different data sets in a single file, separated from each other by double blank lines (as discussed in chapter 3). We can then select a specific such set using index. The every directive can be used to pick out subsets of each data set. Finally, the using directive can be used to choose the data columns for x, y, and z values and to apply data transformations in the usual fashion (see section 3.4).

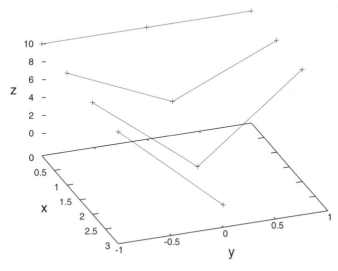

Figure 8.10   The splot command requires all data points to be supplied on a regular grid, with none missing. This figure shows what happens when the last point (at x=3, y=1) has been omitted from the data file in listing 8.2. The splot command is the same as in figure 8.9.

8.4.2   *Matrix format*

The *matrix format* is an alternative file format for data on a regular grid. It's more compact, because the coordinates of the grid points aren't stored in the file; only the z values at the grid locations are kept. The data set from listing 8.2, stored in matrix format, is shown in listing 8.3.

Listing 8.3   The data from listing 8.2 in the more compact matrix format

```
# y1: x1 x2 x3 ...
# y2: x1 x2 x3 ...
# y3: ...
10 10 10 10
10  5  1  0
10 10 10 10
```

Each row corresponds to a single y value, each column to a single x value. We can plot a file in matrix format by appending the `matrix` keyword after the filename in the `splot` command:

```
splot "data2" matrix w linesp
```

If you execute this command, you'll find that we've lost all information on the real x and y coordinates—which makes sense, given that they aren't encoded in the input data at all in this format! This is a serious problem: without coordinates, it's not possible to interpret a graph properly.

If we plot data in matrix format, we therefore have to provide our own coordinates. As it turns out, we can use the `using` directive for this purpose. In the context of the `splot ... matrix` command, there are three pseudocolumns that can be used as part of `using`. Pseudocolumns 1 and 2 refer to the integer index of each data point, counted from zero, while pseudocolumn 3 refers to the actual z value. Put another way, the value of pseudocolumn 1 is the number of the column in the data file, while the value of pseudocolumn 2 is the line number.

It's now very easy to reconstruct the absolute coordinates of each data point in a regular grid from the index of the position through a linear transformation. If x0 and y0 are the absolute coordinates of the first point in the file, and dx and dy are the respective spacings between lattice points, then the absolute coordinates for any point are

```
splot ... matrix using (x0+dx*$1):(y0+dy*$2):3
```

For the example file, the first point is located at (0, -1) in absolute coordinates, and the spacing between consecutive points is 1 in either direction, so this expression reduces to

```
splot "data2" matrix using 1:(-1+$2):3 w l
```

This command will give exactly the same plot as figure 8.9.

The usual `splot` directives apply to the matrix format as well: you can use `index` and `every`. Data transformations can be applied to the z value as well, through pseudocolumn 3.

One final word of advice: when using the matrix format to store data, always, *always* store the absolute coordinates of the first value and the lattice spacings in both directions as a comment in the file itself!

8.4.3 *Smooth surfaces*

Surface plots can be fun, but as we've seen, several things can go wrong, so that `splot` either can't be used at all, or leads to unsatisfactory results:

- Data is scattered (not on a regular grid), so that no regular surface can be drawn.
- Data is sparse, so that the surface consists only of a few elements and is therefore not easy to recognize.
- Data is noisy, so that the surface appears overly bumpy.
- The data file isn't in a suitable format.

Gnuplot provides a slick little facility that takes arbitrary input data and generates a smooth interpolation onto a two-dimensional grid: the `dgrid3d` option.

If `dgrid3d` is on, `splot` doesn't plot the raw data. Instead, it reads the data and then generates an approximation to this data for every point of a regular grid. The number of grid points and some aspects of the interpolation algorithm can be controlled through `set dgrid3d`.[2]

```
set dgrid3d [ {int:nx} [, {int:ny} [, {int:q} ] ] ]

set dgrid3d [ {int:nx} [, {int:ny} ] ]
            [ splines
              | qnorm [ {int:q} ]
              | gauss | cauchy | exp | box | hann
                    [ {flt:dx} [, {flt:dy} ] ] ] ]
```

By default `dgrid3d` is disabled. When enabled, 3D data read from a file are always treated as a scattered data set. A grid with dimensions derived from a bounding box of the scattered data and size as specified by the nx and ny parameters is created for plotting and contouring. The grid is equally spaced in x rows and in y columns; the z values are computed as weighted averages or spline interpolations of the scattered points' z values. In other words, a regularly spaced grid is created and a smooth approximation to the raw data is evaluated for all grid points. Only this approximation is plotted, but not the raw data.

The number of columns defaults to the number of rows, which defaults to 10.

Several algorithms are available to calculate the approximation from the raw data. Some of these algorithms can take additional parameters. These interpolations are

---

[2] Only the first form of the `set dgrid3d` option is available in gnuplot version 4.2; the extended second form is only available in version 4.3 and up.

such that the closer the data point is to a grid point, the more effect it has on that point.

The `splines` algorithm calculates an interpolation based on thin plate splines. It doesn't take additional parameters.

The `qnorm` algorithm calculates a weighted average of the input data at each grid point. Each data point is weighted inversely by a measure of its distance from the grid point raised to the q power. (For arbitrary q, the weights are calculated as the inverse of $dx^q + dy^q$, where dx and dy are the components of the separation of the grid point from each data point. If q takes on the value 4, 8, or 16, gnuplot uses the Euclidean distance when calculating the weight: $(dx^2+dy^2)^{q/2}$.) The power of the norm can be specified as a single optional parameter (it defaults to 1). This algorithm is the default.

Finally, several smoothing kernels are available to calculate weighted averages: $z = \Sigma_i\, w(d_i)\;\; z_i\, /\, \Sigma_i\, w(d_i)$, where z_i is the value of the ith data point and d_i is the distance between the current grid point and the location of the ith data point. All kernels assign higher weights to data points that are close to the current grid point and lower weights to data points further away. Table 8.3 lists all available smoothing kernels.

When using one of the five smoothing kernels from table 8.3, up to two additional parameters can be specified: `dx` and `dy`. These are used to rescale the coordinate differences when calculating the distance $d_i = (\,((x{-}x_i)/dx)^2 + ((y{-}y_i)/dy)^2\,)^{1/2}$, where x and y are the coordinates of the current grid point and x_i and y_i are the coordinates of the ith data point. The value of `dy` defaults to the value of `dx`, which defaults to 1. The parameters `dx` and `dy` make it possible to control the radius over which data points contribute to a grid point *in the units of the data itself.*

Figure 8.11 shows the data from listing 8.2 plotted when smoothed using `dgrid3d` with the Gaussian kernel. (The Gaussian kernel is probably the most generally useful and versatile kernel—unless you have specific reasons to use a different one, it'll probably serve you well in a variety of situations.)

The `dgrid3d` facility isn't perfect. In particular, it can't be turned on and off for individual data sets—either all data sets are smoothed with it, or none. This makes it impossible, for instance, to plot the raw data together with the smooth surface. But

Table 8.3 The smoothing kernels available with `set dgrid3d` for gnuplot versions 4.3 and higher

Keyword	Definition
gauss	$w(d) = \exp(-d^2)$
cauchy	$w(d) = 1/(1+d^2)$
exp	$w(d) = \exp(-d)$
box	$w(d) = 1$ if $|d| < 1$; $w(d) = 0$ otherwise
hann	$w(d) = 0.5\,(1{-}\cos(2\,\pi\,d))$ if $|d| < 1$; $w(d) = 0$ otherwise

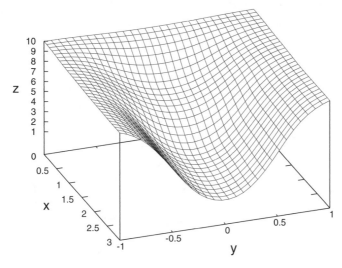

Figure 8.11   The same data as in figure 8.9 but plotted after turning on smoothing using set `dgrid3d 30,30 gauss 0.6,0.6`

overall, `dgrid3d` is a great tool to generate good-looking two-dimensional graphs from otherwise unsuitable data.

8.5   Summary

In this chapter, we've started to explore ways to visualize data that depends on more than one variable. Gnuplot's primary tool for this purpose is the `splot` command, which is an extension of the familiar `plot` command to three dimensions.

The `splot` command can be used to plot surface graphs of functions or data depending on two variables. Using the `set contour` facility and related options, it's possible to add contour lines to a graph, thus making it easier to extract quantitative information from the plot.

The `splot` command can plot either functions or data. Data can only be plotted if it's supplied on a regular grid and is formatted in a suitable format. But even if the data isn't on a grid or is too distorted by noise, the `dgrid3d` facility allows us to draw smooth surfaces representing the data.

But the `splot` command can do more: it can represent numeric values as *color*, adding yet another dimension to our abilities to visualize data. And it's to color, and gnuplot's sophisticated support for smoothly varying color palettes, that we'll turn in the next chapter.

9

Color

We haven't talked much about color yet in this book, so you might be wondering whether gnuplot isn't good at handling it. Quite the opposite! Gnuplot has some clever features to handle *palette-mapped* color plots: plots in which colors are chosen from a continuous spectrum or *palette* and used to express a numeric quantity.

When we briefly discussed color before (in chapter 5), we were only interested in specifying a *single* color at a time: one color for the first data set, a different color for the second data set, and so forth. In this chapter, we take the opposite view: color that varies smoothly, and therefore can be used to indicate continuous changes within a single data set.

But first we must set up the palette that we want to use for our plots. As we'll see, this isn't an easy process, and the `set palette` command we use for this purpose is complicated. In the first part of this chapter, we'll discuss all aspects of defining a palette using `set palette` in detail. If you're in a rush, you might want to skip ahead to section 9.3, where I describe some complete palettes that you can use in your graphs right away, together with some recommendations for good palette design.

I'll then show you how to use palettes to add color to surface plots. In the final section, we look at *density* or *false-color* plots: often the best way to visualize complicated data in two dimensions.

9.1 Defining palettes

For the rest of this chapter, I'll refer to a mapping that assigns a color to each value within a plot range as a *palette* (*color-map* is an alternate expression you may find in the literature). The first thing we must do is to set up the palette we want to use for our plot. We do this using the `set palette` option, but before we can describe its syntax, we must take a brief detour and describe how color can be specified in computer graphics.

9.1.1 Color spaces: a refresher

The most common method to specify a color in computer graphics is through its RGB (red-green-blue) values: a triple of numbers giving the relative intensities of the red, green, and blue components that make up the desired color. In chapter 5, we encountered the compact `#RRGGBB` notation for RGB triples in hexadecimal representation, which is widely used outside of gnuplot (for instance, in Cascading Style Sheets). By convention, RGB values lie between 0 and 255.

This method of describing a color has the advantage that it corresponds directly to the way computer displays operate, but it's not a particularly intuitive way for a *human* to use. (Quickly, what does `#CC6633` look like?)

The HSV (hue-saturation-value) scheme is an alternative to the RGB color description and the most popular intuitive color model. Hue describes the actual shade of the color (by convention, a hue value of zero corresponds to red, followed by yellow, green, cyan, blue, magenta, and purple). The saturation measures the richness of the color, from pale pastel shades to full saturation. Finally, the third element of the HSV triple (value) describes the lightness of the color, from very dark to very bright. All HSV values vary from 0 to 1.

Both ways to describe color are equivalent: mathematical algorithms exist to convert any RGB triple into an HSV triple and vice versa.[1]

This little refresher out of the way, we can now move on to describe the `set palette` command in detail.

---

[1] You can find conversion routines between RGB and HSV color spaces in many texts on computer graphics and on the web. The Wikipedia entry for "HSV Color Space" is a good starting point. The book *Computer Graphics: Principles and Practice* by J. D. Foley, A. van Dam, S. K. Feiner, and J. F. Hughes (2nd ed., 1995) is a classic reference (beware of typos and occasionally wrong or misleading diagrams).

9.1.2   *The palette option*

We use the `set palette` command to map ranges of numeric values to colors. The command is relatively smart, doing a lot of the leg work for us: for instance, it's sufficient to specify only the start and end *values* and the start and end *colors*, and gnuplot will construct a smooth color continuum for all intermediate data values automatically. But if we want to, we can provide detailed descriptions of how the interpolation should be done. Here is its synopsis:

```
set palette [ model [ RGB | HSV ] ]
             [ defined ( {flt:v1} {clr:color1},
                         {flt:v2} {clr:color2}, ... )
               | functions f1(gray), f2(gray), f3(gray)
               | file "{str:filename}" [ using ... ] ]
             [ positive | negative ]
             [ maxcolors {int:n} ]
```

The command can interpret both RGB and HSV triples: use the `model` keyword to indicate which color space to use. The default model is RGB. Note that once a color space has been chosen, this choice remains in effect until a different color space is explicitly selected: this means that we don't have to repeat the `model ...` in every call to `set palette` (although it's often convenient to do so).

There are three different ways to define the mapping from the plot range into the color spectrum. Using `defined`, we provide a list of colors together with their relative positions along the spectrum, and gnuplot will smoothly interpolate between these values. Alternatively, we can provide a set of three functions that transform the plot range into color components using the `functions` keyword. Finally, we can read a list of colors from a file with `file`.

Let's look at these possibilities in a bit more detail.

CREATING PALETTES BY INTERPOLATING BETWEEN INDIVIDUAL COLORS

By using `set palette` with the keyword `defined`, we can build up a palette from a list of individual colors:

```
set palette model RGB defined ( 0 "red", 0.5 "yellow", 1 "green" )
```

We see several things. First of all, we explicitly request the RGB color space. Then we give a set of three values together with their colors.

It's important to understand that the values given to `defined` specify the *relative* positions of the corresponding colors in the resulting spectrum: gnuplot will rescale the spectrum to cover the plot range of the data set automatically, so the palette defined previously will "just work," regardless of whether the values we want to plot lie in the interval [0:1] or not.

On the other hand, the following command will generate quite a different palette:

```
set palette model RGB defined ( 0 "red", 0.1 "yellow", 1 "green" )
```

In this case, the three colors aren't equally spaced along the plot range, but the yellow is much closer to the red end than to the green.

You can use the `test palette` command to generate a picture of the palette we just defined. Color figure 1 shows the resulting test images for the most recent palette definitions.

Colors can be specified in a `defined` gradient in one of three formats: by their name enclosed in quotes (such as `"red"`, `"green"`, and so on), as a hex triple (`"#FF0000"`, `"#00FF00"`, and so on), or as a space-separated triple of floating-point numbers between 0 and 1 (`1 0 0`, `0 1 0`, and so on—this notation is most useful in conjunction with the HSV color model). All three formats are equivalent, and all can be used together in a single command.

In other words, the following commands are equivalent (the alignment tries to indicate corresponding entries):

```
set palette model RGB defined (0 "red",    1 "yellow", 2 "green" )
set palette model RGB defined (0 "#FF0000",1 "#FFFF00",2 "#00FF00" )
set palette model RGB defined (0    1 0 0, 1    1 1 0, 2    0 1 0 )
```

Gnuplot defines a set of 78 predefined colors that can be referenced by name. Using `show palette colornames` lists all names together with their RGB values. Color names only make sense when using the RGB color model—gnuplot will warn you when you attempt to use them together with the HSV model. (Internally, color names are always replaced by their RGB triples, which may not be very meaningful when the HSV model is in effect.)

If you think that having three different color formats to choose from is confusing, realize that they're intended to be used with different color spaces. Color names and hex strings are the normal way to specify colors in the RGB color space. On the other hand, triples of floating-point values make perfect sense for the HSV model.

CREATING PALETTES WITH FUNCTIONS

Whereas `set palette defined` builds up a continuous palette from a discrete set of colors, with `set palette functions` we can define a palette using functions that map the normalized plot range into the color space. Functions work particularly well with the HSV color model, because we can picture smooth curves in the HSV space reasonably well. If we say, "let's increase the lightness steadily, while at the same time drastically reducing the saturation," we have an idea what that looks like, and it's easy to express the desired behavior mathematically.

When using the `functions` keyword, we must provide three functions, one for each component of the chosen model (either RGB or HSV). The functions must map the interval `[0:1]` to `[0:1]`. By convention, the "dummy" variable on these functions isn't called x, but `gray`. Here's an example:

```
set palette model HSV functions gray,1,1
```

The functions here are exceedingly simple: the first function is simply the identity (`f(gray) = gray`), and the second and third functions are constants (`f(gray) = 1`). Don't forget that the dummy variable must be called `gray`. Although this example uses only simple functions, we can use arbitrarily complicated functions here, including user-defined ones.

The preceding example generates a rainbow: we iterate over the entire range of hues, while keeping both saturation and lightness constant at maximum intensity. We'll see more examples of palettes using functions and the HSV space below in section 9.3.

READING PALETTES FROM FILE

The last way to define a palette using set palette that I want to mention involves reading a set of color points from a file specified with the file keyword. This method is similar to set palette defined, except that the colors are read from a file, rather than being given inline.

The set palette file command requires three or four columns. If four columns are given, the first one is interpreted as the location of the corresponding color in the plot range. Columns can be selected with using and the values for the color components read from the file must be in the interval [0:1]. Inline transformations can be applied in the way familiar from the plot command, for instance, to rescale values to fall into the required range. Here's an example that reads in a file containing RGB values from 0 to 255 and rescales them to the unit interval in one go:

```
set palette model RGB file "palette.txt"
                          using ($1/255):($2/255):($3/255)
```

And here's the corresponding file, representing a rainbow (in RGB space):

```
255    0    0    # Red
255  255    0
  0  255    0    # Green
  0  255  255
  0    0  255    # Blue
255    0  255
```

The set palette command has a few more options that you can read about in the standard gnuplot reference documentation. I only want to mention two here: first off, you can invert the order of the color spectrum by supplying the negative keyword to set palette. There's also a corresponding positive keyword to return to the original behavior. Finally, we can limit the number of different colors in the palette through the integer argument to the maxcolors option. This option can be useful when creating large plots for terminals that only allow for a finite number of colors (such as GIF or X11). It has no effect on terminals that allow an infinite set of colors (such as wxt).

QUERYING AND TESTING PALETTES

We've already encountered the test palette command to generate a test image for each palette. We can generate a test image for any terminal and direct it to a file by issuing appropriate set terminal and set output commands, followed by test palette.

Lastly, we can use show palette to obtain information about the current palette settings:

```
show palette [ palette {int:n} [ float | int ]
             | gradient | colornames ]
```

As a convenience, we can export the RGB values of the smooth spectrum that gnuplot generates for us—for instance, to use them in another application. The command show palette palette (note the double use of the word *palette*) takes a mandatory integer argument, which indicates the number of intermediate colors in the exported palette. By default, the output is formatted for humans, but by giving either the int or float keywords, we can obtain a listing that's easier to parse from a program. This list can be exported directly to a file by setting the set print option (see section 4.4.1) to a suitable destination filename first.

The command show palette gradient can be used to show the defined colors and their locations if the palette has been set up using defined. We've already encountered the command show palette colornames, which lists all named colors known to gnuplot.

Now that we understand the mechanics of defining palettes, we can move on and discuss how to create plots that use palettes!

9.2 Creating colored graphs with palettes

Now that we know how to set up a palette, let's discuss how we *use* it. In the following section (section 9.3), I'll show you how to use it *well*.

9.2.1 The pm3d mode

Colored graphs are controlled through the option pm3d (for *palette-mapped three-dimensional*). Actually, pm3d is both a style that can be used inline with splot or set style and an option that can be manipulated with set pm3d. As an option, it has the following set of suboptions:

```
set pm3d   [ at [b|s|t] ]
           [ implicit | explicit ]
           [ hidden3d {idx:linestyle} | nohidden3d ]
           [ interpolate {int:xsteps},{int:ysteps} ]
           [ corners2color
                 [ mean|geomean|median|min|max|c1|c2|c3|c4 ] ]
           [ scansautomatic
             | scansforward | scansbackward | depthorder ]
```

In pm3d mode, gnuplot constructs a surface from colored, nontransparent polygons. Because the polygons are opaque, no explicit hidden-line removal is required—instead, surface areas closer to the observer hide surface areas further away. The resulting effect therefore depends on the order or direction in which the surface has been drawn. Although gnuplot will usually choose a reasonable strategy for drawing surfaces, it helps to keep this point in mind when working in pm3d mode. An example of what a plot using pm3d looks like is shown in figure 9.1.

A colored, opaque surface can be drawn at three positions: at the top of the plotting box, on the plotted surface itself, or at the bottom. The position is specified through the keyword at together with a combination of the letters b (bottom), s (surface), and t (top). Each letter can appear twice (for example, set pm3d at bsb: this is one instance where the way surfaces are drawn in pm3d mode is potentially relevant).

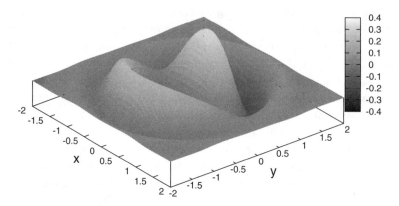

Figure 9.1 **The familiar image from figure 8.2, this time plotted using** pm3d

By default, the command set pm3d puts pm3d into *implicit* mode, meaning that all surfaces drawn with splot will be drawn using colored, nontransparent polygons. If we want to combine colored surfaces together with transparent, wire-mesh surfaces in a single graph, we need to choose the *explicit* mode using set pm3d explicit. In explicit mode, we need to specify the pm3d as part of the splot command:

```
splot f(x,y) w l, g(x,y) w pm3d
```

will plot the function f(x,y) with a transparent wire-mesh, but the function g(x,y) with a colored, opaque surface.

A colored surface can be drawn together with a wire-mesh of the same surface using set pm3d hidden3d. This command takes as an additional, mandatory argument the index of a (previously defined) line style, which will be used for the wire-mesh. When using this plot mode, don't forget to switch off the regular surface and hidden-line removal using unset surface; unset hidden3d.

As an alternative to set dgrid3d (see section 8.4.3), pm3d has a similar interpolating capability, triggered by the keyword interpolate, which takes two mandatory arguments, giving the number of interpolation steps in both x and y directions.

The two remaining directives to the set pm3d command control the way the surface is constructed: the corners2color keyword selects how the color of each polygon is determined from the z coordinates of its four corners: as mean, median, and so on, or by choosing the value from one of the corners directly. The scansforward, scansbackward directives control the direction in which the surface is constructed. The default is scansautomatic and usually doesn't need to be changed.

9.2.2   *The colorbox*

The colorbox is the equivalent of the key (see section 6.4), but for colored plots. It indicates the mapping between colors and numeric values.

The colorbox is only visible in pm3d mode; that is, after a set pm3d command has been issued. Its appearance is controlled through the set colorbox options:

```
set colorbox [ vertical | horizontal ]
             [ noborder | bdefault | border {idx:linestyle} ]
             [ default | user [ origin {pos:orig} ]
                              [ size {pos:size} ] ]
```

The colorbox can be oriented either horizontally or vertically (this is the default). It usually is surrounded by a border, but this can also be customized.

The standard size and position for the colorbox can be chosen using the `default` keyword. Alternatively, the keyword `user` selects customized sizing and placing of the colorbox, indicated through the appropriate optional arguments. For three-dimensional plots, the only permitted coordinate system is the `screen` system (see section 6.2), but for two-dimensional plots (including `set view map` plots), all coordinate systems can be used.

The colorbox can be suppressed using `unset colorbox`. Keep in mind that hiding the colorbox doesn't allow the viewer to extract any quantitative information from your plot, since there's no "obvious" mapping from colors to numbers and vice versa. Don't do it, unless you're sure that the graph is meaningful even without the colorbox.

You can think of the colorbox as just a little plot within a larger one, and so it responds to all commands and options that manipulate plot ranges, axes, and tic marks. For the colorbox, there's only a single axis, running from low values (and the corresponding colors) to high values (and colors). This axis is known as the cb (for *colorbox*) axis. Table 9.1 lists all relevant options. None of these options change the way colors are distributed in the palette; they merely change the way numeric values are assigned to those colors.

Table 9.1 Colorbox options. They control the placement and formatting of tic marks along the colorbox, and are therefore very similar to the corresponding commands for any of the other axes.

Option name	Description	Section
cbrange	Sets the range of numeric values covered by the colorbox, *independently* of the range chosen for the range of z values.	7.2
logscale cb	Distributes numeric values logarithmically across colors.	3.6
cblabel	Assign a text label to the colorbox. (This label will be placed next to the colorbox. If the label is invisible, use set cblabel offset, because the default placement may put the label outside the canvas area.)	6.3.3
format cb	Format string for the tic labels placed next to the colorbox.	7.3.3
cbtics	Controls all aspects of tics for the colorbox (major tic marks).	7.3.1
mcbtics	Minor tic marks for the colorbox.	7.3.2
grid cbtics	Draws grid lines within the colorbox at the major colorbox tic positions.	7.3.5
grid mcbtics	Draws a grid within the colorbox at the minor colorbox tic positions.	7.3.5

Table 9.1 Colorbox options. They control the placement and formatting of tic marks along the colorbox, and are therefore very similar to the corresponding commands for any of the other axes. *(continued)*

Option name	Description	Section
cbdata time	Choose time series mode for the values in the colorbox.	7.5.2
cbdtics	Use weekdays as tic labels for numeric values.	7.5.1
cbmtics	Use months as tic labels for numeric values.	7.5.1

The range of the colorbox can be chosen independently from the z range of the plot. If the range of numeric values covered by the colorbox (as set with the set cbrange option) is larger than the zrange, only a small fraction of the available colors will be used in the plot. Conversely, if the cbrange is smaller than the zrange, those parts of the plot that have z values outside the cbrange will be colored using the color corresponding to the nearest end of the colorbox spectrum.

Setting set logscale cb distributes tic marks (that is, numeric values) logarithmically across the color spectrum leading to a *logarithmic color scale*.

9.2.3   *Other ways to use color*

The pm3d mode is meant to generate colored surfaces in the way that I just described. But because it's so flexible, it can be used in further ways to create attractive graphs. Here are a few ideas.

We can let the apparent height of the surface and the local color of the surface represent different quantities. So far in this chapter, we used color only to enhance the height perception of the surface, but now we let height *and* color represent different quantities. This is done through an additional parameter to the using directive to the splot command:

```
set pm3d at s
splot "data" u 1:2:3:4 w pm3d
```

Here, the first and second column of the data file are taken as x and y coordinates, while the value of the third column is used for the z coordinate (the height) of the surface, and the color is assigned according to the fourth column.

By adjusting the view point, we can achieve other interesting effects. For example, we can plot a function depending only on *one* variable using splot, but viewing it from the side to obtain the appearance of a two-dimensional plot. Why would we do that? Because we can now color the curve depending on its local value! This may be interesting when generating a control chart: if the curve is within the desired range, it's colored green, but as it approaches some threshold, its color changes smoothly to red.

There's a special style to do this: with lines palette (which also works with points or linespoints). Listing 9.1 demonstrates how it's done, and color figure 2 shows the result.

> **Listing 9.1   Drawing a curve using smoothly changing colors (also see color figure 2)**

```
set view 90,0          # View from the side
set isosamples 200,2   # Good resolution along x-axis,
                       #    few points along y-axis

unset ytics            # Not needed
set xtics offset 0,-2  # Push tic marks down from default position

set border 4095        # Turn on all borders
set xyplane 0          # Center the plot within the bounding box

set palette defined ( 0 'red', 0.25 'red', 0.5 'green',
                      1.5 'green', 1.75 'red', 2 'red')

splot sin(x)**3 + 0.3*sin(5*x) w l palette
```

Most of the commands in listing 9.1 should be self-explanatory: first we select a view point that allows us to view the surface from the side (that is, along the direction of the y axis). Because of this, the y axis is no longer visible and we end up with a two-dimensional graph spanned by the x and z axes. To get a smooth curve, we increase the resolution along the x axis, but to improve performance, we reduce the resolution along the y axis to its bare minimum. Because tic marks for the y axis aren't needed, they're switched off (otherwise they interfere with the graph), and tic marks for the x axis are shifted downward, which makes more sense given the selected view point.

But there's also an entirely different way to utilize the pm3d mode: we can do away with the (apparent) elevation of the surface altogether and merely provide a birds-eye view of the surface (by using set view map, introduced in section 8.3.2), but without the contour lines that we described in the previous chapter. Instead, we use color alone to indicate the z value of the data at each point in the plot range. This leads to so-called *false-color* plots and is such a powerful technique that we'll spend the rest of this chapter talking about it.

9.3   Using color for data representation

In a false-color plot, color alone is used to express the magnitude of some quantity. But how do you express a magnitude (that is, a number) as color? There's no obvious or even particularly "natural" way to represent numbers through colors. (Quick: what's larger, green or brown?)

If all information is transmitted by colors alone, without any further visual hinting, the quality of the encoding (colors-to-numbers) becomes critical: a badly chosen mapping won't allow viewers to extract the necessary information from the image.

In the absence of an obvious way to construct such a mapping, it's natural to resort to one of a number of ad-hoc solutions. This is really unfortunate, because—as we'll see—some of the most common encodings are a particular poor choice for virtually *any* data set. Additionally, some of the features that lead to well-designed mappings are rather counterintuitive and not likely to be found by chance.

In the next section, I'd like to summarize some recommendations for good palette design. In the section after that, I put these recommendations to use and describe a number of ready-to-use gnuplot palettes for a variety of different tasks. In section 9.4, we'll look at two case studies and see (literally) how different palettes may hide or highlight certain features of a dataset.

9.3.1   *Thoughts on palette design*

Not a lot of information is readily available on the design of color schemes for visualization tasks, and very little of it is based on actual, empirical research. In this spirit, the following list is certainly not the last word on the matter, but can serve as a good base for further investigation:[2]

- *Be clear about the purpose of the visualization task.*   Are you looking for a truthful representation of the variation of values in the data, or are you more interested in segmenting (categorizing) it into different strata? Are you particularly interested in the features within a certain, limited range of values? Do you want to identify and highlight data points representing specific values (such as outliers)?

  All these tasks are valid, but lend themselves to different palettes. To represent smooth variation, a palette with a continuous spectrum of colors works best, but for segmentation tasks, a palette consisting of several discrete color bands makes more sense. These attributes can be combined, for instance in a palette varying smoothly in the center, but with solid colors once certain thresholds are crossed.

- *Understand the data you're plotting.*   This is somewhat of a corollary to the preceding item. Does the data come from a continuous spectrum of values, or does it consist of a set of discrete values? In either case, is there a natural ordering in the values? (In particular for categorical quantities—such as gender: male, female, unknown—this may not be the case!)

  If the data is discrete, you want to make sure the color bands in your palette include the values in your data set. If the data comes from a continuous spectrum, you may either want a continuous palette or a discrete one, depending on the purpose of the visualization. Finally, if the data is ordered, you want a palette that has some form of visual ordering (such as a black-to-white grayscale).

- *Make sure there are strong visual gradients in those regions of the data where significant and relevant change occurs.*   This is one of the key elements in good palette design. There are two issues here: first of all, there tend to be regions in the data where change is more relevant to the task at hand than in others. What this region is depends all on the data (and the task): are we interested in the detailed behavior in the middle of the dataset, while caring less about the exact behavior near the edges of the spectrum? Or do we mostly want to identify outliers, and are therefore less interested in the variation in the middle ground? Either way, we want to make sure that the strongest *visual* change in the palette

---

[2] This list was partially inspired by a paper entitled "Why Should Engineers and Scientists Be Worried About Color?" by Lloyd A. Treinish and Bernice E. Rogowitz, and its companion papers, all of which can be found on the web.

coincides with those regions that we care about the most. The consequence of this is that palettes which distribute change uniformly across the full range of values will probably not give the most insight into the most relevant parts of our data. (This implies that most palettes generated by some simple mathematical formula, such as the standard rainbow, will be suboptimal.)

The second important insight here is that we need to pay particular attention to those features of a palette that are *perceived* as strong visual change. In section 9.4.1, we'll study a continuous palette from blue over white to red. The strongest impression of visual change occurs where the palette is white, and the same dataset can appear quite differently, depending on the relative location of the white band within the palette. If there's a region in the data that we want to visualize in even greater detail, we want to concentrate many strong visual gradients in that region.

Specialized tasks call for more creativity in the creation of palettes. For example, the data may pass through zero (or some other relevant threshold) in the middle of the spectrum. We want to clearly indicate this threshold, but also show the smooth variation on both sides of it. In such a situation, we may want to have sharp transition (such as a hard red/blue changeover) in the spectrum at the location of the threshold, while letting the colors change smoothly as we go away from the threshold on either side.

To summarize: don't distribute strong visual gradients uniformly over the entire plot range if some regions of the plot range contain much less detail than others. Good palettes will typically not be uniform, and every palette must be tuned for both the current data set and the intended use.

- *If there's ordering in the data, try to find a palette that supports an intuitive sense of ordering.* Color transitions that express a sense of ordering are the grayscale (black to white), the so-called *heat scale* (red to yellow to white), and the blue-to-red palette. More sophisticated, but often particularly useful is the *geo scale* that is familiar from topographic maps (from dark blue over light blue to green and brown to white).

  When using such palettes, make sure you go from "cold" colors to "hot" ones (that is, associate blue with the low values in the plot range and red with the high ones, not the other way around). Also, beware of palettes that seem to wrap around, so that the colors seemingly come full circle with the highest and the lowest values mapping to colors that resemble each other.

  By the way, this item gives yet another reason why the "standard rainbow" is so particularly unfortunate: it maps low values to a hot color (red), proceeds with no sense of ordering via green to blue and then *wraps around*, mapping the highest values to red again!

- *Prefer pastel colors and subtle changes in luminance and saturation.* This is probably the most surprising of all recommendations. Intuitively, you'd expect that bright, fully saturated colors would give the best visual contrast. But this isn't the case. Instead, pastel colors, which are "easier on the eyes," make it easier to detect details and structure in the data. I've had good success with colors that were only 60 to 85 percent saturated. (We'll give some examples later in section 9.3.2.)

Similar considerations apply to changes in brightness (luminance). Quite subtle changes (in the 60 to 100 percent range) are sufficient to bring about clearly distinguishable changes in the palette.[3]

■ *Use changes in luminance for data with lots of fine detail; use changes in hue and saturation for data with smooth, large-scale changes.* This recommendation (which isn't at all obvious) is based on empirical research.[4] It's quite surprising, since it suggests that different changes to a palette have different, but predictable visual effects.

When experimenting with palettes in this way, keep in mind the previous recommendation: quite subtle changes in saturation and luminance are all that is needed! On the other hand, if you crank either of them drastically from 0 to 100 percent, the effect will probably be lost.

Naively, it may seem like a good idea to create palettes in which all three quantities (hue, saturation, brightness) vary concurrently, so as to give the maximum visual change across the spectrum. Based on the previous, it's clear that this doesn't lead to the most suitable palettes: the eye is better than you'd expect at detecting subtle changes. By choosing the most suitable kind of change for any task, we can achieve much better results than with harsh changes.

In section 9.4, I'll discuss two case studies which demonstrate this point in some detail.

■ *Never, ever, publish a false-color plot without showing the mapping of numbers to colors explicitly.* No matter how intuitive you think your chosen color scheme is, keep in mind that there's *no* universally accepted, generally understood mapping from numbers to colors. Without a colorbox, there's a good chance that your graph can't be understood by someone else.

What's more, even if the ordering relation in your color scheme is clear (for example, in a simple grayscale), the mapping of actual numbers to specific colors is impossible to infer without an explicit key. Always provide one!

Now let's put these thoughts into practice by constructing some sample palettes that demonstrate some of these thoughts and ideas. In doing so, we'll also learn how to put gnuplot's set palette feature to good use in a variety of different scenarios.

---

[3] The paper "Escaping RGBland: Selecting Colors for Statistical Graphics" by Achim Zeileis, Kurt Hornik, and Paul Murrell makes a similar point and provides additional references. It can be found on the web.

[4] S. S. Stevens in *Perception and Psychophysics*, Volume 1, p5-8 (1966).

9.3.2 *Some sample palettes*

In this section, I'll introduce and discuss a handful of different palettes. My intention here is twofold: on the one hand, I want to give you a fair number of worked examples to demonstrate gnuplot's `set palette` facility. On the other hand, I want to make some of the principles introduced in the preceding section more concrete. Keep in mind, though, that these palettes are intended only as *starting points*—you'll have to adjust them to fit your particular needs and data sets to get optimal results.

We'll start out with three simple and popular ad-hoc palettes, and then move on to some more sophisticated examples based on the principles discussed earlier.

The simplest palette is the linear grayscale (for all palettes in this section, refer to color figure 3): [5]

```
set palette model RGB defined ( 0 'black', 1 'white' )
```

Just to demonstrate gnuplot's ability to handle different color spaces, here's the same palette, but defined in HSV space, and using functions, rather than named colors:

```
set palette model HSV functions 1,0,gray
```

The three parameters after the `functions` keyword stand for hue, saturation, and value (luminance), respectively. Saturation is set to zero, leading to an achromatic spectrum—that is, a grayscale. Because saturation is zero, the value chosen for the first (hue) parameter doesn't matter.

In the third (luminance) parameter, the brightness is increased in a linear manner. It's tempting to play with other functions that map the `[0:1]` interval to itself, such as `gray**2` or `sqrt(gray)` or even `(1-cos(pi*gray))/2`, to achieve a variety of nonlinear grayscales, but I've found palettes based on simple mathematical functions like these rarely improve the appearance of a graph by much, because they don't give us sufficient control to adapt the palette to the data set. In contrast, in section 9.4.2, I'm going to show you what a hand-tuned grayscale palette can do.

Another simple palette is the so-called *heat scale*:

```
set palette model RGB defined ( 0 'red', 1 'yellow', 2 'white' )
```

Sometimes this palette is made to include black. (Yes, that's a -1 in front of the `black` in the command below. Keep in mind that the values assigned to each color when using `defined` are merely interpreted as the *relative* location of the corresponding color in the palette—the actual values don't matter.)

```
set palette model RGB defined
➥ ( -1 'black', 0 'red', 1 'yellow', 2 'white' )
```

---

[5] For the curious: these palettes were in fact created with gnuplot, using the following command sequence: `unset border; unset key; unset tics; unset xtics; unset ytics; set pm3d; unset cbtics; set colorbox user origin 0.2, 0.05 size 0.6, 0.9; set palette ...; set terminal postscript eps color size 1.25cm, 10cm; set output '...'; splot [0:1][0:1][0:1] 2`. The individual panels were then combined into a single postscript file using the LaTeX array technique explained in chapter 11.

166

Both of these palettes are easy to define and express a sense of ordering. Unfortunately, shades of yellow are particularly hard to distinguish. Also, these palettes embody both drastic luminance and saturation changes (black has a luminance value of zero and white has zero saturation). Overall, they're probably a poor choice for almost any situation.

The final example of an ad-hoc palette is the standard rainbow. It's most easily defined using the HSV color model:

```
set palette model HSV functions gray,1,1
```

As discussed previously, the standard rainbow has a number of problems, the most fundamental one relating to ordering: it maps the warm color red to the lowest values and then progresses to the cold color blue, only to wrap around all the way to red *again*. An improved rainbow changes the ordering to run from blue to red and magenta, while truncating the wrap-around (you may want to plot the function f(x) to see what's going on):

```
f(x) = x < 5./6 ? 2./3 - 4./5*x : 1 - (x-5./6)
set palette model HSV functions f(gray),1,1
```

This is much better, but still has a number of problems. For instance, the green band seems to occupy a disproportionately larger section of the spectrum, compared with the cyan and yellow bands.

Actually, in this form, the rainbow starts to approach the *geo scale*, which is my recommended palette when looking for an ordered, multiband palette. Here's a palette that works quite well:

```
set palette model RGB defined
➡ ( 0 '#3366ff', 1 '#99ffcc', 2 '#339900', 3 '#66ff33',
➡   4 '#996633', 5 '#ff9900', 6 '#ffff33' )
```

This is a hue-based palette: there are no drastic changes in saturation or lightness. It's therefore suitable for data sets with smooth, rather slow changes. In this palette, all colors are pastels: no hue is used at full saturation. You may want to experiment with a similar palette but replace all colors with their fully saturated equivalents. Which palette makes the data come out better? (We'll see another application of this palette below in section 9.4.1.)

Let's look at two examples of saturation-based palettes. The first is a continuous blue/white/red palette:

```
set palette model RGB defined ( -1 'blue', 0 'white', 1 'red' )
```

Depending on the relative location of the white band, the data can appear amazingly different. (Experiment with defined (-1 'blue', 0.5 'white', 1 'red'), and so on.)

As an example of a palette clearly indicating a transition through some sharp threshold value, we can use a "back-to-back" version of the red/blue palette:

```
set palette model RGB defined
➡ ( -1 'white', 0 'blue', 0 'red', 1 'white' )
```

With this palette, there will be an unmistakable, but most of all *sharp* change in hue as data passes through zero. This palette is suitable only for data that varies *continuously* as it goes from positive to negative values: the continuous nature of the transition guarantees that there will be a sharp red/blue boundary separating the two domains. If the data jumps around discontinuously (so that strongly positive regions might be adjacent to strongly negative regions with no area close to zero in between), this palette isn't suitable, because in the resulting graph, we won't be able to distinguish between high and low values, as both of them map to the same color (white).

Both of the preceding (red/blue) palettes are pure saturation palettes, with no change in lightness. They're therefore appropriate to visualize relatively large structures in a data set.

By contrast, here's a luminance-dominated palette, suitable to detect fine details in data:

```
green = 1.0/3.0
blue = 2.0/3.0

set palette model HSV defined
( 0 blue 0.6 0.6, 1 blue 0.5 1, 2 green 0.5 1, 3 green 0.7 0.5 )
```

This palette definition uses the third style of syntax inside the `defined` parentheses, which is particularly useful together with the HSV color model. Each entry consists of four numbers: the first being the relative location, and the following three representing the three components of the chosen color model—that is, hue, saturation, and luminance in this example. To facilitate understanding, I've defined symbolic names for 1/3 and 2/3, which are the hue values for green and blue, respectively.

Although the primary change in this palette is in the luminance values, there's concomitant change in the saturation as well. I found that I had to reduce the saturation toward the middle of the spectrum where the luminance reaches its maximum to achieve a uniform appearance of all colors. If you look closely, you'll also find that the spectrum isn't symmetric in its *values*, although I made a best effort to make it symmetric in its *appearance*. The color blue, for instance, appears much "fuller" than green at equal values of saturation, so I reduced its intensity relative to green. Feel free to experiment further!

All the previous palettes consisted of smooth color changes. Let's take a quick look at a palette consisting entirely of sharp bands of colors:

```
set palette model RGB defined
( 0 'green', 1 'green', 1 'yellow', 2 'yellow', 2 'red', 3 'red' )
```

Such a "traffic-light" palette is suitable for *segmentation* tasks: when we only care whether data points fall into the allowed (green), warning (yellow), or prohibited (red) domain, but don't actually want to follow how the data changes within each band. (In color figure 2, we've seen a similar palette with distinct bands for categorization purposes. There, however, we used smooth transitions between different colors, but restricted the transitions to narrow bands by assigning color locations unevenly across the palette.)

Finally, a completely different example: a continuous grayscale, combined with colored "tree-rings." The grayscale indicates the smooth change of the data, while the discrete tree-rings make it easier to assign specific numeric values to different spots on the graph:

```
hue(x) = x < 1./8. || x > 7./8. ? 0 : (8*x-1)/6.0
sat(x) = x < 3.0/16.0 || x > 15.0/16.0 ? 0 : (1+cos(8*2*pi*x))/2
lum(x) = x < 1.0/16.0 ? 0 : (1+cos(8*2*pi*x))/2
stp(x,y) = x < y ? 0 : 1
w = 0.99
set palette model HSV functions
➥ hue(gray), stp( sat(gray), w ), gray + (1-gray)*stp(lum(gray), w)
```

This example also serves to demonstrate to what extremes you can go when playing with palettes!

Here's how it works: hue increases basically linearly, but has been shifted to make room for the white band. Saturation is zero in most places (so that colors appear achromatic gray), except at multiples of 1/8, where the cosine function has peaks. The step function stp(x,y) cuts off those parts of the peaks that are less than y and promotes the ones greater than y to one—this process narrows the peaks, with the parameter w controlling the width of the color bands. Finally, luminance increases linearly, except for the locations of the color bands, where luminance is switched on fully. Several edge cases have to be dealt with through the ternary ? operator; in particular, color bands right at the edges of the spectrum must be suppressed. The white color band also requires some special handling.

Having seen this, it's sad to say that I've found this palette not to be all that useful—unless the data is very smooth, the color bands are too thin and tend to disintegrate into individual pixels on a grey background. But apart from its immediate use, I find this palette interesting because it shows how different palette elements (smooth gradients and sharp bands, grayscale and color) can be combined in new and creative ways.

To see all of what we just learned in practice, let's study two case studies of custom palette design for two different data sets. The next section is devoted to that.

9.3.3 *Words of caution*

When I was a first-year graduate student, I once did an experiment involving a red laser and a green laser. I plotted the results (naturally enough) in red and green. (On paper. With colored pens. Using special, expensive logarithmic plotting paper. This story doesn't predate gnuplot, but it does predate generally available color printers.) When I showed the graph to one of my professors at the time, he took a look and asked, "Which line is for the red laser?" I responded, somewhat snottily, "Well, the red line is for the red laser and the green one for the green one, of course." (Duh!) He looked at me and said, "I'm color blind." Oops.

Color is a lot of fun and can add a new dimension to our graphs. But it has a number of serious disadvantages, and we need to consider carefully whether the advantages outweigh the drawbacks:

The following color figures are discussed in greater detail in chapter 9, "Color."

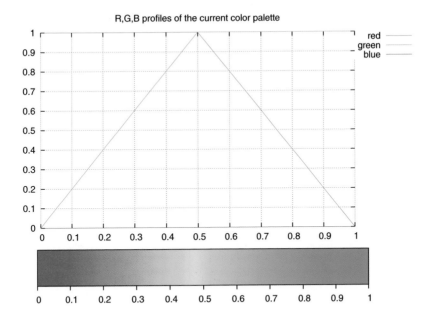

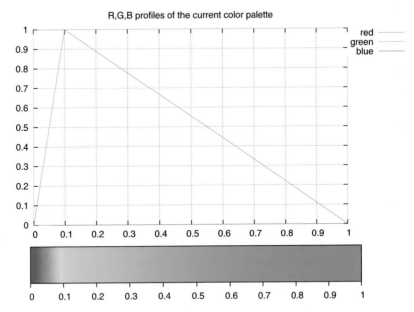

Color figure 1 The result of the `test palette` command for the two palettes defined by `set palette model RGB defined ( 0 "red", 0.5 "yellow", 1 "green" )` (top) and `set palette model RGB defined ( 0 "red", 0.1 "yellow", 1 "green" )` (bottom). The top of each graph shows the intensity levels of the red, green, and blue color components; the bottom shows the spectrum of colors and their position in the spectrum.

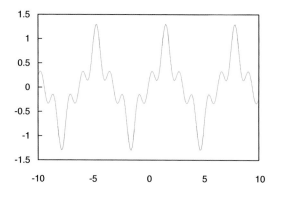

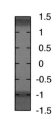

Color figure 2   A control chart: as the plotted value leaves the allowed region, the color of the curve changes smoothly from green to red. This graph was drawn using `pm3d` and the `with lines palette` style. See listing 9.1.

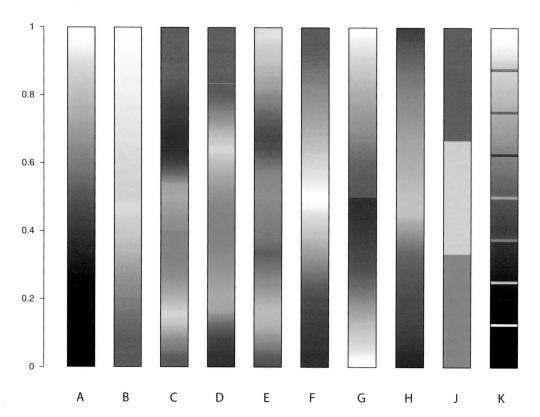

Color figure 3   A collection of sample palettes. See section 9.3.2 for details. A: linear grayscale; B: heat scale; C: standard rainbow; D: improved rainbow; E: geo scale; F: blue/white/red saturation scale; G: blue/red saturation scale with sharp transition point; H: blue/green luminance scale; J: traffic light scale for segmentation tasks; K: smooth grayscale with colored level indicators.

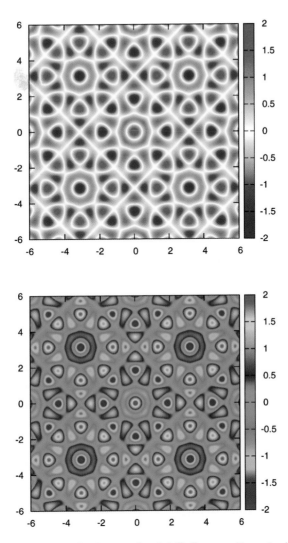

Color figure 4 Color renderings of a function (see section 9.4.1). Compare these graphs to the black-and-white image in figure 9.2. Note how the square symmetry comes out much more clearly in the blue/white/red graph on the top, compared to the black-and-white image, and the additional level of detail discernible in the multi-colored graph on the bottom.

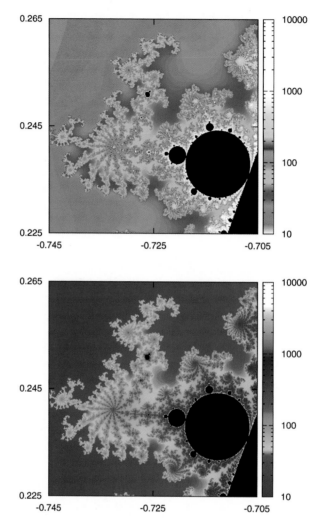

Color figure 5 Color renderings of a section of the Mandelbrot set: a hue-based palette on the top and a luminance-based palette on the bottom. Note how more detail seems to be discernible in the image on the bottom, despite the wider range of colors used in the image on the top. See listing 9.3 for definitions of the palettes and figure 9.3 for a black-and-white version of this plot.

- Color doesn't reproduce well! A graph containing two lines distinguished only by their color will lose most of its values once photocopied. Similarly, offices tend to have powerful, high-speed laser printers—but they (still) usually only print black and white. There's no guarantee that the printout somebody makes of your article containing nicely colored graphs will come out the way it looks on the screen.

- As my embarrassing anecdote demonstrates, about 10 percent of people are at least partially color blind. Relying on color to convey critical (as opposed to supporting) information makes your graphs inaccessible to a significant fraction of viewers.

- Finally, it can be difficult to read *quantitative* information from color. Using well-designed palettes can help, but in the end, colored graphs are great to indicate the "lay of the land" of a data set—once we reach the level of detail that we would like to study quantitative changes in data, we're usually back to two-dimensional xy-plots.

9.4 Case studies

To conclude this chapter on color, let's look at two case studies and see how we can apply what we just learned about palette design. In the first case study, we want to find a palette to represent a smoothly varying, but wiggly function. In the second case study, we're looking for a color scheme suitable for the edge of the Mandelbrot set—an object known to have structure on the finest of scales.

9.4.1 A smoothly varying function

Let's consider a trigonometric function, such as the following:

```
f(x,y,n,m) = cos(n*x)*cos(m*y)+cos(m*x)*cos(n*y)
```

This function depends on the two variables x and y and two parameters. It changes in a regular way, but (depending on the values for the parameters n and m) it wiggles a lot. It's very difficult to get a good picture of this function by taking slices (such as fixing y at some value and then plotting it as a function of x), and in a surface plot, some of the details are guaranteed to be hidden by other parts of the function. So a false-color plot seems to be a good way forward.

For the sake of discussion, let's fix the parameters as follows: n=2 and m=5. (Feel free to play around with other values of n and m. You can get particularly bizarre behavior by adding multiple instances of this function, but choosing different values for the parameters—for example, f(x,y,2,5) + f(x,y,7,3), and so on.)

To do a false-color plot, we need to choose a palette. Let's start with a simple gray-scale. The commands are shown in listing 9.2 and the resulting graph in figure 9.2.

Listing 9.2   A false-color plot, using linear grayscale—see figure 9.2

```
set pm3d                # Turn on pm3d mode
set view map            # Switch to birds-eye view...
set size square         # ... and scale x- and y-axes equally
unset surface           # No need for a surface in a false-color plot!
set isosamples 300      # But we want good resolution.

set palette model RGB defined ( 0 'black', 1 'white' )

splot [-6:6][-6:6] f(x,y,2,5)
```

But this is wrong! The grayscale is a luminance-based palette—for smooth, large-structure data such as this, we should use a saturation- or hue-based palette. So let's give it a try with the blue/white/red palette. The result is shown in color figure 4. The difference from figure 9.2 is stunning!

In particular, the square symmetry of the function is clearly visible now, whereas it wasn't at all obvious before. Also, it's now clear that the function displays a checkerboard pattern, assuming predominantly positive or negative values in adjacent fields of the checkerboard.

More fun can be had by changing the position of the white band in the palette. But wouldn't it be nice to be able to see all the variation in this function in one graph, rather than having to scan through it by moving the white band? This is where a multi-hue palette such as the geo scale comes in.

Give this a shot:

```
set palette defined
➡  ( 0 'magenta', 1 '#0066ff', 2 'cyan', 3 '#009900',
➡    4 'green', 5 '#996633', 6 'orange', 7 'yellow', 8 'red' )
```

This is a geo scale consisting of bright (fully saturated) colors. Now try this:

```
set palette defined
➡  ( 0 'magenta', 1 '#3366ff', 2 '#99ffcc', 3 '#339900',
➡    4 '#66ff33', 5 '#996633', 6 '#ff9900', 7 '#ffff33', 8 'red' )
```

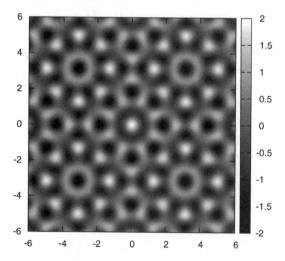

Figure 9.2   A grayscale rendering of a smoothly varying function. Compare this figure with color figure 4. The commands for this plot are in listing 9.2.

This is very similar to the preceding palette, but the colors are less saturated. Compare for yourself—in which one can you see more details? (The pastel version of the plot is shown in color figure 4.) The only colors that aren't pastels are the ones for the most extreme values of the spectrum (magenta and red, in this example). I chose to leave them fully saturated, because they're only used in small, isolated spots of the overall graph, and I wanted to make it easy to detect the distribution of extreme values. In general, the colors are distributed rather uniformly over the entire spectrum, because this matches up with the regularly varying function in this plot.

9.4.2   *A complex figure*

As an example of a graph that includes a lot of fine detail, I've chosen a section from the edge of the Mandelbrot set. The Mandelbrot set is the set of all points in the complex plane for which a certain simple iteration process stays bounded. What's noteworthy here is that the border between points inside the set and outside of it isn't smooth—in fact the border is "infinitely" complicated, showing details at all levels of magnification.[6] For points far from the Mandelbrot set, the iteration will diverge quickly (after just a few steps). But as we approach the border, the iteration will take many more steps before finally diverging. Once inside the set, the iteration doesn't diverge (that's the definition of the Mandelbrot set, after all).

The input to the data visualization project we want to study in this section is a file containing the x and y coordinates of all points in a certain region of the complex plane, together with the number of steps that were required before the iteration diverged. The value 10,000 indicates that the iteration didn't diverge and that the point therefore lies on the inside of the Mandelbrot set. (The iteration is stopped if it hasn't diverged after 10,000 steps, so we know that there won't be any value larger than this threshold.)

We want to use a color scale to indicate how long the iteration lasted before it diverged. The interior of the Mandelbrot set is customarily drawn in black.

Figure 9.3 shows a possible grayscale view of our data set (the corresponding palette can be found in listing 9.3). For the chosen section of the set, most of the detail occurs at iteration counts around 225, which is why I placed the strongest visual gradients in that range. In contrast, the long interval between 1,500 and 10,000 iteration steps is colored in a uniform white, because there are only few pixels in the image falling into this region (mostly the thin white boundaries that you can see around the solid black regions, which belong to the interior or the Mandelbrot set). There's no reason to waste visual gradients on parameter ranges that occupy only a small and not very relevant area of the plot.

Grayscale is of course only the first step. In color figure 5, I show the same data set, plotted with two different palettes, which are also listed in listing 9.3. One is hue-based; the other is luminance-based. According to our guidelines, a luminance-based

---

[6]   This isn't the place to give a detailed introduction to fractals and the Mandelbrot set. Plenty of information is readily available on the Internet—the Wikipedia entry for the Mandelbrot set is a good place to start.

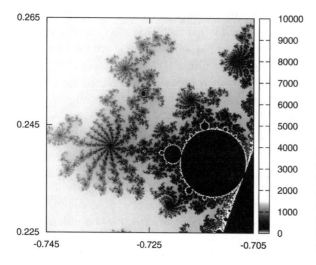

Figure 9.3   A black-and-white rendition of a section of the Mandelbrot set. Note the strongly uneven grayscale, visible in the colorbox. See listing 9.3 for the definition of the palette, and color figure 5 for color renderings of the same image.

palette should be more suitable than a hue-based one for graphs containing a high level of detail, such as this one, and I think this example bears this out—the level of detail can be recognized more clearly when using the luminance-based palette. (This isn't to say that the hue-based version isn't *aesthetically* more pleasing, which brings us back to the first item of the list of recommendations: know your purpose. Are you preparing graphs for illustration or analysis?)

In the two color palettes, I'm employing a weird trick that I should explain. As you can see in figure 9.3, the visual gradient is all bunched up at the low end of the color scale. It would be helpful to expand just the low end of the color scale over the entire colorbox. Unfortunately, we can't simply use `set cbrange [0:1000]` to adjust the scale—this would assign the z values 0 and 1,000 to the ends of the entire palette (thus changing all the mappings from z values to colors), instead of slicing out a section from the palette (while leaving the mappings unchanged).

Instead, I use the `set logscale cb` command to distribute z values in a logarithmic fashion across the spectrum. The last piece of the trick is that I use the *logarithm* of the number of iterations for the location parameter when defining the palette. The logarithm for the location parameter cancels against the log scale for the colorbox, so that the color `#ff6666` is indeed used (in the hue-based palette) to color points corresponding to 20 iteration steps. (If the preceding discussion is too abstract, I suggest you try it yourself in all different ways to see how these different options interact with each other.)

Listing 9.3   Palettes for the Mandelbrot set example. See text for details.

```
# Gray-scale palette
set palette model RGB defined
➡ ( 0 'white', 10 'white', 225 'black', 1500 'white',
➡    9999 'white', 10000 'black' )
```

```
# Hue-based palette
set logsc cb
set palette model RGB defined
➡ ( log(15) 'white', log(20) '#ff6666', log(35) '#cc99cc',
➡ log(50) '#3366ff', log(100) '#99ffcc', log(133) '#339900',
➡ log(167) '#66ff33', log(200) '#996633', log(250) '#ff9900',
➡ log(300) '#ffff33', log(999) 'white', log(9999) 'white',
➡ log(10000) 'black' )

# Luminance-based palette
set logsc cb
blue = 2.0/3.0
green = 1.0/3.0
set palette model HSV defined
➡ ( log(15) blue 0.7 0.6, log(50) blue 0.6 0.9,
➡ log(100) green 0.5 1, log(200) green 0.7 0.5,
➡ log(1000) green 0.9 0.4, log(5000) 0 0 1,
➡ log(9999) 0 0 1, log(10000) 0 1 0 )
```

In fairness, this application isn't really what gnuplot is intended to do. Nevertheless, gnuplot has served us well, because of its nifty support for palettes, and by playing out its core strengths: the ability to handle large data sets and its support for common data formats.

9.5   *Summary*

This was a long chapter, touching on many different issues, not all of them strictly related to gnuplot. So let's summarize what we've learned. First, in regard to gnuplot's support for generating colored graphs:

- The pm3d mode is used to generate images using smooth color scales, by mapping numeric values to be plotted into a continuous spectrum.
- The set palette option can be used to define our own number-to-color mappings. The palette option has a rich syntax and can construct smooth spectra based on just a few fixed values.
- The colorbox is the equivalent to the key for a colored image. Using set colorbox, we can manipulate different aspects of it.

We also discussed some recommendations for the use of color in graphics. Some of the most important items are

- To achieve optimal results, it's almost always necessary to generate a customized palette, adapted to the current data set and the intended visualization task.
- Don't just distribute visual gradients uniformly over the spectrum; instead place them in the region of the most relevant change. Use sharp transitions in the spectrum to indicate relevant thresholds in the data.
- Prefer pastel colors. It's not necessary to make drastic changes in saturation and luminance—the eye can detect gradual changes more easily.

- Prefer saturation-based or hue-based palettes for data with large-scale structures; prefer luminance-based palettes for data containing a great level of fine detail.
- Don't forget to include a colorbox with your graph, showing the mapping of actual numbers to colors.

More than anything, though, the take-away from this chapter is that color can be a lot of fun, and gnuplot (properly used) can make it even more so!

10

Advanced plotting concepts

This chapter covers

- Combining graphs with multiplot mode
- Advanced math features in gnuplot
- Curve fitting

This is the last chapter in which we're going to talk about gnuplot's graphing features. In the next two chapters, we'll talk about different ways of exporting graphs to files and about scripting gnuplot for batch mode, before turning our attention to the things we can find out *using* graphs. But before we can leave gnuplot's plotting commands behind, we still have to finish off some topics that we haven't mentioned so far.

In the next section, I'll introduce gnuplot's `multiplot` feature, a way to combine different plots in a single graph. In the remainder of this chapter, we'll look at ways of visualizing vector fields at other coordinate systems (besides the right-angled, Cartesian system we've been using exclusively so far), and at parametric representations. In the final section, I'm going to introduce gnuplot's built-in curve-fitting capabilities.

Except for the first topic (on `multiplot`), the material in this chapter is rather specialized and involves more advanced math than the rest of this book. Make sure you catch the `multiplot` features, but feel free to skip the rest if it's not relevant to you right now.

10.1 Multiplot

Using gnuplot's multiplot feature, we can combine several plots into a single graph. This can be useful for a number of different purposes:

- To make arrays of related graphs
- To create *insets*: graphs within a graph (for example, to show some details at greater magnification)
- For special effects, such as multiple, clearly separate plots aligned on a common axis

Multiplot mode is enabled like an option through a `set multiplot` command, and remains active until an `unset multiplot` command has been issued. When multiplot mode is active, the usual `gnuplot>` prompt changes and is replaced by a `multiplot>` prompt. All `plot` (or `splot` or `replot` or `test`, but not `test palette`) commands issued at this prompt are directed to the *same* graph, and we can control their relative location by giving additional directives to the `set multiplot` command. Any other option modified while in multiplot mode is applied to *all subsequent* plots. This is the normal gnuplot behavior; multiplot mode doesn't change that. Any option or decoration we want to apply to only one of the plots in a multiplot combination has to be explicitly set before and unset after the respective `plot` command. (This doesn't apply to decorations positioned with `screen` coordinates: since there's only a single `screen` coordinate system even for a multiplot graph, they're *global* objects.)

Different terminals may exhibit different behavior regarding the time when plots become visible. Some show each plot right when the corresponding `plot` has been issued; others may delay generation of the entire array of graphs until multiplot mode is switched off again.

There's one very important limitation to multiplot mode: you can't change the terminal while in multiplot mode! This implies that we have to change the way we usually use gnuplot: it's not possible to build up a graph iteratively using an interactive (screen) terminal, and then, finally, export it to a graphics file format, since this would require a change of terminal before the last step. Instead, the file-based terminal has to be selected *first*, with all other commands following. Personally, I write all my commands to a command file (using a text editor) and then run it using `load`, while using an interactive terminal. When I'm satisfied with the resulting graph, I insert a terminal and output setting at the top of the command file, and run it one final time to export the graph to file. Since multiplot mode is mostly a tool for generating final presentation graphics (as opposed to exploratory data analysis, which must be interactive to be useful), this works quite well.

There's one additional gotcha to be aware of when using multiplot mode: if you want to capture the commands for the plot using `save`, you must issue the `save` command *before* leaving multiplot mode. (Otherwise, only the commands for the last plot in the multiplot set will be saved to file!) And remember to exit multiplot mode using `unset multiplot`, not using `Control-D` (which will terminate gnuplot altogether).

The multiplot feature can be used in two different ways. We can specify the layout of a tabular array of graphs as part of the `set multiplot` command and let gnuplot figure out sizing and positioning of all components in the overall graph automatically. Or we can take control of all aspects of the layout ourselves and arrange the individual graphs using `set size` and `set origin`. All of this will become much clearer once we look at some examples.

The `set multiplot` option has the following suboptions:

```
set multiplot [ title "{str:title}" ]
              [ layout {int:rows},{int:cols}
                [ rowsfirst | columnsfirst ]
                [ downwards | upwards ]
                [ scale {flt:xfactor}[,{flt:yfactor}] ]
                [ offset {flt:xoff}[,{flt:yoff}] ] ]
```

The `title` directive is the equivalent to the `set title` (see section 6.3.3) for regular plots: it can be used to give an overall title to the entire assembly of graphs. (The `set title` command can still be used to assign a title to each of the individual component graphs.) All other directives (besides `title`) are only meaningful in combination with the `layout` keyword, which is a convenience feature to create arrays of graphs easily. In the following sections, we work through some examples of using both the `layout` facility and explicit placing of component graphs.

10.1.1 *Regular arrays of graphs with layout*

The `layout` directive takes two mandatory integer arguments, which describe the number of rows and columns in the resulting array of graphs. This array will be filled with subsequent `plot` commands. We can control the order in which subsequent panels will be filled through the `rowsfirst`, `columnsfirst`, `downwards`, and `upwards` keywords (see figure 10.1). The default is `rowsfirst downwards`.

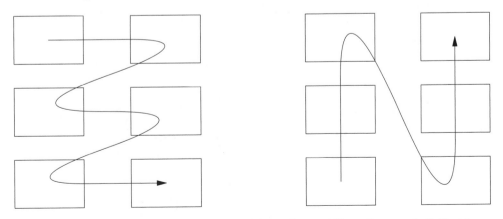

Figure 10.1 Choosing the layout direction in multiplot mode: `rowsfirst downwards` (left) and `columnsfirst upwards` (right)

Individual plots can be scaled and shifted from their (automatically assigned) size and position using the `scale` and `offset` keywords. The arguments to `scale` are multiplicative scale factors for the x and y size of the individual plots (if only one is given, it's applied to both axes). Using the `offset` directive, we can shift all graphs by the same amount; the arguments are interpreted as `screen` coordinates (see section 6.2), so that `offset 0.25, 0.1` shifts everything by a quarter of the overall width of the graph to the right and by a tenth of the height up.

One important limitation: `set multiplot layout` doesn't nest—you can't have a small array of graphs as a panel in a larger array.

The `layout` feature makes it really easy to generate multipanel graphs (as in figure 10.2), as listing 10.1 shows.

Listing 10.1   Creating a regular array with `multiplot layout` (see figure 10.2)

```
t(x,n) = cos(n*acos(x))        # Define some function

set xrange [-1:1]
set yrange [-1:1]

set multiplot title "Chebyshev Polynomials" layout 3,2

plot t(x,1)
plot t(x,2)
plot t(x,3)
plot t(x,4)
plot t(x,5)
plot t(x,6)

unset multiplot                # Don't forget!
```

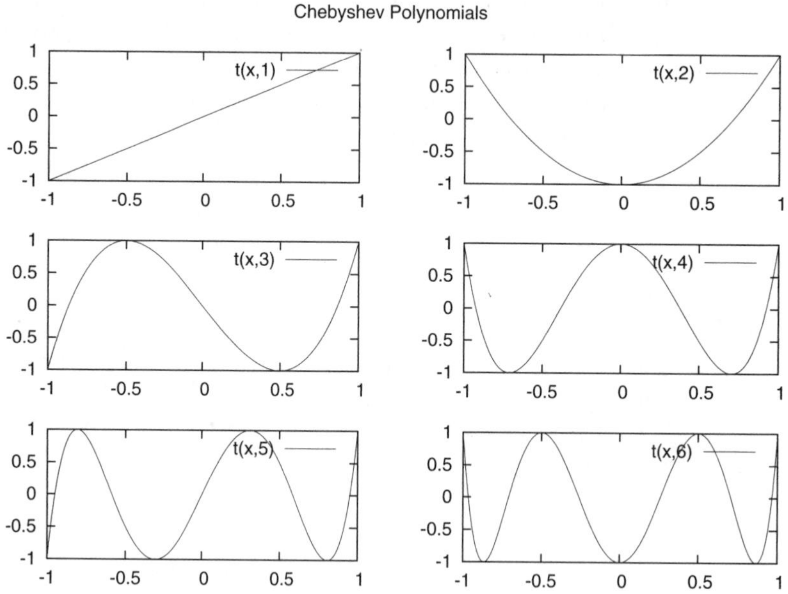

Figure 10.2   A regular array of small plots created in multiplot mode. See listing 10.1.

If we want to have more control over the way individual plots are assembled to form a plot, we can't use `layout`; instead we have to handle everything ourselves using `set size` and `set origin`. Let's look at an example, which lets us demonstrate some fine points that come up when using multiplot mode.

10.1.2 *Graphs within a graph*

Sometimes it's useful to place small graphs inside a larger one, for example to show a detail of the overall graph at greater magnification, or to provide some form of ancillary information (as in figure 10.3). This can't be accomplished using `layout`, so we have to roll our own.

Listing 10.2 shows how it's done.[1] Let's step through this example carefully and point out some details and potential pitfalls.

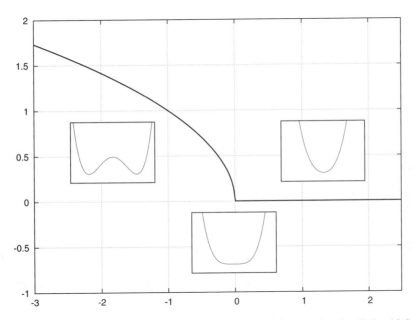

Figure 10.3   A larger graph with insets showing ancillary information. See listing 10.2.

---

[1]   This example is taken from the thermodynamics of phase transitions: if you heat a magnet beyond its *critical temperature*, it loses all magnetization. In the graph, the thick curve shows the magnetization as a function of temperature, while the three insets show the typical form of the *free energy* as a function of the magnetization for three different temperatures: below, at, and above the critical value. Below the critical temperature, the free energy develops two minima at nonzero values of the magnetization, indicating that a magnetized phase is stable. Right at the critical temperature, these two minima coalesce, yielding a curve that's flat at the origin. Above the transition temperature, there's only a single minimum at zero: the magnetization of the sample is now zero.

Listing 10.2   Creating small graphics or insets within a larger graph—see figure 10.3

```
f(x,a) = x<a ? sqrt(a-x) : 0        # Magnetization
g(x,b) = 0.25*x**4 + b*x**2         # Free Energy

set multiplot

set grid
plot [-3:2.5][-1:2] f(x,0) notitle w l lw 3
unset grid

unset tics
unset xtics
unset ytics
unset key
set tmargin 0; set bmargin 0; set rmargin 0; set lmargin 0

set size 0.2

set origin 0.175,0.425
clear
plot [-2.5:2.5][-1.5:2] g(x,-1)

set origin 0.4625,0.125
clear
plot [-2.5:2.5][-0.5:3] g(x,0)

set origin 0.675,0.425
clear
plot [-2.5:2.5][-0.5:3] g(x,1)

unset multiplot
```

1   We define a couple of functions—that's not strictly necessary, but helps to keep the following `plot` commands simple.

2   Switch multiplot mode on.

3   Turn on the background grid, plot the main curve, and then switch the background grid off again.

   This is a standard technique when using multiplot mode: options we want to have active in only some of the plots must be activated only for the actual plot they're supposed to affect.

4   Set some options that will be relevant for *all* of the small inset plots. Since the insets are small, we do away with all decorations, such as tic marks and text labels. We also set all margins to zero at this time.

5   Choose the size of the inset plots, as a fraction of the overall plot size.

6   For each of the insets, choose its location by specifying its origin in `screen` coordinates.

7   By default, gnuplot doesn't clear the area where a second plot will be placed. We must do so explicitly using the `clear` command.

8   Generate the actual inset plot.

9   Repeat the last three steps for all of the insets.

10 Finally, switch multiplot mode off again.

This example demonstrates most of the steps that are typical when combining graphs using multiplot: switching on options only for those plots that require them, clearing the plot area (if necessary and desired), and finally sizing and placing all graphs individually.

Let's look at a second example: rather than placing small plots within a larger one, now we want to place several plots side by side.

10.1.3 *Graphs aligned on a common axis*

Occasionally, we want to show two or more graphs together, aligned on a common axis, to facilitate comparison between curves in both graphs. Of course, we could put all curves into a single plot (as we did in section 7.1), but sometimes doing so would lead to an overly cluttered graph—for example, if we want to compare, not just two curves, but two entire *sets* of curves.

For example, let's assume I want to compare the log-normal probability density function and its cumulative distribution function for a whole set of parameters. I could place all these curves into a single graph, but the graph would appear crowded and it would be difficult to distinguish the curves properly from each other.

Instead, let's put them into two different graphs, aligned on a common axis, as shown in figure 10.4. By now, we know how to create a multipanel plot using multiplot mode (see listing 10.3). The only new details are those that are required to manage the common axis.

Listing 10.3 Showing two plots side by side using multiplot mode—see figure 10.4

```
lgn( x, s ) = exp(-0.5*(log(x)/s)**2)/(x*s*sqrt(2*pi)) # Log-normal
clgn( x, s ) = 0.5*(1+erf(log(x)/(s*sqrt(2))))         # Cumulative

set multiplot layout 2,1


set bmargin 0          # Switch OFF bottom margin of the top panel
set format x ""        # ... and eliminate tic labels for the x-axis

set ytics 0.2,0.2      # Suppress the tic label for y=0 (start,step)

set key bottom
plot [0:2.5][0:1] clgn(x,0.5) t "s=0.5", clgn(x,1) t "s=1.0",
 ➥             clgn(x,5) t "s=5.0"

set bmargin            # Restore the bottom margin
set tmargin 0          # ... but switch of the top one
set format x "%g"      # Also restore the tic labels for the x-axis

set ytics 0,0.2,0.8    # Suppress tic label for y=1 (start,step,stop)

set key top

plot [0:2.5][0:1] lgn(x,0.5) t "s=0.5", lgn(x,1) t "s=1.0",
 ➥             lgn(x,5) t "s=5.0"

unset multiplot
```

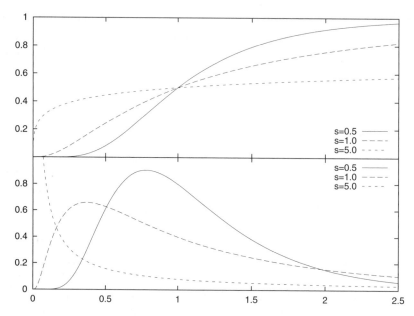

Figure 10.4   Showing two plots side by side using multiplot mode (see listing 10.3)

I want to point out just a few items. This example uses the `set multiplot layout` option, since (after all) both plots are arranged in a regular fashion, but customizes the appearance. In particular, note how the bottom margin of the top graph and the top margin of the bottom graph have been eliminated to give the appearance of a single, two-panel graph.

The other interesting detail concerns the tic marks along the horizontal axis. For the top panel, I wanted regular tic marks, but without the labels, while for the bottom one I wanted both tic marks *and* labels. In addition, I was quite happy to let gnuplot figure out where to place tic marks—I certainly didn't want to specify them individually if I could avoid it. I suppressed tic mark labels (but not the tic marks themselves) in the top panel by choosing `set format x ""` (see section 7.3.3), which tells gnuplot to use an empty string as label. This is a good trick, and is worth remembering (it comes in handy in other situations as well).

There is also a bit of fine-tuning going on in regard to the y axis labels: to make sure that they don't clobber each other, I suppress the first label in the top graph and the last label in the bottom graph (see section 7.3.1 for details of the `set ytics` option).

Lastly, it's easy to compare data for equal "categories" in both panels, since I made sure to use the same line styles for comparable data in each plot.

Plots generated using multiplot mode can be useful when we want to compare different data sets to one another, but placing them all into a single graph would lead to a cluttered appearance. And as we've seen in figure 10.3, we can use multiplot mode to show different aspects of a data set in a single plot. In the rest of this chapter, we'll look at some more mathematically advanced gnuplot features.

10.2 *Higher math and special occasions*

In this section, I'll discuss gnuplot's support for some more advanced mathematical constructs: parameterized curves, non-Cartesian coordinates (such as polar, cylindrical, and spherical coordinates), and support for vectors.

Since this isn't a math book but a book on gnuplot, I will *not* explain these concepts; I'll just show you how gnuplot handles them. This section is best skipped, unless you have a specific need for its contents. Rest assured: if you don't know what I'm talking about, you aren't going to need it.

10.2.1 *Parametric plots*

Parametric plots are only relevant when plotting functions with gnuplot: the concept has no meaning when plotting data from files.

So far, whenever we plotted a function, the function provided a y value (the *dependent* variable) as a function of an x value (the *independent* variable): plot sqrt(x). Alternatively, we can give *two* functions, one for the x and one for the y value, both depending on a common *parameter*, which by convention is called t. For certain kinds of curves, such a parameterization is simpler than the explicit form. The following plot command will draw a circle (after adjusting the aspect ratio appropriately):

```
set parametric
plot [0:2*pi] cos(t), sin(t)
```

This parametric representation is significantly simpler than the equivalent explicit form:

```
unset parametric
plot [-1:1] sqrt(1-x**2), -sqrt(1-x**2)
```

In general, the following two commands will give the same result:

```
unset parametric
plot f(x)

set parametric
plot t, f(t)
```

For parametric plots, there are now *three* relevant plot ranges: trange, xrange, and yrange. The first controls the range of values assumed for the parameter (the dummy variable) t, while the other two are used (as before) to control the range of points that are visible in the plot. All three ranges can be adjusted either explicitly using set trange or the familiar set xrange and set yrange commands (see section 7.2), or inline as part of the plot command. If used inline, the setting for the trange precedes the other two. This is demonstrated in listing 10.4. The resulting plot is shown in figure 10.5.

> **Listing 10.4 Plotting in parametric mode (see figure 10.5)**

```
set parametric
set size square

r(t) = 1 - exp(-0.25*t/pi)    # the radius as function of t

plot [0:25*pi][-1.1:1.1][-1.1:1.1] r(t)*cos(t), r(t)*sin(t)
```

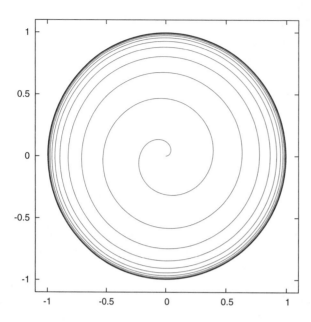

Figure 10.5   A parametric plot. The spiral starts at the origin and approaches the unit circle as the parameter t becomes large. See listing 10.4.

For three-dimensional plots, we obviously need to provide a third function, with all three functions depending on two variables, called u and v, and possessing corresponding options set urange and set vrange.

10.2.2 Non-Cartesian coordinates

Not all coordinate systems are made out of straight lines at right angles to each other. To plot points on a circle, for instance, it makes more sense to use polar coordinates, or to use spherical or cylindrical coordinates for systems possessing those kinds of symmetry. Gnuplot has built-in support for these three symmetries, through the set polar and set mapping facilities. To generate plots using other coordinate systems, we have to resort to inline data transformations or external filters.

Polar mode is enabled using

```
set polar
```

which doesn't take any further options. In polar mode, the independent variable is interpreted as an *angle* and the dependent variable as a *radius*. In polar mode, the independent (dummy) variable is denoted with t (not x), similar to the convention used for parametric plots.

The angle may be given either in radians (multiples of π—this is the default) or in degrees. We can switch between both representations using

```
set angles [ degrees | radians ]
```

The current value of this option affects not only polar plots, but also how the arguments of trigonometric functions are interpreted.

Let's look at an example (see listing 10.5 and figure 10.6). The process to generate attractive plots in polar mode requires several steps, because some artifacts from regular plots must be removed explicitly. Here's the list:

1 Switch to polar mode. Angles will be interpreted as radians (default setting).

2 Select a 1:1 aspect ratio for the diagram.

3 Switch off all parts of the usual decorations: the border, the tic mark labels, and the tic marks themselves. Rather than turning tic marks off entirely, their length is set to zero using the scale directive (this is discussed later in this section).

4 Turn on circular and radial grid lines using set grid polar. The optional argument specifies the angular spacing at which radial grid lines will be drawn.

5 Select a suitable spacing for the circular grid lines using set xtics.

6 Make room for the top and bottom labels by increasing the respective margins.

7 Put labels for the angles on the perimeter of the diagram. Place labels for the radial distances at suitable positions. Using the Symbol font for the Greek letter π requires a terminal in enhanced text mode (see section 11.2.3 for details on enhanced mode).

8 Make sure the key doesn't interfere with the graph by moving it outside the actual plotting region.

9 Plot.

Listing 10.5   Creating a plot in polar mode—see figure 10.6

```
set polar
set size square

unset border
set format x ""; set format y ""
set xtics scale 0; set ytics scale 0

set grid polar pi/8.0
set xtics 0.25

set tmargin 1; set bmargin 1

set label "0{/Symbol p}" at 1,0 offset char 1,0
set label "+0.5{/Symbol p}" at 0,1 center offset char 0,0.5
set label "-0.5{/Symbol p}" at 0,-1 center offset char 0,-0.5
set label "+/-{/Symbol p}" at -1,0 offset char -5,0

set label "0.5" at 0.5*cos(0.84*pi),0.5*sin(0.84*pi) offset char .5,0
set label "1.0" at 1.0*cos(0.83*pi),1.0*sin(0.83*pi) offset char .5,0

set key outside left

plot [-2*pi/3:2*pi/3][-1:1][-1:1] "polar-data" u 1:2 t "Data" w l,
  ➥ 0.27*(2-cos(3*t)+0.75*cos(5*t)) t "Model"
```

The zero angle in this diagram is located on the right of the diagram, not at the top (which is the more commonly used convention for polar plots like this). You can perform the required calculations yourself by subtracting $\pi/2$ from function arguments or making the corresponding inline data transformation when plotting data from a file.

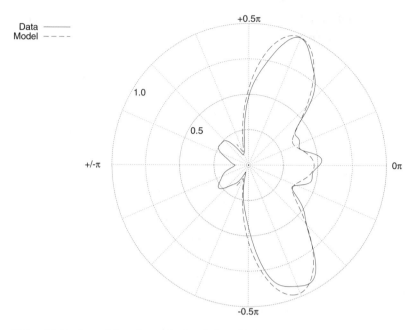

Figure 10.6   A graph in polar mode. See listing 10.5.

While the spacing of the radial lines in the polar grid is controlled through the argument to `set grid polar`, the concentric circular grid lines are controlled through `set xtics`. Specifically, circular grid lines are drawn where major tic marks would be drawn on the x axis—this is also why we mustn't switch off these tic marks entirely using `unset xtics`, but instead merely reduce them to zero length as done in the example.

If you study the commands in listing 10.5 carefully, you'll notice that gnuplot doesn't actually have a polar coordinate system! The positions for the labels, for instance, were given in the `first` coordinate system (see section 6.2), despite the fact that this coordinate system isn't actually visible in the graph, since borders and tic marks have been suppressed. If desired, we can use explicit trigonometric expressions to perform the necessary calculations on the fly, as has been done when placing the radial labels.

In the example, three plot ranges are used as part of the `plot` command. The first corresponds to the `trange` and controls the range of angles for which the function is evaluated. The second and third ranges are the `xrange` and `yrange` respectively, which control (as usual) the visible part of the plot.

There's also the `set rrange` option, which can be used to cut off parts of the data that exceed a desired plot range in the radial dimension. Note that the lower boundary on `rrange` *must* be zero, for example `set rrange [0:0.5]`. It's not possible to select just an intermediate slice of r values (such as 0.25 to 0.75). Similarly, gnuplot will neither warn you if you attempt to plot data containing negative values for the radial variable, nor suppress such data points: instead it'll plot them shifted by π in the angular coordinate. You've been warned!

Polar mode only makes sense for graphs generated using `plot`—the equivalent for graphs created with `splot` is the `set mapping` option:

```
set mapping [ cartesian | cylindrical | spherical ]
```

I'll demonstrate it here only by showing the data set world.dat (which you can find in the demo folder of your gnuplot installation) twice: once plotted using `plot` as a projection into the plane, and once plotted with `set mapping spherical` (see figure 10.7). Check the standard gnuplot reference documentation for further details.

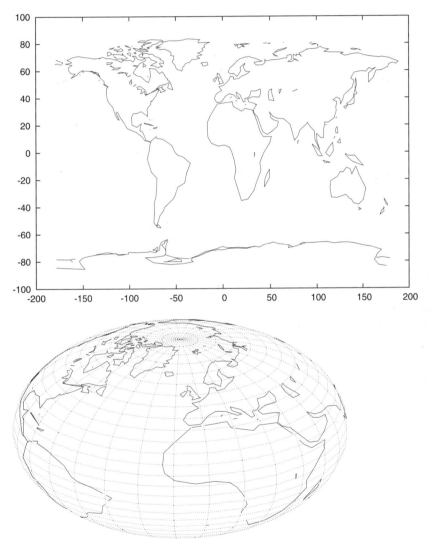

Figure 10.7 Using a spherical coordinate system together with `splot`. On top, the data set has been plotted as a regular two-dimensional plot using `plot`; below it's been plotted (together with a grid) using `set mapping spherical` and `splot`.

10.2.3 *Vector fields*

Vector-valued quantities have both a magnitude and a direction, in contrast to scalars, which only have a magnitude. Simply put, vectors are arrows, while scalars are numbers. Think of a climber in a mountainscape: the local height is a scalar, but the direction that the climber would tumble down (if he let go) is a vector.

Gnuplot has a `with vectors` style, which can be used to plot vector-valued quantities. This style is available for both the `plot` and the `splot` commands.

We must supply additional information when plotting vectors to indicate the direction. For two-dimensional plots using `plot`, gnuplot requires four columns: the first two give the position of the start of each arrow, while the last two give the offset (relative to the start) of the arrow's end. In other words, the columns must represent x, y, dx, and dy, and gnuplot will show the data as arrows from (x, y) to (x+dx, y+dy). All quantities are interpreted as coordinates in the diagram's coordinates.

Figure 10.8 shows an example. The data can be interpreted as the force on a test charge in the presence of three other charges (indicated by dots). By default, gnuplot draws the arrowhead as a fixed fraction of the length of each arrow, so that short arrows have smaller heads. This is shown in the top panel. By contrast, we can supply our own arrow style directives as part of the `plot` command, in which case all arrowheads are drawn with the same size. An example is shown at the bottom of figure 10.8. (You might want to check section 6.3.2 for details on arrow style parameters.)

Similar considerations apply to vectors in three dimensions, only that now we need to supply *six* columns in total. In three dimensions (when using `splot`), the `with vectors` style can be used in creative ways to visualize three-dimensional objects. In particular, together with the mousing capabilities of interactive terminals (see section 8.3.2), this can be quite useful—a lot of visualization power that's usually only achieved with much more complicated programs.

A quick example will help to clarify. Listing 10.6 shows a data file. The top part of the data file gives the coordinates of a pyramid-shaped body. The bottom part of the file shows the edges of the pyramid. The labels A, B, C, and D of the corners help to identify the edges of the body.

Listing 10.6   A data file with coordinates for a simple pyramid—see figure 10.9

```
# End Points
-1 -1  0                    # A
-1  1  0                    # B
 1  0  0                    # C
 0  0  1.75                 # D

# Edges
-1 -1  0        -1  1  0    # A -> B
-1 -1  0         1  0  0    # A -> C
-1 -1  0         0  0  1.75 # A -> D
-1  1  0         1  0  0    # B -> C
-1  1  0         0  0  1.75 # B -> D
 1  0  0         0  0  1.75 # C -> D
```

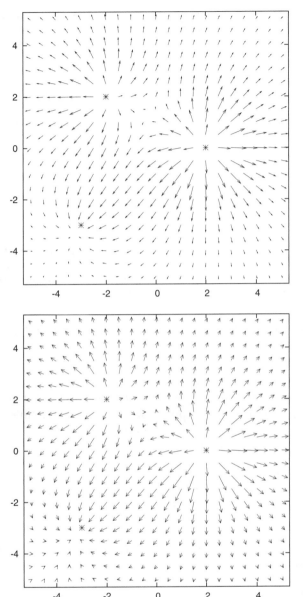

Figure 10.8 Plotting a vector field using with vectors. The top panel shows the gnuplot default, in which the size of the arrowhead is a fixed fraction of the overall length of the arrow. The bottom panel shows the same data plotted using plot "vectors.dat" with vectors head size 0.15,25.

When attempting to plot this data, we need to remember that the with vectors style requires the starting points and the relative offsets of the end points, not the coordinates of the start and end points directly. The commands in listing 10.7 use inline data transformations to convert the coordinates into offsets on the fly. (If you need a reminder how to use the index keyword to pick out different parts from a file, you might want to review section 3.1.1.) The resulting graph is shown in figure 10.9. Try it yourself, and then "grab" the figure with the mouse to rotate. Have fun!

Listing 10.7   The commands used to generate figure 10.9 from the data in listing 10.6

```
unset border
unset tics
unset key
set view 75,35
splot "pyramid.dat" index 0 with points pointtype 7 pointsize 3,
➥ "" i 1 u 1:2:3:($4-$1):($5-$2):($6-$3) with vectors nohead
```

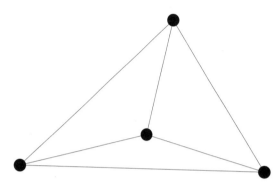

Figure 10.9   The body whose coordinates were given in listing 10.6. Try this yourself, then "grab" this figure with the mouse and try to rotate it!

To close out this chapter on more advanced plotting concepts, we'll look at gnuplot's curve-fitting support. That will be the topic of the next section.

10.3   Curve fitting

Gnuplot includes a facility to perform *nonlinear least-square fits*. This subject, involving a fair amount of data manipulation and descriptive statistics, is actually a little outside gnuplot's primary area of applicability (which is to generate plots of data).

Gnuplot's fitting functionality consists of

- Two commands: `fit` and `update`
- Two options: `set fit logfile` and `set fit errorvariables`; and one environment variable `FIT_LOG`
- Eight gnuplot variables

Before describing how to use the `fit` command and the associated options, let me explain the context and some specific terms.[2]

10.3.1   Background

Assume that we have a set of N data points: (x_i, y_i) and a function $f(x, a_1, ..., a_m)$ of *known functional form*. Note that the function doesn't just depend on the independent variable x, but also on m parameters a_1 through a_m. Fitting this function to the data means finding those values for $(a_1, ..., a_m)$ that optimize a certain *merit function*—a function measuring how well the data is represented by the function. The most

---

[2] An easily accessible, but certainly not sufficient reference for nonlinear least-squares fits is chapter 15 of *Numerical Recipes* (2nd ed., 1992) by W. H. Press, S. A. Teukolsky, W. T. Vetterling, and B. P. Flannery.

common merit function is the sum of the squares of the deviations, which is traditionally referred to as χ^2 (or chi-square):

$$\chi^2 = \Sigma_i^N \, (\, y_i - f(x_i; \, a_1, \, ..., \, a_m) \,)^2$$

We can assign a weight to each term in this sum, such that data points that are known more accurately contribute more strongly to the final sum. We write the weight for the ith term as $1/\sigma_i$, where σ_i is a measure for the uncertainty (such as the standard deviation) of that term. The result is the *weighted least-squares* merit function (also denoted chi-square):

$$\chi^2 = \Sigma_i^N \, (\, y_i - f(x_i; \, a_1, \, ..., \, a_m) \,)^2 / \sigma_i^2$$

The optimal choice of parameters (in a least-squares sense) will minimize this value.[3]

If the function $f(x; \, a_1, \, ..., \, a_m)$ is *linear* in the independent variable—that is, if

$$f(x; \, a, \, b) = a \, x + b$$

then the optimal values of the parameters a and b can be calculated directly from the data (*linear regression*). If the function is not linear in x, but linear in the parameters—for example, $f(x; a, b) = a \sin(x) + b \cos(x)$—a similarly simple relation holds. But if the function is *not* linear in the parameters—for example, $f(x; \, a, \, b \,) = \sin(a \, x)/\text{sqrt}(x+b)$—there's generally no solution to the minimization problem in closed form.

In this case, the merit function must be minimized using an iterative algorithm, in which different values for the parameters are tried repeatedly until the merit function reaches its optimal value. The standard numerical algorithm for this task, which takes into account the specific analytic form of the merit function as a sum of squares, is known as the *Marquardt-Levenberg* method. This is what gnuplot's `fit` command uses.

In the next section, we describe this command in some detail, and then move on to demonstrate it by way of a worked example.

10.3.2 *Using the fit command*

The syntax of the `fit` command is superficially similar to the `plot` command:

```
fit [ {ranges} ]
    {function} "{str:datafile}"
               [ index {int:start}[:{int:end}][:{int:step}] ]
               [ every {int:step}[::{int:start}[::{int:end}]] ]
               [ using {columnspec} ]
               via [ {var1}, {var2}, ... | "{str:parameterfile}" ]
```

The requirements for the format of the data file are the same as for the `plot` command. The `index`, `every`, `using` directives are available for `fit` as well, and so are on-the-fly transformations through the `using` option. Plot ranges can be specified inline, using the syntax familar from the `plot` command.

---

[3] Although the sum of least-squares is by far the most commonly used merit function, it's not the only possible choice. It can be justified on statistical grounds when the noise in the data has certain properties. It has the technical advantage of being simple and analytic everywhere. On the minus side, it tends to overemphasize outliers.

When used with `fit`, the `using` directive can specify one to three columns: if only a single column is given, it's assumed to be the y value. Two columns are interpreted as (x, y) pairs. A third column is interpreted as the standard deviation for the corresponding value and is used to form a weighted-least squares merit function (if the value in the third column is σ, then each term in the sum of squares is multiplied by $1/\sigma^2$).

The function must depend on the dummy variable explicitly, but otherwise can be any valid gnuplot expression. Usually, it'll be a user-defined function. The names of the parameters with respect to which the fit will be performed are specified using the `via` directive. There are two variants: the names of the parameters can be given explicitly as part of the `fit` command, or can be read from a file.

Since nonlinear least-squares require an iterative algorithm, good starting values for all parameters must be selected. With badly chosen starting values, the procedure may require many steps to converge, or diverge altogether.

Values can be assigned to parameters before they're used—any parameter that hasn't been defined is set equal to zero. Alternatively, the parameter file may contain starting values for all parameters, using the following syntax:

```
varname = value
varname = value    # FIXED
```

The comment on the second line forces gnuplot to keep this value fixed during the iteration; that is, the corresponding variable won't be adjusted when attempting to optimize the merit function.

At each step in the iteration, the `fit` command prints out the current values of the fitting parameters, as well as some information about the progress of the iteration. When the algorithm has converged, gnuplot prints out the final values for all fitting parameters, as well some additional information that can be used to interpret the results and evaluate the goodness of the fit and the reliability of the parameter estimates.

At the end of the iteration, the variables are assigned their final values and therefore can be used directly in subsequent plots. Let me give you a quick demonstration of the basic usage right now, and let's look at a more involved example in section 10.3.3.

The basic workflow when using the `fit` command consists of three steps: define a function, then use it as argument to `fit`, and finally plot the function together with the data set using `plot`.

```
f(x) = sin( a*x + b )
fit f(x) "data" u 1:2:(0.25) via a,b

# Many lines of gnuplot output suppressed...

plot "data" u 1:2 w linesp, f(x)   # Plot data together with
                                   #    "best-fit" function
```

After the `fit` command has completed, all the parameters (here: a and b), contain their proper values, so that the function can be plotted without further modification. This is what we do in the final step, where we plot the function (using the fitted values for a and b) together with the data. Also note that we've used a constant value (0.25) for the amplitude of the noise.

Finally, if the list of parameters (and their starting values) has been read from a file, then the resulting values can be written out to a file using the `update` command. This command takes the name of the parameter file as mandatory first argument. If no second argument is given, the input file is renamed by appending .old and the resulting values are written to a file with the original name. Alternatively, if a second filename is supplied, the resulting values are written to this file, while the original file is left untouched.

CONTROL VARIABLES AND OUTPUT VARIABLES

We can control several aspects of the fitting operation through a number of control variables. These are regular gnuplot variables, and we can influence the behavior of the `fit` command by assigning numeric values to these variables.

- `FIT_LIMIT`: The main convergence criterion. If the relative change in the sum of squared residuals between successive iteration steps is less than this value, the iteration stops. Defaults to 10^{-5}.
- `FIT_MAXITER`: Maximum number of iteration steps taken. If set to zero, the algorithm *only* stops on convergence. Defaults to 0.
- `FIT_START_LAMBDA` and `FIT_LAMBDA_FACTOR`: The Marquardt-Levenberg algorithm always attempts to take the largest possible step that will reduce chi-square. A numerical factor (usually called λ or "lambda") controls the size of the step taken and is itself modified by the algorithm as the iteration proceeds. `FIT_START_LAMBDA` is the initial value of lambda at the start of each iteration step; `FIT_LAMBDA_FACTOR` is the factor by which lambda itself is varied when searching for the optimal step size. Controlling these variables can help to achieve convergence in difficult situations.

After the iteration has converged (or has been interrupted), gnuplot sets several variables that can be read out to obtain the results of the fitting procedure:

- `FIT_CONVERGED`: A flag that equals 1 if the iteration converged, 0 if it was interrupted or exceeded the allowed number of steps.
- `FIT_NDF`: The number of degrees of freedom for this fit. It equals the number of data points, less the number of adjustable parameters and is usually denoted v ("nu"): $v = N - m$.
- `FIT_WSSR`: Weighted sum of squares residual, evaluated at the point that the iteration converged to: $\chi^2 = \Sigma_i^N (y_i - f(x_i; a_1, ..., a_m))^2 / \sigma_i^2$.
- `FIT_STDFIT`: sqrt(χ^2 / v).

Also keep in mind that the simplest and most effective way to influence the behavior of the fitting routines is to provide better starting values for the fit parameters. A reasonable selection of starting values will usually obviate the need to fiddle with the control parameters entirely.

OPTIONS AND ENVIRONMENT VARIABLES

Gnuplot writes information about each iteration step of the fitting process to the screen and simultaneously to a file called fit.log. This file is always appended to, so as not to overwrite previous results. The name of this log file can be changed through the option `set fit logfile`, which takes the desired filename as argument. Leaving the filename empty reverts back to the default convention.

A different default name for the log file can be set using the environment variable `FIT_LOG`, which is evaluated when gnuplot first starts up.

Finally, if we activated the option `set fit errorvariables`, then for each fitted parameter, the uncertainty in this parameter will be written to a new variable. This new variable will be named like the parameter, but with the extension _err appended (for example, the error of the fitted parameter a will be contained in a variable called a_err). This option is disabled using `set fit noerrorvariables`.

You can find more information regarding the `fit` command and some of its features not discussed here in the standard gnuplot reference documention.

PRACTICAL ADVICE

Nonlinear least-squares fitting is a pretty complex topic, with many subtle issues. If you want to get serious about it, you'll want to consult a good numerical analysis text, and a good statistics text as well. Here are just a few items of practical advice to get you started. You may also want to take a look at the gnuplot reference documention for further discussion and additional features.

Since the fitting algorithm is an iterative process, it's not guaranteed to converge. If the iteration doesn't converge, or converges to an obviously wrong solution, try to initialize the fitting parameters with better starting values. Unless the variables have been initialized explicitly, they'll be equal to zero, which is often a particularly bad starting value. In special situations, you may also want to try hand-tuning the iteration process itself by fiddling with values of `FIT_START_LAMBDA` and `FIT_LAMBDA_FACTOR`.

All fitting parameters should be of roughly equal scale. If some of the parameters differ wildly (by many orders of magnitude) from one another, the fitting function should be modified to take these factors into account explicitly. (Say, we want to fit $f(x; a, b) = a \cos(b\ x)$ and we know that a is close to 1,000, while b is close to 1; we could either divide the data by 1,000, or write the function as $f(x; a, b) = 1000\ a \cos(b\ x)$ instead.)

The iteration problem becomes mathematically badly conditioned if the fitting function contains several parameters that have similar effects on the behavior of the function. A blatant example is $f(x; a,b) = a \exp(x+b)$, which despite its appearance has only *one* adjustable parameter, since $a \exp(x+b) = (a \exp(b)) \exp(x) = c \exp(x)$. For more complicated models, this kind of cross-correlation may be hard to detect ahead of time.

The number of data points, less the number of adjustable parameters (that is, $N - m$), is known as the *number of degrees of freedom* of the fit, usually denoted v("nu"). The final value of χ^2 (the sum of the squares of the residuals) should be of the same order of magnitude as the number of degrees of freedom for a reasonably good fit.

If you find that the final χ^2 is significantly larger than v, although the fit "looks" good, you may have overestimated the uncertainty in the data points (the σ_i).

10.3.3 *Worked example*

Assume we have a data set like the one in figure 10.10. From other information about the source of the data (for instance the experimental setup), we have reason to believe that the data can be described by a harmonic oscillation:

$f(x; a, b, c, d) = a \, \cos(b \, x + c) + d$

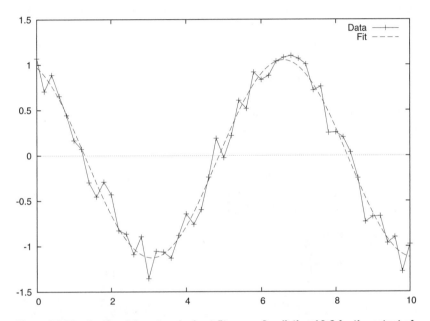

Figure 10.10 **A noisy data set and a best fit curve. See listing 10.8 for the output of the `fit` command.**

Although we have a fair number of data points (namely 51), the data covers only little more than one period of the oscillation, making it impossible to determine the frequency via correlogram analysis, for instance. Furthermore, no transformation of the fitting function suggests itself (inverting trigonometric functions is rarely useful). So a nonlinear fit seems like a reasonable approach, and indeed a fit:

```
fit a*cos(b*x+c)+d "data" u 1:2 via a,b,c,d
```

converges rapidly. The final output is shown in listing 10.8.

Listing 10.8 **The final output of the fit command for the data set shown in figure 10.10**

```
After 5 iterations the fit converged.
final sum of squares of residuals : 0.838001
rel. change during last iteration : -9.32605e-06
```

```
degrees of freedom      (FIT_NDF)                          : 47
rms of residuals        (FIT_STDFIT) = sqrt(WSSR/ndf)       : 0.133528
variance of residuals (reduced chisquare) = WSSR/ndf       : 0.0178298

Final set of parameters          Asymptotic Standard Error
=======================          ==========================

a               = 1.08898        +/- 0.02733      (2.509%)
b               = 0.894293       +/- 0.008294     (0.9274%)
c               = 0.384983       +/- 0.0473       (12.29%)
d               = -0.0368921     +/- 0.01961      (53.16%)
```

Although the fit *appears* quite good, the final χ^2 is *way* too small, suggesting that we overestimated the noise in the data. In fact, since we didn't specify a third column to the `fit` command, gnuplot silently assumed the uncertainty in the data to have an amplitude equal to +/-1 in each data point. Looking at the data (which varies only between -1 and +1 overall) clearly shows this to be wrong.

However, we only have this one data set. If we want to obtain at least an estimate for the amplitude of the noise, we'll have to extract it from the data. To do so, we look at the residuals between the data and the best-fit solution (see figure 10.11):

```
plot "data" u 1:($2 - (a*cos(b*$1+c)+d)) w linesp
```

Immediately we see that there doesn't seem to be a systematic drift in the residuals, giving further confidence in our model. From the graph, we can estimate the amplitude of the noise to be about 0.15. Using this to improve our fit, we try

```
fit a*cos(b*x+c)+d "data" u 1:2:(0.15) via a,b,c,d
```

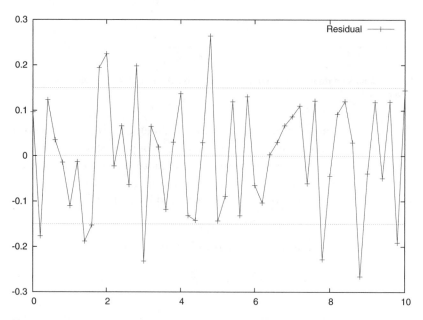

Figure 10.11 The residual between the data and the best fit. For the most part, the residual is bounded in the interval [-0.15:0.15]. See figure 10.10 and listing 10.8.

giving no change in the estimated values of the fitting parameters, but now resulting in a χ^2 of 37.2445.

We can find a "probability" that this model correctly describes the data by evaluating the χ^2 distribution for this value of χ^2 and the number of degrees of freedom. This distribution is tabulated, but we can use gnuplot's built-in `igamma` function to give us the result:[4]

```
print 1.0 - igamma( 0.5*47, 0.5*37.2445 )
```

which equals P = 0.845, suggesting a good fit.

Since the estimate for the constant offset d is small, we may wonder whether the offset might be exactly zero. So we eliminate d from the fitting function and run `fit` again:

```
fit a*cos(b*x+c) "data" u 1:2:(0.15) via a,b,c
```

Now, the final χ^2 equals 40.0481, giving rise to a value of P = 0.786. Still pretty good, but a little less so. What this tells us is that from the data alone, we can't conclusively deduce whether the offset vanishes, or is small but non-zero.

10.3.4 *Should you do it?*

Let me make a bold statement: whenever you find yourself reaching for a nonlinear fit, you're probably up to no good. Hold it—I said *probably*! Let me explain.

There are three reasons why you may find yourself wanting to perform a nonlinear fit:

- To estimate parameter values for an established model
- To find an analytical approximation to a data set
- To select a model from among a set of possible choices

Parameter estimation is a valid application of nonlinear fits, although easily overused. Before reaching for the fitting routine, we should at least have contemplated the following approaches:

- Do closed form solutions exist? Sometimes they do, even if the equations look forbidding. For example, imagine a data set x_i, $0 < i < N$ that we believe to be normally distributed, according to $\exp(-(x_i - m)^2)$. Naively, we may attempt a nonlinear fit here, but in reality, the value of m that will give the best fit is simply the mean of all the values: $m = (1/N)\Sigma_i\, x_i$.
- Can we transform the equation in such a way that it becomes linear? For example, let's assume that we suspect our data to follow a power-law with unknown exponent. Rather than fitting $f(x;a,n) = a\, x^n$, we can take logarithms on both sides, or (equivalently) plot the data on a double-log plot. If the power-law relation holds, the data will fall on a straight line and we can obtain the exponent from the slope of this line. (We showed an example in figure 1.4.)

---

[4] Check for instance *Numerical Recipes*, section 15.1 for more details on this.

- Even if no such a transformation is possible, can we identify and isolate the dominant behavior and perform a transformation to a linear form on that? For example, if we have a model such as $y = a \, \cos(b \, x))/x^n$, and want to determine the optimal value of the parameter n, we're probably much better off taking absolute values and plotting the results on a double-log plot, rather than starting out with a nonlinear fit (which, by the way, will have to be done for all three parameters a, b, and n, although we're only interested in one).

Also, keep in mind that your mathematical model may describe the dominant behavior over some region of the data set well, but may nevertheless be incorrect elsewhere. The fitting process, by contrast, attempts to minimize the χ^2 merit function globally. If the model isn't applicable over some part of the data set, the values obtained from the fit may be less accurate than if the fit had been constrained to only that part of the original data which can be described accurately by the model. You should therefore be careful to perform fits only on those parts of the data set for which the model is good. But how do you decide? This depends on how your data was generated and what you know about the approximations that went into the derivation of your model, among other things. Proceed with caution!

The second reason for attempting nonlinear fits (replacing a noisy data set with a simple analytic expression) looks innocuous enough, but can easily lead to pure evil. Two problems are likely to arise. First of all, it won't be long before it'll be conveniently forgotten that the simple analytical model that was assumed for the fitting procedure has no theoretical justification, and all kinds of unwarranted conclusions will be drawn from it (don't think it won't happen to you!). The second problem is that the fit loses information that can't be restored anymore. Say we think a third-order polynomial ($f(x) = a \, x^3 + b \, x^2 + c \, x + d$) is sufficient to represent the data well enough. But maybe we should really have used a higher-order polynomial. Or maybe an expansion in trigonometric functions. Or something else entirely.

When your goal is to make a noisy data set manageable by finding an analytic formula to describe it, I have three recommendations for you:

- If you want to evaluate the function at arbitrary points, you really are talking about a (much simpler) interpolation problem. You can use local two- or three-point interpolation formulas if the data is smooth, or something like a spline if it's noisy.

- If you want to represent the data, try an expansion in basis functions (orthogonal polynomials or trigonometric functions). This has a couple of advantages. The expansion coefficients can be found through explicit (noniterative) expressions, avoiding all problems of nonconvergence of an iteration. And furthermore, the expansion is a systematic process that can be pushed to any desired degree of accuracy by calculating higher and higher terms. At the same time, it gives you a built-in criterion for the goodness of the approximation: if the coefficients of subsequent terms are sufficiently small, the expansion can be truncated safely.

- Only if the data is close to linear (that is, it doesn't look like the data in figure 10.10) should you attempt a fit to a low-order polynomial. I'd caution strongly against representing more complicated looking data sets with intricate mathematical functions.

Finally, attempting to select one model from a set of candidates based purely on a nonlinear fit is simply exceptionally hard, and rarely all that conclusive. In particular, never blindly believe the numeric "goodness of fit" values calculated from the final residuals and the χ^2 distribution. Instead, plot the residuals and look for systematic deviations from zero: if there are any, that's a strong sign that your model is incomplete or just plain wrong. This is another reason why a transformation to a linear model (if one exists) is so powerful: deviations from linearity are much easier to spot than deviations from more complicated curves. If the transformed data falls on a straight line, that provides strong proof for the validity of the model implied by the transformation!

So, in summary: if you find yourself reaching for nonlinear fits, there are almost certainly better ways to achieve your purpose. They may require more work, but the added confidence in the results should be well worth the effort. As a final rule of thumb, I'd say this: don't do a nonlinear fit unless you've completed one of the alternative approaches. Once this has been done, a nonlinear fit can be a convenient way to speed up the process or to polish the values.

But only then.

10.4 *Summary*

In this chapter we looked at a variety of advanced techniques for specialized situations. It may well be that you'll never need any of them—but if you do, you'll be glad they're there!

First, we discussed gnuplot's multiplot mode, which allows us to combine several plots into a single graph. Typical applications are regular arrays of small graphs, placed next to each other for easy comparison, or insets of smaller graphs in a larger one to highlight details or special features.

Then we moved on to a number of topics of somewhat higher mathematical sophistication, such as parametric plots, non-Cartesian coordinates, and plots of vector fields.

In the final section, we discussed gnuplot's built-in facility to perform nonlinear fits in some detail, and I tried to give some recommendations on how to use it most appropriately.

In the next chapter, we'll learn all there is to know about gnuplot's ways of generating output: its `terminal` facility.

Terminals in depth

This chapter covers
- Exporting graphics using terminals
- Generating standard graphics file formats
- Generating print-quality output
- Customizing interactive terminals

Gnuplot supports more than 70 *terminals*: devices for which it can produce output. This may seem daunting, but the reality is that most of them are obsolete today—the number of terminals that are relevant is (thankfully) much smaller.

We can divide the currently used terminals broadly into three groups: terminals that produce output in a standard graphics file format (bitmaps: GIF, JPG, PNG; scalable vector graphics: SVG), terminals that produce output primarily for print (PostScript and PDF), and terminals for interactive use.

Terminal handling used to be a bit messy, but a lot of effort has been made to streamline the user interface in recent releases (version 4.2 and higher). Today, most terminals follow similar conventions and share a common set of options.

In this chapter, I'll first review the steps required to export plots to graphics file formats and make some additional suggestions on how this process can be improved (we touched on this briefly in chapter 2). I'll then describe the most commonly found terminal features by themselves. In the sections dealing with individual terminals, we can then concentrate on features specific to each terminal.

11.1 Exporting graphs to file

The `set terminal` command controls the type of the currently active output device, including all its options. As we've already seen in chapter 2, this necessitates a multistep process to export a graph to a file:

1 Preserve the current (interactive) terminal setting, using `set terminal push`.
2 Switch to the desired export terminal type, including all necessary options.
3 Set the output filename using `set output`.
4 Generate the plot using `plot` or `replot`.
5 Restore the previous (interactive) terminal with `set terminal pop`.
6 Direct output back to the interactive terminal using `set output` without a filename.

The pseudoterminals `terminal push` and `terminal pop` are very helpful in this context, because they preserve not only the type, but all selected settings for the interactive terminal.

We can greatly improve the efficiency of this process by combining all of these steps into a command script, such as the one in listing 2.3. In listing 11.1 I show you a slightly improved version, which not only exports the plot to a graphics file, but also saves the commands to a gnuplot command file at the same time.

Listing 11.1 An improved export script

```
save "$0.gp"       # Save commands to file
set t push         # Store current terminal settings
set t png $1       # Set terminal type to PNG, taking additional
                   #   options from second argument
set o "$0.png"     # Set output file name
replot             # Generate plot
set o              # Restore output to interactive terminal
set t pop          # Restore interactive terminal settings
```

We'd invoke this script using `call`, for example like this (export.gp is the filename of the script in listing 11.1):

```
call 'export.gp' 'myplot'
```

The script will append the appropriate file extensions (.gp or .png) to the base name supplied in the `call` command. As a bonus feature, this script can take an additional (second) argument, which is passed straight to the `set terminal` command. In this way, it's still possible to pass additional options to the export terminal, like so:

```
call 'export.gp' 'myplot' 'size 160,100'
```

This will result in a PNG image, which is much smaller than the default.

It should be clear from this example that this `call` macro trick is extremely versatile. For example, you might find it convenient to read the desired terminal type (such as PNG, PDF, or SVG) as an argument, rather than hard-coding in the script itself. You might want to supply default values for common terminal options. In section 12.2.4, we'll see further possibilities.

11.2   Common terminal options

Some settings exist for all terminals (although there may be small variations in syntax), and we summarize them here so that we don't have to repeat this information for each individual terminal.

11.2.1   Size

Remember when we talked about the `set size` command back in chapter 6? There, we made the distinction between the size of the *canvas* and the size of the *plot* on the canvas, and explained how to adjust the size of the plot using `set size`. Now it's time to talk about ways to set the size of the canvas.

Almost all terminals have a `size` option, which can be used to fix the size of the resulting canvas. (Some interactive terminals are exceptions to this rule, since for those terminals the size of the plot window is determined by the platform-dependent windowing system, and not under the control of gnuplot.) The size can be given in pixels (for bitmap terminals) or in inches or centimeters (for printable output, such as PostScript and PDF).

11.2.2   Fonts

Fonts aren't handled by gnuplot itself—instead, gnuplot relies on the capabilities of the output devices and their driver libraries. What gnuplot can do with fonts, therefore, depends not so much on gnuplot itself, but on the font-handling capabilities of the installed system libraries (and, of course, on the selection of installed fonts).

Most terminals allow you to declare a *default font*, usually using the `font` keyword. This font will be used for all text labels, unless explicitly overridden using the special commands available in enhanced mode (see the next section). The default font is also relevant, because the average size of its characters is used to define the `character` coordinate system, and because it is used to set the size of the graph's margins (see section 6.6.2). For variable-width fonts, gnuplot makes a best-effort attempt to determine the average character size, either by using the nominal font size in printer points (PostScript) or by sampling the size of a test string (libgd-based bitmap terminals).

Several terminals can use PostScript Type 1 or TrueType fonts, if the underlying libraries support them. Check the following sections on individual terminals for details.

11.2.3   Enhanced text mode

All contemporary terminals support *enhanced text mode*, which allows additional formatting options: mainly support for sub- and superscripts, and for font changes. (If a font name can't be resolved, gnuplot selects a standard font instead.) Changing the font makes it possible to use symbols in graph labels that aren't part of regular fonts: for example, the standard PostScript Symbol font includes Greek letters and many special math characters (see figures B.1 and B.2 in appendix B for a list of available symbols). Enhanced text mode is off for all terminals by default; we must explicitly enable it when choosing a terminal using the `enhanced` keyword.

In enhanced text mode, certain characters are used as control characters and influence the way text is formatted. Table 11.1 lists all special characters.

Table 11.1 Control characters for enhanced text mode

Control character	Example	Result	Description
{}			Grouping and scoping.
^	x^2	x^2	Superscript.
_	A_{ij}	A_{ij}	Subscript.
@	x@^s_i	x_i^s	Alignment of sub- and superscripts.
	x@_i^{-3/2}y	$x_i^{-3/2}y$	Put the shorter one *first*...
	x@^{-3/2}_iy	$x_i^{-3/2}y$	... rather than last.
~	~B/	₿	Overlay the two following characters or groups.
	~x{.6-}	$\bar{x}$	Overlay a – character on previous character, raised by 0.6 times the current character size.[a]
{/ }	{/Times Hello}	Hello	Change font.
{/Symbol }	{/Symbol abc}	αβχ	Use Symbol font.
{/= }	{/=20 A}	A	Select an absolute font size (size in printer points).
{/* }	{/*0.5 A}	A	Change font size relative to enclosing font.
	{/Symbol=24 G}	Γ	Font family and size selections can be combined.
&	[&{abc}]	[ ]	Space, corresponding to the length of the enclosed argument.
\NNN	\101	A	Select a symbol, using its octal code.
\			Escape special characters within *single* quoted strings.[b]
\\			Escape special characters within *double* quoted strings.[b]

a. Overlay operator doesn't nest inside PostScript terminals.
b. Not available for PostScript terminals.

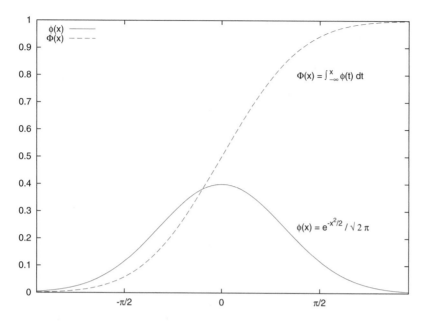

Figure 11.1 **Enhanced text mode. See listing 11.2.**

Curly braces ({...}) are used both to group several characters together and to limit the effect of a font declaration to the contents of the braces only. They can be left off for single-character sub- and superscripts.

Let's look at some examples of enhanced mode (see listing 11.2 and figure 11.1). Most of the commands should be clear; I only want to point out a few details. Enhanced mode can be used anywhere that gnuplot expects a string: in the example, we use it in the labels, for the x tics, and for the entries in the graph's key. The scope of a font selection can be limited using curly braces. We use this several times, for example in expressions such as {/Symbol f}(x), which prints the first character using the Symbol font, but the last three using the regular font.

A word of warning: enhanced mode works best for simple applications, such as sub- and superscripts, and simple font changes (mostly to get access to Greek letters and a few other special characters). But complicated, nested expressions may not always work out the way you expected them to, in particular when using one of the PostScript terminals (see the footnotes in table 11.1).

As part of the documentation that comes with the gnuplot distribution, you'll also find a document titled ps_guide.ps, which contains more information on enhanced mode.

Listing 11.2 Enhanced text mode example—see figure 11.1

```
set terminal ... enhanced    # Don't forget to turn on enhanced mode!
set label 1
➡    "{/Symbol f}(x) = e^{-x^2/2} / {/Symbol \326 2 p}" at 1.2,0.25
set label 2
```

```
➡    "{/Symbol F}(x) = {/Symbol \362 @_{-\245}}^x &{i} {/Symbol f}(t) dt"
➡    at 1.2,0.8

set key top left

unset xtics                      # Switch off default xtics
set xtics ( "{/Symbol p}/2" pi/2, "0" 0, "-{/Symbol p}/2" -pi/2 )

plot [-3:3] exp(-0.5*x**2)/sqrt(2*pi) t "{/Symbol f}(x)",
➡          norm(x) t "{/Symbol F}(x)"
```

11.2.4 *Miscellaneous appearance options*

Several of the terminals have options that can be used to influence the way graph elements are drawn.

Using rounded, line ends and joins of two lines are rounded off; using butt forces rectangular line ends and sharp angles where lines join. Both butt and rounded only make sense for line widths greater than one.

The solid keyword can be used to force all lines to be drawn solid. The opposite is dashed. These options are occasionally useful when switching between color and monochrome terminals. For example, interactive terminals (these days) are usually color terminals, so all lines are drawn with solid line styles and distinguished by their colors. When exporting a graph to a monochrome PostScript terminal, for instance, the colors are translated into different dash styles. Often, this is just what we want. But sometimes it leads to poor results, for example if our graph includes boxes filled with dash patterns (as in figure 5.7)—the boxes are distinguished by their different fill patterns, and we don't want the fill patterns themselves to be drawn with dashed lines. Using the solid option forces all lines to be drawn with solid lines, as desired.

Several terminals offer the possibility of scaling line widths globally using the linewidth option. Its argument is a floating-point number, which is used to scale all line widths used in the graphs. The dashlength option is similar: it can be used to control the length of dashes (for dashed line styles) globally.

11.2.5 *Flushing output channels*

Finally, a word of warning: don't assume that the gnuplot plot or replot commands will automatically flush their output buffers to file! This isn't a problem with bitmap terminals, but can lead to frustrating problems with file formats that can contain more than one graph in a single file (among them PostScript, PDF, and SVG). I've also encountered this sort of problem with terminals that generate output which requires postprocessing (for instance, by LaTeX).

In short, when the plot or replot command returns, the output files may still be incomplete and not yet ready to be used as input to other programs.

There's a simple remedy, though: the next set terminal or set output command is guaranteed to flush any open output buffers. Therefore, when generating (for example) PostScript files, issue a set output after each plot or replot command. Note that quitting gnuplot does *not* necessarily flush open files! (But set output always seems to work.)

11.3 *Standard graphics file formats*

Gnuplot can generate images in the most popular image file formats. In this section, we'll look first at bitmap formats (GIF, JPG, PNG), and then at the vector-oriented SVG format.

11.3.1 *Bitmaps*

All bitmap formats (GIF, JPG, PNG) are generated using Tom Boutell's libgd library, and therefore the options available depend on the capabilities of your local libgd version. You may also want to check the libgd documentation for further details (http://www.libgd.org).

All three terminal options take a common set of options, available for all formats, as well as options specific to the capabilities of each file format. The common options are

```
set terminal XXX [ size {int:x},{int:y} ] [ [no]crop ]
                 [ tiny | small | medium | large | giant ]
                 [ font [ {str:name} [ {int:size} ] ]
                      | [ "{str:path} [, {int:size} ]" ] ]
                 [ [no]enhanced ]
                 [ rounded | butt ]
                 [ {color0} {color1} {color2} ...]
```

Here, XXX stands for gif, jpeg, or png.

The size of the resulting image (in pixels) is controlled by the size directive, defaulting to 640 x 400 pixels. Unless set size has been set, gnuplot will size the actual plot (including margins, tic marks, and other decorations) to fill this image. Using the crop option, any white background margins around the image can be cropped to the smallest possible image size. A cropped image isn't scaled up to the specified size after cropping, resulting in an image of smaller size (in pixels) than requested by size. We'll see an example in listing 11.4 later in this chapter.

The GD library provides five basic named fonts (tiny: 5 x 8 pixels; small: 6 x 12 pixels; medium: 7 x 13 pixels [boldface]; large: 8 x 16 pixels; and giant: 9 x 15 pixels). These fonts can neither be scaled nor rotated around arbitrary angles.

Much better-looking results can be obtained if the GD library has been built with support for TrueType fonts. (Look for the option +GD_TTF in the output of show version long.) In this case, both TrueType (.ttf) and Adobe Type 1 (.pfa) fonts can be used.

The font directive takes either the name of a font file (without the extension), optionally followed by the desired font size, or full path name to the font file enclosed in quotes, possibly followed by the desired size after a comma (see listing 11.3). In the latter case, the filename must include the extension, while in the former case, it must not. In either case, the font specification is case sensitive. The set terminal command will print an error message if the desired font couldn't be found.

> **Listing 11.3 Two equivalent ways to specify the fonts to be used by the PNG terminal**

```
set t png font FreeSans 11
set t png font "/usr/share/fonts/truetype/FreeSans.ttf, 11"
```

If no explicit path to the font file is supplied, standard locations as well as the list of directories given by the GDFONTPATH environment variable are searched. (Note that gnuplot's fontpath option applies only to PostScript terminals and has no affect for bitmap images.) If no font is specified, gnuplot checks the GNUPLOT_DEFAULT_GDFONT environment variable for a font name or font file. The font size defaults to 12 point.

In any case, the selection of available fonts (and their installation location) depends on your local system, so it's difficult to make recommendations that are guaranteed to work everywhere. I've achieved good results with the TrueType font Free-Sans (at 11pt), which is a rather tight and compact sans serif font. It's part of the freefont project (http://www.gnu.org/software/freefont/) and should therefore be available to anyone. To use it, I use the following command:

```
set terminal png font "FreeSans,11"
```

Finally, a color map for the image can be given explicitly. The first color (color0) will be used for the background, the second color for the border, the third for the axes (when using set zeroaxis, for instance). All remaining colors are used for consecutive line types. The format for the color specification is *different* from the format used elsewhere by gnuplot. The required format here consists of a color specification as a hex string, preceded by the letter x, for example xFF0000 for red, and so on.

GIF

Since the expiration of the Unisys patent, libgd does generate GIF images. The options for the gif terminal are the common options given previously. In addition, it supports a transparent option, which makes the first (background) color transparent. Default is notransparent.

```
set terminal gif ...
                [ [no]transparent ] [ animate [delay {int:time}] ]
```

Animated GIFs can be created using animate. Subsequent plots sent to a terminal set up with set terminal gif animate are used as successive images in the animation. By default, the delay between images is 1/100 of a second. This delay can be changed using the delay option, which expects an integer argument, giving the desired delay in units of 1/100 of a second. The next set output or set terminal command terminates the animation sequence.

PNG

The PNG terminal supports the common options, as well as some options specific to the PNG image format:

```
set terminal png ...
                [ [no]transparent ] [ [no]interlace ]
                [ [no]truecolor ]
```

The transparent option is the same as for GIF (PNG alpha-channel support for partial transparency isn't supported by the gnuplot interface). The PNG image format supports interlacing, so that a partially received image is visible, albeit at reduced quality. Interlacing of the created image can be enabled using interlace; it's off by default.

Finally, PNG images can draw their colors either from a fixed-size palette or support *true-color* images with eight bits per red, green, and blue channel. By default, `truecolor` is disabled.

JPG

The JPG terminal supports all the common options, as well as the `interlace` option we just discussed in the context of the PNG terminal:

```
set terminal jpeg ...
               [ [no]interlace ]
```

EXAMPLE: CREATING THUMBNAILS

As a hands-on demonstration of some of the options we just introduced, let's assume that we want to generate thumbnail versions of our plots. They should be tiny, but still show the most dominant features of the plot. This is actually an interesting example, because it demonstrates some of the difficulties when generating output for specific purposes.

Let's assume we export the full plot to a PNG file of the standard size (640 x 400 pixels) and would like a thumbnail of size 64 x 40. If we scale text down correspondingly, the characters will be too small to read (in particular on the web, given the limited resolution of computer monitors). So we'll leave all textual information (tic marks and so forth) off.

Furthermore, we want to export a *cropped* image, since at 64 x 40 pixels, we don't have any room to waste on empty margins. But if we set the terminal to `set terminal png size 64,40 crop`, the final image file will end up being 24 x 13 pixels only—remember that the image size isn't scaled up when using `crop`.

We therefore have to add the margins onto the image size we specify in the `set terminal` command, to end up with an image of the desired size. The sequence of commands in listing 11.4 will do the trick.

Listing 11.4   Creating thumbnails: all non-essentials removed

```
unset xtics          # Switching off all textual information...
unset ytics
unset key
set terminal png size 104,67 crop
set output "thumb.png"
replot
```

The resulting image file is 64 x 40 pixels, exactly as desired.[1]

11.3.2 *SVG*

The SVG terminal generates images in scalable vector graphics format:

```
set terminal svg [ size {int:x},{int:y} [ fixed | dynamic ] ]
                 [ font "{str:name} [, {int:size} ]" ]
```

---

[1] The same effect can be achieved by setting all margins to a small number, such as `0.1`, and specifying the terminal without the `crop` feature. Note that you can't set the margin width to zero, because this will make the output routine fail. (This bug has been fixed in gnuplot version 4.3.)

```
[ fontfile "{str:filename}" ]
[ [no]enhanced ]
[ rounded|butt ] [ linewidth {flt:factor} ]
```

By default, gnuplot creates an image of 600 x 480 pixels with fixed size. Choosing the `dynamic` keyword leads to an image that can be dynamically resized by the application used to view the SVG file.

A font name and size (in points) can be specified (the defaults are Arial, 12pt). Note that the size specification must be part of the string argument giving the name of the font. Fonts aren't embedded into the SVG file, so the SVG viewer may replace a different font when rendering the image. It's also possible to embed a link to a font file in the SVG file, using the `fontfile` option. Gnuplot will search for this file in the directories pointed to by the GNUPLOT_FONTPATH environment variable.

The `linewidth` directive takes a floating-point argument: the width of all lines in the graph will be increased by the corresponding factor.

11.4   *Print-quality output*

Gnuplot has excellent support for generating print-quality graphs. Most of them are built on top of gnuplot's powerful PostScript terminal, which I am going to describe next. After that, we'll take a look at the rather symbiotic relationship between gnuplot and LaTeX: how to include PostScript graphs generated with gnuplot into a LaTeX document, and vice versa—how to include text typeset using LaTeX into a gnuplot graph.

11.4.1 *PostScript*

Gnuplot's PostScript terminal is very powerful, with many options that can be configured individually:

```
set terminal postscript [ landscape | portrait | eps ]
                        [ color | mono ] [ blacktext | colortext ]
                        [ simplex | duplex | defaultplex ]
                        [ size {flt:x}[in|cm], {flt:y}[in|cm] ]
                        [ [font] "{str:name}" [ {int:size} ] ]
                        [ [no]enhanced ]
                        [ solid | dashed ]
                        [ linewidth | lw {flt:factor} ]
                        [ dashlength | dl {flt:factor} ]
                        [ rounded | butt ]

set terminal postscript [ fontfile [add|delete] "{str:filename}"
                        | nofontfiles ]
```

The `landscape` and `portrait` options chose the orientation of the plot on the page. The default is `landscape`. If the image will be used inside some other document (for example, to illustrate a text document), instead of being sent directly to a printer by itself, we usually want to generate Encapsulated PostScript using the `eps` option.

The resulting graph may either use color (`color`) or be black and white (`mono` or monochrome—this is the default). We can force text to be black (`blacktext`), even in a graph using color. The opposite is `colortext`. By default, the PostScript terminal uses different dash patterns to distinguish between line types. When generating colored PostScript output, we may therefore want to use the `solid` option as well: the appearance of the graph will be clearer when all lines are drawn as solid and distinguished by their color alone.

Plots can be printed on only one side of the paper (`simplex`) or on both sides (`duplex`). Choosing `defaultplex` uses whatever the printer is set to. If the printer isn't capable of printing double-sided, this option is ignored. Of course, the `duplex` option only makes sense if there's more than one graph in the file.

The size of a PostScript image can be specified in either inches or centimeters (`in` or `cm`). The default size for raw PostScript is 10 x 7 inches; the default for EPS is 5 x 3.5 inches. The correct dimension of the bounding box for the chosen size is calculated correctly and written to the PostScript file.

We can specify a font by giving its name (such as Helvetica, Times, or Palatino) as a string argument. We can include the desired size of the font (in points) after the font name:

```
set terminal postscript "Helvetica" 12
```

This is now the default font. If enhanced text mode is enabled, we can select a different font for individual text elements, such as labels or key entries (see section 11.2.3).

For all fonts that we use in a PostScript plot, only the font name is embedded in the file, and the font isn't resolved until the document is rendered (printed or viewed). Font information must be available at that time. There are two ways we can guarantee a portable PostScript document. We can restrict ourselves to one of the 35 basic PostScript fonts, which are supported directly by all PostScript-capable devices. Alternatively, we can embed the font information necessary to render the font in the PostScript file itself, via the PostScript terminal's `fontfile` functionality.

The argument to `fontfile` is the name of a font file (*not* a font name), possibly including path information. Only a single file can be specified per invocation of `set terminal postscript fontfile`, but the command can be used repeatedly to add several font files to the PostScript document.

Gnuplot attempts to find the file in the directories listed on the gnuplot font path. The font path may either be set using the `set fontpath` command or via the `GNUPLOT_FONTPATH` environment variable. If neither is set, gnuplot looks for the file in the platform-dependent default locations. If the file is found, gnuplot will report both the name of the font contained in the file, as well as the file's absolute location:

```
set fontpath '/usr/share/fonts'
set terminal postscript fontfile 'Type1/1047013t.pfa'

Font file 'Type1/1047013t.pfa' contains the font 'LuxiMono'.
Location:
    /usr/share/fonts/Type1/1047013t.pfa
```

We need to specify the reported name of the font when we want to use it. For instance, *assuming enhanced text mode is enabled*, we can now say

```
set label "{/LuxiMono This is my text!}" at 0,0
```

We can use either PostScript Type 1 fonts or TrueType fonts. Gnuplot can handle ASCII-encoded Type 1 fonts (file extension .pfa) directly, but for binary-encoded Type 1 fonts (.pfb) or TrueType fonts (.ttf), gnuplot requires external helper programs. Check the standard gnuplot reference documentation or the special documentation on PostScript that's part of the standard gnuplot distribution if this is of relevance to you.

The PostScript terminal includes a PostScript prologue at the beginning of each PostScript file it generates. It expects to find a file containing the prologue in a standard location, or alternatively, in the directories specified by the environment variable GNUPLOT_PS_DIR. By pointing this variable to a directory containing your own version of the prologue file, it's possible to customize the resulting PostScript files. (The command `show version long` will display the current search path for prologue files.)

There's more information regarding gnuplot's PostScript capabilities in the gnuplot standard reference documentation and the psdoc directory in the gnuplot documentation tree.

11.4.2 *Using PostScript plots with LaTeX*

One very common use of PostScript graphs is to include them as illustrations in a LaTeX document. In this section, I give a couple of cookbook-style recipes. First, I describe how to include a regular PostScript file as an image in a LaTeX document. Then we discuss gnuplot's special `epslatex` terminal, which allows us to combine PostScript graphics with LaTeX text in the same illustration, so that we can use the full power of LaTeX for mathematical typesetting in gnuplot graphs.

INCLUDING AN EPS FILE IN A LaTeX DOCUMENT

If we want to include a PostScript file in another document, it's usually best to use an EPS (Encapsulated PostScript) file, rather than "raw" PostScript. Encapsulated PostScript contains some additional information regarding the size and location of the graph, which can be used by the embedding document to position the image properly.

As an example, let's assume we want to include the graph from figure 11.1 in a LaTeX document. We'd have to export the graph to EPS, using the following commands:

```
... # plot commands
set terminal postscript eps enhanced
set output 'enhanced.eps'
replot
```

There are different ways to import this PostScript file into a LaTeX document. Here, we use the `graphicx` package for this purpose. The LaTeX document is shown in listing 11.5.

> **Listing 11.5   A LaTeX document that imports enhanced.eps. See figure 11.2.**

```
\documentclass{article}
\usepackage{graphicx}

\begin{document}

\section{The First Section}
```

```
Here is a very short paragraph. The plot will be included
after this paragraph.

\begin{figure}[h]
  \begin{center}
    \includegraphics[width=10cm]{enhanced}
  \end{center}
  \caption{A Postscript file, included in \LaTeX}
\end{figure}

And here is a second paragraph. The graph should have
been included before.

\section{The Second Section}

The second section really contains only a very short
text.
\end{document}
```

The `graphicx` package provides the `\includegraphics` command, which takes the name of the graphics file to include as mandatory parameter. (The filename extension isn't required and it's recommended that you omit it.) The `\includegraphics` command takes a number of optional parameters as key/value pairs, which allow us to perform some useful operations on the image as it's included: we can trim, scale, and rotate it. Here, we adjust its size ever so slightly (from 5 inches down to 10 cm).[1] The final appearance of the document after processing it with LaTeX is shown in figure 11.2.

USING THE EPSLATEX TERMINAL

In the previous example, we included a PostScript file containing enhanced mode text in a LaTeX document. This seems inconvenient, to say the least: since LaTeX has such powerful capabilities to format text (and mathematical expressions specifically), we should find ways to use them to lay out our text, rather than dealing with the much more limited possibilities available through the enhanced text mode.

The `epslatex` terminal does exactly that: it splits a gnuplot graph into its graphical and its textual components. The graph is stored as EPS file, while the text is saved to a LaTeX file. We then include this LaTeX document, which in turn imports the PostScript file, into our LaTeX master file.

An example will make this more clear. Let's re-create the graph from figure 11.1, this time using LaTeX formatting commands instead of enhanced text mode (see listing 11.6—see listing 11.2 for a version of this graph using enhanced text mode).

> **Listing 11.6 Combining gnuplot and LaTeX using the `epslatex` terminal**

```
set label 1
➥ '$\phi(x) = \frac{1}{\sqrt{2 \pi}} e^{-\frac{1}{2} x^2}$'
➥ at 1.2,0.25
set label 2 '$\Phi(x) = \int_{-\infty}^x \phi(t) dt$' at 1.2,0.8

set key top left Left    # Interchange line sample and explanation
```

---

[1] There are many more options—check your favorite LaTeX reference for details. A good place to start is *Guide To LaTeX* (4th ed.) by H. Kopka and P. W. Daly, Addison-Wesley, 2004.

1   The First Section

Here is a very short paragraph. The plot will be included after this paragraph.

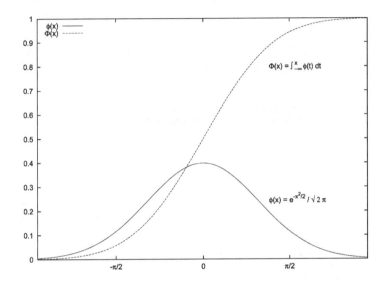

Figure 1: A Postscript file, included in LaTeX

And here is a second paragraph. The graph should have been included before.

2   The Second Section

The second section really contains only a very short text.

1

Figure 11.2   The final appearance of the LaTeX document shown in listing 11.5. Note the labels using enhanced text mode in the included gnuplot graph.

```
unset xtics
set xtics ( '$-\pi/2$' -pi/2, '$0$' 0, '$\pi/2$' pi/2 )

plot [-3:3] exp(-0.5*x**2) /sqrt(2*pi) t '$\phi(x)$',
➡          norm(x) t '$\Phi(x)$'

set terminal epslatex
set o "epslatex.tex"    # Name of output LaTeX file with extension!
replot
```

The text for labels and tic marks that we're adding to the graph now contains LaTeX directives. In particular, note the $...$, which indicate *math-mode* in LaTeX, and which are required for many of the special mathematical formatting commands.

The epslatex terminal generates *two* files: the actual graph (as EPS file) and the text (as LaTeX file). Gnuplot expects the full name (including extension) of the LaTeX file as output device when using the epslatex terminal (see the second-to-last line in listing 11.6).

Listing 11.7 A LaTeX document that imports epslatex.eps. See figure 11.3.

```
\documentclass{article}
\usepackage{graphicx}

\begin{document}

\section{The First Section}

This is a different document. We will include a \LaTeX\ file
containing the graph below.

\begin{figure}[h]
  \begin{center}
    \input{epslatex}
  \end{center}
  \caption{A Postscript file included in \LaTeX, with \LaTeX\ labels}
\end{figure}

And here is a second paragraph. The graph should have
been included before.

\section{The Second Section}

The second section really contains only a very short
text.

\end{document}
```

The LaTeX master file is shown in listing 11.7. Note how similar the document is to the one in listing 11.5. We again must explicitly require the graphicx package at the beginning of the document. We then use \input (instead of \includegraphics—that's the only difference) to include the LaTeX file written by gnuplot. Again, it's recommended to omit the extension—LaTeX will look for a file with .tex extension. The appearance of the final document (after LaTeX processing) is shown in figure 11.3.

1   The First Section

This is a different document. We will include a LATEX file containing the graph below.

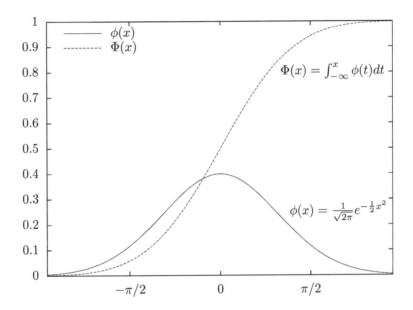

Figure 1: A Postscript file included in LATEX, with LATEX labels

And here is a second paragraph. The graph should have been included before.

2   The Second Section

The second section really contains only a very short text.

1

Figure 11.3   The final appearance of the LaTeX document shown in listing 11.7. Note the true LaTeX labels and tic marks on the graph. Also see figure 11.2.

Now that we've seen how the epslatex terminal is used, we can take a closer look at its features. The complete set of options is here:

```
set terminal epslatex [ standalone | input ]
                      [ header "{str:header}" | noheader ]
                      [ color | mono ] [ blacktext | colortext ]
                      [ size {flt:x}[in|cm], {flt:y}[in|cm] ]
                      [ [font] "{str:latexfont}" [ {int:size} ] ]
                      [ solid | dashed ]
                      [ linewidth | lw {flt:factor} ]
                      [ dashlength | dl {flt:factor} ]
                      [ rounded | butt ]
```

With two exceptions (more on them later), this is a strict subset of the syntax for the postscript terminal, but a few options that make no sense for epslatex (such as duplex) aren't available.

Two options are new (compared to the postscript terminal). If we select standalone, the generated LaTeX document is complete and can be compiled by itself. In other words, it doesn't have to be included into another LaTeX document for further processing. This way, we can create standalone graphics with LaTeX-style annotations.

In standalone mode, the name of the generated EPS file is modified by appending -inc to the base name: the two files written by epslatex would be called (for example) graph.tex and graph-inc.eps (so that the resulting graph, which combines both plot and text, can simply be called graph.eps). The default value for this option is input, which generates an incomplete LaTeX document for inclusion in a master file, as shown earlier.

The other new option is the header option. With it, an arbitrary set of LaTeX commands can be added into the LaTeX file containing the text component of the plot. We could use this, for instance like this:

```
set terminal epslatex header "\\bfseries"
```

to print all text within the plot as boldface.

If the file gnuplot.cfg is found by LaTeX when processing a standalone file, it's included into the preamble of the document. It's included *before* the argument to the header option, so the latter can be used to override global settings from the gnuplot.cfg file.

Finally, the font option changes its meaning for the epslatex terminal, compared to the postscript terminal. Instead of the names of PostScript fonts, epslatex obviously expects names for LaTeX fonts. The font description consists of three parts: the font name, the font series, and the font shape. All three parts are optional, but the commas are mandatory. Two quick examples:

```
set terminal epslatex "cmr,b,it" # ComputerModern, Bold, Italic
set terminal epslatex ",,sc"     # Surrounding font, with Small Caps
```

The size of the font can be given after the font description: set terminal epslatex "cmr" 14. Check your favorite LaTeX reference for more details.

FURTHER TRICKS WITH LaTeX AND GNUPLOT

Here's a great trick I learned from Toshihiko Kawano's excellent gnuplot page.[1] Imagine you have several PostScript plots that you want to combine into a single graph, so that individual plots become tiles in an array of graphs. If these are individual gnuplot plots, you could use `multiplot`, but what if some of the graphs are only available as PostScript files, or multiplot mode is unavailable or impractical for some reason?

The tabular effect can be achieved easily using the LaTeX `tabular` environment:

1 Make sure all the individual image files are properly trimmed EPS files.
2 Create a LaTeX document similar to the one in listing 11.8.
3 Process this document using LaTeX.
4 Use the `dvips` utility with the `-E` flag to turn the resulting DVI file into Encapsulated PostScript.

Done!

Listing 11.8 Bundling several PostScript images into an array using LaTeX

```
\documentclass{article}
\usepackage{graphicx}

\begin{document}

\pagestyle{empty} % Suppress page numbering

\begin{tabular}{cc}
  \includegraphics{img1} & \includegraphics{img2} \\
  \includegraphics{img3} & \includegraphics{img4}
\end{tabular}

\end{document}
```

This is just one example of combining gnuplot PostScript output with LaTeX. Further applications are possible. Just keep in mind that you must explicitly require the `color` package in your LaTeX files if you want to process colored PostScript graphics.

Also, don't forget that classic LaTeX can't generate PDF files directly (use `dvipdf` to translate DVI files to PDF). And vice versa, `pdflatex` can't process PostScript graphics files. Such files must usually be converted to PDF format before `pdflatex` is run.

Finally, let me remind you once more of the need to flush gnuplot output buffers explicitly when using the PostScript or `epslatex` terminals (see section 11.2.5).

11.4.3 PDF

Compared to its PostScript capabilities, gnuplot acquired support for PDF rather recently. The `pdf` terminal was added in gnuplot release 4.0. It relies on the `pdflib` library, which is a commercially developed product.

The current development version of gnuplot (version 4.3) contains a new PDF terminal `pdfcairo` based on the Cairo graphics library, which promises to be the best way to generate PDF output from within gnuplot. Check the standard gnuplot reference documentation or the gnuplot web site for updates.

---

[1] http://t16web.lanl.gov/Kawano/gnuplot/index-e.html

11.5 *Interactive terminals*

In contrast to the large range of options available for file-based terminals, interactive terminals are rather straightforward.

Gnuplot can have multiple plot windows open at any given time (on all platforms except Microsoft Windows), although only one of the windows will receive plot commands at any time. We can create a new plot window by specifying the terminal ID (which is just an integer expression) when choosing the terminal. To distinguish between multiple plot windows, we can give them a title, which will (depending on the window manager) be displayed in the window's header bar. (This is the title of the *window* only and has nothing to do with the title that can be placed on the plot using set title.) To switch between open windows, use set terminal together with the terminal ID to select the active terminal. The keyword close in a set terminal command will close the identified window. (Depending on the window manager, the window may persist until it has received mouse or keyboard focus for the first time after the set terminal ... close command has been issued.)

Plot windows are automatically raised and receive input focus when a new plot is drawn. This behavior can be disabled using the noraise option, so that keyboard focus stays with the command window even when a plot is issued. (I highly recommend this—it makes interactive work go surprisingly more smoothly. Unfortunately, for some of the terminals, the window won't be redrawn until it receives an event from the windowing system, making this option much less useful.)

When the persist option has been enabled, plot windows will stay up even when gnuplot is exited (or prevent gnuplot from terminating completely until all plot windows have been closed explicitly).

Three commands can be used to manipulate interactive terminals directly: raise, lower, and clear. The first two take an optional window identifier as optional argument. The clear command (which always acts on the most currently active terminal) is useful even for noninteractive terminals: it clears the plot area (and forces a form-feed or page break for noninteractive terminals). We've already encountered it in conjunction with multiplot mode (in section 10.1.2).

11.5.1 *wxt*

The wxt terminal is a relatively recent addition to gnuplot. It's based on the wxWidgets widget set and uses the Cairo and Pango libraries for graphics and text representation. Because wxWidgets and the other libraries are *cross-platform*, the wxt terminal promises the availability of a single interactive terminal for all three of the current operating systems.[1]

---

[1] The operational word here is *promise*. At the time of this writing, the wxt terminal doesn't work for Mac OS X. A project to make wxt available on the Mac is underway, but the problem proves hard and progress is slow.
   The wxt terminal does work for Windows, but you may have to search for prebuilt binaries with support for it (as of mid 2008, the "official" binaries distributed on the gnuplot home page are built without it). For example, the Windows port of the Octave project includes a version of gnuplot with support for wxt. You can download it from the Octave Forge web site, accessible through the Octave project's home page.

The wxt terminal is still classified as experimental by the gnuplot developer team, but it's arguably the best interactive terminal currently available (at least for the Linux/Unix platform). It creates very high-quality graphics (using anti-aliasing to avoid jagged edges on sloped lines, for instance) and provides some useful interactive menus. I recommend it highly!

```
set terminal wxt [ {int:winid} ] [ title "{str:title}" ]
                  [ [no]enhanced ]
                  [ font "{str:name} [,{int:size}]" ]
                  [ [no]persist ] [ [no]raise ] [ [no]ctrl ]

set terminal wxt {int:winid} close
```

The only option requiring explanation at this point is the ctrl option. Usually, a plot window can be closed using the q key and focus be directed back to the command window using the spacebar when the plot window is active. Setting the ctrl option binds these functions to the key combinations ctrl-q and ctrl-space, respectively, allowing other commands to be bound to the single keystrokes.

11.5.2 *x11*

The x11 terminal is gnuplot's classic Unix terminal for interactive use:

```
set terminal x11 [ {int:winid} ] [ title "{str:title}" ]
                  [ [no]enhanced ]
                  [ font "{str:fontspec}" ]
                  [ [no]persist ] [ [no]raise ] [ [no]ctrlq ]
                  [ solid | dashed ]

set terminal x11 [ {int:winid} ] close
```

See section 11.5.1 on the wxt terminal for the meaning of the ctrlq (or ctrl) option.

If gnuplot is used with the x11 terminal, it'll honor several standard X11 options and resources (such as geometry) given on the command line when gnuplot is first started. Check the standard gnuplot reference documentation if this is relevant to you.

11.5.3 *aqua*

The aqua terminal is a native Mac OS X terminal for gnuplot. It relies on Aqua-Term.app:

```
set terminal aqua [ {int:winid} ] [ title "{str:title}" ]
                   [ size {int:x} {int:y} ]
                   [ [no]enhanced ]
                   [ font "{str:name} [,{int:size}]" ]
                   [ solid | dashed ] [ dl {flt:dashlength} ]
```

It supports the standard options for interactive terminals.

11.5.4 *windows*

The windows terminal for use on Microsoft Windows platforms doesn't allow multiple plot windows to be open at the same time:

```
set terminal windows [ color | monochrome ]
                     [ [no]enhanced ]
                     [ font "{str:name} [,{int:size}]" ]
```

11.6   *Other terminals*

As mentioned in the introduction to this chapter, gnuplot supports a *lot* of terminals—many more than I discussed in this chapter. While most of them are no longer relevant, there are some that may be of use in specialized situations.

There are many more terminals that generate commands suitable for LaTeX processing than I described here. If you're interested, you might want to check out the standard gnuplot reference documentation for eepic, latex, pslatex, pstricks, texdraw, and tpic.

Besides LaTeX, gnuplot supports some other graphical command languages. Check out the fig, tgif, and gpic (for PIC processing) terminals.

Finally, a true classic: the dumb terminal (see figure 11.4). This is a terminal for character-oriented output devices. It uses characters to draw an ASCII-art rendition of the plot—useful when you want to run gnuplot remotely over a telnet connection. (Don't laugh—I've done that.)

For all of these terminals, see the standard gnuplot reference documentation.

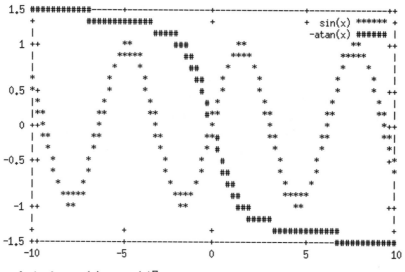

```
gnuplot> plot sin(x), -atan(x)
```

Figure 11.4   The dumb terminal

11.7 *Summary*

In this chapter, we studied all the different devices and file formats for which gnuplot can generate output. Although gnuplot supports some 70 different formats, only a few are really relevant today, and those can be grouped into three major groups:

- Standard graphic file formats: bitmap and SVG
- PostScript for print-quality output
- Interactive terminals for Linux/Unix, Windows, and Mac OS X

Most of the time, the defaults for terminal options are well chosen and don't require much customization. An exception is the enhanced text mode, which enables all kinds of additional formatting options for textual labels on the plot. Depending on the font selection on your local computer, you may also want to customize the default font for terminals, in particular for the bitmap terminals (GIF, PNG, JPG).

Finally, for those who are familiar with LaTeX, the `epslatex` terminal makes it possible to use LaTeX's text (and in particular, math) formatting capabilities together with gnuplot's plotting facilities to achieve particularly high-quality PostScript plots for publications or other printable documents.

Macros, scripting, and batch operations

12

This chapter covers

- Understanding strings and string macros
- Calling other programs from gnuplot
- Calling gnuplot from other programs
- Configuring your workspace
- Gnuplot for the web

In the preceding 11 chapters, we've studied almost every command or option that can be used from within gnuplot. But up to this point, our discussions always assumed that we'd be running gnuplot interactively: actually entering commands at the gnuplot prompt, viewing the plot on the screen, and then entering more commands.

But sometimes that's not what we want. For instance, we may have a large number of data sets and just want to convert all of them to plots using the same `plot` command. Or we may have a `cron` job running nightly to scan web server logs and want it to also generate some plots showing the number of hits per hour. Or we might want to use gnuplot as a *graphing engine* from within some other program, possibly even a web script.

In all these situations, we want to run gnuplot in the background, without human intervention. In this chapter, we study ways to do this, and also look at other things we can do with gnuplot that aren't primarily interactive: macros, configuration, and the ability to interact with other programs.

12.1 Strings and string macros

The string-handling capabilities that gnuplot acquired in release 4.2 make it possible to construct command lines programmatically in a number of ways.

First of all, anywhere a command expects a string, a *string expression* can be substituted as well. For instance, this will work just fine:

```
file = "data.txt"       # Assign string "data.txt" to variable
desc = "My Data"        # Assign description to a variable

plot file title desc    # Equivalent to:
                        #    plot "data.txt" title "My Data"
```

Functions that return a string can also be used. Here, we use a function to provide the file extension for us:

```
f( x ) = x . '.txt'
plot f( 'data' )        # Plots the contents of "data.txt"
```

The example is whimsical, of course, but it's easy to come up with more useful applications. The string functions (see chapter 4) will often be helpful in this context.

When we want to replace a part of a command line where gnuplot doesn't expect a string, we can't use a string variable (or string expression) directly. Instead, we must resort to a string *macro*. String macros let us insert the contents of string variables at arbitrary positions within a gnuplot command. Here's an example:

```
set macro                    # Turn macro expansion ON

cols  = "using 1:3"          # Assign a string variable
style = "with lines 3"       # Assign another one

plot "data" @cols @style     # Equivalent to:
                             #    plot "data" using 1:3 w lines 3
```

The symbol @ in front of a variable name indicates that the value of the variable should be interpolated into the command line at the current location. The command line is evaluated after all string macros have been expanded.

Be aware that gnuplot must have been compiled with macro expansion enabled (you can test this by running show version long—look for +MACROS), and macro processing must have been explicitly switched on using set macro within your gnuplot session. (It's off by default.)

We can play all kinds of games with string macros. In the previous example, we used it simply to avoid having to repeat the column specification. Obviously, we could do the same thing to define mnemonic names for custom styles. We can even define entirely new commands:

```
redblue =
➥ "set pm3d; set palette defined( 0 'blue', 1 'white', 2 'red' )"
```

Now it suffices to say

```
set macro

@redblue
splot cos(x)*sin(y)
```

Macros aren't evaluated within quotes (either single or double), but we can usually achieve the desired effect through simple string manipulations. This example shows both situations:

```
set macro

tool = "(made with gnuplot)"    # String variable

set title "My plot @tool"       # Macro expansion does not work...
set title "My plot " . tool     # but string concatenation is fine!
```

Only string *variables* are evaluated when prefixed with an @, but more general string *expressions* aren't. The return value from a string function must therefore always be assigned to a variable before it can be evaluated. Using such a two-step process, we can write string functions that are able to process arguments. For example, here we define a function that takes a filename and then prepares a command line consisting of all commands necessary to export a plot to the indicated file as PNG:

```
export( file ) =
➥ sprintf("set t push;set t png;set o '%s';replot;set o;set t pop",
➥ file );
```

We'd use it like this:

```
set macro

cmd = export( 'out.png' )    # setup
@cmd                         # evaluate
```

You might want to compare this version with the version we gave in section 2.2 earlier.

Macro expansion can provide convenience by allowing us to define and then reuse certain repetitive expressions. We may even want to predefine certain macros so that they're available whenever we start a gnuplot session. That's a topic we'll pick up again in section 12.5.

12.2 *Calling other programs from gnuplot*

Gnuplot can't do everything by itself; therefore it's sometimes helpful to execute an external program from within gnuplot. There are several ways to do this: we can spawn a subshell to execute commands in; we can evaluate an external command, capturing its output so that we can use it in the current the gnuplot session; and, finally, we can establish a direct interprocess-communication (IPC) channel between gnuplot and external programs using pipes (if available).

A word of warning: since all the material in this section is about interacting with the system *outside* of gnuplot, this material is necessarily somewhat platform dependent. In particular, section 12.2.3 only applies to Unix-based computers (including Linux and Mac OS X).

12.2.1 Executing a command in a subshell

We can simply execute a command in a subshell through the `system` command:

```
system "ls"                    # Shows directory contents
system "lpr -P laser plot.ps"  # Sends file 'plot.ps'
                               #     to printer 'laser'
```

Output of the subprocess is always directed to the interactive terminal.

Whereas the `system` command executes an external program in a subshell, the `shell` command suspends the current gnuplot session and starts an interactive shell. Quitting the shell (typically by typing `exit` or `Control-D`) resumes the gnuplot session. The `shell` command is somewhat of a legacy from days before windowing systems—today, we're more likely to pop up a shell in another terminal window, rather than suspending the process in the current window. But the command is there if we need it.

12.2.2 Capturing the output of a subprocess

Besides the `system` *command*, there is also a `system( "..." )` *function*. The latter takes a command as argument, executes it as a subprocess, and returns its output as a string (in contrast to the `system` command, which always directs any output from the subprocess to the interactive terminal). For example, if we wanted to capture the current date and time information in astring variable, we can use the `system()` function and the Unix `date` utility:

```
now = system( "date" )  # Capture timestamp in variable 'now'
set label now at 0,0    # Use variable for a label
```

The `system( "..." )` function is very versatile and can be used in some creative ways.

Let's assume that we have a bunch of log files with really opaque filenames, such as rL0Y20zC+Fzt72VPzMSk2A.vv-markim.log. The filenames themselves aren't helpful, but each file contains a header line with the calendar date of the day the log was taken, for example # 2007-11-01. We can now use the Unix `grep` facility to find the file containing the desired date:

```
file = system( "grep -l '2007-11-01' *" )
```

The `-l` (list) option forces `grep` to return only the name of any matching file, and the star operator (`*`) instructs the Unix shell to look in all files in the current directory for matches. We can take this a step further, because we can use the `system()` function wherever gnuplot expects a string. Therefore, we can use it in place of the filename as part of the `plot` command directly, like so:

```
plot system( "grep -l '2007-11-01' *" ) u 1:2 w lp
```

This example should give you an idea of the kinds of things you can do with the `system()` function.

There's another (older) way to execute a subprocess and capture its output that's occasionally still useful—namely, to execute a command via *back ticks*.

Back ticks or back quotes (decimal ASCII code 96—typically bound to the leftmost key in the top row on the keyboard) may be familiar from Perl and some Unix shells. The command in back quotes is executed, and its output replaces the back-quoted text (including the back quotes). Back quote substitution can be used anywhere, except inside of single-quoted strings.

In general, the `system()` function is more versatile than back ticks, and the preferred way to capture output from a subprocess. But back ticks have the advantage that they can occur inside of double-quoted strings, whereas the output from the `system()` function would have to be concatenated explicitly to the string. In other words, the following two commands are equivalent:

```
set label 1 "Today: `date`" at 0,0
set label 2 "Today: " . system( "date" ) at 0,1
```

For simple string substitutions such as these, back ticks can be a convenient shorthand. For more complicated operations, the `system()` function is the better choice.

12.2.3 *Input/output redirection (Unix only)*

The following functionality is only available on platforms supporting the `popen()` system call (all Unix and Unix-derived operating systems, but not Windows).

All gnuplot commands expecting a filename as argument can also take the name of a process, preceded by either < (for input) or | (for output). For example, instead of reading from a file, we can read from a *process*:

```
plot "< a.out"
```

Here, `a.out` is some command that writes data that we want to plot to standard output.

Equivalently, we can send output to a process via a pipe, instead of a file, for example to send a plot directly to a printer:

```
set terminal postscript
set output "| lpr -P laser"
```

The first version (input) is occasionally useful to apply an external filter to the data: for example, to sort the data before it is plotted:

```
plot "< sort data.txt"
```

But be aware that each invocation of a command spawns a separate subprocess. A command like `plot "< a.out" u 1:2, "< a.out" u 1:3` will run the `a.out` process twice. So if you want to grab multiple columns, it probably makes more sense to dump the results into a file first.

12.2.4 Example: watermarking plots

To conclude this section, let's look at an example that demonstrates some of the things we can do with the techniques we just learned.

Let's revisit the export macros that we first introduced in section 2.2 and extended in section 11.1. Now I'm going to show you a version that automatically includes a *watermark* at the bottom of each page, with the filename, the current username, and a timestamp (Unix only—sorry).

Listing 12.1 shows one possible implementation. Let's step through it:

1 First of all, save the current commands (*before* adding the timestamp) to file, so that the plot can be re-created later.

2 Generate the watermark and save it to a string variable called `watermark`. To create the watermark, we call the Unix commands `whoami` and `date` in back ticks. Their return values will be interpolated into the string.

3 Place the watermark on the plot. I give it the huge label ID `9999`, so as not to clobber any existing labels.

4 The watermark is placed into the bottom-left corner, using a very small font (6pt). Note the `screen` coordinates (see section 6.2), which we can use to indicate an absolute position for the label, independent of the plot range.

5 I increase the bottom margin to 3 character heights. The default in the absence of an `xlabel` (see section 6.3.3) is 2.

6 Now follow the same commands to change the terminal, plot to it, and restore it. This is familiar from section 2.2.

7 Finally, I restore the session by removing the watermark label and restoring the bottom margin to automatic sizing.

If we place these commands into a file called export.gp, then we could call it like this:

```
call "export.gp" "graph"
```

The resulting plot would be placed into a file called graph.png.

One caveat: if the size of the bottom margin has been changed from its default value, either explicitly through a `set bmargin` command or implicitly through a `set xlabel` command, this macro may lead to strange results, because this script can't detect such changes. Instead, it specifically requests a fixed margin size, clobbering any previous settings. Not the biggest problem in the world—just be aware!

Listing 12.1 Script to export a plot to a PNG file with a watermark

```
save "$0.gp"    # save the current commands to file w/o watermark

watermark = "File $0.png - Generated by `whoami` at `date`";
set label 9999 watermark at screen 0.02,0.02  font "FreeSans, 6"

set bmargin 3   # increase bottom margin to make room for watermark

set t push      # save the current terminal settings
set t png font "FreeSans, 11"  # change terminal to PNG,
                          #    choosing a decent font
```

```
set o "$0.png"   # set the output filename to the first option
replot           # repeat the most recent plot command
set o            # restore output to interactive mode
set t pop        # restore the terminal

watermark = ''   # revert to previous state...
unset label 9999
unset bmargin
```

Executing a subprocess from within a gnuplot session can be a convenient technique to get access to functionality that gnuplot itself doesn't offer. But now we're turning to the opposite task: calling gnuplot from a separate application, to provide graphing capabilities that the parent application itself doesn't possess.

12.3 *Calling gnuplot from other programs*

Up to this point, we've always assumed that we were running gnuplot *interactively*, with a human user entering commands at the gnuplot prompt. But sometimes it makes sense to run gnuplot as a background process to execute some well-defined, possibly repetitive task.

There are two ways that this can be done. We can run gnuplot unattended as a batch job, for example if we want to generate plots automatically for a large number of data files. Or we may want to use gnuplot's plotting capabilities to give graphics functionality to some other program. In this case, gnuplot serves as a graphing back-end or graphing engine and is controlled by some master program.

Given the way gnuplot is implemented, the latter is always a variation of the batch mode mentioned earlier. Therefore, this is what we need to understand first.

12.3.1 *Batch operations*

Running gnuplot in batch mode is straightforward: any files listed after the gnuplot command itself are expected to contain gnuplot commands. They're executed in the order specified, as if they had been loaded using load. (In the following, commands following a shell> are meant to have been entered at a *shell* prompt. Commands without a prefix are entered at the gnuplot prompt.)

The following three commands are all equivalent:

- Using command-line arguments:
    ```
    shell> gnuplot plot1.gp plot2.gp plot3.gp
    ```
- Reading from standard input:
    ```
    shell> cat plot1.gp plot2.gp plot3.gp | gnuplot
    ```
- From within a gnuplot session:
    ```
    load "plot1.gp"
    load "plot2.gp"
    load "plot3.gp"
    ```

Gnuplot doesn't start an interactive session when invoked with command-line arguments: it just processes all commands (including any plot commands) and terminates. This implies that *plots sent to an interactive terminal will usually not be visible*, or rather, they're visible for a tiny moment as gnuplot opens the terminal window, draws the graph, and immediately closes the plot window again and exits. It's a common mistake to forget to set appropriate (file-based) terminal and output options in gnuplot batch files!

We can force an interactive session by using the special filename - (hyphen) on the command line, for example after running a setup script. Upon terminating the interactive session, the commands in the teardown script will be executed:

```
shell> gnuplot setup.gp - teardown.gp
```

Batch files usually contain some options (such as set title, and so on), selection of terminal and output file, and a plot command. It's good form to end them with the reset command, which returns all options to their default values. (The only options not affected by reset are set output and set terminal, as well as set loadpath and set fontpath. See section 12.5 in this chapter for the latter two options.)

Another helpful technique when writing batch files (and even more so when calling gnuplot from other programs, as we'll see in a moment) is the use of the special filename - as part of the plot command (see 4.5.4). Remember: the command plot "-" tells gnuplot to read data from the current source; that is, from the same input device from which the most recent command was read. So if the command was read from a batch file, plot "-" will expect to find the data *in the batch file*, like so:

```
# Batch file bat1.gp
set t png
set o "out.png"
plot "-" u 1:2 w linesp
1 2
2 5
3 6
4 3
10 0
```

and we'd invoke it like this:

```
shell> gnuplot bat1.gp
```

Alternatively, if gnuplot read the commands from standard input, it expects to read the data from standard input as well:

```
shell> cat bat2.gp data.txt | gnuplot
```

Here, the file bat2.gp contains only commands; all the data is in file data.txt.

This latter technique shows how to use gnuplot from another program: pipe the commands to gnuplot, followed by the data to plot. Let's look at a few examples in the next section.

12.3.2 *Invoking gnuplot from other programs*

The methods in the preceding section work well if the data we want to plot already exists as files somewhere. But what if the data comes out of a calculation performed by a computer program or is contained in a database that needs to be queried? Do we have to write it to file and then invoke gnuplot on it?

The answer is no—if we're on a Unix or Unix-like system that allows *pipes*. In this case, we can pipe the data straight from the program that calculated or retrieved it directly into gnuplot. Listing 12.2 shows a simple way to do so in Perl; listing 12.3 shows a slightly more complicated one using Python. The main differences between these examples concern the way Perl and Python handle subprocesses and have little to do with gnuplot itself.

Listing 12.2   Calling gnuplot from a Perl program using a file handle

```
open PROC, "| /usr/bin/gnuplot "
  || die "Could not start gnuplot: $!";

print PROC "set xlabel 'Time'; set ylabel 'Amplitude';";

print PROC "set o 'graph.png';";
print PROC "set t png;";

print PROC "plot '-' u 1:2 t 'data' w l\n";

for( $x = 0.0; $x  <= 10.0; $x += 0.1 ) {
  $y = exp(-$x/5)*sin( $x );
  print PROC "$x $y\n";
}
print PROC "e\n";

close PROC;
```

Perl allows us to open a subprocess as a file handle—in the same way we'd open a file—provided the first character in the filename is a pipe symbol (|). We can then write anything to this file handle using print. In the first line of listing 12.2, we open gnuplot as a subprocess and assign it to the file handle PROC. We then proceed to write some gnuplot options to this file handle, including the essential terminal information and output filename, followed by the plot command. The plot command is told to read from the special file *dash* (-), which means that it expects the data to follow inline. The data stream is terminated by the single letter e, and then the file handle is closed, which terminates the gnuplot subprocess. If we forget to close the file handle explicitly, Perl won't terminate while gnuplot is still running!

Listing 12.3   Calling gnuplot from Python—note how we send *two* data sets to plot

```
import os
import math

gp = os.popen( '/usr/bin/gnuplot', 'w' )

gp.write( "set output 'graph.png'; set terminal png;" )
gp.write( "plot '-' u 1:2 w lines, '-' u 1:2 w lines\n" )

x = -5.0
while( x <= 5.0 ):
    gp.write( "%f %f\n" % ( x, math.sin(x) ) )
    x += 0.5
gp.write( "e\n" )
```

```
x = -5.0;
while( x <= 5.0 ):
    gp.write( "%f %f\n" % ( x, math.cos(x) ) )
    x += 0.5
gp.write( "e\n" )

gp.close()
```

In Python, we can use the popen() function in the os module to obtain a file-like object that represents the gnuplot subprocess. Make sure to open this object in *write mode*, by passing a 'w' as second argument to popen(). (Alternatively, we could've used the subprocess module, which is new in Python 2.4.)

In contrast to listing 12.2, in listing 12.3 we plot two data sets. Each must be terminated with an e on a line by itself.

Using gnuplot in such a way from another program works quite well, but can appear a bit fickle at first because we need to re-create exactly those conditions that are usually fulfilled by input coming from the interactive command-line environment. Diagnosing glitches in this area isn't helped by error messages, which are intended for interactive use. Here's a checklist of trouble spots to look for when things don't work out at first:

- Commands must be separated from one another by *explicit* semicolons or newlines. A common mistake is to write code like this (also see listing 12.2):

```
print PROC "set key";     # WRONG - missing newline or semicolon!
print PROC "set border";
```

  The two set commands *appear* to be broken down onto two separate lines, but gnuplot will see them as one consecutive string. This will work:

```
print PROC "set key\n";    # RIGHT - explicit newline
print PROC "set border";
```

  Instead of the newline, a semicolon could've been used as well.

- The line containing the plot command *must* be terminated by an explicit newline. Gnuplot doesn't parse the command line, and consequentially doesn't start waiting for data until it has encountered a newline.

- You *must* use an explicit using directive when using the special filename - to tell gnuplot how to parse the incoming data stream.

- For each occurrence of - in the plot command, there *must* be a separate data stream. Gnuplot will continue to interpret incoming characters as data until it has encountered a corresponding number of end-of-file characters.

- Don't forget to separate data lines from one another using newlines as well.

One final comment: when generating many graphs from the same program, it is usually a good idea to start gnuplot only once and use it for all of the graphs, rather than starting a separate gnuplot process for each of them. This doesn't matter much when preparing two or three graphs, but when the number of graphs is large, the time savings are significant. Just make sure to reset all relevant options (and specifically the output filename) between invocations of the plot command.

12.3.3 *Example: creating a font table*

Scripting can be used together with gnuplot for other purposes besides plotting data. In listing 12.4, a Perl script builds up a lengthy command line, consisting of labels that demonstrate every character in a character set, using two different fonts. (The resulting graphs can be found in figure B.1 and figure B.2 in appendix B.) This command line is then piped to gnuplot, which generates the desired PostScript output. Note that it's not necessary to call gnuplot as a subprocess: we could've dumped the command line to a file and then called gnuplot on it in batch mode: `gnuplot cmd.gp`.

In this example, gnuplot is used strictly as a PostScript generator: none of its data-handling and graphing capabilities are utilized. This technique of building up a lengthy and possibly complicated command line programmatically is a good trick, which is well worth remembering.

Listing 12.4   A Perl script that uses gnuplot as PostScript generator

```
$k = 32; # + 128;
for $i ( 0..3 ) {
  for $j ( 0..23 ) {
    ( $x, $y ) = ( 2*$i, 23-$j );
    $cmd .= sprintf("set label '%o' at %f,%f right;", $k, $x, $y);
    $cmd .= sprintf("set label '{\\%o}' at %f,%f;", $k, $x+0.3, $y);
    $cmd .= sprintf("set label '{/Symbol \\%o}' at %f,%f;",
                    $k, $x+0.8, $y);
    $k++;
  }
}

$cmd .= "unset border; unset xtics; unset ytics; unset key;";
$cmd .= "set t po eps enh font 'Helvetica' 20 size 4.9in,4.5in;";
$cmd .= "set o 'font-table1.eps';";
$cmd .= "plot [-.2:6.8][0:23] -1\n";

open PROC, "| /usr/bin/gnuplot" or die "Could not start gnuplot: $!";
print PROC $cmd;
close PROC;
```

12.4 *Slideshows with pause and reread*

As we've seen, when gnuplot reads its commands from a batch file, it usually doesn't enter into an interactive session, immediately closing any interactive terminal windows after completing a plot. But using the `pause` command, we can force interactive terminals to persist until either a fixed length of time has gone by or a user event (such as a mouse click) has occurred. The `pause` command takes the number of seconds to wait (-1 will wait until a carriage return is encountered) and an optional string argument, which will be printed to the command window:

```
pause {int:seconds} [ "{str:message}" ]
```

Another command that's frequently useful in this context is `reread`. The `reread` command instructs gnuplot to begin executing the current batch file from the beginning, basically resulting in an infinite loop. (We'll see in a minute how to stop it.)

Why is this useful? Imagine you have a program that performs some long-running calculation. Every 30 seconds, the program appends its results to an output file and you want to watch the data in this file as it accumulates. Using pause and reread, this is now easy. We write a batch file along the following lines:

```
plot "data" u 1:2 w l
pause 30
reread
```

Now all we have to do is to load this file, and gnuplot will refresh the plot periodically.

There's a second form of the pause command that waits until a specific user event has occurred:

```
pause mouse [ {eventmask} ] [ "{str:message}" ]
```

The event mask can contain any combination of the following keywords, separated by commas: keypress, button1, button2, button3, and any. If pause was terminated through a keyboard event, the ASCII value of the selected key will be stored in the gnuplot variable MOUSE_KEY and the corresponding character in the variable MOUSE_CHAR. If a mouse event occurred, the mouse coordinates will be stored in the variables MOUSE_X, MOUSE_Y or MOUSE_X2, MOUSE_Y2, respectively, and available for further processing.

The pause command is also useful when using gnuplot as the graphing engine for some other program: it forces output to be generated for the interactive terminal. Listing 12.5 shows one possible application. The Perl script in the example uses gnuplot as a graphing backend. After each graph is drawn, gnuplot waits, using pause mouse keypress, until a keyboard event has occurred in the active plot window, at which point the program redraws the graph with different parameters.

Listing 12.5   Using gnuplot from Perl while capturing user input with pause mouse

```
open PROC, "| /usr/bin/gnuplot" or die "Could not start process: $!";

print PROC "set o; set t wxt; set o;\n";
print PROC "set bmargin 3;\n";
print PROC "set label 'Press key (not Space!) to continue' ",
           "at screen 0.02,0.02 tc rgb 'red'\n";

for $a ( 1..20 ) {
  print STDERR "$a\n";
  print PROC "plot '-' u 1:2 w linesp;\n";
  for $x ( -10..10 ) {
    print PROC "$x ", sin($a*$x), "\n";
  }
  print PROC "e\n";
  print PROC "pause mouse keypress\n";
}
close PROC;
```

There are some additional commands that are useful in this context. I'll only mention the if command which allows conditional execution. The if command together with a counter can be used to terminate an otherwise infinite `reread` loop. Check the standard gnuplot reference documentation for further details.

12.5   Configuring your workspace

On startup, gnuplot reads a number of environment variables if they're defined. They're described in table 12.1.

Gnuplot also attempts to read a startup file, called .gnuplot on Unix (and Mac OS) and GNUPLOT.INI on Windows. Gnuplot searches for this file first in the current directory, then in the home directory (as defined by the corresponding environment variable). Once a file has been located, searching doesn't continue. The file is executed (using `load`) before any other files or commands are read from the command line, standard input, or an interactive terminal. In general, settings in the initialization file override environment variables.

Table 12.1   The environment variables that gnuplot reads on startup. Unless otherwise specified, the variables have the same name on all platforms.

Name (Unix and Mac OS X) ▶ Name (Windows, if different)	Description
GNUTERM	The name of the terminal to be used. (Compare the `set terminal` command.)
GNUHELP	The path to the online help file gnuplot.gih.
GNUPLOT_LIB	Additional directories to be searched for data and command files. (Compare the `loadpath` variable.)[a]
GDFONTPATH and GNUPLOT_DEFAULT_GDFONT	Search path used by terminals based on the GD library (PNG, GIF, and JPG) to locate font files, and a default font to be used with these terminals, respectively.
GNUPLOT_FONTPATH	Search path used by the PostScript terminal to locate font files. (Compare gnuplot's `fontpath` variable.)[a]
GNUPLOT_PS_DIR	Used by the PostScript terminal to locate custom prologue files.
FIT_SCRIPT and FIT_LOG	Name of a file to execute when gnuplot's `fit` (discussed in section 10.3) command is interrupted, and the name of the log file maintained by `fit`, respectively.
HOME ▶ GNUPLOT and USERPROFILE	The directory to search for a .gnuplot initialization script if none is found in the current directory.
PAGER ▶ n/a	The name of pager program to use.
SHELL ▶ COMSPEC	The name of the shell to spawn in response to the gnuplot `shell` command.

a. Path entries are separated from one another using a colon (:) on Unix, and a semicolon (;) on Windows.

The initialization file can be used to customize your gnuplot environment. Listing 12.6 shows what an initialization file might look like.

Most of the entries should be clear. Two features we haven't yet seen are the `set loadpath` and `set fontpath` options. Both can be used to specify additional search paths that will be examined by gnuplot whenever appropriate. The `loadpath` will be searched for command files (read by `load` and `call`) *and* for data files (as read by `plot` and `splot`). The `fontpath` is used by the PostScript terminal to locate additional font files. Note that the bitmap terminals which are based on the GD library do *not* examine `fontpath`. Use the GDFONTPATH environment variable for these terminals!

Path entries on both `loadpath` and `fontpath` are separated from each other using a platform-dependent separator: the colon (`:`) on Unix and Mac OS, and the semicolon (`;`) on Windows.

Many of the entries in listing 12.6 either add some basic functionality not provided out of the box by gnuplot (such as a function for the logarithm to an arbitrary base: `logb( x, base )`) or set up my personal preferences where I find the default settings unsatisfactory (for example, `set isosamples 30` and `set hidden3d`). An interesting application is the selection of a better default font for bitmap terminals: the terminals remember their `font` attribute, so that the call `set terminal png` implies my preferred font selection as well.

The entries regarding arrow styles are intended as examples of the kinds of things you might want to explore if you have a recurring need: I define two custom arrow styles that I can now simply refer to when placing an arrow on the graph. To facilitate this, I invent symbolic names for the styles, so that I can now refer to them by their descriptive names, rather than having to memorize which style had index 1 and which index 2. Instead, I can simply (and clearly) say (as is short for `arrowstyle`):

```
set arrow from 0,0 to 2,0.5 as @scale
```

I need to use gnuplot's new macro functionality here, because gnuplot won't accept a variable (containing an integer value) as argument to `arrowstyle`. But the detour through the string expressions that's evaluated when encountered works quite well.

The last entries define custom keyboard and mouse bindings. That's a new topic (we mentioned it briefly before in section 4.5.3), and we'll devote the entire next section to it.

Listing 12.6 A personalized .gnuplot initialization file

```
# Path to my personal library of gnuplot snippets
set loadpath "/home/janert/lib/gnuplot"

# Turn on macro expansion
set macro

# Define some useful constants and functions
e     = 2.7182818284590452354
euler = 0.5772156649015328606

log2(x)       = log(x)/log(2.0)
```

```
logb(x, base) = log(x)/log(base)

# Adjust sample quality
set samples 300

set isosamples 30
set hidden3d

# Set a default font for GD based terminals
set terminal png font FreeSans 11
set terminal gif font FreeSans 11
set terminal jpeg font FreeSans 11

# Select my preferred interactive terminal
set terminal wxt

# Custom arrow styles
scale = '1'      # Symbolic names for styles!
diamond = '2'

set style arrow 1 heads size screen 0.0075, 90
set style arrow 2 head size screen 0.02, 15, 165 filled

# Palettes
falsecolor = "set pm3d; set view map; set size square;
➡ unset surface; set isosamples 100"
gray = "set palette model RGB defined ( 0 'black', 1 'white' )"
bluered =
➡ "set palette model RGB defined ( 0 'blue', 1 'white', 2 'red' )"

# Mouse and Key Bindings

# 1) Toggle logarithmic axes
is_log_x = 0;
is_log_y = 0;

bind 'y' "if(is_log_y) is_log_y=0; unset logsc y; replot;
➡ else is_log_y=1; set logsc y; replot";
bind 'x' "if(is_log_x) is_log_x=0; unset logsc x; replot;
➡ else is_log_x=1; set logsc x; replot";

# 2) Place arrows using the mouse
bind ">" "call 'arrow1.plt'";
```

12.5.1 *Creating custom hot key bindings*

The bind command is used to bind gnuplot commands to specific keystrokes. These commands will be executed if the corresponding keyboard event takes place while the *plot* window has keyboard focus. They don't apply when the command window has focus.

```
bind
bind!
bind [allwindows] "{str:keys}" "{str:command}"
```

The bind command has several formats. If it's used without any arguments, it reports all currently effective key bindings. Appending an exclamation point to the command name restores the default key bindings.

Custom bindings can be registered by passing two arguments to the `bind` command: the first is the key (possibly in combination with one or several of the control keys); the second is the command to be executed. Quotes aren't strictly necessary if either the key or the command consists of a single token. It's possible to bind commands to special keys—see listing 12.7 for the symbolic names of some function keys you might want to know, and the standard gnuplot reference documentation for the `bind` command for the complete list. If the optional `allwindows` option has been given, the binding applies to all plot windows, active or not.

Listing 12.7   Symbolic names of some of the function keys available

```
# Control keys:
ctrl
alt

# On main key block:
"Tab"   "Escape"   "Return"

# On arrow-block:
"Home"   "End"    "PageUp"    "PageDown"
"Left"   "Up"    "Down"    "Right"

# Function keys:
"F1" ... "F12"
```

Here are two quick examples. The first binds the `replot` command to the R key (that is, the `Shift-r` combination), the second places an arrow and a label on the plot in response to the key combination `Control-a` (that is, a lowercase *a*):

```
bind R "replot"
bind "ctrl-a" "set arrow from 0,0 to 1,1;
➥ set label 'northeast' at 1,1; replot"
```

When mousing is active (using `set mouse`), clicking into a plot window will set several variables in your current gnuplot session (see table 12.2). These variables can be accessed in the commands bound to keys using `bind`.

Table 12.2   These variables are set whenever a mouse or keyboard event occurs when a plot window is active, provided that mousing has been enabled using `set mouse`.

Variable name	Description
MOUSE_X	x coordinate at the time of the mouse event (measured in `first` coordinate system)
MOUSE_Y	y coordinate (in `first` coordinate system)
MOUSE_X2	x coordinate (measured in `second` coordinate system)
MOUSE_Y2	y coordinate (in `second` coordinate system)
MOUSE_BUTTON	ID of the mouse button clicked (1, 2, or 3)
MOUSE_SHIFT	Nonzero if the `Shift` key was pressed when the event occurred

Table 12.2 These variables are set whenever a mouse or keyboard event occurs when a plot window is active, provided that mousing has been enabled using `set mouse`. *(continued)*

Variable name	Description
MOUSE_CTRL	Nonzero if the `Control` key was pressed when the event occurred
MOUSE_ALT	Nonzero if the `Alt` (`Meta`) key was pressed when the event occurred
MOUSE_KEY	ASCII code of the key that was pressed
MOUSE_CHAR	The character value of the key that was pressed
MOUSE_KEY_WINDOW	ID of the plot window that received the event

The last two entries in listing 12.6 should give you some idea of how the `bind` command can be used to create additional interactive functionality within gnuplot.

The first of these shows a way to toggle some setting using `bind`—in this case, toggling the logarithmic scaling for either the x or the y axis. Since we can't read out the value of a gnuplot option (such as `set logscale`) programmatically, we have to introduce a *variable* (`is_log_x` in this example) to keep track of the current value of the toggle switch. The actual switching between the states is performed through the `if` statement. The action is bound to a key, so that pressing the key while a plot window has keyboard focus will trigger the action.

This works well; the only problem occurs if we interchange toggling using the hot key and using the `set logsc` command. Since the latter won't update the `is_log_x` variable, the two methods can get out of step. Hitting the hot key twice will bring everything back in sync.

The second example is more involved and demonstrates how we can combine the `bind` command, mouse variables, and external command scripts to create our own gnuplot "commands."

I want to be able to place arrows using *only the mouse*. Gnuplot doesn't provide built-in support for this. What can I do?

First I use the `bind` command so that pressing the selected hot key (which is >, because it looks like an arrow) will load and execute a first command file, which is called arrow1.plt. The contents of this file is shown in listing 12.8. You can see that this file, when loaded, will wait for mouse input (using `pause mouse`), prompting the user appropriately. If the user clicks the left mouse button, it saves the coordinates of the mouse pointer at the time of the click and loads a second external command file, called arrow2.plt, which is shown in listing 12.9. When the second file is executed, it waits for the user to select the endpoint coordinates of the arrow, again using the mouse, and creates the arrow using the newly entered endpoint and the saved start point coordinates from the previous step. If the user doesn't click the left mouse button at either step, the command sequence terminates.

Although both these examples are quite useful by themselves, my main intention here is to give you some pointers for your own development of custom key bindings, commands, and macros. Have lots of fun!

Listing 12.8   The contents of the file arrow1.plt—see listing 12.6

```
pause mouse any "\n      Start point (Button-1) ? "
if( MOUSE_BUTTON == 1 ) my_x = MOUSE_X; my_y = MOUSE_Y;
⇒                       print "From ", my_x,my_y; call 'arrow2.plt';
⇒ else print "Never mind...";
```

Listing 12.9   The contents of the file arrow2.plt—see listing 12.6

```
pause mouse any "     End point (Button-1) ?   "
if( MOUSE_BUTTON == 1 ) print "To   ", MOUSE_X,MOUSE_Y;
⇒                       set arrow from my_x,my_y to MOUSE_X,MOUSE_Y;
⇒                       replot;
⇒ else print "Never mind...";
```

12.6   Gnuplot for the web

As a final application of gnuplot scripting, let's see how we can use gnuplot to draw dynamic graphics for inclusion in web pages. (This section assumes basic familiarity with CGI programming and HTTP.)

The simple (but not necessarily wrong) approach would be to let gnuplot generate whatever graphics are required and write them to file. A web page can then include a tag linking to this file. If there's any chance that the same graph will be requested several times, this would probably be the right way to go about it. In contrast, if the graph will never be needed again, we now have the problem of having to clean up the graphics files that get generated every time a user visits our site. Can't we make do without ever writing anything to disk?

We can, and I'll show you two different ways to do so, depending on your circumstances.

12.6.1   Using Gnuplot as a CGI script

The first version I'd like to show you is a variation of the batch processing we encountered in section 12.3.1. The principle is simple: what if the gnuplot batch file were called as a CGI script?

Listing 12.10 shows a simple web page, including an <img> tag. Look closely at the src attribute of this tag: the attribute doesn't point to an image file, but to a command script that will generate the required graph on the fly.

Listing 12.10   The web page (HTML file) that references a dynamically generated image

```
<html>
  <head></head>

  <body>

    <h1>Our Page</h1>
    <img src="graph.cgi">

  </body>
</html>
```

Listing 12.11 shows the contents of the command file graph.cgi, which is nothing more than a gnuplot batch file. It couldn't be any simpler.

Listing 12.11   A gnuplot batch file that can be used as a CGI script

```
#!/usr/bin/gnuplot

set t png
set o

set print '-'
print "Content-Type: image/png\n"

plot "data.txt" u 1:2 w linesp
```

Let's step through the command file:

1   In the first line, we tell the system which command interpreter to use for this file—in our case, it happens to be gnuplot.

2   We set the terminal type (PNG) and then direct output to standard output. According to the CGI spec, the web server will return the output of the CGI script to the requesting client (typically, a web browser).

3   Set the output channel for text to standard output as well, using the special file-name *dash* (-) (see section 4.4.1).

4   Print the header line containing the MIME type of the following message body, as required by the HTTP spec. Note the single newline terminating the header line: gnuplot's `print` command will add another one, so that the header is separated from the body of the response by a line containing only a newline—again, as required by the HTTP spec. (We are cheating here a little bit: according to the HTTP spec, line breaks should be indicated using the CR-LF character combination. Nevertheless, this script will work for most modern web servers and browsers.)

5   Finally, the `plot` command, showing the contents of some data file in the desired way.

This method (though cheeky) works well if we don't need to parse any input data sent from the client. I can imagine a situation where we know exactly what data to display; we just want to make sure that the most recent version of the data is used.

Two points to remember:

- Make sure the command file has the executable bit set.
- Depending on your local web server configuration, this script must be placed into a special directory (such as cgi-bin) or must have a certain extension (such as .cgi). Check with your local system administrator.

Next, let's look at the more general case.

12.6.2 *Using gnuplot as a subprocess to a CGI script*

While the previous example was an application of the batch processing model of section 12.3.1, in this section we apply the subprocess approach of section 12.3.2 to the web.

We can reuse the HTML file from listing 12.10, but use a different CGI file (see listing 12.12). The CGI file is straightforward—we use the standard CGI Perl module, which gives us access to any input parameters that may have been specified as part of the URL. Then we call gnuplot as a subprocess, using the PROC file handle to access it. In contrast to listing 12.2, we direct gnuplot's output to standard output (set o), so that the web server will send it along to the client. Everything else should be familiar from the examples we've seen before.

Listing 12.12 Using gnuplot as a subprocess from a Perl CGI script

```perl
#!/usr/bin/perl

use CGI;

$q = new CGI;

# Possibly do something interesting with input parameters...
# ....

print $q->header( 'image/png' );

open PROC, "| /usr/bin/gnuplot" or die "Cannot start gnuplot: $!";

print PROC "set t png; set o;";
print PROC "plot '-' u 1:2 w linesp\n";

for( $x=0; $x<=10; $x+=0.1 ) {
    $y = $x*sin($x);
    print PROC "$x $y\n";
}
print PROC "e\n";

close PROC;
```

12.7   Summary

This long chapter concludes our introduction to gnuplot proper. Although gnuplot doesn't provide a full-blown programming environment, it plays well with programs written in other languages, and can be customized and extended in various ways.

Specifically, we've discussed the following features:

- Gnuplot's new macro facility allows gnuplot to evaluate string expressions. This makes it possible to parameterize even those parts of a command where a string variable can't be used. To use it, macro evaluation has to be turned on explicitly using set macro, and string expressions to be evaluated as macros must be prefixed using the @ character.
- The defaults for many options can be changed through startup customization. Gnuplot reads a set of environment variables at startup and also processes the

contents of a startup file (if found), which can be used to set up personal preferences, adjust to the local installation environment, and to introduce useful extensions to the basic gnuplot functionality.

- There are different ways to call other programs from within gnuplot. They differ mostly in how output from these auxiliary programs is handled: the `system` command directs output to the command window, while back ticks return the output of the subprocess as a string. On platforms supporting it, interprocess communications via pipes is available.

- Although we think of gnuplot primarily as an interactive plotting environment, it's possible to run it entirely in the background as a batch job. Gnuplot reads files containing gnuplot either from the command line or from standard input.

- Since gnuplot can read commands and (inline) data from standard input, it can be used in command-line pipelines. When called from other programs, IPC via pipes is a convenient way to use gnuplot as graphing engine for programs written in other programming languages.

- Limited functionality exists to customize how users interact with generated interactive graphics. We can bind commands to specific keys and capture certain kinds of mouse input.

- Gnuplot can be used to serve up dynamically generated images from a web server. If we don't need to process individual, dynamic user input, it's sufficient to use an appropriate gnuplot batch file as server-side script. Using a wrapper in a general-purpose programming language, which employs gnuplot as graphing engine, gives us much greater flexibility.

Now that we know *how* to use gnuplot, I want to spend some time discussing *what* can be done with it. This is what the next (and last) part of this book is about: applications of graphical analysis. Stay tuned.

Part 4

Graphical Analysis with Gnuplot

We can now take gnuplot for granted and discuss how it can be used to solve problems using graphical methods.

Chapter 13 discusses different kinds of plots and their uses. It also explains how to produce them with gnuplot.

Chapter 14 turns its attention away from the tools and towards the problems we are trying to solve. It explains how to understand data with graphs, emphasizing practices such as iteration and transformation, as well as various housekeeping tasks.

Chapter 15 is a reminder that the purpose of any analysis is to arrive at a set of correct conclusions.

Fundamental graphical methods

13

This chapter covers
- Investigating relationships
- Representing counting statistics
- Visualizing ranked data
- Exploring multivariate data

In this chapter and the next, I want to shift my attention: I'll now largely take gnuplot for granted, and concentrate on *applying* it to problems. Nevertheless, whenever appropriate, I'll take the opportunity to show you how a certain effect can be achieved with gnuplot. In this chapter I want to talk more generally about different graphical methods and the kinds of problems they're applicable to. In the next chapter, I'm going to take a number of different problems and walk you through the different steps that the analysis may take. If you will, this chapter introduces *la technique*, while the next chapter explains *la méthode* (with a nod to Jacques Pépin).

When faced with a new data set, there are two questions that usually dominate. The first one is, how does one quantity depend on some other quantity—how does y vary with x? The second question (for data sets that include some form of statistical noise) asks, how is some quantity distributed—what's the character of its randomness? We'll look at graphical methods suitable for either question in the next two sections. In the last two sections of this chapter, I'll discuss two particularly challenging problems: ranked data, and methods applicable to large, unstructured, multivariate data sets.

13.1   Relationships

For many data sets, we're interested in the question of whether one quantity depends on another, and if so, how: does y grow as x grows, or does it fall, or does y not depend on x to begin with?

13.1.1   Scatter plots

A *scatter plot* is the first step in finding the answer. In a scatter plot, we just show unconnected symbols, located at the position given by x and y. It's an easy way to get a feeling for an otherwise unknown data set.

AN EXAMPLE: CAR DATA

Listing 13.1 shows the first few lines from a sample data set, containing 26 attributes for 205 different car models that were imported into the US in 1985.[1] The 14th column gives the curb-weight in pounds, and the last (26th) column the price (in 1985 dollars). We can use a scatter plot as in figure 13.1 to see how weight varies as a function of price.

In this case, the input file isn't whitespace separated, but comma separated. Instead of transforming the input file to space separated, it's more convenient to use gnuplot's `set datafile separator` option to plot this data file:

```
set datafile separator ","
plot "imports-85.data" u 26:14
```

Listing 13.1   A few lines from the Automobile data set (truncated)—see figure 13.1

```
1,158,audi,gas,turbo,four,sedan,fwd,front,105.80,192.70,71.40,55.90,...
0,?,audi,gas,turbo,two,hatchback,4wd,front,99.50,178.20,67.90,52.00,...
2,192,bmw,gas,std,two,sedan,rwd,front,101.20,176.80,64.80,54.30,2395...
0,192,bmw,gas,std,four,sedan,rwd,front,101.20,176.80,64.80,54.30,239...
0,188,bmw,gas,std,two,sedan,rwd,front,101.20,176.80,64.80,54.30,2710...
...
```

We can clearly see that weight goes up as the price increases, which is reasonable. We should also note that there are many more low-price/low-weight cars than heavy, premium vehicles. For budget cars, weight seems to increase in step (linearly) with price for a while, but for higher-priced vehicles, the gain in weight levels off. This observation may have a simple explanation: the price of mass market vehicles is largely

---

[1] This example comes from the "Automobile" data set, available from the UCI Machine Learning Repository: Asuncion, A. and Newman, D.J. (2007). UCI Machine Learning Repository [http://www.ics.uci.edu/~mlearn/MLRepository.html]. Irvine, CA: University of California, School of Information and Computer Science.

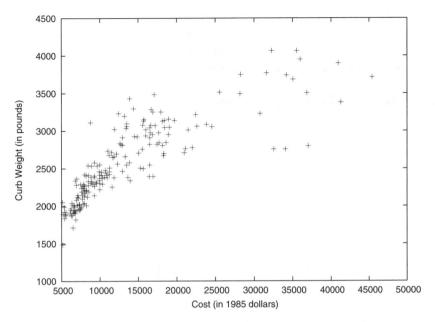

Figure 13.1   Curb weight versus price for 205 different cars. See listing 13.1.

determined by the cost of materials, so that a car that's twice as big (as measured by its overall mass) is also twice as expensive, whereas the price of luxury cars is determined by higher quality (fancier materials such as leather seats, and additional options such as more electronics), rather than by sheer bulk.

It's tempting to try to find a mathematical model to describe this behavior, but the truth of the matter is that there's not enough data here to come to an unambiguous conclusion. Various functions of the form $a\,(x\text{-}b)^{1/n} + c$ or even $a\log(x\text{-}b) + c$ fit the data about equally well, but the data alone doesn't allow us to determine which one would be the "correct" model.

USING SCATTER PLOTS

This example demonstrates what to look for when examining a scatter plot. The first question usually concerns the nature of the relationship between x and y. Does y fall as x grows or vice versa? Do the points fall approximately onto a straight line or not? Is there an oscillatory component? Whatever it is, take note of it.

The second question concerns the strength of the relationship, or, put another way, the amount of noise in the data. Do the data points jump around unpredictably as you go from one x value to the next? Are there outliers that seem to behave differently than the majority of the points? Detecting outliers is important: gone unnoticed, they'll mess up most statistical quantities (such as the mean) you may want to calculate later. And sometimes outliers indicate an interesting effect—maybe some subgroup of points follows different rules than the majority. Outliers in scatter plots should never go uninvestigated.

A third aspect to look out for in a scatter plot is the distribution of points in either dimension. Are points distributed rather uniformly, or do they cluster in a few locations? If so, do we understand the reason for the clustering, or is this something we need to investigate further? There may be a lot of information even in a humble scatter plot!

A MORE COMPLICATED EXAMPLE: THE 1970 DRAFT LOTTERY

Be warned that correlations aren't always trivial to detect. Figure 13.2 shows a famous data set, which I'll explain in a minute. But first, what do you think: is there a correlation between x and y?

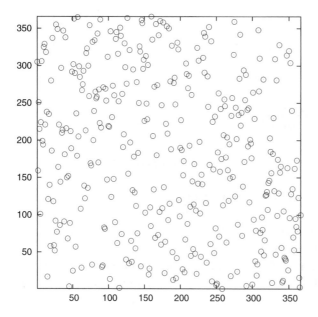

Figure 13.2 Is there any correlation between x and y in this data?

Here's the story behind the data: during the Vietnam war, men in the US were drafted into the armed forces based on their birth dates. Each possible birth date was assigned a *draft number* from 1 to 366, and men were drafted in order of their draft numbers. To ensure fairness, draft numbers were assigned to birth dates using a lottery process. Yet, allegations quickly arose that the lottery was biased, such that men born later in the year had a higher chance of being drafted early.

Figure 13.2 shows the draft numbers (as they'd been assigned by the lottery process) as a function of the birth dates. If the lottery had been fair, there should be no detectable pattern in the data.

Figure 13.3 shows the same data, but this time together with two interpolation curves, drawn using `plot ... smooth`. The curves clearly slope downward, indicating that there's a trend in the data: the later in the year the birth date falls, the lower (on average) the draft number. It was later found that the procedure used in the lottery process to mix entries was insufficient to achieve true randomness. In

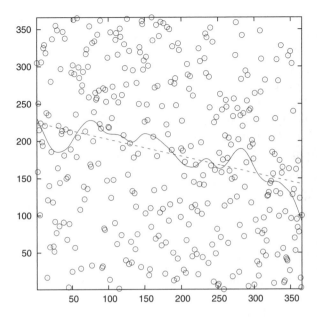

Figure 13.3 The 1970 draft lottery. Birth date (as day after Jan 01st) on the horizontal axis, draft number on the vertical axis. The lines are weighted spline approximations, with different weights. The data is the same as in figure 13.2.

later draft lotteries, this process was improved and the lottery produced truly random results.[2]

Using an interpolating line as in figure 13.3 can be a useful tool to discover otherwise invisible behavior when the input data is very noisy. It's often useful when the "stiffness" of the interpolating line can be varied continuously: If the line is very soft, it'll follow all the bumps in the data; if it's too stiff, if may flatten out relevant features in the data set. Iteration, visual inspection, and judgment are critical. In the figure, I've used gnuplot's `smooth acsplines` weighted spline feature, with two different weights: 10^{-4} for the wobbly line and 10^{-15} for the straight line (`plot "data" using 1:2:(1e-4) smooth acsplines`). The smaller the weight, the less each individual data point influences the local shape of the curve. Therefore, as the weight goes to zero, the approximation becomes increasingly global, just showing the overall trend. For more information on using locally smooth approximations to detect features and trends in data, you might want to check out the *Lowess* (or *Loess*) family of algorithms. Cleveland's books mentioned in appendix C are a good starting point.

A NOTE ON SPLINES

Splines are a way to provide a smooth approximation to a set of points. The points are called *knots*.[3]

---

[2] The 1970 draft lottery is a famous example in statistical analysis and has been analyzed in many places, for example in the introductory textbook *Introduction to the Practice of Statistics* by D. S. Moore and G. P. McCabe. The description of the lottery process can be found in *The Statistical Exorcist* by M. Hollander and F. Proschan and is well worth reading. The raw data can be found in StatLib's Data and Story Library at http://lib.stat.cmu.edu/DASL/Stories/DraftLottery.html.

[3] I'd like to thank Lucas Hart for helpful correspondence regarding this topic.

Splines are constructed from piece-wise polynomial functions, which are joined together in a smooth fashion. In the case of *interpolating* splines, the resulting curve is forced to pass *exactly* through all knots; in the case of *smoothing* or *approximating* splines, the resulting curve will in general *not* pass through the individual knots. Because in the latter case the curve doesn't have to pass through any points exactly, it can be less wiggly.

Both interpolating and approximating splines must fulfill the same smoothness conditions, but in addition, the approximating spline must strike a balance between the following two conditions:

- Passing close to the knots
- Not being too wiggly

These conditions are expressed in the following functional, which is minimized by the approximating spline *s(x)*:

$$J[s] = \int (s'')^2 \, dx + \Sigma_i^N \, w_i \, (\, s(x_i) - y_i \,)^2$$

where (x_i, y_i) are the coordinates of the knots, the w_i are the weights attached to each knot, and the prime indicates a derivative with respect to x. In this functional, the first term is large if $s(x)$ is wiggly, and the second term is large if $s(x)$ doesn't pass close to the knot points. (The form of the first term comes from a physical analogy: if the spline were made out of a real material, such as a thin strip of wood or metal, the first term would be related to the total bending energy of the strip.)

The balance between these two terms is controlled through the weight parameters w_i: if the w_i are small, the first term dominates, and the resulting spline approaches a straight line (which happens to coincide with the least-squares linear regression line for the set of knots). If the weights are large, the second term dominates and the spline approaches the interpolating spline (which passes exactly through all knots).

Another way to think about the weights is to write $w_i = 1/d_i^2$, where d_i is a measure for the uncertainty in the data of point i (such as the standard deviation in this point). We'd expect that the spline will pass through the interval $[y_i-d_i, y_i+d_i]$ at x_i. The higher our confidence in one point, the smaller we can choose this interval, and therefore the larger the weight w_i will be. By choosing $d_i = 0$ for one of the points, we can even force the curve to pass through this point exactly, although we can let the spline float more freely for the other points. Although we may choose different weights for each point, we can also use the same weight for all points, if we know all points to the same accuracy. This is what was done for all examples in this book.

One important remark: the way $J[s]$ is written in our example, the size of the second term depends on the number of knots—if you double the number of knots, the size of the second term will be (approximately) twice as large. By contrast, the first term does *not* depend on the number of knots. If the number of knots grows, the second term will therefore become larger relative to the first one, and the resulting spline will be more wiggly.

To maintain the original balance between wigglyness and closeness of approximation, the weights must be increased accordingly for data sets containing a larger number of points. Equivalently, you might want to take the number of points into account explicitly by writing $w_i = u_i/N$, where u_i is the actual weight and N is the number of knots. With this choice for w_i, the balance between both terms will be maintained regardless of the number of knots in the data set. [4]

SCATTER PLOTS WITH LABELS: CAR DATA, AGAIN

We can add an additional dimension to a scatter plot by using gnuplot's `with labels` style. Let's come back to the car data from listing 13.1. The data set contains many more attributes than just weight and price. Column 4, for instance, gives the type of fuel used: gas or diesel. We want to include this information in our graph. Maybe diesel-powered vehicles tend to be heavier at a given price point?

We could split the data set apart (using external text-editing tools) into one set containing all diesel engines and one containing all others, and then plot these two data sets using different plot symbols. For a presentation graph, that's exactly what we should be doing, but while we're still experimenting, that's awfully inconvenient. Instead, we'll use the information in the column itself as part of the graph.

We could simply use the value of the fourth column as plotting symbol: `plot "imports-85.data" u 26:14:4 w labels`, but there are too many records in the data set so that the strings would start overlapping each other badly. So instead, we just make the diesel cars stand out more (see figure 13.4), using gnuplot's string functions:

```
plot "imports-85.data" u 26:14,
⮕  "" u 26:14:(stringcolumn(4) ne 'gas' ? 'D' : '') w labels
```

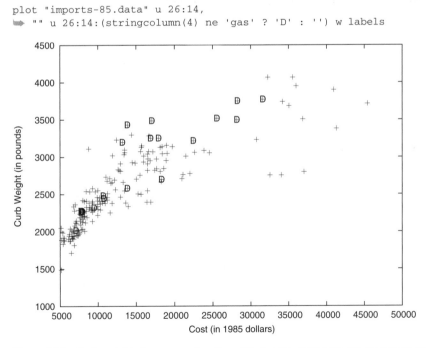

Figure 13.4   Curb weight of cars as a function of their price. Cars with diesel engines are indicated with the letter *D*. Note the distribution of diesel engines relative to gas-powered cars.

---

[4] More information on splines can be found in chapter 1 of *Handbook on Splines for the User* by E. V. Shikin and A. I. Plis (CRC Press, 1995).

The `stringcolumn(4)` function returns the value of column 4 *as a string*, which is then compared to the standard fuel (namely "gas"). Only if the fuel isn't regular gasoline, a text label ("D" for diesel) is placed onto the graph in addition to the usual plot symbol.

And, yes, overall diesel-powered vehicles seem to be slightly on the heavy side. We should also take note that diesel is most prevalent in the mid-price sector: there are a few cheap diesels, but none of the true luxury cars use it.

13.1.2 *Logarithmic scales*

Logarithmic scales are one of the most versatile tools in the graphical analyst's toolbox. I introduced them already in section 3.6.1 and discussed how they work. Now let's put them into action.

Logarithmic scales serve three purposes when plotting:

- They rein in large variations in the data.
- They turn multiplicative deviations into additive ones.
- They reveal exponential and power-law behavior.

To understand the meaning of the first two items, let's study the daily traffic pattern at a web site. Figure 13.5 shows the number of hits per day over approximately three months. There's tremendous variation in the data, with alternating periods of high and low traffic. During periods of high traffic, daily hit counts may reach close to half a million hits, but then fall to very little traffic shortly thereafter. On the scale of the graph, the periods of low traffic seem barely different from zero, with little fluctuation.

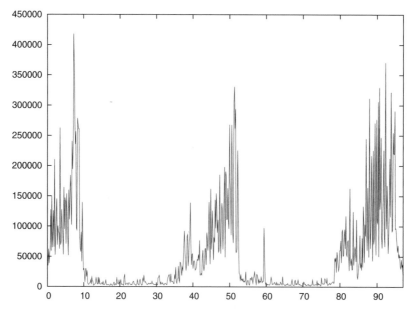

Figure 13.5   Traffic patterns at some web site. Daily hit count versus day of the year. Note the extreme variation in traffic over time.

In figure 13.6 we see the same data, but now on a semi-logarithmic scale. The logarithmic scale helps to dampen the extreme variation of the original data set (two orders of magnitude), so that we can now see the structure both during the high- and the low-traffic season. That's the first effect of logarithmic plots: they help to make data spanning extreme ranges visible, by suppressing high-value outliers and enhancing low-value background.

Furthermore, we can see that the *relative* size of the day-to-day fluctuations is about equal during both phases. The absolute size of the fluctuations is quite different, but their size as a percentage of the average value is roughly the same (very approximately, during low season, traffic varies between 2,000 and 20,000 hits a day, a factor of 10; whereas during high season it varies between 30,000 and 300,000 hits a day, again a factor of 10). That's the second effect of logarithmic plots: they turn multiplicative variations into additive ones.

Figure 13.7 tries to demonstrate the last point in a different way. The bottom panel shows the web traffic on consecutive days (like figure 13.5), displaying great seasonal variance, but the top panel shows the ratio of the difference in traffic on consecutive days divided by the actual value—*(current day - previous day)/current day*—which does *not* exhibit a seasonal pattern: further proof that the daily fluctuation, viewed as a percentage of the overall traffic, is constant throughout.

Finally, let's look at a curious example that brings together two benefits of logarithmic plots: the ability to display and compare data of very different magnitude, and the ability to turn power-law behavior into straight lines.

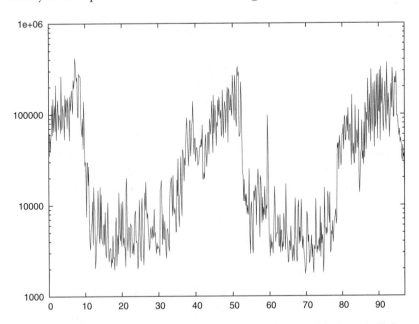

Figure 13.6   The same data as in figure 13.5, but on a semi-logarithmic scale. Note how the high-traffic outliers have been suppressed and the low-traffic background has been enhanced. In this presentation, data spanning two orders of magnitude can be compared easily.

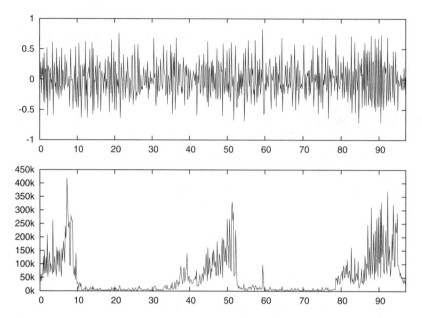

Figure 13.7   Bottom panel: hits per day over time (as in figure 13.5); top panel: change in traffic between consecutive days, divided by the total traffic. Note how the relative change (top panel) doesn't exhibit any seasonal pattern, indicating that the relative size of the variation is constant.

Mammals come in all shapes and sizes, from tiny rodents (the smallest known land mammal is the Pygmy Shrew, which weighs only a few grams, but some bats found in Thailand are apparently smaller still) to the largest of whales (weighing several hundreds of tons). It's a curious empirical fact that there seem to be fixed relationships between different metabolic quantities—basically, the larger an animal is, the slower its bodily functions progress. Figure 13.8 shows an example: the duration (in seconds) of a single resting heartbeat, as a function of the typical body mass. The regularity of the data is remarkable—spanning *eight orders of magnitude* for the mass of the animal. What's even more amazing is how well the data is represented by the simple function $T \sim m^{1/4}$. This law isn't limited to the examples shown in the graph: if you added further animals to the list, they'd also fall close to the straight line (I didn't just pick the best ones).

The existence of such scaling relations in biological systems has been known for a long time and seems to hold generally. For example, it turns out that the typical lifetime of a mammal also obeys a quarter-power scaling law relation against the body mass, leading to the surprising conclusion that the total number of heartbeats in the life of a single organism is fixed—no matter what the typical resting heart rate is. (In case you care, the number comes out to about 1.5 billion heartbeats during a typical lifetime.)

Recently these observations have been explained in terms of the geometrical constraints that must exist in the vascular networks (the veins and arteries), which supply nutrients to all parts of the organism.[5] As it turns out, you can derive the quarter-power scaling laws starting from only three simple assumptions, namely that the support network must be a space-filling fractal, reaching all parts of the organism; that the terminal capillaries where nutrients are actually exchanged are the same size in all animals; and finally that organisms have evolved in such a way that the energy required for the transport of nutrients through their bodies is minimized. I think it's amazing how such a powerful result can be derived from such simple assumptions, but on the other hand, we shouldn't be surprised: generally applicable laws (such as the quarter-power scaling in this example) must stem from very fundamental assumptions disregarding any specifics.

Let's come back to figure 13.8. The double-logarithmic scales make it possible to follow the data over eight orders of magnitude. (Had we used linear scales, all animals except for the whale would be squished against the left side of the graph—literally crushed by the whale.) So again, logarithmic scales can help to deal with data spanning a wide range of values. In addition, the double-logarithmic plot turns the power law relationship $T \sim m^{1/4}$ into a straight line and makes it possible to read off the exponent from the slope of the line. I explained how this works in detail in section 3.6.1 and won't repeat it here.

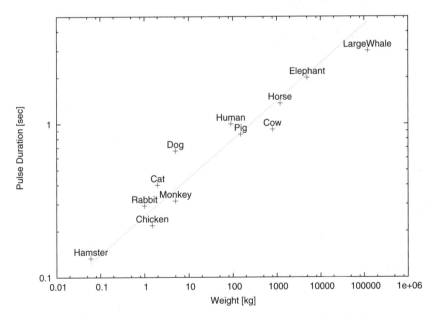

Figure 13.8 Allometric scaling: the duration of a average resting heartbeat as a function of the typical body mass for several mammals. Note how the data points seem to fall on a straight line with slope 1/4.

---

[5] The original reference is the paper "A General Model for the Origin of Allometric Scaling Laws in Biology" by G. B. West, J. H. Brown, B. J. Enquist in the journal *Science* (Volume 276, page 122 (1997)). Additional references can be found on the web.

Finally, figure 13.8 is a nice example for the power of gnuplot's `with labels` plot style. The graph was generated using

```
plot "mammals" u 2:3 w points, "" u 2:(1.1*$3):1 w labels
```

The first part of the command draws the symbols (`with points`); the second adds the labels. All the labels are shifted a bit upward so as not to obscure the symbols themselves. In this example, the vertical offset is *multiplicative*, because of the logarithmic scale of the graph (remember: logarithms turn multiplicative offsets into linear ones).

13.2 Counting statistics

Besides detecting relationships between quantities, we may want to understand how data points that are somehow random are distributed. Are data points spread out evenly or are they clustered in a few spots? Are distributions symmetric or are they skewed? How much weight is contained in the tails of a distribution, compared to its center?

Let's say we have a file containing a set of measurements—these can be anything: interarrival times for requests at a web server, completion times of database queries, weights of potatoes, heights of people—whatever. What can we say about them?

13.2.1 Jitter plots and histograms

One easy way to get a visualization of a collection of random points is to generate a *jitter plot*, which is really a one-dimensional scatter plot, but with a twist (as in the bottom part of figure 13.9).

This graph was created by shifting each data point vertically by a random amount. (The `rand(0)` function returns a random number in the range [0:1].) If we'd just plotted the data in a true, one-dimensional fashion, too many of the points would've overlapped, making it difficult to detect clustering. Such jittering by a random amount is a good trick to remember whenever creating scatter plots of larger data sets!

```
plot "random-points" u 1:(0.25*rand(0)-.35)
```

We can see that the distribution of points is skewed. It's strictly bounded by zero on the left, with points clustering around one, and as we move to the right, points become increasingly sparse. But it's hard to say something more definite by just looking at the jitter plot. For instance, is there a second cluster of points between three and four? This does seem possible, but it's hard to tell for sure using this representation.

The next step when investigating the properties of a distribution usually involves drawing a histogram. To create a histogram, we assign data points to buckets or *bins* and count how many events fall into each bin. It's easiest to make all bins have equal width, but with proper normalization per bin, we can make a histogram containing bins of differing widths. This is sometimes useful out in the tails of a distribution where the number of events per bin is small.

Gnuplot doesn't have an explicit histogramming function, but we can use the `smooth frequency` functionality (see section 3.2) to good effect. Recall: `smooth frequency` sorts the x values by size, and then plots the sum of y values per x value. That's what we need to build a histogram.

In the following code, I introduce a function `bin(x,s)` of two parameters. The first parameter is the x value we'd like to bin, and the second parameter is the bin width. Note that the bins obtained in this way are flush left—you can use the `binc(x,s)` function for bins centered at the bin value.

The `smooth frequency` feature forms the sum of all y values falling into each bin. If all we care about is the overall shape of the histogram, we may supply any constant, such as `(1)`, but if we want to obtain a normalized histogram (one including a total surface area equal to unity), we need to take into account the number of points in the sample and the bin width. You can convince yourself easily that the proper y value for a normalized histogram is

*1/(bin-width * number-of-points-in-sample)*

We can use the `with boxes` style to draw a histogram (see figure 13.9), but we want to fix the width of the boxes in the graph to coincide with the bin width. (By default, the boxes expand to touch their neighbors, which leads to a faulty graphical representation if some of the internal bins are empty.) The bin width is 0.1 and there are 300 points in the sample. (We have to count them ourselves—unfortunately, gnuplot currently doesn't have the ability to report the number of records in a data file.)

```
bin(x,s)  = s*int(x/s)
binc(x,s) = s*(int(x/s)+0.5)

set boxwidth 0.1
plot "random-points"
⟿ u (bin(1,0.1)):(1./(0.1*300)) smooth frequency with boxes
```

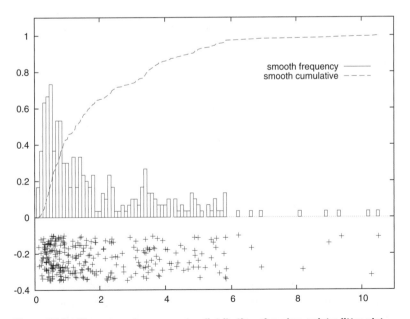

Figure 13.9 **Three ways to represent a distribution of random points: jitter plot (bottom), histogram (with boxes), and cumulative distribution function (dashed line)**

Before leaving this section, I should mention another graphical device you may encounter in the literature, the so-called *box-and-whiskers* plot or *box plot* for short. Basically, a box-plot is similar to the `with candlesticks` style (see section 5.2.3), with the box representing the upper and lower quartiles (see section 13.2.4 if you aren't familiar with percentiles). The "whiskers" extending from the central box are a measure of the outliers and may represent, for example, the 10 and 90 percent percentiles.

I must say that I never use box plots for the purpose of representing a single distribution of points. They give you all the hassles of a graph, but don't add much information that couldn't be expressed by the sheer percentile numbers alone. Furthermore, if I'm looking for a graphical representation, a histogram or even a jitter plot tells me so much more than a box plot. This comment doesn't apply to situations where I want to compare a large number of distributions, such as the time series plots, where box plots can be very useful.

13.2.2 *Kernel density estimates*

The apparent simplicity of the histogramming method hides some pitfalls. The first concerns the width of the bins: make them too narrow and the resulting histogram will be bumpy; make them too wide and you lose relevant features. There's also ambiguity in regard to the placement of the bins: is the first bin centered at zero (or any other value) or flush left there? The overall appearance of the histogram can depend quite sensitively on these details!

A better method to generate distribution curves from individual data points goes under the name *kernel density estimation*. Rather than counting how many data points fall into each bin, we place a strongly peaked, but smooth function (a *kernel*) centered at the location of each data point. We then sum the contributions from all these curves and plot the result. Mathematically, the kernel estimate $f(x)$ for a data set consisting of N points x_i is

$$f(x) = (1/N)\Sigma_i^N \ (1/h) \ K(\ (x\text{-}x_i)/h \ )$$

Here, $K(x)$ is any smooth, peaked, normalized function, and h is the *bandwidth*: a measure of the width of the kernel function. A popular example is the Gaussian kernel:

$$K(x) = (2 \ \pi)^{-1/2} \exp(\text{-}x^2/2)$$

The current development version of gnuplot (version 4.3) contains code to generate such curves, using the `smooth kdensity` functionality. It works in much the same way as the `smooth frequency` feature we saw earlier:

```
plot "random-points" u 1:(1./300.):(0.05) smooth kdensity
```

The first column specifies the location; the second gives the weight each point should have. For a normalized histogram, this should be the inverse of the number of data points—since the kernel functions are normalized themselves, you don't have to worry about the bandwidth at this point as you did for histograms using `smooth frequency`. The third parameter is optional and fixes the bandwidth of the kernels. If it's omitted (or negative), gnuplot calculates a default bandwidth, which would be

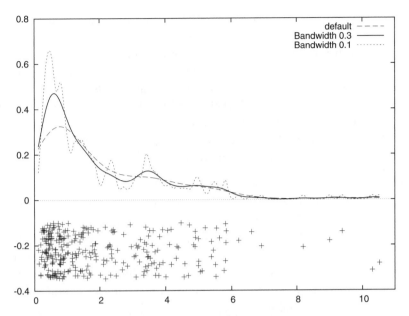

Figure 13.10 An alternative to histograms: kernel density estimates using smooth `kdensity`. Curves for three different bandwidths are shown. A bandwidth of 0.3 seems to give the best trade-off between smoothing action and retention of details. Note how it brings out the secondary cluster near x=3.5.

optimal if the data were normally distributed. This default bandwidth tends to be quite conservative (that means, rather broad).

Figure 13.10 shows several curves drawn using `kdensity` for the same data set we've already seen in figure 13.9, for a variety of bandwidth parameters. Studying this graph carefully, we may conclude that there's indeed a second cluster of points, located near 3.5. Note how the choice of bandwidth can hide or reveal features in the distribution of points.

13.2.3 *Cumulative distribution functions*

Histograms and density estimates have the advantage of being intuitive: they show us directly the probability for a certain value to occur. But they have some disadvantages when it comes to making quantitative statements. For example, based on the histogram in figure 13.9, it's hard to determine how much "weight" is in the tail of the distribution: how likely are values larger than 4 to occur? How about values larger than 6? We can guess that the probability will be small, but it's hard to be more precise. To answer such questions, we need to know the *area under the histogram* within certain bounds. In other words, we want to look at the *cumulative distribution function* (or simply *distribution function* for short).

The value of the cumulative distribution function at position *x* gives us the fraction of events that have occurred with x_i less than *x*. In figure 13.9, I already showed the distribution function together with the histogram. To repeat: the value of the cumulative distribution function at position *x* is equal to the area under the (normalized) histogram from its left border to the position *x*.

Cumulative distribution functions are part of the current development version of gnuplot (version 4.3), and are accessible using `smooth cumulative`. The `smooth cumulative` feature is similar to `smooth frequency`: first, all points are sorted in order of ascending *x* value, then the sum of all *y* values to the left of the current position is plotted as smoothed value. To obtain a normalized distribution function, we must supply 1/*number-of-points* as *y* value. In contrast to histograms or density estimates, distribution functions don't depend on a width parameter.

```
plot "random-points" u 1:(1./300.) smooth cumulative
```

Cumulative distribution functions can be a little unintuitive at first, but they're well worth becoming familiar with. They make it easy to answer questions such as those raised at the beginning of this section. From figure 13.9 we can immediately see that there's a 3 percent chance of finding a point at *x* > 6 and about a 15 percent chance for *x* > 4. We can also find more proof for the second cluster of points between 3 and 4: at this point, the distribution function seems to make a jump, indicating an accumulation of points in this interval.

The cumulative distribution function is sufficiently useful that you may want to dump it into a file, in order to study it in its own right. Listing 13.2 shows how to do that and also demonstrates a good graphical method to check whether the points in a data set are normally (Gaussian) distributed. If they are, the resulting plot will be a straight line. Moreover, we can read off the width of the Gaussian from the slope of the line and the location of the Gaussian from the intersection of the line with the y axis. (Here's how it works: if the data points were normally distributed, then the cumulative distribution function would be the Gaussian one, so that $y = \Phi((x-\mu)/\sigma)$, where $\Phi()$ stands for the Gaussian distribution function, μ is the mean and σ is the standard deviation. Now operate on both sides with the inverse of the distribution function: $\Phi^{-1}(y) = (x-\mu)/\sigma$. Rearranging terms, we end up with $\sigma \Phi^{-1}(y) + \mu = x$. A similar argument also holds for non-Gaussian distributions functions, although few of them have a closed form for the inverse of their distribution functions, and μ and σ need to be taken as the appropriate location and scale parameters for the distribution under consideration.)

Listing 13.2 Testing whether a cumulative distribution function is normal

```
plot "data" u 1:(1./100.) s cumul  # Distribution function of
                                   #     original data

set table "cdf" # Re-direct output to file 'cdf'
replot          # ... write to file
unset table     # ... and switch file output off again.

plot "cdf" u (invnorm($2)):1 w l   # Should be straight line
                                   #    if data is Gaussian
```

13.2.4 *Consider using median and percentiles*

When faced with a random distribution of points or events, it's natural to look for some form of summary statistics that'll give a good estimate for the *location* of the distribution and its *spread*. The best-known measures of location and spread are the *mean* and the *standard deviation*:

$$\mu = (1/N) \Sigma_i^N x_i$$

$$\sigma = [(1/N) \Sigma_i^N (x_i - \mu)^2]^{1/2}$$

One major reason for their popularity is the relative ease with which they can be calculated. Both can be found by iterating over the data set, updating the sum $\Sigma_i^N x_i$ and the sum of squares $\Sigma_i^N x_i^2$ (it's not hard to show that the standard deviation can be found from the sum and the sum of squares: $\sigma^2 = (1/N) (\Sigma_i^N x_i^2) - \mu^2$). In particular, it's never necessary to manipulate the entire data set at once; elements need only be accessed one by one and in any order.

The problem is that mean and standard deviation may not be good estimators of location and spread. If the distribution of points is asymmetrically skewed, the mean won't be a good measure of the location, and if the distribution has so-called *fat tails* (so that relatively many events occur far away from the center), the standard deviation won't be of much value. If the distribution is bi- or multimodal (has more than one peak), both of these measures are basically meaningless.

I therefore strongly recommend that you become familiar with the median and percentile statistics. To find the median, sort all values in ascending order: the median is the element exactly in the middle, so that half of all points are below the median and the other half above it. (This rule holds if the overall number of points is odd. If it's even, take the average of the two points closest to the middle.) Percentiles work in a similar fashion: the *10 percent percentile* is the value below which 10 percent of points fall, and so on. The lower and upper quartiles are the values below which 25 and 75 percent of points fall, respectively.

The median is a much more reliable estimator of the true center of the distribution in the presence of asymmetry than the mean. For the same reason, the quartiles are a better measure of the spread than the standard deviation. The latter are also much less sensitive to the occasional "crazy" outlier (in contrast to the standard deviation).

The problem with median and percentiles is that they're computationally expensive: the entire data set must be read and sorted. In particular, this requirement makes it impossible to process a data set point by point—instead, the entire file must be slurped and processed at once.

Many actual distributions that one encounters in the wild aren't well represented by mean and standard deviation. Skewed and multimodal distributions are the rule rather than the exception. Heavy-tail phenomena occur frequently and their effects tend to be important; outliers, both real and accidental, are widespread and need to be dealt with. Any one of these effects renders mean and variance nearly useless, but the median and quartiles will tend to hold up in these situations. Use them!

13.3   *Ranked data*

Imagine I give you a list of the countries in the European Union, together with their land area (in square kilometers) and population numbers. How would you represent this information? How would you represent it *graphically*?

The particular challenge here is that *the independent variable has no intrinsic ordering*. What does this mean?

Given the name of a country, the value of the area measure is fixed; hence the name is the independent variable and the area is the dependent variable. We're used to plotting the independent variable along the x axis and observing the behavior of the dependent variable with it. But in this case, there's no natural ordering of the independent variable. Sure, we can order the states alphabetically by their names, but this ordering is entirely arbitrary and bears no relationship on the data. (We wouldn't expect the size of a state to change if we gave it a different name, would we?) Also, the ordering would change if we were to translate the names to a different language. But the information that we want to display depends on the areas, and shouldn't be affected by the spelling of the country names in any way.

For data like this, the only ordering that's intrinsic to the data itself is in the values of the dependent variable. Therefore, a graphical representation of this data should be ordered by the dependent variable, not the independent one. Such plots are often called *dot plots*, but I tend to think of them as *rank-order plots*. Figure 13.11 shows an example.

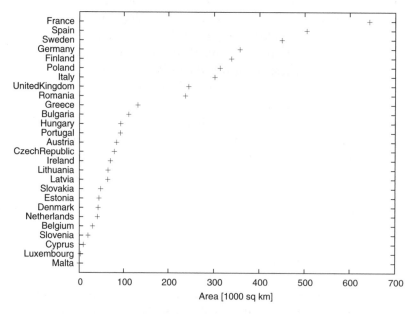

Figure 13.11   A rank-order plot. Because there's no natural ordering in the independent variable (in this case, the country names), we sort the data by the dependent variable to emphasize the structure in the data.

If the input file is sorted by the appropriate quantity, we can generate such plots easily using gnuplot's facility for reading tic labels from the input file. Given an input file containing the names and areas in two columns,[6] such as this:

```
France      643427
Spain       504782
Sweden      449964
Germany     357021
Finland     338145
...
```

the entire plot can be generated using the following command:

```
plot [][26:1] "data" using 2:0:ytic(1)
```

The `ytic(1)` function selects the values in column 1 as tic labels for the y axis (see section 7.3.4), and the pseudocolumn 0, which evaluates to the line number in the input file, is used as the corresponding vertical coordinate (see section 3.4.2). The inverted y range places the first line in the file at the top of the graph instead of the bottom.

This is the basic idea. We could've plotted the state names along the x axis instead, but then we'd need to rotate the labels, to make sure they don't overlap. Unfortunately, rotating the labels by 90 degrees (so that they run vertically) makes them hard to read. A good trick is to rotate them by some angle so that they run diagonally (we'll see an example in figure 13.13). But the initial layout, with the names running down the y axis, is the easiest to read.

What if we want to show and compare multiple data sets, such as the land area and the population? The best strategy is to declare a primary data set, which determines the ordering for all others. In figure 13.12, we can see an example. The points of the secondary data set (the population in millions) have been connected by lines to make them stand out more. Additionally, the x axis has been scaled logarithmically, which is often useful with dot-plots of this sort. We can see that overall the population count follows the area, but there are some notable outliers: the northern Scandinavian countries Sweden and Finland are thinly populated, whereas the so-called Benelux countries (Belgium, Netherlands, and Luxembourg) have an exceptionally high population density.

Dot- or rank-order plots are useful whenever the dependent variable has no natural ordering. On the other hand, if the dependent variable can be ordered, even if it's nonnumeric (such as the categories *Strong Dislike, Dislike, Neutral, Like, Strong Like*), we should use the information in our graphs and order data points by the independent variable.

---

[6] All data in this section comes from the *CIA World Factbook*, because I was unable to find this data in a suitable format on the European Union's official web site.

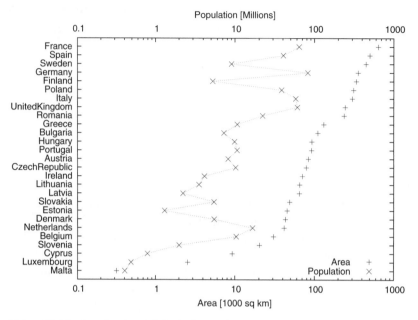

Figure 13.12   A rank-order plot displaying a primary and a secondary data set for comparison. The country names are sorted according to the primary data set (the area); the points in the secondary data are connected by lines to make them easier to distinguish. Note the logarithmic scale for the horizontal axes.

13.4   *Multivariate data*

Sometimes we don't even know what to look *at,* much less what to look *for.* This problem typically arises for large, somewhat disparate sets of data. For example, later in this section we'll look at a data set containing measurements for more than 200 individual samples of glass. For each bit of glass, nine different quantities have been measured. In such a situation, it's not at all clear where to begin. What quantity should we plot as a function of which other? Which one will tell us the most about the data in the sample? Our first task is therefore to find which quantities are the most relevant. We can then study how the other quantities vary with them. It would also be nice to be able to break the original data set up into a handful of groups, so that the records within each group are somehow similar. But first we'd have to find the criteria by which the data could be classified!

In this section, we study two different graphical methods that have been suggested for problems of this kind: parallel coordinate plots and star plots.

13.4.1   *Parallel coordinate plots*

The purpose of a parallel coordinate plot is to visualize *all* measurements for a large number of records *simultaneously.* The price we pay is a highly unintuitive and not very pretty graph. A parallel coordinate plot is strictly a tool for graphic discovery, not for presentation or communication.

Let's imagine we have a data set of n records, where each record consists of k measurements of different quantities. Each record is therefore a point in a k-dimensional space: each measured quantity spans a separate *dimension*. To construct a scatter plot, we'd have to pick two (or at most three) of these dimensions as axes of the plot. In a parallel coordinate plot, we instead assign a fixed location along the x axis to each of the measured quantities. For each record, the value of this quantity is taken as the y coordinate at the corresponding x location. All points from a single record are then connected with straight lines.

An example will make this more clear. Let's look at a data set of more than 200 individual samples of glass taken from crime scenes.[7] For each glass sample, nine quantities were measured: the refractive index and the content of substances such as sodium, silicon, iron, and so on. Each of these quantities is assigned a position along the x axis, and the reported value is used as y coordinate. Figure 13.13 shows the resulting plot after only a single record has been plotted; figure 13.14 shows it after all records have been added, with the original record highlighted.

We can now examine this plot for possible structure in the data set. We look for clusters or gaps along one of the marked x values. Those can be used to classify data sets into groups. We can also look for outliers and for correlations among data sets: positively correlated quantities show up as parallel (or nearly parallel) lines, whereas negative correlation is indicated by lines crossing each other.

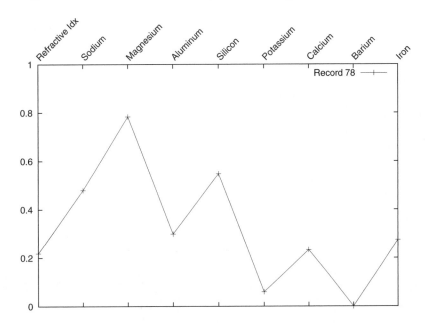

Figure 13.13   A single record in a parallel coordinates plot

---

[7] This example comes from the "Glass Identification" data set, available from the UCI Machine Learning Repository: Asuncion, A. and Newman, D.J. (2007). UCI Machine Learning Repository [http://www.ics.uci.edu/~mlearn/MLRepository.html]. Irvine, CA: University of California, School of Information and Computer Science.

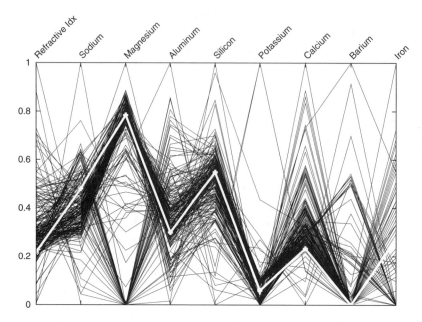

Figure 13.14   All records in a parallel coordinates plot. The record from figure 13.13 is highlighted.

The data set in figure 13.14, for instance, exhibits clustering along the third axis (measuring magnesium content). Taking this as a hint, I separate the records into two sets: one with high magnesium content and one with low magnesium content. In figure 13.15, I show only the records with high magnesium content, which allows us to identify additional characteristics. For example, the records shown in figure 13.15 can be partitioned again based on the potassium content. It also appears as if records with high potassium content have a low calcium concentration. On the other hand, iron exhibits no clustering whatsoever. In this way, we can proceed and detect those criteria (such as high or low magnesium content) that can be used to classify records.

There are a few technical points that need to be discussed. The first concerns the best data input format for this kind of plot. Listing 13.3 shows the first few lines of the original data set. Each row contains one record; the individual measurements are separated by commas. The first entry in a line is the index of that record, followed by the nine measurements. The last entry is a check digit, which we'll ignore.

Listing 13.3   The beginning of the Glass Identification data set

```
1,1.52101,13.64,4.49,1.10,71.78,0.06,8.75,0.00,0.00,1
2,1.51761,13.89,3.60,1.36,72.73,0.48,7.83,0.00,0.00,1
3,1.51618,13.53,3.55,1.54,72.99,0.39,7.78,0.00,0.00,1
4,1.51766,13.21,3.69,1.29,72.61,0.57,8.22,0.00,0.00,1
5,1.51742,13.27,3.62,1.24,73.08,0.55,8.07,0.00,0.00,1
...
```

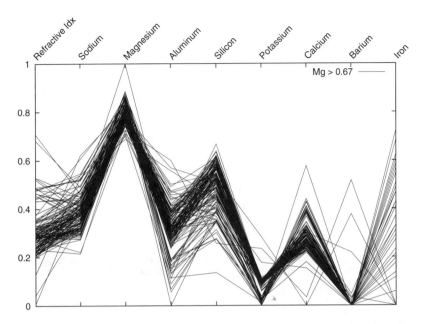

Figure 13.15   A subset of records: only those records from figure 13.14 are shown in which the magnesium concentration exceeds 0.67. Note the secondary structure in this subset: there are two distinct clusters of data characterized by their concentration of potassium and calcium.

This format isn't ideal for the kind of plot we have in mind. It would be much better if all measurements for a single record would form a column instead of a row. I therefore transform the original data set using the short Perl program shown in listing 13.4 to a more suitable format. The first few rows of the transformed data set are shown in listing 13.5.

In the transformed data set, each record has been turned into a data block, with individual data blocks separated from each other using two blank lines. This means that we can now plot each data block individually using the `plot ... index` facility (see section 3.1.1).

The transformation script also rescales the original values to lie in the unit interval [0:1]. Although not strictly necessary, this is usually a good idea to make different measured quantities comparable. Finally, the appearance of a parallel coordinates plot depends on the specific ordering of the dimensions along the x axis. You may want to try out different permutations to see how this changes the image.

Listing 13.4   Perl script to transform listing 13.3 to the format in listing 13.5

```
while( <> ) {
  chomp;
  push @r, [ split "," ];
}
```

```
for $i ( 1..scalar( @{ $r[0] } )-1 ) { # For each column...
  ( $min, $max ) = ( 100000, 0 );       # ... find min and max
  for $j ( 0..scalar @r-1 ) {           # ... over all rows.
    $min = $r[$j][$i] < $min ? $r[$j][$i] : $min;
    $max = $r[$j][$i] > $max ? $r[$j][$i] : $max;
  }
  for $j ( 0..scalar @r-1 ) {      # Rescale this column in all rows
    $r[$j][$i] = ($r[$j][$i] - $min)/($max-$min);
  }
}

for $r ( @r ) {
# unless( $r->[3] > 0.67 ) { next; } # Optional filter logic
  for $i ( 1..scalar( @{ $r[0] } )-1 ) {
    print "$i\t", $r->[$i], "\n";
  }
  print "\n\n";
}
```

Listing 13.5   The transformed data set, ready for plotting

```
# ColumnIndex    RescaledValue
1                0.43
2                0.43
3                1
4                0.25
5                0.35
6                0.00
7                0.30
8                0
9                0
10               0

1                0.28
2                0.47
3                0.80
4                0.33
5                0.52
6                0.07
7                0.22
8                0
9                0
10               0

...
```

Finally, I've collected the most pertinent commands I used to create figure 13.13 in listing 13.6. The most interesting aspect is the way x tic labels are handled. I use explicit text labels rotated by 45 degrees. I also use the secondary x axis (at the top), rather than the primary axis, because the textual labels align better along the top than at the bottom. Additionally, the size of the top margin has been adjusted manually to make room for the rotated text labels.

> **Listing 13.6   Commands to generate figure 13.13 from the data in listing 13.5**

```
unset xtics
set tmargin 5
set x2tics rotate by 45 offset 0 mirror
➡ ( 'Refractive Idx' 1, 'Sodium' 2, 'Magnesium' 3, 'Aluminum' 4,
➡    'Silicon' 5, 'Potassium' 6, 'Calcium' 7, 'Barium' 8, 'Iron' 9 )
plot [1:9][0:1] "data" i 78 u 1:2 w linesp t 'Record 78'
```

13.4.2 *Multivariate analysis*

The study of problems involving the simultaneous consideration of several related statistical quantities is called *multivariate analysis*. The first, and often the most important, goal of multivariate analysis is to find any kind of structure in the data, and thereby simplify the problem. This leads to classification, clustering, or projection techniques, some of them quite sophisticated.[8]

Multivariate analysis is hard, and graphical methods quickly seem to reach their limits. (I think parallel coordinate plots can't be regarded as anything but a kludge, but much weirder techniques have been suggested. The idea behind Chernoff-faces, for example, is to encode each quantity as a facial feature in a stylized human face: size of the mouth or distance between eyes, and so on. The observer then tries to find the faces that are "most similar" or "least similar" to one another.) For much larger data sets, one may resort to computationally intensive methods, which go under the name of *data mining* or more specifically *pattern recognition* and *machine learning*.[9] The latter set of methods is a highly active area of research.

I must say that I experience a certain degree of discomfort with the "random search" character of some multivariate methods. The purpose of data analysis is to gain insight into the problem domain that the data came from, but any brute-force method that isn't guided by intuition about the problem domain runs the risk of being about the numbers only, not about the actual system that the data came from originally.

The analysis we did earlier on the glass data set (see listing 13.3) is a case in point: we found that records can be classified according to their magnesium content—but what does that tell us about the original problem? This isn't at all clear at this point. We'll have to go back and understand more about the context in which this data was collected.

Multivariate classification methods, such as the parallel coordinates technique introduced here, can be a useful starting point when faced with large and unsystematic data sets, or any time we don't have good intuition about the actual problem

---

[8] Two short and accessible introductory texts are *Multivariate Statistical Methods: A Primer* by Bryan F.J. Manly (Chapman & Hall, 3rd ed., 2004) and *Introduction to Multivariate Analysis* by Chris Chatfield and A. Collins (Chapman & Hall, 1981).

[9] Three introductory texts, in approximate order of increasing sophistication, are: *Pattern Recognition and Machine Learning* by Christopher M. Bishop (Springer, 2007); *Pattern Classification* by Richard O. Duda, Peter E. Hart, David G. Stork (Wiley-Interscience, 2nd ed., 2000); and *The Elements of Statistical Learning* by T. Hastie, R. Tibshirani, J. H. Friedman (Springer, 2003).

domain. We can use these methods to develop strategies for more detailed analysis, but we must make sure to tie the results back to the original problem. The purpose of data analysis is insight into the problem domain, not insight into the data!

13.4.3 *Star plots*

Star plots are basically parallel coordinate plots in polar coordinates. Instead of showing many records in a single plot, it's more common to draw a single star plot for each record and to compare the resulting images. They're therefore more suited for smaller data sets (fewer records). Figure 13.16 shows a star plot for some of the records of the glass samples data set. The commands (involving both polar coordinates and multiplot mode) are shown in listing 13.7.

The advantage of star plots over parallel coordinate plots is that they give the viewer more of a sense of a recognizable shape. In figure 13.16, for instance, we can easily distinguish the three records of the top row as being similar to one another, while the three records in the bottom row are clearly different from both the top row and from each other.

Listing 13.7   Commands for a star plot array—see figure 13.16

```
set polar
set size square

unset border

set format x ""; set format y ""
set xtics scale 0; set ytics scale 0

set grid polar 2.0*pi/9.0
set xtics 0.25

unset key

set style data linesp

set multiplot layout 2,3

set label 1 '77' at graph 0,0.95
plot [0:2*pi][-1:1][-1:1] "stardata" i 77 u (2*pi*($1-1)/9.):2

set label 1 '78' at graph 0,0.95
plot [0:2*pi][-1:1][-1:1] "stardata" i 78 u (2*pi*($1-1)/9.):2

set label 1 '79' at graph 0,0.95
plot [0:2*pi][-1:1][-1:1] "stardata" i 79 u (2*pi*($1-1)/9.):2

set label 1 '105' at graph 0,0.95
plot [0:2*pi][-1:1][-1:1] "stardata" i 105 u (2*pi*($1-1)/9.):2

set label 1 '174' at graph 0,0.95
plot [0:2*pi][-1:1][-1:1] "stardata" i 174 u (2*pi*($1-1)/9.):2

set label 1 '184' at graph 0,0.95
plot [0:2*pi][-1:1][-1:1] "stardata" i 184 u (2*pi*($1-1)/9.):2

unset multiplot
reset
```

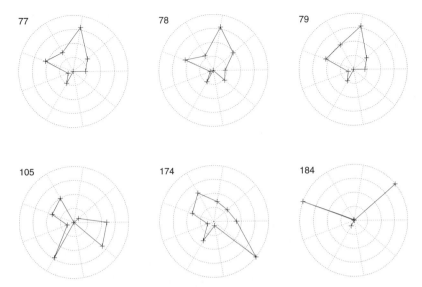

Figure 13.16   **Star plot of six individual records from listing 13.3. The records in the top row are more or less similar to one another, but the records in the bottom row belong in very different categories.**

13.4.4 *Historical perspective: computer-aided data analysis*

In this chapter, we talked about some more modern techniques for data analysis: using the median (instead of the mean), kernel density estimates (instead of histograms), parallel coordinate plots (for multivariate data). All these techniques have something in common that sets them apart from their "classical" counterparts: they *require* a computer to be practical.

I already commented on this when discussing the median (which requires sorting the entire data set, compared to the mean, which only requires a running sum of totals). Similar considerations apply to the kernel density estimate: a histogram only requires counting the number of events in each bin, whereas the kernel method requires an evaluation of the kernel function for each data point *and* for each sample point at which the curve should be drawn. And the parallel-coordinate plot is intended for data sets that are too large for manual techniques, anyway.

But this is only the beginning. Once we fully embrace the computer as a readily available and fully legitimate tool, what other methods for visual exploration become possible? The short answer is: we don't know yet. There are some new ideas that have started to come out of research in computer-assisted data visualization, some good, some certainly misguided. Time and experience will tell which is which.

One possible direction for the development of new visualization techniques is the ability to interact dynamically with a plot. For instance, a concept known as *brushing* involves two different views on a single, multivariate data set. When selecting a subset of points with the mouse in one view, the corresponding points in the other view are highlighted simultaneously. This technique can be used to investigate structure in multivariate data sets. (I can also imagine applications to the parallel-coordinate plots we discussed.)

Gnuplot isn't suitable for such applications, but some academic software systems are freely available for experimentation. If you're interested, you might want to check out GGobi (www.ggobi.org) or Mondrian (www.rosuda.org/mondrian). The book *Graphics of Large Datasets* by A. Unwin, M. Theus, and H. Hofmann (Springer, 2006) also contains many useful pointers in this regard.

13.5   *Summary*

In this chapter, we started with the most fundamental questions we may pose to a data set, and discussed ways to answer them using graphical methods:

- For questions about the functional relationships between two quantities, we'll usually use a scatter plot of some form. We also discussed how a smooth curve approximation can help to detect structure in noisy data.

- For data sets of random points, we're mostly interested in the distribution of the points. Questions of this sort quickly take us into the territory of statistics, and I introduced jitter plots, histograms and kernel density estimates, and cumulative distribution functions.

- Data sets for which the independent variable has no natural sort order pose particular challenges. I suggested rank-order plots, in which we utilize the sort order of the *dependent* variable as the best way to visualize such data sets.

- Finally, we looked at unstructured, multivariate data sets. Here, our ambition was much more modest: rather than making definitive statements about the data, we were satisfied merely to find some form of structure in the data, which can help partition the data set into smaller and more uniform fragments.

In passing, I mentioned several mathematical concepts that are of particular usefulness during analysis. First we discussed logarithms, which are always helpful with data spanning many orders of magnitude, and which can reveal exponential and power-law behavior in data. Although I first discussed logarithms in connection with scatter plots, they're more generally useful, for example for rank-order plots. I also discussed the problems that may arise from the uncritical use of classical summary statistics (such as mean and standard deviation) and recommended instead statistics based on the median and percentiles. And finally, I tried to put the purpose and challenges of multivariate statistics into perspective.

In the next chapter, we'll get more specific and work through some particular problems in much more detail. Stay tuned.

14

Techniques of graphical analysis

In this chapter, I want to show you some more specialized techniques that are helpful when analyzing data graphically. We'll look at a few examples in more detail, so that I can explain the different steps and the rationale behind them.

There are a few overarching ideas I want to convey here. First and foremost is the importance of *iteration*: the need to plot data, learn something about it, and plot it again in a different manner, until we've learned whatever was possible from it.

Another theme in this chapter is the importance of *transformations*, either mathematical transformations that we apply to the data, or (and this is a topic we haven't touched on before in this book), visual transformations in which we change the overall appearance of the plot to make features in the data stand out. It turns out

273

that our human perception of features in a graph can be helped or hindered by the way that data is presented, and in changing the appearance of a plot, we attempt to find the format that lets us recognize certain features most easily.

This chapter is also a good place to talk about some other housekeeping activities that help with the organization of our work. And I'll close with a short checklist for presentation graphics.

14.1 *The core principle of graphical analysis*

Here's what I believe to be the core principle of graphical analysis:

Plot exactly what you want to see!

That sounds trite, doesn't it? But it isn't, for a number of reasons.

First off, it's often not at all obvious what to look at from the outset. Very often, it's only when we look at data that we come up with new ideas about the data and therefore new ways that we want to plot it. When dealing with a truly new data set, I've found that frequently I don't know what to look for until I see it! Hence the importance of iteration, to bring out the relevant information in a data set.

Secondly, initially data isn't necessarily in the form that brings out its most important features most clearly; therefore we might have to apply some transformation before graphing it. Maybe we shouldn't plot the data itself, but its logarithm instead. Or maybe its standardized *z-score*. Or we don't actually care about the data itself, but the difference between two data sets, so that we should plot this difference instead. And so on.

Finally, we need to understand how our minds process visual information, and use this information to present data in a way that makes it easiest for us to recognize features in a data set that we care about. If we want to see the change in a data set, we should choose the plot ranges in such a way that the graph only includes the values over which change happens. If instead we want to understand the global behavior of the same data set, we need to choose plot ranges wide enough to include the entire data set. We'll see more sophisticated examples later.

I stress this simple principle, to *plot what you want to see*, because it's so frequently overlooked—maybe precisely because of its simplicity. But if you look at some of the well-publicised examples of bad information graphics, you'll find that often what makes them bad is that they *don't* show what you really want to see. Maybe the relevant quantity is the difference between two signals, but the two individual signals are shown separately instead. Or the relevant information is the relative change of some quantity about a baseline, but the total value of the quantity is shown instead. Or only a specific subset of all data points is relevant, but all points are shown instead. Based on what I've seen, this seems to be the single most frequent *fundamental* problem with information graphics—much more serious than the superficial problems with missing labels or inappropriate line widths that so much of the debate concentrates on.

I'd also like to stress that finding out what's most relevant is often not easy. Take your time. Think about it. Try it several times. It's *supposed* to be hard. That's why it's fun!

In this chapter, I'm not trying to show you "the one right way to do it," because all I've seen has taught me that no such thing exists. Instead, I want to suggest ways to think about graphing data and how we can use graphs to relate to and understand data.

14.2 Iteration and transformation

Let's look at a few examples that require multiple plots, and typically some data transformations as well. The first example is a study in iteration: we plot the same data set several times. Each plot reveals some structure or behavior in the data, which we remove in the next step to see whether there's evidence of weaker (secondary) structure. After several iterations, we'll have extracted all useful information and will be left with an apparently random collection of points that doesn't suggest any further structure. In the second example, I'm going to discuss the importance of making data sets from different sources comparable to one another by normalizing them. In the last example, we'll take a look at the dangers of truncating or censoring data and the sometimes hidden ways these issues can occur when working with data.

14.2.1 A case study in iteration: car data

Our first example concerns a data set we already know from listing 13.1. Besides the weight and the price, it contains many more attributes for each car, including values for cars' fuel consumption in miles per gallon (mpg), both for city traffic and for highway driving. On a lark, I plotted both against the price (see figure 14.1).

There are a lot of points in this plot, many of which overlap at least partially. Since we want to compare the distribution of data points for inner-city and highway driving, we need to be able to distinguish between points for either case most clearly. For these reasons, I've chosen open and filled circles as symbols. There is empirical evidence[1] that among geometric shapes, circles remain identifiable most clearly even when partially overlapping, and that open and filled symbols provide greater contrast than symbols of different shapes.

This is certainly a minor point, but I'd like to emphasize how attention to even such an apparent detail can make a difference in the visual usefulness of even a modest scatter plot!

Also keep in mind that this entire discussion is only relevant because of the black-and-white restriction imposed by the printed book: in an interactive session using a color terminal, we'd use highly contrasting colors (such as red and green) to help us distinguish between the two data sets.

Looking at figure 14.1, I was struck by the similarity in behavior between city and highway uses, so I plotted one against the other to see more clearly how they behave relative to each other. I found that the points seem to fall on a straight line. This is shown in figure 14.2, where I've also added the linear function $f(x) = x$ for comparison.

---

[1] See *The Elements of Graphing Data* by William S. Cleveland, Hobart Press (1994) and references therein.

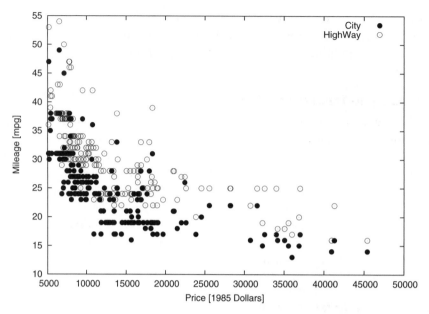

Figure 14.1   Mileage (in miles per gallon) for city and highway use of 205 cars versus their price (1985 data)

This graph is quite interesting by itself. It tells us that the highway mileage grows in step with the mileage for city use. The only difference is that we seem to get a few more miles per gallon on the highway than in the city. (It's not entirely clear yet how many more miles.) I find this mildly surprising: I would've expected cars with overall high consumption to turn into disproportional guzzlers on the highway. But they don't appear to.

The functional form suggested by figure 14.2 is

highway-mpg = city-mpg + const

To verify this, I looked at the residual between the data and the functional form; in other words, I plotted the difference between the highway mileage and the city mileage as a function of the city mileage. If the preceding equation holds, I'd expect the residuals to be scattered about the value of the (as yet unknown) constant, without a significant trend. The result is shown in figure 14.3, where I've also added a weighted spline to indicate the trend (if any), similar to the process we used in section 13.1.1. Because in this plot many points coincide, I've added a small random component to both x and y values, and chosen open circles (again), which remain most clearly visible even when partially overlapping. There's no discernible overall trend, and we can read off the difference in mileage between city and highway use: we get about 5.5 miles more to the gallon on the highway.

This is admittedly not the most fascinating result in the world, but it's interesting how we arrived at it by purely graphical means. Also, observe how each step in this (mini) analysis was based directly on the results of the preceding one.

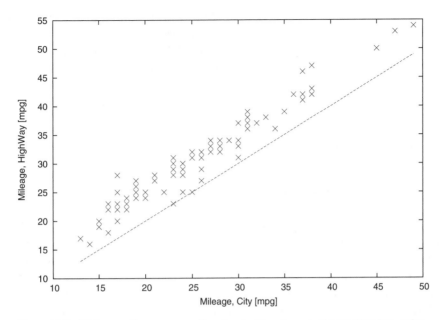

Figure 14.2   Highway mileage versus city mileage. Also shown is the function *f(x) = x* for comparison. (See figure 14.1.)

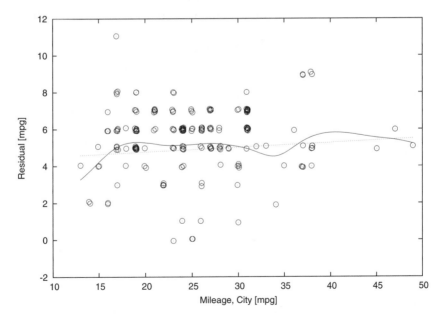

Figure 14.3   The residual after subtracting the postulated functional form from the data in figure 14.2. Note how there doesn't seem to be a significant trend in the residuals, suggesting that the functional form represents the data well.

There's one additional interesting tidbit in this example. If you fit a straight line through the points in figure 14.3, you'll find that it displays a weak upward slope, suggesting that high consumption vehicles do in fact need disproportionately more fuel in the city. But if you compare it with the smooth trend line in the graph, it becomes apparent that the upward slope is due mostly to the existence of a few outliers on the very left of the graph. Excluding them, no overall trend can be detected.

14.2.2 *Making data comparable: monitoring quantities in a control chart*

Imagine you're in charge of a factory or some production plant. You're responsible for the smooth running of the operation, so you want to monitor the most relevant metrics constantly.

To keep things simple, let's say there are just three parameters that really matter: the overall productivity (units per hour), the completion time for each unit (in minutes), and the defect rate (the ratio of defective units to the total number of units produced). You might want to plot them together on a control chart, so that you can immediately see if one of them starts running out of the allowed zone. But most of all, you want to be able to *compare* them against each other: is one parameter consistently performing better than the other ones? Is one of the parameters on a slippery slope, getting worse and worse, relative to the other ones? And so forth.

A naive way to achieve this effect is to just plot the three parameters in a single chart. The result is shown in figure 14.4 and is probably *not* what you wanted!

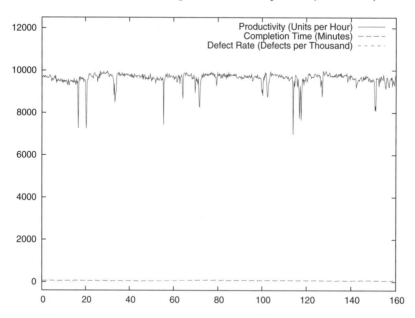

Figure 14.4   A control chart, showing three very different quantities simultaneously. What's wrong with this picture?

The problem is that the three parameters assume very different values: productivity is typically around 10,000 units per hour, assembly time is on the order of an hour, and the defect rate should be very, very small.

So, what to do? One possible solution might be to use a logarithmic scale for the y axis (see section13.1.2) and this is indeed a valid approach. But in our example, we run into trouble with it, because the defect rate is in fact often zero (no defects found), and logarithms are undefined at zero.

What other ways do we have to make the three data streams comparable? We can subtract an offset (for example, the value that they have first thing in the morning). But that won't do the trick, because it's not just the overall magnitude that matters, but also the range of values over which each parameter fluctuates. The productivity ranges from as low as 7,000 units per hour to almost 10,000 units per hour. The assembly time hovers around one hour, plus or minus thirty minutes, while the defect rate is always smaller than 0.001 (one defect per thousand items).

So after we've shifted the values to have a common starting point, we need to divide by the range of possible values to make the three quantities really comparable. The resulting graph is shown in figure 14.5.

This example serves to make a more general point: before you can compare different quantities, you have to make sure to make them comparable. A strong hint that something is missing can come from a consideration of the units of the quantities involved. Look at figure 14.4, for example. What units are plotted along the y axis? The three quantities that are so innocuously graphed together are measured in three

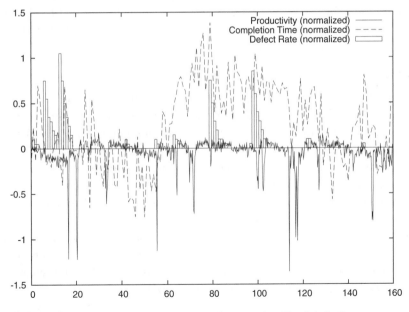

Figure 14.5 A control chart showing normalized metrics. The data is the same as in figure 14.4.

totally different systems of measurement, so that the absolute numbers plotted in the figure have no meaning relative to each other.

A general strategy to make data comparable is to perform a linear transformation on it: first *shift* the curves to have a common starting point, then *scale* them to make the fluctuations comparable:

$z_i = (x_i - m) / s$

Here, m is the offset, and s is a measure of the *spread*.

What to use for m and s is somewhat arbitrary and depends on the specifics of the data. One reasonable possibility is to use the (long-term) mean for m and the standard deviation for s. (With these choices for m and s, the quantity z is sometimes called the *standardized value* or *z-score* by statisticians.)

$m = (1/N) \Sigma_i x_i$

$s = \text{sqrt}((1/N) \Sigma_i(x_i^2) - m^2)$

But this isn't the only possible choice. In other situations it might make sense to take m as the minimum of all values, and to make s be the range between the maximum and the minimum:

$z_i = (x_i - min(x_i)) / (max(x_i) - min(x_i))$

This transformation makes particular sense when there's a well-defined minimum and a similar maximum value. In our example, we know that the defect rate can never be negative, so zero is an obvious choice for the lower limit, and we may know from experience that rarely are there more than 5 defects per 1,000 items, giving us a reasonable maximum value. (Be aware that transforming a quantity by subtracting the mean will lead to a variable that assumes both positive and negative values, while subtracting the minimum value will lead to a strictly positive variable.)

14.2.3 *Honor the data: truncation and responsiveness*

Figure 14.6 shows the finishing times of the winners in a marathon event from when the event was first conducted until 1990.[2] In general, we see that the finishing times have decreased over time—the top athletes are getting better every year. The changes are particularly dramatic for the women's results since they started competing in 1966.

Also shown are the "best-fit" straight-line approximations to the data, and they seem to represent the data quite well. The only issue is that according to those fits, women should overtake men sometime in the early '90s—and then continue to get dramatically faster. Is this a reasonable conclusion?

This example attempts to demonstrates two important points when working with data. The first one is the need to be sensitive to the structure and quality of the data. For the data in figure 14.6, fitting a straight line provides only a very coarse—and as we'll see, misleading—approximation of the real behavior.

---

[2] This example was inspired by the book *Graphic Discovery* by Howard Wainer, Princeton University Press (2005).

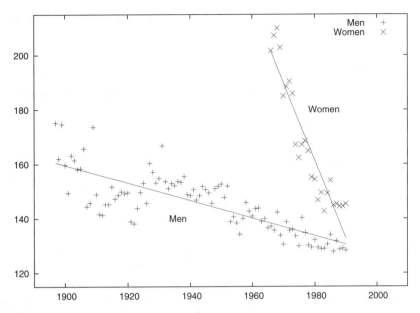

Figure 14.6 Finishing times (in minutes) for the winner of a marathon competition (up to the year 1990), together with the best straight-line fit. Will women overtake men in the coming years?

You need to remember that by fitting a straight line, you've chosen one specific model to represent the data. At this point, you're no longer analyzing the data with the intention of revealing the information contained in it, but are making a very specific statement about its surmised behavior. Before making such a strong statement, you should have sufficient evidence for the applicability of the particular model selected. And coming back to the current example, there certainly doesn't seem to be any strong theoretical reason why athletic performance should follow a straight line as a function of time.

To understand the structure of the data, we might instead attempt to represent the data by some "soft" local approximations, such as weighted splines. Some experimentation with the weights will tell us much about the structure of the data: does the overall shape of the approximation curve change drastically as we vary the weighting? Which features are the most robust, and which disappear most quickly? Typically, significant features tend to be rather robust under transformations, while less relevant features are more transient.

Figure 14.7 shows the same data as figure 14.6, but instead of a straight line, a soft spline has been used to represent the data. This approximation suggests that women's performance starts to level off in the late '80s, and the results from years after 1990 corroborate this observation. Note that the spline approximation is based *only* on years up to and including 1990, but not on later data points.

The second point I want to make is this: be very careful when truncating or rejecting data points—for whatever reason. But we didn't actually *reject* any data points, you say? Yes, we did: we didn't include any result past the year 1990 in our analysis. But they hadn't happened yet when the analysis was done, you say. Fair enough—but reject them we did.

Rejecting, truncating, and censoring of data takes many forms.

- *Outlier removal*—This is probably the most readily understood case. Often a data set will contain a few isolated points that just seem "way off," and you may want to remove them, so as not to distort the overall result. Just be very careful. Try to avoid automatic outlier removal, and never allow data points to be removed silently. No point should be removed from a sample without a (visible) audit trail. (There's a story that the detection of the hole in the ozone layer was delayed by several years, because on-board software on the survey satellite kept silently rejecting the low ozone readings as outliers.[3])

- *Sampling bias*—This is the most insidious form of data censoring, because often you won't even know that you're doing it. A few examples: a survey conducted over the phone will be biased, because it excludes everyone who doesn't have a phone, or doesn't answer (or doesn't answer at the time the survey is conducted). A study of mutual funds available today will show unjustifiably high returns on average, because it doesn't include funds that have been closed or merged away because of poor performance. Polling children for the number of siblings will give a wrong number of children per household because it excludes households without children. One of the best publicized cases of data censoring is related to the space shuttle Challenger accident: by restricting analysis to only those flights exhibiting damage to the O-rings (effectively *removing* cases with no damage to the O-rings from the analysis), it appeared as if temperature wasn't a significant influence on the occurrence of defects.

- *Edge effects*—Another form of truncation occurs naturally at the edge of the plot range. Data points very close to the edge should always be regarded with suspicion, simply because we don't know how the curve would continue if it were to extend beyond the plot range. (In experimental setups, points near the edge may also have higher uncertainty because we're reaching some technical limit of the apparatus: if there were no such limit, the data would extend further.)

In figure 14.6, the problem is such an edge effect. Figure 14.7 tells us how the story ends: the performance of female runners has begun to level off in the late '80s, just when figure 14.6 was drawn.

But in fact the story doesn't end there. We've merely pushed out the edge by another 15 years—how things progress from here is hard to predict. Has the time of dramatic improvements come to an end or will it continue? Incidentally, there are several places along the men's curve that would have suggested a similar flattening of the curve earlier in time. For example, cover the points to the right of 1950 (or 1977),

---

[3] "Ozone Depletion, History and Politics" by Brien Sparling, available at http://www.nas.nasa.gov/About/Education/Ozone/history.html.

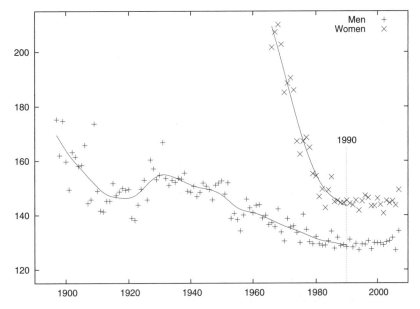

Figure 14.7 **The same data as in figure 14.6, together with a weighted-splines fit. The fit is based only on points prior to 1990, but the actual finishing times for the following years are also shown. The softer spline clearly reveals the leveling off of the women's results well before 1990.**

and you'd be forgiven for guessing that performance had reached a stable plateau—only to see a dramatic improvement within the next few years! (Similar observations can be made for the records in other sports as well.[4])

What causes the apparently steady improvement in athletic performances in a variety of sports? One surprising answer might be simply that an increased number of people are trying! The number of humans on Earth continues to grow, and therefore the likelihood that one of them is a tremendous athlete also increases—even if the overall performance of all of humanity doesn't change. A study[5] showed that a large part of the year-over-year improvement in athletic performance can be attributed to this effect alone.

One last mystery, before leaving this example behind: what happened in the years 1910–1930? Why did the winning time suddenly drop significantly (to levels that wouldn't be attained for another 40 years), and then abruptly increase again after a few years? We can't tell, but it makes you wonder whether the length of the course wasn't too well established in those early years. Another indicator is the strong fluctuation of data points from one year to the next for all years prior to 1930: maybe time wasn't taken very carefully then. But that's speculation—we can't tell from the data available.

---

[4] See for example the delightful *Teaching Statistics—A Bag of Tricks* by Andrew Gelman and Deborah Nolan, Oxford University Press (2002).

[5] "A Statistician Reads the Sports Pages: One Modern Man or 15 Tarzans?" by S. M. Berry in *Chance*, Vol 15/2, p. 49 (2002).

14.3 *Changing the appearance to improve perception*

Even if we've found the most appropriate combination of quantities to look at, the amount of information we extract from a graph still depends on the way the data is presented. The way we perceive a plot depends on our human, visual-psychological perception of it. To get the most out of a graph, we should therefore format it to improve the way it will be perceived.

Whether we're aware of it or not, in looking at a plot we always tend to engage in *comparisons*. Is this line longer than that? Is this part of the curve steeper than that? Is the area underneath this function larger than the area underneath that function? And so on.

To gain the maximum insight from a plot, we therefore want to find a representation of the data that facilitates such comparisons as much as possible. In this section, I want to give you some ideas how this can be achieved.

14.3.1 *Banking*

The idea of *banking* (or *banking to 45 degrees*) goes back to W. S. Cleveland, who demonstrated in a series of controlled experiments that our ability to compare angles is greatest for angles that are close to 45 degrees.[6] In other words, if we want to assess and compare the slopes of lines on a graph, we'll do best if the graph is sized in such a way that most of the lines are roughly going diagonally across it.

In a way, this is just a confirmation of something that you probably have been doing intuitively already. Whenever you've found yourself adjusting the plot ranges of a graph to get its aspect ratio right (as opposed to narrowing the plot ranges to "zoom in" on some region), you've probably been "banking." Figure 14.8 shows a silly example of what I mean: both panels show the function $f(x) = 1/x$. In the top panel, the y range is very large, so that the plot is dominated by vertical and horizontal line segments (keep in mind that the curve is built up from many straight line segments, connecting adjacent data points) leading to an unsatisfactory impression of the graph. In the bottom panel, the y range has been constrained, so that more of the graph is occupied with line segments close to 45 degrees. That's a form of banking.

Figure 14.9 shows a more interesting data set: the number of sun spots observed annually, for the 300 years from 1700 to 1999. The number of sun spots observed varies from year to year, following an irregular cycle of about 11 years.

Because of the large number of cycles included in the graph, vertical (or almost vertical) line segments dominate the graph, making it hard to recognize the structure in the data. Figure 14.10 shows exactly the same data, but now the aspect ratio of the plot has been changed so that the raising and falling edges of the curve are close to 45 degrees. We can now easily recognize an interesting feature in the data, namely, that the number of sun spots during each cycle rises quickly, but tends to fall more slowly.

---

[6] See *The Elements of Graphing Data* by William S. Cleveland, Hobart Press (1994) and references therein.

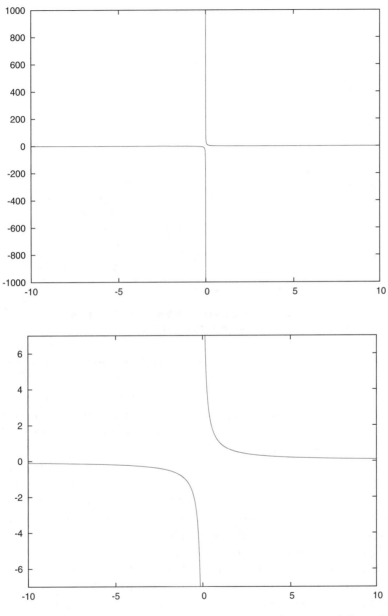

Figure 14.8 Banking: two plots of the function $1/x$. In the bottom panel, the vertical plot range has been constrained so that the average angle of line segments is approximately 45 degrees.

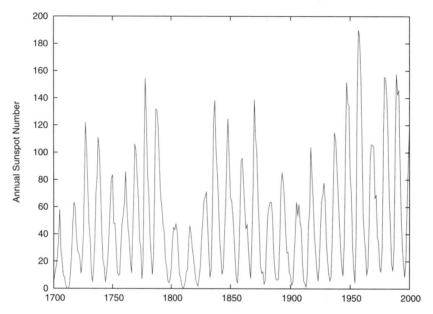

Figure 14.9 **Annual sunspot numbers for the years 1700 through 2000. What can
you say about the shape of the curve in this representation?**

(There's the visual comparison, referred to earlier!) We wouldn't have been able to
spot this from the representation of the data in figure 14.9.

In figure 14.10, I adjusted the aspect ratio of the entire plot (using `set size ratio`
`0.075`), not just the plot range. Just extending the y range by the required amount to
compress the data in the vertical direction sufficiently would've led to a graph with an
inappropriate amount of unused, wasted space.

Personally, I'm unhappy with the graph in figure 14.10. Through the banking process, we've made some important structure in the data visible, yet we've lost a lot of
detail by shrinking the y axis down to almost nothing. In figure 14.11 I show a third
way to render the data: the continuous time series has been broken up, and subsequent centuries have been shifted horizontally and vertically to make it possible to
look at all of them at the same time. (Note that all the shifting can be done as part of
the `plot` command, without the need to chop up the data file: plot [1700:1800]
`"data" u 1:2 w l, "" u ($1-100):($2+200) w l 1, "" u ($1-200):($2+400) w l 1, 200`
`w l 0, 400 w l 0.`) I think this graph (a *cut-and-stack* plot) strikes a good balance

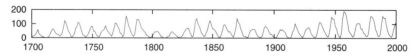

Figure 14.10 **The same data as in figure 14.9, plotted at an aspect ratio which
banks lines to 45 degrees**

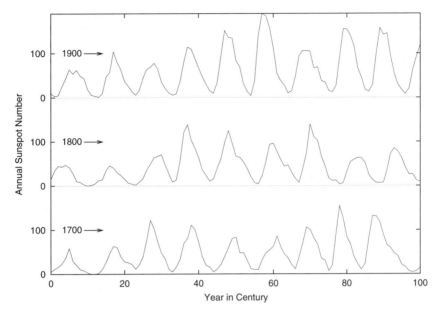

Figure 14.11   A third representation of the sunspot data from figure 14.9: a cut-and-stack plot

between the desire to find the optimal aspect ratio for the plot and the desire to choose the optimal plot range for the data.

Banking is a valuable tool. In particular, I find it helpful because it draws our attention to the importance of the apparent slopes of lines on a graph. Nevertheless, it must be used with judgment and discretion. Taken by itself, it can lead to graphs with strongly skewed aspect ratios (such as figure 14.10), which can be inconvenient to handle and which make comparisons between different parts of the graph (such as the left and the right sides in figure 14.10) difficult.

14.3.2 Judging lengths and distances

Look at figure 14.12. It shows the inflows and outflows to and from a storage tank over time. For the interval considered here, the inflows are always greater than the outflows, so that the tank tends to fill up over time, but that's not our concern right now. (Let's say the tank is large enough.)

Instead, let's ask for the *net inflow* as a function of time—the inflow less the outflow at each moment. Could you draw it? Does it look at all like the graph in figure 14.13? In particular, did your graph contain the peak between 6 and 7 on the horizontal axis? How about the relative height of the peak?

This example shows how hard it is to estimate accurately the vertical distance between two curves with large slopes. The eye has a tendency to concentrate on the *shortest* distance between two curves, not on the *vertical* distance between them. The shortest distance is measured along a straight line perpendicular to the curves. For

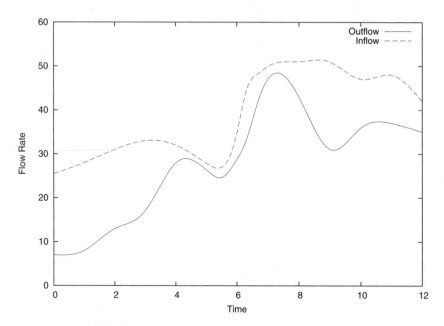

Figure 14.12   Inflow and outflow to and from a storage tank. What's the net flow to the tank?

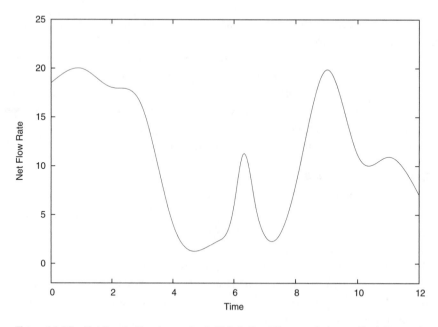

Figure 14.13   Net flow to the storage tank. This is the difference between the inflow and the outflow (see figure 14.12).

nearly horizontal curves, this is reasonably close to the vertical distance, but as the slopes become more steep, the difference becomes significant. (Because we're interested in the difference between the two flow rates at the same point in time, we're looking specifically for the vertical distance between the two curves.)

Figure 14.14 demonstrates the same point. Looking at the plot, the conclusion seems inevitable that the distance between the two curves varies, being largest close to the maxima and minima of the two curves, and in general increasing from left to right. Yet, in reality, the vertical distance between the two curves is exactly constant over the entire plot range: the graph shows the same function twice, shifted vertically by a constant amount.

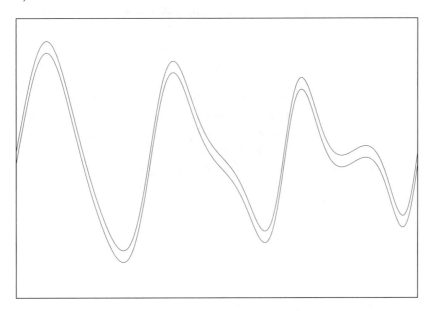

Figure 14.14   The same curve plotted twice, shifted by a small vertical amount. Note how the distance between the two curves seems to vary depending on the local slope of the curves.

14.3.3 *Enhancing quantitative perception*

Our ability to recognize differences between graphical elements depends not on the absolute, but on the relative size of the differences. In other words, we have an easier time determining which of two line segments is longer if they're 1 and 2 inches long, respectively, rather than if they're 11 and 12 inches long—the absolute difference is the same, but the relative difference is much smaller in the second case. (You may find references to *Weber's Law* or *Steven's Law* in the literature.)

We can leverage this observation to make it easier to detect differences in our graphs, for example by using a reference grid. Rather than having to compare features of the graph directly to each other, we can instead compare differences between points on the graph and nearby grid lines. As long as the grid is sufficiently fine, those differences will be smaller than the features themselves and their relative sizes therefore easier to estimate accurately.

An example will clarify. In figure 14.15, we see two curves, one above the other. Both seem to be similar to each other, exhibiting two local maxima (indicated by arrows) for example, but shifted horizontally and vertically relative to each other. But just by looking at this figure, though, it's hard to decide just how similar the two curves are.

Figure 14.16 shows exactly the same data, but now a reference grid has been added. We can use this grid to help us compare specific features of both curves. For example, we can now easily see that the vertical distance between the two maxima is approximately the same for both curves (about 2.5 vertical units), but that the intermediate minimum is shallower for the bottom curve. The horizontal distance between the maxima, on the other hand, is nearly equal between the top and bottom curves. And so on.

This is a somewhat different use for grid lines than the usual one, which is to make it easier to read off specific numeric values from the plot of a curve. Here, we're not interested in actual numbers (which is why I quite intentionally left the tic labels off), but only in the relative distances between points on the curve.

There's of course nothing special about grid lines here; they're merely the most convenient way to achieve our purpose. Alternatively, we could've placed some arrows of equal length next to the maxima of both curves and used them as yardsticks for comparisons.

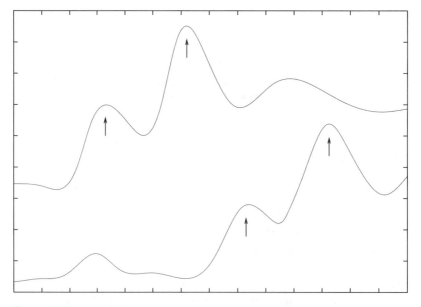

Figure 14.15   How similar are the two curves to each other?

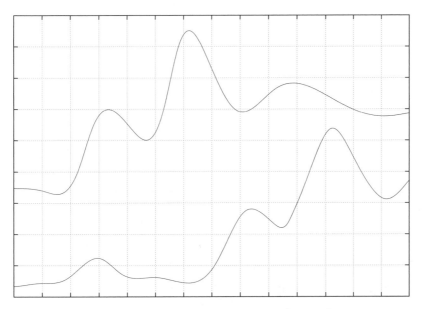

Figure 14.16 **The same curves as in figure 14.15. The reference grid helps to make detailed comparisons between curves.**

14.3.4 *Plot ranges and the matter of zero*

Plots should have meaningful plot ranges, showing those parts of the data that the viewer is most likely going to be interested in at a reasonable resolution. It may not be possible to convey all the meaning appropriately with a single choice of plot ranges, so don't be shy about showing two or more views of the same data set, for instance an overview plot and a detailed close-up of only a small section of the entire data set.

A long-standing, and largely unfruitful discussion concerns the question of whether zero should be included in the range of a graph. The answer is simple: it all depends.

If you're interested in the total value of a quantity, you probably want to include zero in your range. If you care only about the variation relative to some baseline other than zero, then don't include zero.

Figure 14.17 demonstrates what I mean. Both panels of the graph show the same data. One tells us that the total variation is small, compared to the overall value. The other panel tells us that there has been a steady increase from left to right. Both views are valid, and each gives an answer to a different question.

Plot ranges are a bit more of a concern when several graphs need to be compared against each other. In such a situation, all graphs should have the same scale to facilitate comparison; in fact, using different scales for different graphs is a guaranteed path to confusion (because the difference in scales will go unnoticed or be conveniently forgotten). And if one of the graphs legitimately includes zero, then all of them will have to do the same.

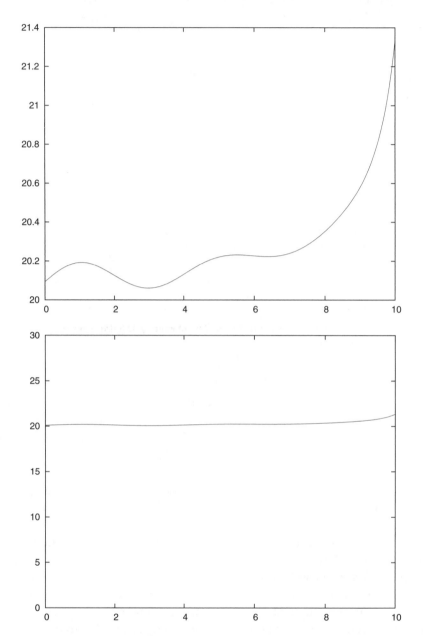

Figure 14.17   The effect of plot ranges. The data in both panels is the same, but the vertical plot range is different. The top panel shows only the variation above a baseline; the bottom panel shows the global structure of the data. Either plot is good, depending on what you want to see.

14.3.5 *A tough problem: the display of changing compositions*

A hard problem without a single, good solution concerns the graphical representation of how the breakdown of some aggregate number into its constituent parts changes over time (or with some other control variable). Examples of this type are often found in "general interest" domains. Let's consider the Earth's population, for example. Its overall magnitude changes over time, but its breakdown by continent is changing as well. Or consider pre-election opinion polls: the way votes are distributed across different candidates continues to change over time. The second example is different than the first, in that the total sum of all parts is fixed (namely, 100 percent), whereas the earth's overall population is changing together with the breakdown by continent.

A popular way to represent such information is to draw a *stacked graph*: we order the individual components in some way (more on this later), and then add the numbers for each subsequent component to all previous ones.

Let's look at an example. A company manufactures four different products, labeled A, B, C, and D. Figure 14.18 shows the number of parts manufactured per day in a stacked graph, meaning that the line labeled *B* gives the sum of produced parts of type A *and* B. The topmost line shows the total number of units produced per day.

A graph of this sort can be desirable if the composition changes dramatically over time, because it can give an intuitive feeling for the size of the relative changes. But it's hard to extract quantitative information from stacked graphs if the variation is small relative to the absolute values. Consider figure 14.18 again. For which of the four products has production increased over time, and by how much? We can only answer this question accurately for product A, because for all the other products, the changing baselines make comparisons difficult, if not impossible.

So why not show the production numbers for the four product lines individually, in a nonstacked representation? Figure 14.19 shows the whole dilemma: all the magnitudes are similar, and so the curves overlap, making the graph both unattractive and

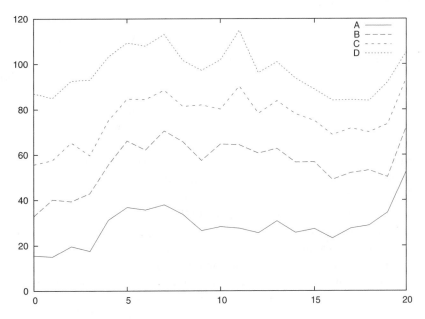

Figure 14.18   A stacked graph. Each line represents the sum of the current quantity and all previous quantities.

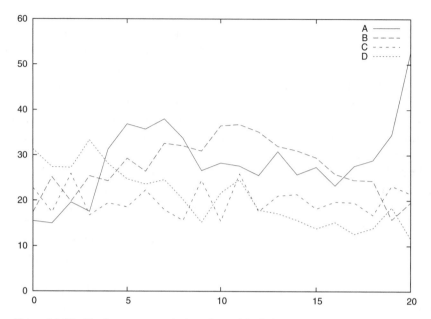

Figure 14.19   The four components from figure 14.18, but now not shown stacked

hard to read. Of course, this problem only gets worse as the number of components increases.

Figure 14.20 is yet another attempt to represent the same information: as an array of individual graphs, one for each of the product lines. This graph makes the differences in the production numbers for the four components very clear: A fluctuates, but grows strongly; B has gone up and down; C stays flat, while D has fallen continuously. The price we pay is the smaller scale of each graph. Of course we could blow each of the individual panels up to full size, but this seems like overkill for this information. As usual, it's a trade-off.

As I said in the introduction to this section, I think there's no single best approach for problems of this kind. The main take-away from this example is that stacked graphs (as in figure 14.18) easily hide trends in component parts of aggregate numbers, and we should consider alternative ways of visualizing this information. Individual graphs, either as a panel (like figure 14.20) or as a combined graph (figure 14.19) are often a better idea, possibly augmented by an additional graph showing just the total sum of all components. If aggregate numbers are required (for example, production of A and B), it's easy enough to read off the (approximate) numeric values from the individual graphs and add them—easier than to perform the visual subtraction required in figure 14.18 to get back to the individual quantities.

Make sure to draw the individual graphs to the same scale, so that quantities from different panels can be compared directly to each other.

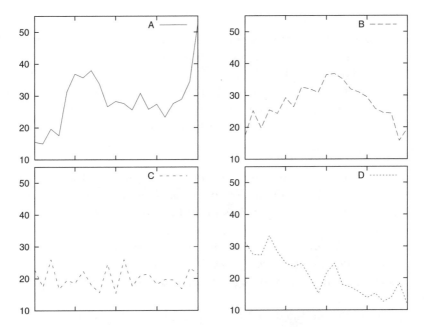

Figure 14.20 **The four components shown in individual graphs. Note that all graphs are drawn to the same scale, so that they can be compared to each other directly.**

Stacked graphs can be a good idea if we're only interested in the intermediate sums (which are pictured directly), but not in the constituent parts. To consider an example from manufacturing again, we may want to show how many parts were machined to within 5 percent of the specification, how many were within 10 percent, and how many within 25 percent. In such a situation, it's less likely that someone will ask for the number of parts that were more than 10 but less than 25 percent out of spec. But even in this example, there's trouble: someone is guaranteed to ask for the number of parts that were off by *more* than 25 percent (and therefore had to be rejected), which brings us back to the beginning.

This last example highlights another interesting question in regard to stacked graphs: the sort order. In the last example, the problem itself determines the natural sort order: smallest deviation first. But in the example in figures 14.18 through 14.20, no such natural sort order is present. In such cases, it's best to place the components with the least amount of variation first, to preserve the stability of the baseline as much as possible. The graph in figure 14.18 intentionally violates this recommendation—have you noticed how the rapid raise in component A toward the right side of the graph compounds the difficulty in assessing the changes in the other three quantities (see the discussion in section 14.3.2)?

This examples emphasizes that for some graphing problems no happy solution exists, which would combine a maximum of clarity and precision with a minimum of required space, while being intuitive and unambiguous at the same time. Don't be afraid to make trade-offs when necessary.

14.4   Housekeeping

Besides actually looking at graphs, there's a need for some other activities, which I tend to think of as housekeeping. Many of them involve the handling and organization of input and output files.

Most of these ideas amount to no more than motherhood and apple pie, meaning that you almost certainly know all of this already. But then again, as with motherhood and apple pie, a second serving doesn't hurt. Consider this dessert.

14.4.1   The lifecycle of a graph

It's helpful to have a sense for the life expectancy of your graphs: short (seconds to days, for interactive exploration and ongoing work), intermediate (days to weeks, for intermediate results), and long (weeks to infinity, for final results and public consumption).

Treat graphs differently, based on their expected lives: for short-lived graphs, ease of use is the predominant concern. Nothing should stop you from redrawing the graph, changing the range or plotting style, or a transformation. Any amount of "polishing" is too much.

For graphs in the intermediate bracket, polishing is still not required, but contextual descriptions (title, units, key) become important: not necessarily to communicate such details to others, but to serve as reminder to yourself, should you find yourself coming back to your work after a few days or weeks of absence. (It's amazing how quickly even essential details can be forgotten.)

For long-lived graphs, and those published or presented publicly, different rules apply. Such graphs belong to "presentation graphics" proper, and I'll have a bit more to say about that topic in section 14.5.

14.4.2   Input data files

Data files should be reasonably *self-contained* and *self-explanatory*. Let me explain.

When I was looking for data sets to use as examples for this book, I checked out quite a few publicly accessible data set libraries on the web. On one of them, I found a data set that, according to the description on the web site, contained annual sunspot numbers for a certain specified range of years. I downloaded the corresponding file together with several others data sets from the web site, and only then started to examine the contents of each file in detail.

Each file consisted of only a single column, containing the dependent variable—and nothing else! Looking at these files alone, it was no longer possible to determine which one contained what, be it sunspot numbers or carbon-dioxide concentration in the atmosphere, or some other data set. Since even the independent variable was missing, I couldn't even tell whether I was looking at monthly or yearly data, and in any case, for what time frame.

In other words, the sheer act of downloading a file turned it into instant garbage, by irrevocably separating it from the information that gave it meaning!

To avoid such embarrassments, it's generally a good idea to keep the basic information that's necessary to understand the data contained in the data set as part of the data file itself, typically as a block of comments near the beginning of the file. (I find it more convenient to have this information at the top of the file than at the end.) The information contained in such a header is more or less the same information that we'd put onto a graph itself in the form of textual labels and descriptions.

Most important is a description of the file format. It should at least include a description of the content of all columns, together with the units used. It's nice if it also contains a brief overall "headline" description of the file. If there's ancillary information that would be required to recreate the data set, it should also be included: things such as parameter settings for the experimental apparatus, or starting values and the version number for the simulation program that was used to calculate the data. If the data was downloaded from the web, I always make sure to keep a reference to the source URL in the file itself.

I also recommend you be rather generous when it comes to the inclusion of "redundant" information. The sunspot data I mentioned earlier is an interesting example. The lack of data for the independent variable (namely, the date) made it more difficult to use and understand the contents of the file. Given the starting value and the increment, it's trivial to reproduce it, but it's generally much more convenient to have all this information available already.

The ability to reproduce a data file if necessary is critical. Should you combine data from several sources into a single data set, or manually edit a data set to remove glitches, keep the originals. And stick a note in the combined file explaining its origins. More likely than not, you'll have to come back and do it all over again at some point. Remember: if you delete the originals, they're gone forever.

Unless there are extenuating circumstances (and even in most cases when there are), prefer plain text files over binary formats. The advantages of plain text are just too numerous: plain text is portable across all platforms (despite the annoying newline character issue), and can be manipulated using standard tools (editors, spreadsheets, scripting languages). A corrupted text file can be repaired easily—not so for a binary file. A text file is by construction more self-explanatory than a binary file will ever be. And finally, text files compress nicely, and therefore don't have to take up much disk space.

Some statistics packages keep their data sets in proprietary binary formats, and I've found the constant need to invoke a special, proprietary program just to view the contents of a file a major inconvenience, and the dependence on the operations provided by the package for all data manipulation tasks an unwelcome hindrance to my work.

If you have a legitimate need for a binary file format, at least use an existing standard, for which quality libraries are easily available. Ad-hoc binary formats are almost certainly a bad idea.

Something we don't tend to think of often are clerical errors: typos, incorrectly named files, data entered into the wrong column, wrongly recorded units—that sort of thing. They're apparently more common than you might think: Cleveland and Wainer[7] give interesting examples of odd entries in well-known data sets and provide convincing arguments that explain these entries as due to clerical errors, such as the interchange of digits, or the inadvertent switching of columns for the data points in question.

I'm not sure whether the move to electronic data manipulation (from paper and pencil) has made errors of this sort more or less likely. My hunch is that individual errors (interchange of two digits, for example) have become much less likely, while the probability for catastrophic errors (such as the mislabeling of entire files or columns) has gone up. The good news is that such catastrophic errors are possibly found much more quickly; the bad news is of course that computers are much more tolerant of complete nonsense than most humans are.

Finally: make sure critical data is backed up frequently. (I once accidentally deleted data that had taken weeks to compute. Praise your system administrators!)

14.4.3 Output files

The most important advice (again) is to make plots reproducible. Don't just export to a printable format and move on. It's almost guaranteed that you'll want to redraw the graph, with minor modifications, as more data becomes available or the understanding of it grows. Always save the plotting commands and options to a file before moving on.

Use an appropriate file format: PNG or GIF (possibly SVG) for the web; PostScript, EPS, or PDF for print publications. I routinely create both PostScript and bitmap versions of all graphs at the same time, so that I'm all set for all possible applications. This means that I end up with at least three files for each plot I make (commands, bitmap, print). Adopting a naming convention (such as always using the same basename for all three files) helps.

14.5 Reminders for presentation graphics

This book isn't primarily about presentation graphics, but about graphical analysis. There's already plenty of advice on presentation graphics, and you'll have no difficulty finding it, but not much of it appears to be based on rigorous studies. Nevertheless, the advice is often worded assertively, if not emotionally, and there's an unfortunate (and ultimately unhelpful) tendency toward the derision of work considered inadequate. Given the lack of rigorous evidence, tastes and personal opinions naturally play a large role.

I don't intend to add to this debate. Instead, I'd like present a list of reminders concerning details that are easily (and inadvertently) forgotten when preparing a graph for publication. Most of them concern the inclusion of *contextual* information, which can't be inferred from the graph itself, but which is nevertheless important for

---

[7] See section 6.4 in *Visualizing Data* by W. S. Cleveland, Hobart Press (1993) and the introduction to *Graphic Discovery* by H. Wainer, Princeton University Press (2005) for details.

understanding. By "publication" I mean any form of wider distribution of the graph: anything leaving the immediate group of coworkers who were involved in its creation, and in particular any use with a long expected lifetime.

These aren't commandments, but reminders. Use your own good judgment.

- Axes should be labeled. The labels should describe the quantity plotted and should include the units of measurement. Don't leave this information to a separate figure caption. Keep in mind that the graph may be separated from its context, so that information contained only in the caption may be lost. The caption should be used to describe salient features of the graph, not to give vital information about the plotted data itself.

- Choose meaningful, self-explanatory labels. If you must use abbreviations that aren't in common use, explain them, ideally on the graph itself, not in the caption (see previous item). (In a recent book on data graphing, I found a figure of a histogram in which the buckets were labeled *Married, Nvd, Dvd, Spd,* and *Wdd.* I marveled about the possible meaning of *Nvd* for quite a while. The abbreviations were explained neither in the text nor in the figure caption.)

- If there's more than one line in a graph, explain what each of the lines represent; either through a key, or using an explicit label referring to each line. If using a key, make sure the key entries are meaningful.

- If there's ancillary information, consider placing it onto the graph itself, rather than supplying it only in the caption.

- When publishing a false-color plot, *always* include the associated color scale in the graph. No matter how intuitive the chosen palette may appear to you, remember that there's no universal and unambiguous mapping from numbers to colors and vice versa.

- Describe the meaning of errorbars. Do they show the calculated standard deviation of the sample population? Do they represent interquartile ranges? Or do they indicate the limits of resolution of your experimental apparatus? This information can't be inferred from the graph, but must be explained through textual information.

- Use an appropriate measure of uncertainty. Don't show standard deviations for highly skewed or multimodal populations just because they're easy to calculate.

- Don't forget the basics. Choose meaningful plot ranges. Make sure that data isn't obscured by tics, keys, labels, or arrows.

- Don't be shy about choosing a different font if the default font looks ugly. Given the importance of textual information on a graph (labels, tic marks, keys), make the necessary effort to ensure that all text is clearly readable, even after the graph has been reproduced and possibly reduced in size a few times. (On the other hand, making labels too big or too bold can easily ruin the overall appearance of a plot. Experiment!)

In general, sans-serif fonts (such as Helvetica) are preferred for standalone pieces of text, whereas serif fonts (such as Times Roman) are considered more suitable for body text. Since labels on a graph tend to be short, this suggests using a good sans-serif font in plots. (I also find that sans-serif fonts enhance the visual clarity of a graph, whereas serif fonts don't, but others may disagree. Judge for yourself.)

- Don't use bit-mapped graphics formats (PNG, GIF, JPG) in print publications. Use vector formats such as PostScript, EPS, PDF, or SVG instead.
- Proofread graphs. Common spots of errors include typos in textual labels, switched data sets or interchanged labels, and omitted qualifiers (milli-, kilo-, and so on) for units.

14.6 Summary

In this chapter, we worked through some case studies in more detail and emphasized some more specialized techniques that are helpful when analyzing data through graphs.

I stressed the need to normalize data from different sources to make it comparable, and to be particularly careful when truncating or censoring data sets. It's important to understand the structure of the data before postulating specific mathematical models, to avoid drawing conclusions that are unsupported by the evidence.

I discussed some specific techniques that can be used to allow us to recognize features in the data, such as banking of curves to 45 degrees, or the use of a reference grid to help make detailed comparisons between different parts of a plot.

Two unifying themes of the chapter are the importance of iteration and the need to change the overall appearance of the graph to facilitate human perception of the displayed data. Rarely do we know at the outset what it is we want to see: the questions arise—and are answered—as we continue to work with the data.

Coda: Understanding data with graphs

But in the end, the most important thing is to draw the right conclusions from the available evidence.

During World War II, a program was launched to explore the possibility of equipping fighter planes with additional armor as protection against ground-based anti-aircraft fire.[1] To determine where on the airplane to place the armor, fighter planes returning from combat missions were investigated for bullet holes. In figure 15.1, the areas where bullet holes were found are shown shaded; areas without bullet holes are left white.

Given this evidence, where would *you* put additional armor?

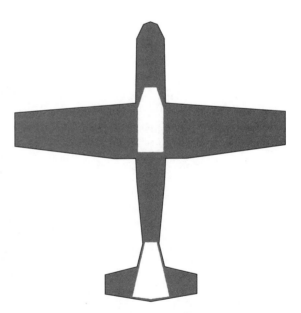

Figure 15.1 Schematic outline of a fighter airplane. Areas where bullet holes were found on machines returning from combat missions are shaded. Where would you recommend additional armor to be placed?

---

[1] The inspiration to this story stems from the book *Graphic Discovery* by Howard Wainer, Princeton University Press (2005).

The not-so-obvious obvious answer is to add the armor in those areas where *no* bullet holes were found. Why? Because airplanes are subject to hits everywhere, but if the hits strike in the white areas in figure 15.1, *the airplane doesn't come back* from its mission. (Statisticians speak of *survivorship bias.*) Therefore, those are the most vital areas of the machine and should receive the best possible protection.

So, let this be our final lesson. Evidence, be it graphical or otherwise, is just that: mere data. But actual *insight* arises only through the correct *interpretation* of those facts.

appendix A:
Obtaining, building,
and installing gnuplot

The easiest way to install gnuplot on your local computer is to download and install a precompiled package. If you're running Linux, there's a good chance gnuplot is already installed; if not, you'll have no difficulty finding an RPM or Debian package on the net. There are Fink packages for Mac OS X, and precompiled binaries for Windows as well. In section A.2 we consider some of these options in more detail.

If you'd like to be totally up to date and have access to the newest features, or if you want to start hacking on gnuplot yourself, you'll have to build from source. Section A.3 in this appendix is will help you get started.

A.1   *Release and development versions*

Gnuplot versions are generally labeled by a three-part version number, indicating major, minor, and bug-fix releases. Bug fix releases are prepared as needed (roughly twice a year). Minor releases introduce new features, but preserve backward compatibility for existing gnuplot command scripts. Major releases may break backward compatibility. The development version of a minor release is indicated by an odd version number, which is incremented to the next even number on promotion to a "released" version.

Gnuplot is a mature project—for the 4.x.x major release series, minor releases are a few years apart, and the core developer team is very conscientious about not introducing instability into released versions. On the other hand, new and exciting features continue to be added to gnuplot all the time, so there are good reasons for learning how to build gnuplot from source.

A.2   Installing a prebuilt package

Installing a prebuilt package is usually straightforward and mostly dependent on your choice of package manager.

A.2.1   Linux

Usually, the easiest way to install new software on a Linux box is to use the standard administration tool that comes with your local Linux distribution.

On RPM-based distributions, you can also download an RPM file explicitly and then install it (as root) using

```
rpm -i gnuplot-XXX.rpm
```

where you should replace gnuplot-XXX.rpm with the exact name of your downloaded package file.

On Debian-based systems, you can simply execute

```
apt-get install gnuplot
```

but be warned that gnuplot for Debian-based systems is usually built without the GNU readline library (due to strict interpretations of the differences in the GNU and the gnuplot licenses), so that you might want to build gnuplot from source instead.

A.2.2   Mac OS X

At the time of this writing, a version of gnuplot packaged as DMG (or Mac Installer) file is not generally available. The most convenient way to install gnuplot on a Mac OS X computer is via fink. Fink is a package manager based on apt-get, and you can use it to install gnuplot with the command

```
sudo fink install gnuplot
```

If you have a development environment installed, you can also use MacPorts. Mac-Ports does not install prebuilt packages; instead, it builds a gnuplot binary from scratch, resolving and downloading required libraries as needed. If you have MacPorts installed and configured, the following command will build and install gnuplot on your computer:

```
sudo port install gnuplot
```

Both commands will prompt you for the root password, which you should enter. Once gnuplot has been successfully installed using either method, you can run it by issuing the command gnuplot in the Terminal window.

A.2.3   Windows

The easiest way to install gnuplot on Windows is to use the precompiled package available from the download section of the gnuplot website at www.gnuplot.info. At the time of this writing, the most recent version available was gnuplot 4.2.5. Simply download the file gp425win32.zip and unpack it into a directory of your choice. (The file gp425win32x11.zip is for people who use Cygwin on Windows.)

Inside the zip file, you will find four folders (bin, contrib, demo, and docs), as well as some files containing the gnuplot license, a list of the most recent updates, and several files with installation instructions. The most important one of these is README.Windows, which contains Windows-specific instructions.

No further installation is required. To run gnuplot, simply execute (double-click) the prebuilt binary wgnuplot.exe in the bin folder. A new window will pop up, containing the familiar gnuplot command prompt. The window has some additional menus, which provide shortcuts to many of the gnuplot commands.

The bin directory contains some additional gnuplot executables, which are intended to emulate Unix "pipes". You can use TrueType fonts with bitmap or PostScript terminals, provided you specify the path to the local font directory (typically C:\WINDOWS\FONTS when you call set terminal. Refer to the README.Windows file for additional details.

A.3   *Building from source*

If you want to build gnuplot from source, you have two choices: either you can download and build an officially *released* version of gnuplot, or—if you want to be truly on the cutting edge—you can download and build the latest *development* version.

Released versions of gnuplot can be downloaded as source tarballs from the gnuplot home page at www.gnuplot.info. There, you can also find precompiled binaries for several non-Unix platforms.

A.3.1   *Obtaining the development version from CVS*

The development version of the gnuplot source tree is kept in CVS at www.sourceforge.net. To get a copy of the development version from the repository, follow these steps:

1 Create a directory on your local drive and change into it. You can name it any way you like.

2 Login to the CVS repository:

```
cvs
➥ -d:pserver:anonymous@gnuplot.cvs.sourceforge.net:/cvsroot/gnuplot
➥ login
```

Simply hit Enter when prompted for a password. (This step is only necessary the first time around.)

3 Check out the source tree:

```
cvs
➥ -d:pserver:anonymous@gnuplot.cvs.sourceforge.net:/cvsroot/gnuplot
➥ checkout gnuplot
```

You may want to set the environment variable CVSROOT to

```
:pserver:anonymous@gnuplot.cvs.sourceforge.net:/cvsroot/gnuplot
```

(How you do this depends on the shell you're using). If CVSROOT is set, you don't need to repeat the cvs-directory as part of the CVS command-line using the -d option.

The checkout command creates a directory called gnuplot in the current directory. We'll examine its contents next.

A.3.2 Layout of the source tree

Whether you downloaded and unpacked a tarball of a released version or checked out the current development version from CVS, you should now have a directory called gnuplot (or similar) on your local drive. Inside this directory you'll find (listing only the most important files and directories):

config/   Files required by the automake/autoconf utility, which is used to configure the build process to the local environment.

demo/   A large set of gnuplot demos and the data files required by them.

docs/   Source files for the gnuplot reference documentation. Documentation for gnuplot is maintained in a markup language that's specific to gnuplot. Help files in common formats (HTML, TeX, GNU Info, and so on) are built from the master file (called gnuplot.doc), as is the gnuplot online help feature. An explanation of the markup format can be found in the README file in the docs/ directory.

lisp/   Emacs-Lisp files, that allow Emacs to be used as a front end for gnuplot.

src/   The actual source tree.

Copyright   The gnuplot copyright and license.

INSTALL   Gnuplot build and installation instructions. Very detailed.

INSTALL.gnu   Documentation for the GNU autoconf/configure utility.

NEWS   Overview of new features, changes, and fixes in the current version of gnuplot.

README   The overall gnuplot Readme file (slightly out of date).

README.1ST   A short file with updates on issues with external libraries that are used by gnuplot (notes on conflicting licensing models, and so forth).

A.3.3 Building and installing

Specific build instructions are platform dependent. Because of the great variability of Unix platforms, the instructions for building on Unix are the most complex.

UNIX

Building gnuplot from source on Unix requires that the standard Unix development tools are installed. Besides a C compiler and make, this also includes the autoconf/automake utility, which is used during the configuration step to probe many aspects of the local build environment and to create a localized Makefile. Building is then a rather painless process using make.

Configure

When building from source, it's necessary to set up your build script first. To do so, change into the gnuplot directory and execute ./prepare to create a configure script. (This step is only required when building the development version of gnuplot; the release versions already include a usable configure script.)

In either case, run ./configure in the gnuplot directory to create a Makefile.

The configure script takes a large number of command-line options, which are described in detail in the INSTALL file. Here, I mention just the ones that you'll most likely want to tinker with. For the majority of options, the defaults are just fine.

--prefix=PREFIX   This controls where the gnuplot executable, library, and documentation files will be installed. The default is /usr/local. If you don't have root permission on your box, or if you'd like to maintain a local version of the development version, you might want to provide a different path here.

There are many more options that control the installation location of executable, library, and documentation files independently. Check the INSTALL file for details.

--with-readline   Gnuplot comes with its own minimal version of a readline library (which provides command-line editing capabilities, command completion, and a history feature). You can select this version using --with-readline or using --with-readline=builtin (this is the default). If instead you'd like to use the more powerful GNU readline library, use --with-readline=gnu, or --with-readline=DIR, where DIR is the path to a (nonstandard) directory containing the GNU readline library. Note that the GNU readline library is released under a different license than the rest of gnuplot.

--with-gd=DIR   Gnuplot uses Tom Boutell's GD library for common bitmap terminals (PNG, GIF, JPG). This option can be used to provide a path to the directory containing the library.

--with-pdf=DIR   As of release 4.2, gnuplot uses the PDFlib Lite library (www.pdflib.de). Check the file README.1ST for more details.

As of version 4.3, gnuplot ships with a new terminal pdfcairo, which generates PDF output and is based on the Cairo graphics library, making this option obsolete.

--with-wx-config=DIR   This is required if you want to build gnuplot with support for the wxt terminal, using the wxWidgets set. The value of this option must be the name of a directory containing a utility called wx-config, which is part of the wxWidgets distribution.

--with-cwdrc   This indicates whether gnuplot should check the current working directory for a .gnuplot file on startup. Usually disabled for security reasons.

The configuration step produces a long list of output, describing the local environment that will be used during the build process. It's worth skimming this output: if the configuration utility doesn't seem to find libraries that you know are available, you might have to change some of the defaults using additional command-line options described in the INSTALL file.

Also be aware that you'll need the *devel* packages for many of the required libraries, if you want to build gnuplot from source, not just the *release* packages. In particular the devel packages required for the wxt, cairo, and pango libraries might not be installed on your local system by default.

Build and install

If the configuration step has completed successfully, building gnuplot is very simple: just execute make from within the gnuplot directory. Compilation (on a reasonably current system) takes only a few minutes.

If the compilation was successful, execute make install to install the gnuplot binary, its documentation, and any required auxiliary files into the specified locations. You may want to follow this by make distclean to remove many of the temporary files left over from the build process.

WINDOWS

To build gnuplot for Windows, you must have a development environment installed. Assuming that you have Visual C++, you can compile gnuplot by stepping into the src directory and executing

```
nmake -f ..\config\makefile.nt
```

If you're using a different compiler (such as the Windows or Cygwin port of gcc), the process is similar, but you'll need to use a different Makefile. Check the INSTALL file for more details.

MAC OS X

There are two ways to build gnuplot for Mac OS X: either via a manual process similar to the one used for Unix/Linux, or using Fink. Here, I'll give some pointers for the first case only (not using Fink).

You'll need to have a development environment installed (typically Xcode from Apple's Developer Tools collection, although having merely compiler and linker will do).

You'll also need either AquaTerm or X11 installed. (Gnuplot will compile without them, but the only interactive terminal you will be able to use will be the dumb terminal. File terminals, on the other hand, will work.)

X11 is a standard installation option for Mac OS X, unless you're running Leopard or newer, on which it's already preinstalled by default. AquaTerm can be downloaded either as source code or as precompiled binary from SourceForge (available at http://aquaterm.sourceforge.net).

Once either one of these is installed and is detected during the configure step, the build process is the same as for all other Unix platforms.

There are reports that recent versions[1] of OS X ship with a broken version of the GNU readline library. These problems won't be detected during the configure step, but will lead to compile-time errors later. There are two workarounds: you can use gnuplot's own (minimalistic) version of the readline library: ./configure --with-readline=builtin; or you can replace Apple's version of the library with the GNU version before building.

---

[1] As of June 2008.

appendix B:
Gnuplot reference

B.1   Command reference

Commands are grouped by topic and sorted alphabetically within each section.

B.1.1   Running gnuplot

`exit`	Terminate gnuplot session. `exit`

`help`	Access the online help. `help [{enum:topic}]` Full documentation: section 4.5.1.

`history`	List the command history.
	`history [quiet] [{int:max}] ["{str:filename}" [append]]` `# show`
	`history ?"{str:cmd}"` `# search`
	`history !"{str:cmd}"` `# execute`
	Full documentation: section 4.5.2.

`print`	Evaluate one or more expressions and print result as text.
	`print {expression} [, {expression}, ... ]`
	Comments
	  ■ By default, output is sent to standard error.
	  ■ Output can be redirected using `set print`.
	Full documentation: section 4.4.
	See also `set print`.

`quit`	Terminate gnuplot session. `quit`

B.1.2   File system

cd	Change current directory.

```
cd "{str:path}"
```

pwd	Print the current working directory to screen.

```
pwd
```

B.1.3   Saving and loading commands

call	Load commands from a file and execute them.

```
call "{str:filename}" [ {val}, ... ]
```

Comments

- Up to ten optional parameters can be specified to `call`. Their values are available inside the called script in the variables $0 through $9.
- Inside the script, the variable $# holds the number of parameters passed to `call`.
- `call` must be the last command on a multi-command line.

Full documentation: section 2.2 and section 12.2.4.

load	Load commands from file and execute them.

```
load "{str:filename}"
```

Comments

- `load` must be the last command on a multi-command line.

Full documentation: section 2.2.

save	Save details of the current session to file.

```
save "{str:filename}"
save [ functions | variables | set | terminal ] "{str:filename}"
```

Comments

- `functions` writes only user-defined functions to file.
- `variables` writes only user-defined variables to file.
- `set` writes only the values of all currently defined options to file. The values of the `terminal` and `output` options are written out as comments.
- `terminal` writes only the current `terminal` setting and `output` file name to file (uncommented).
- Without any of the optional constraints, all user-defined functions and variables, the current values of all options, and the last `plot` command are written to file. The values of the `terminal` and `output` options are written out as comments.
- The special filename *hyphen* (-)redirects to standard output.

Full documentation: section 2.2.

B.1.4   Plotting

plot	Plot function or data (two-dimensional plot).

```
plot [ {ranges} ]
        [ {function} | "{str:filename}" ]
                     [ index {int:start}[:{int:end}][:{int:step}] ]
                     [ every {int:step}[::{int:start}[::{int:end}]] ]
                     [ using {columnspec} ]
```

```
[ axes [ x1y1 | x1y2 | x2y1 | x2y2 ] ]
[ title [ "{str:explanation}" | {int:col} ]
  | notitle ]
[ smooth [ unique | frequency | bezier | sbezier
           | csplines | acsplines ] ]
[ with {stylespec} ]
```
```
[, ... ]
```

Comments

- Ranges are given as pairs in brackets: [min:max]. Leaving an entry empty leaves the corresponding limit unchanged; supplying a * turns on autoscaling for that limit.

  Up to two ranges can be supplied: one to limit the x range, and one to constrain the y range.

  In parametric mode, up to three ranges can be supplied. The first measures the range of the parameter; the following two are as before.

- A function can be supplied, depending on a dummy variable called x in regular mode, or t in parametric mode. (The name can be changed using set dummy.)

- A text file containing data to plot can be specified.

  Supplying an empty filename reuses the most recently named file in the same plot command.

  The special filename *hyphen* (-) indicates that data should be read from the same device that the command was read from (usually standard input—the terminal in interactive mode).

- index selects which data set(s) in the input file should be plotted. Data sets are separated from each other by double blank lines in the data file. Data sets are counted starting at zero.

- every controls how lines in multiline records should be read.

- using selects which columns should be used for x and y values, and possibly other values as well (style-dependent). Column numbers start at 1.

  The pseudocolumn with column number 0 contains the line number (starting at zero) in the current data set, resetting to zero when encountering a double blank line. The pseudocolumn with column number -2 contains the index of the current data set, which is incremented whenever a double blank line is found.

  If a column number is enclosed in parentheses, the expression within the parentheses is evaluated and the result is used as if it were the column value. Within such an expression, the value of each column can be accessed by prefixing the column number with a dollar sign ($).

- axes indicates which set of axes the current data file or function should be plotted against.

- title takes a string that will be placed as explanation into the graph's key. Supplying an empty string or the notitle keyword suppresses the key entry.

- If the set key autotitle columnhead option has been enabled, title takes an integer argument that will be interpreted as a column number. The first noncomment line in the column indicated will be used as explanation in the graph's key.

- smooth applies a smoothing algorithm:
  - unique sorts points by x value and replaces multiple data points having the same x value with the average of the y values.

— frequency sorts points by x value and replaces multiple data points having the same x value with the sum of the y values.

— bezier calculates the Bézier curve through all data points.

— sbezier applies the unique transformation and then calculates the Bʔzier curve for the result.

— csplines applies the unique transformation, then calculates a natural cubic spline interpolation, passing exactly through all data points.

— acsplines applies the unique transformation, then calculates a weighted cubic spline approximation. The weights must be supplied through an additional column.

As of version 4.3, gnuplot contains two additional smoothing algorithms, cumulative and kdensity, which calculate the cumulative distribution function and the Gaussian kernel density estimate (a form of smooth histogram) for the data set.

■ A number of inline styles can be specified following with; see chapter 5 for details.

Full documentation: chapter 2 and chapter 3 for basic usage; chapter 5 for style information.

---

replot   Repeat the last plot or splot command.
```
replot
```
See also the standard gnuplot reference documentation for additional options.

---

splot   Plot function or data (three-dimensional plot).
```
splot [ {ranges} ]
        [ {function} | "{str:filename}" ]
                    [ index {int:start}[:{int:end}][:{int:step}] ]
                    [ every {int:step}[::{int:start}[::{int:end}]] ]
                    [ using {columnspec} ]
                    [ title "{str:explanation}" | notitle ]
                    [ with {stylespec} ]
        [, ... ]
```
Comments

■ The syntax is similar to the plot command, except where the additional dimension needs to be accommodated (additional range and column specs).

■ Some options available for the plot command aren't available for splot: smooth and axes.

Full documentation: chapter 8 and chapter 9.

B.1.5   *Managing options*

---

set   Set an option.
```
set ...
```
Full documentation: section 4.1.

---

show   Display information about the current session.
```
show ...
show plot
show [ variables [all] | functions ]
show [ all | version ] [ long ]
```

Comments
- Can be used with any option to see the current value of that option.
- `show plot` displays the most recent `plot` command.
- `variables` and `functions` display only user-defined variables and functions.
- `variables all` displays user-defined and gnuplot internal variables.
- `show version` and `show version long` display information about the version of gnuplot installed and its compile-time options.

Full documentation: section 4.1.

`reset`	Reset all options to their system defaults.

`reset`

Comments
- Leaves the following plot-related options unchanged: `terminal` and `output`.
- Leaves the following configuration-related options unchanged: `fontpath` and `loadpath`.

Full documentation: section 4.1.

`unset`	Disables an individual option or resets it to its default state.

`unset ...`
Full documentation: section 4.1.

B.1.6 *Subprocesses*

`shell`	Spawns an interactive shell.

`shell`

Comments
- Exit the shell to return to the gnuplot session.

Full documentation: section 12.2.

`system`	Executes a shell command and displays its output on the screen.

`system "{str:shellcmd}"`
Full documentation: section 12.2.

(back ticks)	A shell command enclosed in back ticks is executed and its output evaluated as an expression and returned.

`` `{str:shellcmd}` ``
Full documentation: section 12.2.

B.1.7 *Terminal handling*

`clear`	Clears the current output device.

`clear`

Comments
- Clears the current output device as set by `set output`.
- Particularly useful when using multiplot mode to generate images with insets.

See also `set multiplot`.

`lower`   Lowers a plot window.

    lower {int:winid}

Comments

■ Lowers the named plot window, or the currently active one if no window ID has been supplied.

`raise`   Raises a plot window.

    raise {int:winid}

Comments

■ Raises the named plot window, or the currently active one if no window ID has been supplied.

`test`   Generates a test image, demonstrating the capabilities of the currently chosen terminal.

    test
    test palette

Comments

■ `test` generates a standard test image, demonstrating line styles and point types, using the currently chosen settings of `set terminal` and `set output`.

■ `test palette` generates a test image of the currently active pm3d color mapping, using the currently chosen settings of `set terminal` and `set output`.

■ Both `set terminal` and `set output` must have been set to appropriate values prior to executing the `test` command.

Full documentation: section 5.1.2 for `test` and section 9.1.2 for `test palette`.

B.1.8   *Curve fitting*

`fit`   Performs a numerical, nonlinear least-squares fit.

    fit [{ranges}]
        {function} "{str:datafile}"
                    [index {int:start}[:{int:end}][:{int:step}]]
                    [every {int:step}[::{int:start}[::{int:end}]]]
                    [using {columnspec}]
                    via [{var1}, {var2}, ... | "{str:parameterfile}"]

Comments

■ Most of the syntax is similar to the syntax for the `plot` command and many of the data selection and transformation directives available for `plot` are also available for `fit`.

■ Both the function to fit and a file with the data must be supplied. The function must depend on the dummy variable explicitly.

■ The parameters named in the `via` clause are varied to obtain the best fit result.

Full documentation: section 10.3.

See also `set dummy`.

`update`   Writes the current values of the best-fit parameters to the named file.

    update "{str:filename}"

Comments

■ This command is only useful in conjunction with the `fit` command.

■ The format of the output file is such that it can be used as input file in the `via` directive of the `fit` command.

Full documentation: section 10.3.

See also the standard gnuplot reference documentation for further options.

B.1.9   *Miscellaneous*

bind   Change or display hot key bindings.
```
bind
bind!
bind [allwindows] "{str:keys}" "{str:command}"
```
Comments
- `bind` without any arguments displays all currently defined key bindings.
- `bind!` restores default key bindings.
- `bind` with two arguments defines a new key binding. The first argument must be the key (possibly in combination with control keys); the second argument must be the name of the command to invoke.
- The `allwindows` keyword makes the hot key active for all windows, active or not.

Full documentation: section 12.5.1.

See also `set mouse` and the standard gnuplot reference documentation for additional details.

if   Conditional execution of commands.
```
if ({condition}) {command}
    [; else if ( {condition} ) {command} ]
    [; else {command} ]
```
Comments
- The condition will be evaluated. If it's nonzero, the commands following it will be executed; otherwise the secondary condition (if present) is evaluated, and so on.
- Can be used with a counter to stop an infinite `reread` loop.

See also sections 12.4 and 12.5 and the standard gnuplot reference documentation for more details.

pause   Prints a message to the screen, then waits until a timer expires or a user event occurs.
```
pause {int:seconds} [ "{str:message}" ]
pause mouse [ {eventmask} ] [ "{str:message}" ]
```
Comments
- `pause -1` will wait until the return key is hit; `pause 0` won't wait at all.
- The eventmask must be a comma-separated combination of `keypress`, `button1`, `button2`, `button3`, and `any`. The character code (in case of a keyboard event) or the mouse coordinates (in case of a mouse event) are made available through the variables `MOUSE_KEY`, `MOUSE_CHAR` `MOUSE_X`, `MOUSE_Y`, `MOUSE_X2`, and `MOUSE_Y2`.

Full documentation: section 12.4.

reread   If used within a file containing gnuplot commands, forces gnuplot to read the file again from the beginning.
```
reread
```
Comments
- The `reread` command will continue rereading the current command file in an infinite loop, until explicitly terminated using `if`.

- Can be used to generate animated slideshows.
- The `reread` command has no effect if used at the interactive gnuplot prompt.

Full documentation: section 12.4.

B.2   Function reference

For nonelementary functions with ambiguous notations, I've given a pointer to the defining relationship in *Handbook of Mathematical Functions* by M. Abramowitz and I. Stegun (Dover Publications, 1965), quoted as A&S. (The full content of the book can be found on the web, for instance at http://www.nr.com/aands/ and http://www.convertit.com.)

B.2.1   Square root, exponential function, logarithms

Function	Description
`sqrt(x)`	Square root function
`exp(x)`	Exponential function
`log(x)`	Natural logarithm (base e)
`log10(x)`	Common logarithm (base 10)

All functions can handle complex arguments.

B.2.2   Trigonometric functions

Function	Description
`sin(x), cos(x), tan(x)`	Trigonometric functions.
`asin(x), acos(x), atan(x)`	Inverse trigonometric functions.
`atan2(y, x)`	Evaluates to `atan(y/x)`, but uses the signs of both arguments to determine the resulting quadrant. Arguments must not be complex.

Depending on the value of the `set angles` option, angles are either interpreted in radians or in degrees.

All functions can handle complex arguments, except where indicated.

B.2.3   Hyperbolic functions

Function	Description
`sinh(x), cosh(x), tanh(x)`	Hyperbolic functions
`asinh(x), acosh(x), atanh(x)`	Inverse hyperbolic functions

All functions can handle complex arguments.

B.2.4 *Bessel functions*

Function	Description
besj0(x)	Bessel function of the first kind of order 0
besy0(x)	Bessel function of the second kind of order 0
besj1(x)	Bessel function of the first kind of order 1
besy1(x)	Bessel function of the second kind of order 1

Arguments to Bessel functions are given in radians and must not be complex.
(A&S 9.1.1)

B.2.5 *Error integral and related functions*

Function	Description
erf(x)	Error function (A&S 7.1.1)
erfc(x)	Complementary error function (A&S 7.1.2): erfc(x) = 1 - erf(x)
inverf(x)	Inverse error function
invnorm(x)	Inverse normal distribution function
norm(x)	Normal (Gaussian) distribution function (A&S 26.2.2): norm(x) = 0.5*(1+erf(x/sqrt(2)))

All functions accept complex arguments, ignoring the imaginary part.

B.2.6 *Gamma function and related functions*

Function	Description
gamma(x)	Gamma function (A&S 6.1.1)
ibeta(p, q, x)	Incomplete beta function (A&S 6.6.1)
igamma(a, x)	Incomplete gamma function (A&S 6.5.1)
lgamma(x)	Natural logarithm of gamma function: lgamma(x) = log(gamma(x))

All functions accept complex arguments, ignoring the imaginary part.

B.2.7 *Miscellaneous mathematical functions*

Function	
abs(x)	Absolute value for real or complex x.
ceil(x)	Smallest integer not less than x (as floating-point value).
floor(x)	Largest integer not greater than x (as floating-point value).
int(x)	Integer part of x, truncated to zero.
lambertw(x)	Lambert-W Function (the inverse of f(w) = w exp(w)). Argument must not be complex.
rand(x)	Random number generator (see table 3.1).
sgn(x)	Sign function (-1 if x < 0; 0 if x = 0; 1 if x > 0).

All functions accept complex arguments, ignoring the imaginary part (except for abs()).

B.2.8 *Functions for complex arguments*

Function	
abs(x)	Absolute value of x: sqrt(real(x)**2 + imag(x)**2)
arg(x)	Phase angle of x: atan(imag(x)/real(x))
imag(x)	Imaginary part of x
real(x)	Real part of x

B.2.9 *String functions*

Function	Description
exists("x")	Takes a variable name as string and returns 1 if a variable with that name has been defined, 0 otherwise.
strlen("str")	Takes a string and returns the number of characters in the string.
substr("str", i, j)	Takes a string and two integers and returns the substring indicated by the two arguments. Equivalent to str[i:j]. The argument i is the position of the first character in the substring, the argument j is the position of the last character in the substring. Character positions start at 1.
strstrt("str", "key")	Takes two strings. Returns the index of the first character of the string key in the string str, or zero if not found. Character positions start at 1.

Continued on next page

Function	Description
`words( "str" )`	Takes a string. Strips leading and trailing whitespace, then breaks the string into tokens on whitespace. Returns the number of tokens found. Newlines and tabs are interpreted as whitespace only if the string was double-quoted.
`word( "str", n )`	Takes a string and an integer. Strips leading and trailing whitespace, then breaks the string into tokens on whitespace. Returns the nth token found. (Tokens are counted starting at 1, not at zero.) Newlines and tabs are interpreted as whitespace only if the string was double-quoted.
`sprintf( "format", ... )`	Returns a formatted string. Equivalent to the `sprintf()` function in the C standard library.
`gprintf( "format", ... )`	Returns a formatted string. Similar to `sprintf()`, but uses gnuplot's format specifiers. Compare section 7.3.3 on `set format` for details.
`system( "command" )`	Takes a shell command as string and executes it in a subshell. Returns the output of the shell command. (More detail in chapter 12.)

B.2.10 *Column manipulation functions*

The following functions are only useful as part of a `using` directive.

Function	Description
`column(x)`	Takes the number of a column as integer and returns the current value of that column as a *number*.
`stringcolumn(x)`	Takes the number of a column as integer and returns the current value of that column as a *string*.
`valid(x)`	Takes the number of a column as integer and returns 1 if the current value of that column is valid.

B.2.11 *Time column handling functions*

Function	Description
`timecolumn(x)`	Takes the number of a column as integer and parses the column value according to `set timefmt`. It returns the result as a numeric value, which can be supplied to the time handling functions (such as `tm_sec(x)`, and so forth) for interpretation. The function requires that `set _data time` *not* be enabled for the columns in question. This function can only be used as part of a `using` directive.

Continued on next page

Function	Description
tm_sec(x), tm_min(x), tm_hour(x), tm_mday(x), tm_mon(x), tm_year(x), tm_wday(x), tm_yday(x)	These functions take the value returned from timecolumn(x) and extract individual elements of date/time information from it. The functions return seconds, minutes, hours, day of month (1...31), month (0...11), year (including the century part), day of week, day of year, respectively.

B.3   Operator reference

Operators are grouped by the number of operands they take: unary, binary, and ternary.

B.3.1   Unary operators

In order of decreasing precedence.

Operator	Example	Argument type	Description
!	!a	int	logical NOT
~	~a	int	one's complement
!	a!	int	factorial
−	-a	any numerical	unary minus
+	+a	any numerical	unary plus

B.3.2   Binary operators

In order of decreasing precedence.

Operator	Example	Argument Type	Description
**	a**b	any numerical	exponentiation
*	a*b	any numerical	multiplication
/	a/b	any numerical	division
%	a%b	int	modulo
+	a+b	any numerical	addition
−	a-b	any numerical	subtraction
<	a<b	any numerical	less than
<=	a<=b	any numerical	less than or equal to
>	a>b	any numerical	greater than

Continued on next page

Operator	Example	Argument Type	Description
>=	a>=b	any numerical	greater than or equal to
==	a==b	any numerical	numerical equality
!=	a!=b	any numerical	numerical inequality
&	a&b	int	bitwise AND
^	a^b	int	bitwise XOR
|	a|b	int	bitwise OR
&&	a&&b	int	logical AND
||	a||b	int	logical OR
.	a.b	string	string concatenation
eq	a eq b	string	string equality
ne	a ne b	string	string inequality

The logical operators `&&` and `||` short-circuit, meaning that the second argument is only evaluated if the truth of the entire expression isn't determined after evaluating the first argument.

B.3.3 *Ternary operator*

The ternary operator

```
a ? b : c
```

evaluates its first argument (which must evaluate to an integer). If true (nonzero), the second argument is evaluated and returned; otherwise, the third argument is evaluated and returned.

B.4 *Option reference*

Options are grouped by topic and sorted alphabetically within each section.

B.4.1 *Configuration*

`datafile` Controls how certain aspects of a data file will be interpreted when read by gnuplot.

```
set datafile commentschar ["{str:chars}"]
set datafile separator [ "{str:char}" | whitespace ]
set datafile missing ["{str:str}"]
```

Comments
- `whitespace` is the default. In this mode, columns may be separated from each other by any number of space or tab characters.
- If not using `whitespace`, only a single character can be declared as separator at any given time.
- Separator characters aren't interpreted as separators within quoted strings.

Full documentation: section 4.2.

`decimalsign`   Changes the character to be used as decimal sign.

```
set decimalsign [ "{str:char}" | locale [ "{str:locale}" ] ]
```

Comments

- If an explicit string is given, it'll be used as decimal sign.
- If a locale is specified, the locale-dependent decimal sign will be used.

See also the standard gnuplot reference documentation.

Example:
```
set decimalsign ","
set decimalsign locale
```

`encoding`   Selects the character encoding.

```
set encoding [ default | iso_8859_1 | iso_8859_2 | iso_8859_15
               | koi8r | koi8u | cp437 | cp850 | cp852 | cp1250 ]
```

Comments

- `iso_8859_1` is equivalent to the PostScript encoding ISO-Latin-1 and is commonly used for Western European languages.
- `iso_8859_2` is used for Central and Eastern European languages.
- `iso_8859_15` is similar to `iso_8859_1`, but includes the euro symbol.
- `koi8r` (Russian) and `koi8u` (Ukrainian) are Cyrillic encodings.
- The other encodings are used by MS-DOS, OS/2, and MS Windows.

See also the standard gnuplot reference documentation.

`fit`   Defines the filename to which the `fit` command writes its output. Also controls whether the `fit` command will populate certain variables in the current gnuplot session.

```
set fit [ logfile "{str:filename}" ] [ [no]errorvariables ]
```

Full documentation: section 10.3.

See also the `fit` command.

`fontpath`   The path searched by PostScript terminals for font files.

```
set fontpath [ "{str:path}" ]
```

Comments

- This option is only relevant to PostScript terminals.
- The path value must be suitable for the local platform (for example, with respect to the choice of path separator character).
- Bitmap terminals based on the `libgd` library don't use this option. They inspect the `GDFONTPATH` environment variable instead.

Full documentation: section 11.4.

See also section 12.5 on environment variables.

`historysize`   Sets the number of commands retained in the command history buffer.

```
set historysize {int:size}
```

Comments

- Only available when gnuplot was built with support for the GNU readline library.

Full documentation: section 4.5.2.

loadpath   General gnuplot search path, used to locate command and data files.

```
set loadpath [ "{str:path}" ]
```

Comments
- The directories in the loadpath are searched after the current working directory.
- The path value must be suitable for the local platform (for example, with respect to the choice of path separator character).
- If the environment variable GNUPLOT_LIB is set, its contents is appended to loadpath.

See also section 12.5.

macros   Enables macro expansion.

```
set macros
```

Comments
- Only available when gnuplot was built with support for macro substitution.

See also section 12.1.

mouse   Enables mouse actions.
See also the standard gnuplot reference documentation.

B.4.2   Math

angles   Selects whether angles are interpreted as radians (default) or degrees.

```
set angles [ radians | degrees ]
```

Comments
- This option affects how the arguments of trigonometric functions are interpreted.
- This option is relevant in polar mode (set polar) or when using cylindrical or spherical coordinates (set mapping).
- This option has no effect on Bessel or hyperbolic functions.
- Inverse hyperbolic functions of complex arguments require set angles radians.

See also set polar, and set mapping.

dummy   Sets the name of the dummy variable in plot commands.

```
set dummy {varname1} [, {varname2} ]
```

Comments
- By default, the name of the dummy variable for the plot command is x (or t in parametric or polar mode).
- By default, the name of the dummy variables for the splot command are x and y (or u and v in parametric mode).

mapping   Chooses the coordinate system for the splot command.

```
set mapping [ cartesian | cylindrical | spherical ]
```

See also section 10.2.2.

parametric   Switches to parametric mode.

```
set parametric
```

Full documentation: section 10.2.1.

---

polar   Switches to polar mode.

`set polar`

Comments

- Not supported for `splot`.

Full documentation: section 10.2.2.
See also set `mapping`.

---

samples   The number of points at which a function is evaluated for a plot.

`set samples {int:samples1} [, {int:samples2} ]`

Comments

- Defaults to `set samples 100`.
- The second parameter is only relevant for `splot`.

Full documentation: section 3.5.
See also set `isosamples`.

---

zero   Threshold for small values.

`set zero {expression}`

Comments

- Gnuplot won't plot a point if its imaginary part is greater in magnitude than the zero threshold.
- Defaults to 1.0e-8.
- `set zero 0` is legal.

See also the standard gnuplot reference documentation.

B.4.3   *Appearance*

---

border   Controls whether a border is drawn around the plot region.

```
set border [ {int:mask} ] [ front | back ]
          [ [ linewidth | lw {int:width} ]
            [ linetype | lt {idx:type} ]
          | [ linestyle | ls {idx:style} ] ]
```

Comments

- The `mask` parameter is used to turn individual sides of the border on or off. For two-dimensional plots, the mask values are 1=bottom, 2=left, 4=top, 8=right. For three-dimensional plots, see table 8.2.

Full documentation: section 6.6.2 and section 8.3.1.
See also set `margin`.

---

clip   Suppresses data points near the edge of the graph and lines connecting data points outside the graph area.

```
set clip points
set clip [ one | two ]
```

Comments

- `set clip points` suppresses individual data points which would touch or overlap the graph's border. Only relevant for styles using individual plot symbols, such as `with points` or `with linespoints`.
- The effect of `set clip points` depends on the current symbol size.

- If `set clip one` is active, line segments are drawn if at least one of their endpoints falls into the visible plot range.
- If `set clip two` is active, line segments are drawn even if neither of their endpoints falls into the visible plot range.

Full documentation: section 3.5.

See also `set offsets`.

`logscale`   Switches on log-scaling for the selected axes.

```
set logscale [ {enum:axes} ] [ {flt:base} ]
```

Comments

- The `axes` parameter must be any one of the following indicators: x, y, x2, y2, z, or cb. If omitted, all axes are assumed.
- The base defaults to 10.

Full documentation: section 3.6.

`margin`   Sets the empty margins around the graph.

```
set bmargin [ {int:margin} ]    # bottom margin
set lmargin [ {int:margin} ]    # left margin
set tmargin [ {int:margin} ]    # top margin
set rmargin [ {int:margin} ]    # right margin

show margin                     # show current settings
```

Comments

- The units are character widths and heights using the default font for the current terminal.
- A negative value instructs gnuplot to revert to the computed default value.

Full documentation: section 6.6.2.

See also `set border`.

`multiplot`   Turns on multiplot mode.

```
set multiplot [ title "{str:title}" ]
              [ layout {int:rows},{int:cols}
                [ rowsfirst | columnsfirst ]
                [ downwards | upwards ]
                [ scale {flt:xfactor}[,{flt:yfactor}] ]
                [ offset {flt:xoff}[,{flt:yoff}] ] ]
```

Comments

- `layout` creates a regular grid of plots. `rowsfirst`, `columnsfirst`, `downwards`, and `upwards` control the order in which the grid is filled.
- `scale` and `offset` apply size scaling and translation from the default position.
- If `layout` isn't used, `set origin` and `set size` must be set explicitly for each subgraph.

Full documentation: section 10.1.

See also `set origin`, `set size`, and the `clear` command.

offsets	Offsets puts an empty boundary around the data inside an autoscaled graph. In other words, the autoscaled plot ranges are extended to make room for the offsets in addition to the data.

```
set offsets [ {flt:left} [, {flt:right}
                   [, {flt:top} [, {flt:bottom}]]]]
```

Comments

■ Left and right offsets are given in x axis units, top and bottom offsets in y axis units.

See also the standard gnuplot reference documentation.

origin	Fixes the origin of the graph on the canvas.

```
set origin {flt:x}, {flt:y}
```

Comments

■ Coordinates must be given in the `screen` coordinate system.

Full documentation: section 6.6.1.
See also set `size`.

size	Fixes the size of the graph on the canvas.

```
set size [ [no]square | ratio {flt:r} | noratio ]
           [ {flt:x} [,{flt:y}] ]
```

Comments

■ set size `x,y` scales the graph relative to the canvas.

■ For positive values of r, set size ratio r generates a graph with an aspect ratio equal to r. (The aspect ratio is the ratio of the y axis length to the x axis length.)

■ For negative values of r, set size ratio r generates plots in which the ratio of the y and x axis units equals the absolute value of r.

■ `square` is equivalent to `ratio 1`.

Full documentation: section 6.6.1.
See also set `origin`.

B.4.4   Decorations

arrow	Place an arrow on the graph.

```
set arrow [{idx:tag}] [ from {pos:from} ][ [to|rto] {pos:to} ]
                       [ [ arrowstyle | as {idx:style} ]
                         | [ [ nohead | head | backhead | heads ]
                            | [ size {flt:length} [,{flt:angle}]
                                 [,{flt:backangle}] ]
                            [ filled | empty | nofilled ]
                            [ front | back ]
                            [ [ linetype | lt {idx:type} ]
                              [ linewidth | lw {int:width} ]
                              | [ linestyle | ls {idx:style} ] ]
                         ]
                       ]
```

Full documentation: section 6.3.2.

key   Configure the key (or legend) of the graph.

```
set key [ on|off ] [ default ]
        [ [ at {pos:position} ]
          | [ inside | lmargin | rmargin | tmargin | bmargin ] ]
        [ left | right | center ] [ top | bottom | center ]
        [ vertical | horizontal ] [ Left | Right ]
        [ [no]reverse ] [ [no]invert ]
        [ [no]autotitle [columnheader] ] [ [no]enhanced ]
        [ samplen {flt:len} ] [ spacing {flt:factor} ]
        [ title "{str:text}" ]
        [ width {int:chars} ] [ height {int:chars} ]
        [ [no]box [ [ linetype | lt {idx:type} ]
                    [ linewidth | lw {int:width} ]
                    | [ linestyle | ls {idx:style} ] ] ]
```

Comments
- left, right, top, bottom, and center can be used in any combination as shorthand to indicate the desired position of the key.
- vertical and horizontal control the arrangement of line samples in the key.
- Left and Right control the alignment of the textual explanations within the key.
- reverse places the explanation to the right of the line sample.
- inverse reverses the vertical stacking of all items in the key.
- autotitle columnheader takes the explanations from the first noncomment line in the data file.

Full documentation: section 6.4.

label Places a text label on the graph.

```
set label [{idx:tag}] [ "{str:text}" ] [ at {pos:location} ]
                      [ left | center | right ]
                      [ rotate [ by {int:degrees} ] | norotate ]
                      [ font "{str:name}[,{int:size}]" ]
                      [ [no]enhanced ] [ front | back ]
                      [ textcolor | tc [ {clr:colorspec}
                                       | lt {idx:type}
                                       | ls {idx:style} ] ]
                      [ point lt|pt {idx:pointtype}
                              | ps {idx:pointsize} | nopoint ]
                      [ offset {pos:off} ]
```

Comments
- left, center, and right control the text alignment.
- point places a symbol at the position named in the label.

Full documentation: section 6.3.3.

object Places a graphics object on the graph.

```
set object [{idx:tag}] rectangle [ from {pos:from} [to|rto] {pos:to}
                                 | center|at {pos:ctr}
                                   size {pos:extent} ]
                                 [ default ]
                                 [ front | back | behind ]
                                 [ fillcolor | fc {clr:color} ]
                                 [ fillstyle | fs {idx:style} ]
                                 [ linewidth | lw {flt:width} ]
```

Comments

- Rectangles can be defined by specifying to corners diagonally across from each other using to (absolute coordinates of both corners) or rto (relative coordinates of second corner).

- Alternatively, the center of the rectangle can be fixed using at, followed by the width and height.

- behind draws the rectangle behind all other graph elements (so that the rectangle becomes the graph's background).

Full documentation: section 6.3.4.

---

timestamp   Places a timestamp using the current time and date into the left margin of the graph.

```
set timestamp ["{str:format}"]
              [ top | bottom ] [ [no]rotate ]
              [ offset {pos:offset} ]
              [ font "{str:name}[,{int:size}]" ]
```

Comments

- The format string uses the same syntax as the set timefmt option. The default is "%a %b %d %H:%M:%S %Y".

- rotate rotates the label by 90 degrees.

See also set timefmt.

---

title   Places a textual title centered at the top of the plot.

```
set title [ "{str:text}" ]
          [ font "{str:name}[,{int:size}]" ][ [no]enhanced ]
          [ textcolor | tc [ {clr:colorspec}
                           | lt {idx:type}
                           | ls {idx:style} ] ]
          [ offset {pos:off} ]
```

Full documentation: section 6.3.3.

B.4.5   *Style*

A color specification begins with the keyword rgbcolor (or rgb for short), followed by a string, which can either be the name of a color known to gnuplot, or a hex string, preceded by a # character, giving the RGB components of the desired color.

```
rgbcolor "{str:colorname}"
rgbcolor "{#RRGGBB}"
```

Use show palette colornames for a list of available color names.

See the standard gnuplot reference documentation for additional ways to specify color.

---

set style   Controls global style aspects.

```
set style data {enum:style}
set style function {enum:style}
set style increment [ default | userstyles ]
```

Comments

- set style data sets the default style for data read from a file.

- set style function sets the default style for plotting functions.

- set style increment controls how gnuplot chooses line types or line styles when plotting several data sets or functions with the same plot command. default cycles through the predefined line types available for the current terminal; userstyles prefers user-defined custom line styles if available, falling back to predefined line types if no line style with the required index is available.

Full documentation: section 5.1.3 and section 5.3.

`set style arrow` Creates custom arrow styles.

```
set style arrow {idx:index} default

set style arrow {idx:index} [ nohead | head | backhead | heads ]
                           [ size {flt:length} [,{flt:angle}]
                                  [,{flt:backangle}] ]
                           [ filled | empty | nofilled ]
                           [ front | back ]
                           [ [ linetype | lt {idx:type} ]
                             [ linewidth | lw {int:width} ]
                             | [ linestyle | ls {idx:style} ] ] ]
```

Comments
- Creates a custom arrow style for the desired index. Styles defined in this way can then simply be called as part of a `set arrow` command.

Full documentation: section 6.3.2.

See also `set arrow`.

`set style fill` Sets aspects of the global fill style.

```
set style fill [ empty | solid [{flt:density}] | pattern [{idx:n}] ]
               [ border [ {idx:linetype} ] | noborder ]
```

Comments
- There's only a single fill style, which applies globally.
- The fill style applies to box styles and to the `filledcurves` style.
- `solid` takes a density parameter between 0 (empty) and 1 (solid).
- `pattern` takes an integer parameter referring to one of the patterns available for the current terminal.

Full documentation: section 5.2.2.

See also the `test` command.

`set style histogram` Enables the interpretation of input data for histograms.

```
set style histogram [ clustered [ gap {flt:gap} ]
                    | errorbars [ gap {flt:gap} ]
                                [ linewidth | lw {int:width} ] ]
                    | rowstacked | columnstacked
```

Comments
- `clustered` plots each *row* in the input file as a separate histogram (histogram boxes are placed side by side).
- The `gap` parameter controls the spacing between distinct histograms, as a multiple of the width of an individual histogram box.
- `errorbars` is similar to `clustered`, but adds an errorbar on top of each box in the histogram.
- `rowstacked` builds a stacked histogram from each row in the input file (histogram boxes are stacked on top of each other).
- `columnstacked` builds a stacked histogram from each column in the input file (histogram boxes are stacked on top of each other).

Full documentation: section 5.2.2.

`set style line`   Creates custom line styles.

```
set style line {int:index} default
set style line {int:index} [ [ linetype  |  lt ] {idx:linetype} ]
                           [ [ linewidth |  lw ] {flt:linewidth} ]
                           [ [ pointtype |  pt ] {idx:pointtype} ]
                           [ [ pointsize |  ps ] {flt:pointsize} ]
                           [ [ linecolor |  lc ] {clr:colorspec} ]
```

Comments
- Creates a custom line style for the desired index.

Full documentation: section 5.3.

`set style rectangle`   Sets aspects of the global style for rectangle objects.

```
set style rectangle [ front | back | behind ]
                    [ fillcolor | fc {clr:color} ]
                    [ fillstyle | fs {idx:style} ]
                    [ linewidth | lw {flt:width} ]
```

Full documentation: section 6.3.4.

See also: `set object`.

OPTIONS

`bars`   Controls the size of the tic mark at the end of errorbars.

```
set bars [ small | large | fullwidth | {flt:mult} ]
```

Comments
- The parameter is a multiplier, relative to the default length.
- `small` is equivalent to 0.0; `large` is equivalent to 1.0.

Full documentation: section 5.2.3.

`boxwidth`   Controls the width of boxes for box styles.

```
set boxwidth [ {flt:size} ] [ absolute | relative ]
```

Comments
- The parameter can be an absolute box width in x axis units using the `absolute` keyword.
- The parameter can be a multiplier relative to the default box width using the `relative` keyword. The default width is the width that makes each box touch adjacent boxes.

Full documentation: section 5.2.2.

`pointsize`   Controls the size of plotting symbols.

```
set pointsize {flt:mult}
```

Comments
- The parameter is a multiplier, relative to the default point size.

Full documentation: section 5.2.1.

B.4.6 Axes

Several options related to axes exist in different forms, applicable to the different axes that may exist in a plot. The respective axis is referenced as part of the option name. For the options described in this section, the specific axis indicator has been replaced by an underscore (_). When calling such an option, the underscore must be replaced with one of the values from the following table.

Prefix	Applicable axis
x	Primary x axis
y	Primary y axis
x2	Secondary x axis
y2	Secondary y axis
z	z axis
cb	colorbox

A screen location can be specified in five different coordinate systems. Each part of a coordinate specification can be prefixed individually with a keyword identifying the coordinate system it refers to. (See section 6.2 for more detail.)

Identifier	Description
first	The primary coordinate system (bottom and left).
second	The secondary coordinate system (top and right). Not available for three-dimensional plots.
graph	The graph area proper. The bottom-left corner of the graph has coordinate (0,0); its top-right corner has coordinate (1,1).
screen	The entire screen area. The bottom-left corner of the graph has coordinate (0,0); its top-right corner has coordinate (1,1).
character	Positions in character widths and heights from the origin (0,0) of the screen area. Coordinates depend on the font size of the default font for the current terminal.

---

autoscale Enables automatic selection of plot ranges for axes.
See also set _range and the standard gnuplot reference documentation.

---

format Sets the number format to be used for tic labels.
  `set format [ x | y | x2 | y2 | xy | z | cb ] [ "{str:format}" ]`

Comments
  - Omitting the axis specifier will apply the formatting to all axes.
  - The format string uses `printf()`-like conversion specifiers. See table 7.2.
  - Additional conversion specifiers are available for date/time information. See table 7.3 and table 7.4.
  - An empty format string leads to a tic mark without a tic label.
  - This option also determines the output format when using the `set table` option.

Full documentation: section 7.3.3 and section 7.5.2.
See also set table.

grid Draws a reference grid at the tic mark positions across the plot area.

```
set grid [ [no]_tics ] [ [no]m_tics ]
           [ layerdefault | front | back ]
           [ polar [ {flt:angle} ] ]
           [ [ linetype | lt {idx:majortype} ]
             [ linewidth | lw {flt:majorwidth} ]
             | [ linestyle | ls {idx:majorstyle} ] ]
           [, [ linetype | lt {idx:minortype} ]
              [ linewidth | lw {flt:minorwidth} ]
              | [ linestyle | ls {idx:minorstyle} ] ]
```

Comments

- Grid lines can be enabled/disabled for major and minor tic marks individually, using no_tics (major) and nom_tics (minor).
- The grid can be drawn in front of (front) or behind (back) the data.
- layerdefault is only relevant for three-dimensional plots and may interfere with set hidden3d. Check the standard gnuplot reference documentation for details.
- polar draws a circular grid suitable for polar coordinates.

Full documentation: section 7.3.5.

See also set polar.

_label Places a label on the axis.

```
set _label ["{str:text}"] [ offset {pos:offset} ]
                          [ font "{str:name}[,{int:size}]" ]
                          [ textcolor | tc [ {clr:color}
                                              | lt {idx:type}
                                              | ls {idx:style} ] ]
                          [ [no]enhanced ]
                          [ rotate by {int:degrees} ]
```

Comments

- This option is a special case of the more general set label command with specific defaults.

Full documentation: section 6.3.3.

See also set label.

---

m_tics Controls the placement of minor tic marks.

```
set m_tics [ {int:intervals} | default ]
```

Comments

- Minor tic marks are never labeled.
- By default, minor tic marks are drawn for logarithmic axes, but not for linear axes.
- The optional parameter counts the number of subintervals between major tics; the number of minor tic marks generated is one less than this number.
- To place minor tic marks at specific locations, use set _tics.
- Don't confuse with _mtics, which is used in time series mode.

Full documentation: section 7.3.2.

See also set _tics.

_range   Sets the plot range.

```
set _range [{flt:min}:{flt:max}]    # Including the [..] brackets!
```

Comments

- Omitting the value for either minimum or maximum limit leaves the corresponding setting unchanged.
- The colon (:) must be supplied, even if one of the limits is omitted.
- Using a star (*) turns on autoscaling for that limit.
- In addition to the usual axes prefixes, there are additional variants of this option: trange, urange, vrange for parametric mode; and rrange for polar mode.

Full documentation: section 7.2.

See also set autoscale and the standard gnuplot reference documentation for additional options.

_tics   Controls placement and appearance of tic marks and tic labels.

```
set _tics [ axis | border ]
          [ [no]mirror ]
          [ in | out ]
          [ scale [ default | {flt:major} [,{flt:minor}] ] ]
          [ [no]rotate [by {flt:ang}] ]
          [ offset {pos:offset} | nooffset ]
          [ font "{str:name} [,{int:size}]" ]
          [ textcolor | tc {clr:color} ]
          [ add ]
          [ autofreq
            | {flt:incr}
            | {flt:start}, {flt:incr} [,{flt:end}]
            | ( ["{str:label}"] {flt:pos} [ 0 | 1 ]
                [, ["{str:label}"] ... ] ) ]
```

Comments

- Only major tic marks are labeled.
- By default, tic marks are drawn on the border, but can also be placed on the axis (the location where one of the coordinates is zero).
- By default, tic marks are mirrored on the opposing border.
- By default, tic marks are drawn to extend into the graph area from the border, but can also made to extend outward.
- scale takes one or two numeric arguments, which are interpreted as multiplicative factors to adjust the size of tic marks relative to their default size. If no value for the scale of the minor tic marks is given, minor tic marks are drawn half as long as major tic marks.
- Tic labels can be rotated or shifted from their default positions.
- Using the add keyword, all subsequent tic mark requests are added to the already existing ones. When omitting add, the current tic mark request will clobber previous settings.
- Tic marks can be autogenerated using autofreq.
- If only a single numeric argument is given, it's interpreted as an increment for tic mark placement, starting at zero.
- If two or more numeric arguments are given, they're interpreted as starting value and increment, treating the optional third argument as end value.

- Individual tic marks can be placed by giving their label, followed by their location in regular parentheses: ("0.5" 0.5). To set several tic marks this way, separate them by commas inside the parentheses: ("0.5" 0.5, "1.0" 1.0). An optional third parameter can be given to indicate whether the tic mark is supposed to be drawn as major (0) or minor (1).
- set tics (without axis prefix) applies settings to all axes.

Full documentation: section 7.3.1.

---

ticscale   Deprecated—use set tics scale instead.

---

zeroaxis   Draws axes on the graph itself.

```
set _zeroaxis [ [ linetype | lt {idx:type} ]
                [ linewidth | lw {flt:width} ]
                | [ linestyle | ls {idx:style} ] ]
```

Comments
- Axes are drawn at locations where at least one of the coordinates has value zero.

Full documentation: section 7.3.5.

DATE/TIME

---

locale   Determines the language and formatting of tic labels when using set _dtics or set _mtics.

```
set locale ["{str:locale}"]
```

Comments
- The argument must be a locale designation available on the current platform. (On Unix, the command locale -a lists all available locales.)
- This option is only used when using either the set _dtics or the set _mtics option to generate textual tic labels for the names of weekdays or months (respectively).

Full documentation: section 7.5.1.
See also set _dtics and set _mtics.

---

timefmt   Determines the way date/time information in a data file will be parsed.

```
set timefmt "{str:format}"
```

Comments
- This option has no effect unless time series mode has been enabled using set _data time.
- This option determines how entries in an input file will be read; it doesn't influence output formatting.
- The format string uses scanf()-like conversion specifiers. See table 7.3 and table 7.4 for available conversions.

Full documentation: section 7.5.2.

_data   Switches time series mode on or off.

```
set _data [ time ]
```

Comments
- If used with the keyword time, time series mode is enabled for that axis. Values in the data file will be parsed according to the format specified by set timefmt. (Output is controlled by set format.)
- If used without the time keyword, reverts back to normal processing.

Full documentation: section 7.5.2.
See also set timefmt and set format.

`_dtics` Interprets numeric input values as days of the week and uses weekday names as tic labels.

`set _dtics`

Comments
- Input value 0=Sunday, ..., 6=Saturday.
- Overflows are converted modulo 7.
- Weekday names are locale dependent, according to the value of `set locale`.

Full documentation: section 7.5.1.

See also `set locale` and `set _mtics`.

`_mtics` Interprets numeric input values as months of the year and uses month names as tic labels.

`set _mtics`

Comments
- Input value 1=January, ..., 12=December.
- Overflows are converted modulo 12.
- Month names are locale dependent, according to the value of `set locale`.

Full documentation: section 7.5.1.

See also `set locale` and `set _dtics`.

B.4.7   *Three-dimensional plots*

`dgrid3d` Constructs a smooth surface approximation to an arbitrary set of points.

`set dgrid3d [ {int:nx} [, {int:ny} [, {int:q} ] ] ]`

Comments
- The first two parameters control the number of node points for the approximation surface.
- The third parameter controls the order of the approximation.
- Additional smoothing kernels are available in gnuplot version 4.3 and later.

Full documentation: section 8.4.3.

`hidden3d` Enables hidden-line removal for surface plotting (surfaces will appear opaque).

`set hidden3d [ offset {int:offset} ] [ trianglepattern {int:mask} ]`

Comments
- `offset` takes an integer argument, which specifies how far the internal style counter will be advanced to determine the line style that will be used for the back side of the drawn surface. An offset of 0 means that both front and back will be drawn using the same style.
- `trianglepattern` takes an integer as argument, which will be interpreted as a bitmask and controls which lines of each surface element will be drawn (0: lines parallel to x axis; 2: lines parallel to y axis; 4: diagonal lines).

Full documentation: section 8.2.1.

`isosamples` Controls the number of points at which a function of two variables will be evaluated to generate a surface plot.

`set isosamples {int:xlines} [, {int:ylines} ]`

Comments
- This option is irrelevant when plotting data from a file.

Full documentation: section 8.2.1.

surface   Enables surface plots.

           `set surface`

           Comments

           ■ `unset surface` can be used to suppress the plotting of an actual surface, for instance
             to generate pure contour plots.

           Full documentation: section 8.2.1.

view   Controls the view point for three-dimensional plots.

```
set view [ {flt:polar} [, {flt:azimuthal}
                           [, {flt:scale} [, {flt:z_scale} ]]]]
```

           `set view map`

           Comments

           ■ Angles are measured in degrees.

           ■ `polar` is the polar angle and is restricted to `[0:180]`.

           ■ `azimuthal` is the azimuthal angle and is restricted to `[0:360]`.

           ■ `scale` is a multiplicative scaling factor for the size of the overall plot, relative to the
             default size.

           ■ `z_scale` is a multiplicative scaling factor for the apparent "height" of the plot, rela-
             tive to the default height.

           ■ `map` is shorthand for `set view 0, 0, 1, 1` and places the view point straight above the
             plotted surface.

           Full documentation: section 8.3.2.

xyplane   Controls the elevation of the plotting surface above the base plane of the surrounding box.

           `set xyplane [ at {flt:zvalue} | {flt:frac} ]`

           Comments

           ■ `set xyplane at` draws the base plane at the z value named as argument.

           ■ `set xyplane` (without `at`) controls the elevation of the plot surface above the base
             plane as a fraction of the total z range. The argument is interpreted as a fraction of
             the overall z range of the plot.

           ■ This option used to be known as `set ticslevel`.

           Full documentation: section 8.3.1.

CONTOUR PLOTS

clabel   Defines the format for the numeric explanation placed in the key for each contour line.

           `set clabel [ "{str:format}" ]`

           Comments

           ■ Only relevant when drawing contour lines using `splot`.

           ■ The format string uses `printf()`-like conversion specifiers.

           Full documentation: section 8.2.2.

           See also `set contour` and `set format`.

cntrparam Controls aspects of contour lines.

           `set cntrparam [ linear | cubicspline | bspline ]`

           `set cntrparam [ points {int:q} ]`
           `set cntrparam [ order {int:q} ]`

           `set cntrparam levels [ auto [{int:n}]`

```
                          | discrete {flt:z0} [, {flt:z1} [, ...]]
                          | incremental
                                  {flt:start}, {flt:inc} [, {flt:end}] ]
```

Comments

- linear, cubicspline, bspline select the interpolation algorithm for lines drawn between adjacent points.
- points controls the number of interpolation points for each spline segment. Only relevant for cubicspline and bspline. Cannot be combined with any other option in a single set cntrparam call.
- order determines the order of the bspline approximation. Only relevant for bspline. Cannot be combined with any other option in a single set cntrparam call.
- levels auto determines z levels at which contour lines will be drawn automatically. The integer parameter can be used to express the preferred number of levels, but gnuplot will adjust this number so as to draw contour lines at "round" values of z.
- discrete draws contour lines only at the explicitly named values of z.
- incremental draws contour lines at z values beginning at the first numeric parameter, incrementing by the second numeric parameter. A third parameter can be used to limit the range of z values for which contour lines will be drawn.

Full documentation: section 8.2.2.

---

contour   Enables drawing of contour lines and determines where they are drawn.

```
set contour [ base | surface | both ]
```

Comments

- base draws contour lines on the base of the drawing box.
- surface draws contour lines on the surface itself.
- both draws contour lines both on the base and on the surface.

Full documentation: section 8.2.2.

COLOR PLOTS (PM3D MODE)

---

colorbox   Controls the appearance of the colorbox in pm3d plots.

```
set colorbox [ vertical | horizontal ]
              [ noborder | bdefault | border {idx:linestyle} ]
              [ default | user [ origin {pos:orig} ]
                               [ size {pos:size} ] ] ]
```

Comments

- The colorbox can be drawn horizontally or vertically.
- The colorbox can be positioned automatically (default) or explicitly by the user (user). For three-dimensional plots, the only allowed coordinate system is the screen system, but for two-dimensional plots (including set view map plots), all coordinate systems can be used.

Full documentation: section 9.2.2.

---

palette   Defines a mapping between values in the z range and colors.

```
set palette [ model [ RGB | HSV ] ]
            [ defined ( {flt:v1} {clr:color1},
                        {flt:v2} {clr:color2}, ... )
              | functions f1(gray), f2(gray), f3(gray)
              | file "{str:filename}" [ using ... ] ]
            [ positive | negative ]
```

```
                 [ maxcolors {int:n} ]
show palette [ palette {int:n} [ float | int ]
                 | gradient | colornames ]
```

Comments

- `defined` maps a list of colors to their relative positions along the z range.
- `functions` evaluates three functions, which must map `[0:1]` to `[0:1]`, for the three components of the selected color space. The dummy variable must be called `gray`.
- `file` reads colors and their positions from the named file. A `using` directive can be supplied.
- `show palette palette` with an integer argument n prints a list of n colors to the output device as set by `set print`.
- `show palette gradient` displays the relative locations and colors supplied to `defined`, if the palette has been set up this way.
- `show palette colornames` prints all symbolic color names known to gnuplot.

Full documentation: section 9.1.2.

See also the standard gnuplot reference documentation for additional options.

---

pm3d   Enables palette-mapped mode (colored surfaces).

```
set pm3d  [ at [b|s|t] ]
              [ implicit | explicit ]
              [ hidden3d {idx:linestyle} | nohidden3d ]
              [ interpolate {int:xsteps},{int:ysteps} ]
              [ corners2color
                     [ mean|geomean|median|min|max|c1|c2|c3|c4 ] ]
              [ scansautomatic
                | scansforward | scansbackward | depthorder ]
```

Comments

- `at` determines where a colored surface should be drawn (bottom, surface, top).
- By default, pm3d operates in *implicit* mode, so that all surfaces drawn with splot will be drawn using colored, nontransparent polygons. If only some surfaces should be colored, use `set pm3d explicit` and use `with pm3d` as part of the `splot` command.

Full documentation: section 9.2.

B.4.8   Output

---

output   Redirects output to a file or device.

```
set output [ "{str:filename}" ]
```

Comments

- Empty filename directs output to standard output. This value must be set for interactive terminals.

See also the standard gnuplot reference documentation.

---

print   Redirects textual output and output from the `print` command to a file or device.

```
set print [ "{str:filename}" ] [ append ]
```

Comments

- Empty filename directs output to standard error.
- The special filename - (hyphen) directs output to standard output.
- The `append` keyword causes output to be appended if the file already exists.

Full documentation: section 4.4.1.

table   Generates a textual representation of the data points, rather than a graph.

```
set table [ "{str:filename}" ]
```

Comments

- If no filename is given, output is sent to the current value of set output.
- The current setting of set format is used to format the output.

Full documentation: section 4.4.2.

---

terminal   Selects the output format for graphical output.

See separate section on terminal handling in this appendix (section B.4.9).

---

termoption   Change suboptions on the current terminal device.

```
set termoption [no]enhanced
set termoption font "{str:name} [, {int:size} ]"
```

Comments

- set termoption can be used to change a single option for the current terminal, without requiring a full set terminal command.
- Only a single option can be changed with each invocation of set termoption.
- Currently, only the font and the enhanced mode options can be changed using set termoption.

See section on terminal handling in this appendix (section B.4.9).

B.4.9 *Terminals*

ENHANCED TEXT MODE

Enhanced text mode allows for advanced formatting options, such as sub- and superscript, as well as font changes. In enhanced text mode, several characters assume a special meaning.

Control character	Example	Result	Description
{}			Grouping and scoping.
^	x^2	x^2	Superscript.
_	A_{ij}	A_{ij}	Subscript.
@	x@^s_i	x_i^s	Alignment of sub- and superscripts.
	x@_i^{-3/2}y	$x_i^{-3/2}y$	Put the shorter one *first...*
	x@^{-3/2}_iy	$x_i^{-3/2}y$	... rather than last.
~	~B/	$\not\!\!B$	Overlay the two following characters or groups.
	~x{.6-}	$\bar{x}$	Overlays - on previous character, raised by 0.6 times the current character size.[a]

a. Overlay operator doesn't nest inside PostScript terminals.

Continued on next page

Control character	Example	Result	Description
{/ }	{/Times Hello}	Hello	Change font.
{/Symbol }	{/Symbol abc}	αβχ	Use Symbol font.
{/= }	{/=20 A}	A	Select an absolute font size (size in printer points).
{/* }	{/*0.5 A}	A	Change font size relative to enclosing font.
	{/Symbol=24 G}	Γ	Font family and size selections can be combined.
&	[&{abc}]	[ ]	Space, corresponding to the length of the enclosed argument.
\NNN	\101	A	Select a symbol, using its *octal* code.
\			Escape special characters within *single* quoted strings.[b]
\\			Escape special characters within *double* quoted strings.[b]

b. Not available for PostScript terminals.

SYMBOL FONT

Enhanced text mode allows font changes within a textual label. Of particular interest is the standard PostScript Symbol font, because it contains many characters frequently used in mathematical contexts.

Figures B.1 and B.2 show the following (using the default encoding for the PostScript terminal):

- Each character's ASCII code in *octal* representation (suitable for use with enhanced mode)
- The corresponding character using a standard text font (Helvetica)
- The corresponding character using the Symbol font

code	Helv	Sym	code	Helv	Sym	code	Helv	Sym	code	Helv	Sym
40			70	8	8	120	P	Π	150	h	η
41	!	!	71	9	9	121	Q	Θ	151	i	ι
42	"	∀	72	:	:	122	R	P	152	j	φ
43	#	#	73	;	;	123	S	Σ	153	k	κ
44	$	∃	74	<	<	124	T	T	154	l	λ
45	%	%	75	=	=	125	U	Y	155	m	μ
46	&	&	76	>	>	126	V	ς	156	n	ν
47	'	∋	77	?	?	127	W	Ω	157	o	ο
50	(	(	100	@	≅	130	X	Ξ	160	p	π
51	)	)	101	A	A	131	Y	Ψ	161	q	θ
52	*	∗	102	B	B	132	Z	Z	162	r	ρ
53	+	+	103	C	X	133	[	[	163	s	σ
54	,	,	104	D	Δ	134	\	∴	164	t	τ
55	-	−	105	E	E	135	]	]	165	u	υ
56	.	.	106	F	Φ	136	^	⊥	166	v	ϖ
57	/	/	107	G	Γ	137	_	_	167	w	ω
60	0	0	110	H	H	140	`	‾	170	x	ξ
61	1	1	111	I	I	141	a	α	171	y	ψ
62	2	2	112	J	ϑ	142	b	β	172	z	ζ
63	3	3	113	K	K	143	c	χ	173	{	{
64	4	4	114	L	Λ	144	d	δ	174	|	|
65	5	5	115	M	M	145	e	ε	175	}	}
66	6	6	116	N	N	146	f	φ	176	~	~
67	7	7	117	O	O	147	g	γ	177		

Figure B.1 Character codes, part 1. Columns are ASCII code (octal), Helvetica, Symbol Font.

code	Helv	Sym	code	Helv	Sym	code	Helv	Sym	code	Helv	Sym
240		€	270	,	÷	320	—	∠	350	Ł	⎧
241	¡	ϒ	271	„	≠	321		∇	351	Ø	⎡
242	¢	′	272	"	≡	322		®	352	Œ	⎢
243	£	≤	273	»	≈	323		©	353	º	⎣
244	⁄	/	274	…	…	324		TM	354		⎧
245	¥	∞	275	‰	|	325		Π	355		⎨
246	ƒ	ƒ	276		—	326		√	356		⎩
247	§	♣	277	¿	⌐	327		·	357		|
250	¤	♦	300		ℵ	330		¬	360		
251	'	♥	301	`	ℑ	331		∧	361	æ	⎫
252	"	♠	302	´	ℜ	332		∨	362		∫
253	«	↔	303	^	℘	333		⇔	363		⎧
254	‹	←	304	~	⊗	334		⇐	364		|
255	›	↑	305	¯	⊕	335		⇑	365	ı	⎩
256	fi	→	306	˘	∅	336		⇒	366		⎞
257	fl	↓	307	·	∩	337		⇓	367		|
260		°	310	¨	∪	340		◊	370	ł	⎠
261	–	±	311		⊃	341	Æ	⟨	371	ø	⎫
262	†	″	312	°	⊇	342		®	372	œ	|
263	‡	≥	313	˛	⊄	343	ª	©	373	ß	⎭
264	·	×	314		⊂	344		TM	374		⎤
265		∝	315	˝	⊆	345		Σ	375		⎬
266	¶	∂	316	˷	∈	346		⎛	376		⎦
267	•	•	317	ˇ	∉	347		|	377		

Figure B.2 Character codes, part 2. Columns are ASCII code (octal), Helvetica, Symbol Font.

BITMAP TERMINALS

`set terminal XXX`   Common options for all bitmap terminals based on the GD library.

```
set terminal XXX [ size {int:x},{int:y} ] [ [no]crop ]
                 [ tiny | small | medium | large | giant ]
                 [ font [ {str:name} [ {int:size} ] ]
                      | [ "{str:path} [, {int:size} ]" ] ]
                 [ [no]enhanced ]
                 [ rounded | butt ]
                 [ {color0} {color1} {color2} ...]
```

Comments

- `size` of the image in pixels.
- `crop` trims empty space around the graph, possibly resulting in an image smaller than `size`.
- Built-in fonts: `tiny`: 5 x 8 pixels, `small`: 6 x 12 pixels, `medium`: 7 x 13 pixels (bold face), `large`: 8 x 16 pixels, and `giant`: 9 x 15 pixels). These fonts can't be scaled or rotated.
- If libgd was built with support for TrueType fonts, either TrueType (.ttf) or Adobe Type 1 (.pfa) fonts can be used. Specify either the font name (for example, FreeSans) or the full name to a font file (for example, `"/usr/share/fonts/truetype/FreeSans.ttf"`).
- A color map can be specified explicitly. The first color (`color0`) will be used for the background, the second color for the border, the third for the axes (when using `set zeroaxis`, for instance). All remaining colors are used for consecutive line types. The format for the color specification consists of a hex string preceded by the letter x, for example `xFF0000` for red, and so on.

Full documentation: section 11.3.1.

`set terminal gif`   GIF output.

```
set terminal gif ...
                    [ [no]transparent ] [ animate [delay {int:time}] ]
```

Full documentation: section 11.3.1.

`set terminal png`   PNG output.

```
set terminal png ...
                    [ [no]transparent ] [ [no]interlace ]
                    [ [no]truecolor ]
```

Full documentation: section 11.3.1.

`set terminal jpeg`   JPG output.

```
set terminal jpeg ...
                    [ [no]interlace ]
```

Full documentation: section 11.3.1.

POSTSCRIPT TERMINALS

`set terminal postscript`   PostScript output.

```
set terminal postscript [ landscape | portrait | eps ]
                        [ color | mono ] [ blacktext | colortext ]
                        [ simplex | duplex | defaultplex ]
                        [ size {flt:x}[in|cm], {flt:y}[in|cm] ]
```

```
                              [ [font] "{str:name}" [ {int:size} ] ]
                              [ [no]enhanced ]
                              [ solid | dashed ]
                              [ linewidth | lw {flt:factor} ]
                              [ dashlength | dl {flt:factor} ]
                              [ rounded | butt ]
     set terminal postscript [ fontfile [add|delete] "{str:filename}"
                               | nofontfiles ]
```

Comments

- A single file can contain multiple graphs, except when creating Encapsulated Post-Script (eps).
- Size given in either inches or centimeters. Defaults to 10 x 7 inches; 5 x 3.5 inches for EPS.
- Examines the values of the fontfile option and the GNUPLOT_FONTPATH environment variable to find font files.
- The name of a PostScript font can be specified to set the default font for the terminal.
- fontfile takes the name of a font file and embeds the font information (not just the font name) in the PostScript file.

Full documentation: section 11.4.1.

See also set fontpath.

---

set terminal epslatex   PostScript graphics with LaTeX text and labels.

```
     set terminal epslatex [ standalone | input ]
                           [ header "{str:header}" | noheader ]
                           [ color | mono ] [ blacktext | colortext ]
                           [ size {flt:x}[in|cm], {flt:y}[in|cm] ]
                           [ [font] "{str:latexfont}" [ {int:size} ] ]
                           [ solid | dashed ]
                           [ linewidth | lw {flt:factor} ]
                           [ dashlength | dl {flt:factor} ]
                           [ rounded | butt ]
```

Comments

- Generates two files: a PostScript file and a LaTeX file.
- The full name of the LaTeX file (including extension .tex) should be set via set output. An Encapsulated PostScript file with the same base name but with the extension .eps will automatically be created, containing the graphics part of the plot.
- The argument to header will be placed verbatim in the header of the generated LaTeX file.

Full documentation: section 11.4.2.

See also set terminal postscript.

INTERACTIVE TERMINALS

---

set terminal wxt   Interactive terminal using the wxWidgets widget set.

```
     set terminal wxt [ {int:winid} ] [ title "{str:title}" ]
                      [ [no]enhanced ]
                      [ font "{str:name} [,{int:size}]" ]
                      [ [no]persist ] [ [no]raise ] [ [no]ctrl ]

     set terminal wxt {int:winid} close
```

Full documentation: section 11.5.

`set terminal x11`   Interactive terminal using the standard X11 libraries.

```
set terminal x11 [ {int:winid} ] [ title "{str:title}" ]
                 [ [no]enhanced ]
                 [ font "{str:fontspec}" ]
                 [ [no]persist ] [ [no]raise ] [ [no]ctrlq ]
                 [ solid | dashed ]
set terminal x11 [ {int:winid} ] close
```

Full documentation: section 11.5.

`set terminal aqua`   Interactive terminal for Mac OS X.

```
set terminal aqua [ {int:winid} ] [ title "{str:title}" ]
                  [ size {int:x} {int:y} ]
                  [ [no]enhanced ]
                  [ font "{str:name} [,{int:size}]" ]
                  [ solid | dashed ] [ dl {flt:dashlength} ]
```

Full documentation: section 11.5.

`set terminal windows`   Interactive terminal for MS Windows.

```
set terminal windows [ color | monochrome ]
                     [ [no]enhanced ]
                     [ font "{str:name} [,{int:size}]" ]
```

Full documentation: section 11.5.

MISC

`set terminal svg`   SVG (scalable vector graphics) output.

```
set terminal svg [ size {int:x},{int:y} [ fixed | dynamic ] ]
                 [ font "{str:name} [, {int:size} ]" ]
                 [ fontfile "{str:filename}" ]
                 [ [no]enhanced ]
                 [ rounded|butt ] [ linewidth {flt:factor} ]
```

Comments

- Creates a fixed-size image of 600 x 480 pixels by default.
- `dynamic` generates an image that can be resized by the viewer. `fixed` by default.
- `fontfile` will embed font information (not just the font name) in the output file.
- Examines the GNUPLOT_FONTPATH environment variable for font files.

Full documentation: section 11.3.2.

appendix C:
Resources

C.1   Web sites and mailing lists

The official web site for the gnuplot project is www.gnuplot.info. There you'll find the official documentation, including the extensive and helpful FAQ as well as links (not always current) to other sites and related projects.

Community support is available through the newsgroup comp.graphics.apps.gnuplot and the mailing list gnuplot-info@lists.sourceforge.net. There's also a mailing list for gnuplot developers: gnuplot-beta@lists.sourceforge.net.

Very helpful, with many examples of more advanced uses, is the "not-so-frequently asked questions" list, maintained by Toshihiko Kawano at the Los Alamos National Lab: http://t16web.lanl.gov/Kawano/gnuplot/index-e.html.

And if you're curious to see how far you can push gnuplot, I suggest you take a look at Bastian Maerkisch's brilliant "99 Bottles of Beer" implementation: http://99-bottles-of-beer.net/language-gnuplot-1598.html.

C.2   Books

These are books on topics relevant to the material in this book that I've found helpful and interesting.

C.2.1   Graphics and graphical analysis

The Elements of Graphing Data by William S. Cleveland. Hobart Press (1994).

Probably the definitive reference on graphical analysis (as opposed to presentation graphics). Much of the material in chapter 13 and chapter 14 has been influenced by Cleveland's careful approach. There's also a companion volume, *Visualizing Data* (1993), by the same author.

Creating More Effective Graphs by Naomi B. Robbins. Wiley (2005).

A catalog of graph types with commentary. This book is in part based on Cleveland's work and makes many of the same points, but it may be much easier to find.

Visual Revelations by Howard Wainer. Copernicus/Springer (1997); *Graphic Discovery* by Howard Wainer. Princeton University Press (2005).

> Two collections of short essays on statistical graphics, written in an entertaining, semi-popular style. Many good ideas and interesting case studies can be found here, but also a lot of editorializing about various issues.

The Visual Display of Quantitative Information by Edward R. Tufte. Graphics Press (2nd Ed, 2001); *Envisioning Information* by Edward R. Tufte. Graphics Press (1990); *Visual Explanations: Images and Quantities, Evidence and Narrative* by Edward R. Tufte. Graphics Press (1997).

> A series of best-selling books with an emphasis on presentation graphics.

Graphics of Large Data Sets by Antony Unwin, Martin Theus, Heike Hofmann. Springer (2006).

> A research monograph, describing some of the current thinking regarding the visualization of large data sets, both in the number of records and in the number of dimensions: parallel-coordinate plots, tree-maps, dynamic graphics. Accessible, interesting.

Information Dashboard Design by Stephen Few. O'Reilly, (2006).

> Much interesting (and current) information on good ways to present information visually, with an emphasis on business uses.

Visualizing Data by Ben Fry. O'Reilly (2007).

> This book describing the Processing environment—a Java tool that allows the user to create graphs programatically—was written by the tool's creator. Graphs may be complex and involve animation or dynamic interaction.

C.2.2   Statistics

An Introduction to Mathematical Statistics and Its Applications by Richard J. Larsen and Morris L. Marx. Prentice Hall (4th ed, 2005)

> An excellent introductory textbook. The authors manage to strike a very nice balance between practical applications and mathematical depth. The emphasis of this book is more on mathematical development, rather than on practical applications. The text contains a large number of uncommonly interesting examples.

The Statistical Sleuth by Fred L. Ramsey and Daniel W. Schafer. Duxbury (2002).

> An undergraduate textbook which emphasizes practical application of statistical methods to a variety of data analysis problems. Strongly emphasizes the distinction between randomized and observational studies and contains a particularly careful discussions of the steps required to arrive at definitive (in a statistical sense) statements about a set of data points.

Statistics for Technology: A Course in Applied Statistics by Chris Chatfield. Chapman & Hall (1983).

> A compact introduction to classical statistics for readers who are mostly interested in applications. Despite the practical bend, this is no mere collection of cookie-cutter recipes, but a thorough introduction to both the theory and the application of statistics. Not a textbook, but a guide for a self-motivated audience.

All of Statistics by Larry Wasserman. Springer (2004).

> A post-graduate reference for people who already know statistics. Includes many modern topics. Beware that necessary context may be lost due to the extreme terseness of the presentation.

Data Analysis: A Bayesian Tutorial by D. S. Silva with J. Skilling. Oxford University Press (2006).

> An accessible introduction to the Bayesian view point of statistics.

e-Handbook of Statistical Methods by NIST/SEMATECH: www.nist.gov/stat.handbook

> A valuable online resource published by the National Institute for Standards and Technology (NIST). Broad coverage of statistics from an engineering point of view, including topics not usually covered in introductory treatments (such as time series modeling and reliability estimation).

C.2.3   *Mathematical methods and modeling*

How to Model It by Anthony M. Starfield, Karl A. Smith, and Andrew L. Bleloch. Burgess Publishing (1994).

> The best introduction into the application of mathematics to real-world problems for the general audience that I'm aware of. In each chapter, the authors present one problem, and then proceed to devise various approximate answers to the question posed by the problem, achieving better accuracy at each step. The range of topics and methods is impressive. Out of print, but easily available used.

Used Math by Clifford E. Swartz. American Association of Physics Teachers (1993).

> If you need a refresher on college math, with a bend toward applications, this book is a good choice. The selection of topics—and most of the examples—reveal the author's background in physics, but the material presented here is generally applicable and useful.

Industrial Mathematics by Charles R. MacCluer. Prentice-Hall (2000).

> A catalogue of more advanced mathematical techniques helpful in data analysis and model building. The choice of topics is excellent, but the presentation often seems a bit aloof and too terse for the uninitiated. Very expensive.

An Introduction to Mathematical Modeling by Edward A. Bender. Dover (1978, 2000).

> Short and idiosyncratic. A variety of problems are investigated and mathematical models developed to help answer specific questions. Requires only basic math skills, the emphasis being on the conceptual model building process.

Problem Solving: A Statistician's Guide by Chris Chatfield. Chapman & Hall (1995).

> A thorough discussion of the data analytical thought process. Includes typically neglected topics such as data gathering. The book consists of three parts: a general exposition, a set of well-posed problems with discussion, and a sketchlike overview of statistical techniques.

C.3   *Other open source tools*

If you're dealing with data and graphics, here are some additional tools you might find helpful. This list is by no means comprehensive. For a project to be listed here, first of all I had to be aware of it. Then, the project had to be

- Free and open source
- Available for the Linux platform
- Active and mature
- Available as a standalone product and allowing interactive use (this requirement eliminates libraries and graphics command languages)

- Reasonably general purpose (this eliminates specialized tools for molecular modeling, bio-informatics, high-energy physics, and so on)
- Comparable to or going beyond gnuplot in at least some respects

C.3.1 *Math and statistics programming environments*

R   The R language and environment (www.r-project.org) are in many ways the de facto standard for statistical computing and graphics using open source tools. R shares with gnuplot an emphasis on iterative work in an interactive environment. It's extensible, and many user-contributed packages are available from the R website and its mirrors. R is famous for its graphics capabilities. Its learning curve is rather steep.

An alternative project, with an emphasis on time series analysis and financial applications, is gretl. Gretl uses gnuplot as graphics backend.

Octave   Octave is a high-level programming language, primarily for "classic" numerical applications (linear algebra, quadrature, differential equations, and so forth). It provides an interactive command-line environment or can be used for batch processing. Octave uses gnuplot for graphical output.

Scilab is an alternative project, maintained by the INRIA national research institute in France.

Maxima   Maxima is a system for symbolic calculations, including integration and differentiation, Taylor series expansion, differential equations, fractions, and vectors. It includes support for high- and arbitrary-precision numerical calculations as well. It uses gnuplot for graphical output.

A relatively new project for symbolic computation, maintained by researchers at the University of Washington, is SAGE.

C.3.2 *Graphing tools*

OpenDX   Started by IBM in 1991 as "Visualization Data Explorer," this project was donated to the open source community in 1999. Giving off a distinctly early-1990s feel (everything opens in a separate Motif window) and using somewhat unfamiliar and crude GUI metaphors, this program isn't easy to learn. But it offers many features not often found otherwise, including support for surface, volume, and flow visualization, as well as the ability to interact with graphs dynamically.

SciDAVis   SciDAVis is a fork of the QtiPlot project. Both combine spreadsheet-like functionality, including the ability to load, edit, and save data, with plotting and analysis capabilities in a WYSIWYG environment. This, together with the availability of non-graphical analysis functions (interpolation, Fourier transforms, numeric integration) positions these projects as expressions of a design philosophy very different from gnuplot.

kst   Although it can handle other types of plots as well, this program is particularly suited for the real-time visualization and analysis of streaming data. It features an impressive set of spectral analysis tools and rich support for color. Documentation appears spotty.

Grace   Grace (Xmgr, xmgrace) has long been a mainstay of Unix-based plotting programs. It's GUI-based and has numerical analysis capabilities (fitting, Fourier transforms, numerical integration, joining and sorting), as well as a built-in scripting language. In contrast to gnuplot, its central work unit is the individual graph, not the data file. Grace doesn't read data files natively, but "imports," then stores, all data, together with the commands that make up a plot, in its own native file format. This, together with the way the user interface is designed, makes Grace appear to be more of a graph-preparation program, rather than a tool for visual exploration.

index

X

X11 308
x11 terminal 219
xticlabels() function 122
xyplane option 142, 336

Y

yticlabels() function 122, 263

Z

z value 280

zero axes 123
zero included in range 291
zero option 324
zeroaxis option 334
z-score 274